I0753043

Advanced Tattoo Art

REVISED

How-to Secrets from the Masters

Doug Mitchel

Published by:
Wolfgang Publications Inc.
PO Box 223
Stillwater, MN 55082
www.wolfpub.com

Legals

First published in 2013 by Wolfgang Publications Inc.,
PO Box 223, Stillwater MN 55082

ISBN-13: 978-1-941064-38-2

Advanced Tattoo Art REVISED How-to Secrets from the Masters

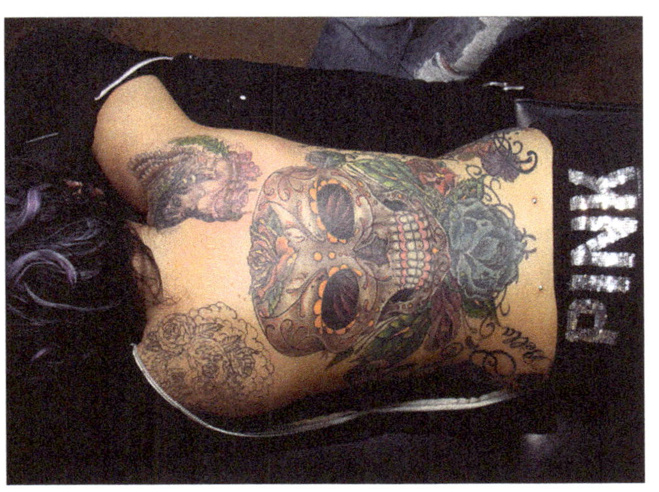

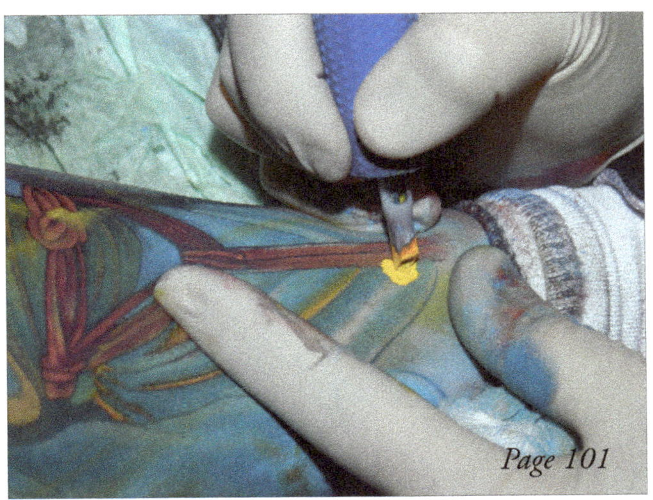
Page 101

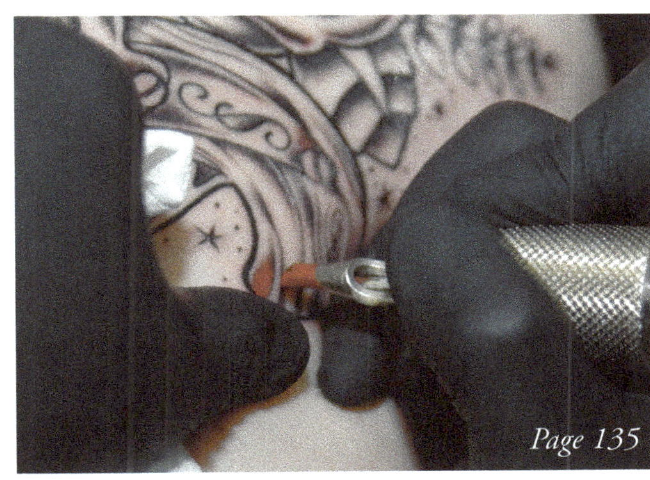
Page 135

Acknowledgements

Producing a book like this requires the time and patience of many individuals. Not only did each tattoo artist allow me to hover over them for hours as they created art on skin, they also did the leg work necessary to provide a willing recipient for each piece. It is only with cooperation of this level that a book of any sort can be created, and for that I thank them all.

From the Publisher

Doug Mitchel is a rather prolific journalist, one with over twelve titles to his name. And while this is the first collaboration between Doug Mitchel and Wolfgang Publications, it won't be the last. Some people can write and some can take photographs. Only a limited number can do both. Of that limited number, an even smaller number can organize their material in a logical fashion and turn it in on time. Doug fits all these criteria.

The format we've used for this book is part how-to and part photo-essay. I've always thought that if you want to know how to do something - be it brick laying or tattooing - you need to start by studying with the person who does it all day long. Thus Doug spent hours and days with a variety of well-known and highly skilled Tattoo artists, following their every move. Doug's well-done photo sequences follow the artist from the initial sketch though all the steps necessary for the creation of a finished and colorful tattoo.

We've given each artist a chapter to show what it is they do and how they do it. Included in each chapter is a Q&A, which is really just one more opportunity for the artist to share with a larger audience their preference for materials and any special tricks they've learned along the way.

In the end, this book is mostly photographs, hundreds and hundreds of very detailed photographs that show first, the outlining, and then the application of each color.

So whether you're looking for how-to information, to launch a new career, or new ideas for your current tattoo business, or you're simply fascinated with tattoos in any shape or form - there's information here sure to satisfy. And for all of this we have Doug Mitchel to thank.

Timothy Remus

Perspective & History

Tattoos Then and Now

Placing images on the human body is hardly a new craft, but the recent popularity of tattoo art seems to have reached critical mass. You can barely turn on the television, open up a magazine or view a stranger's arm without seeing evidence of this trend. While the art has earned the acceptance of the public and adoration of many, it is a form of artistic and ritual illustration that has survived for thousands of years.

Some historians point to a period that may

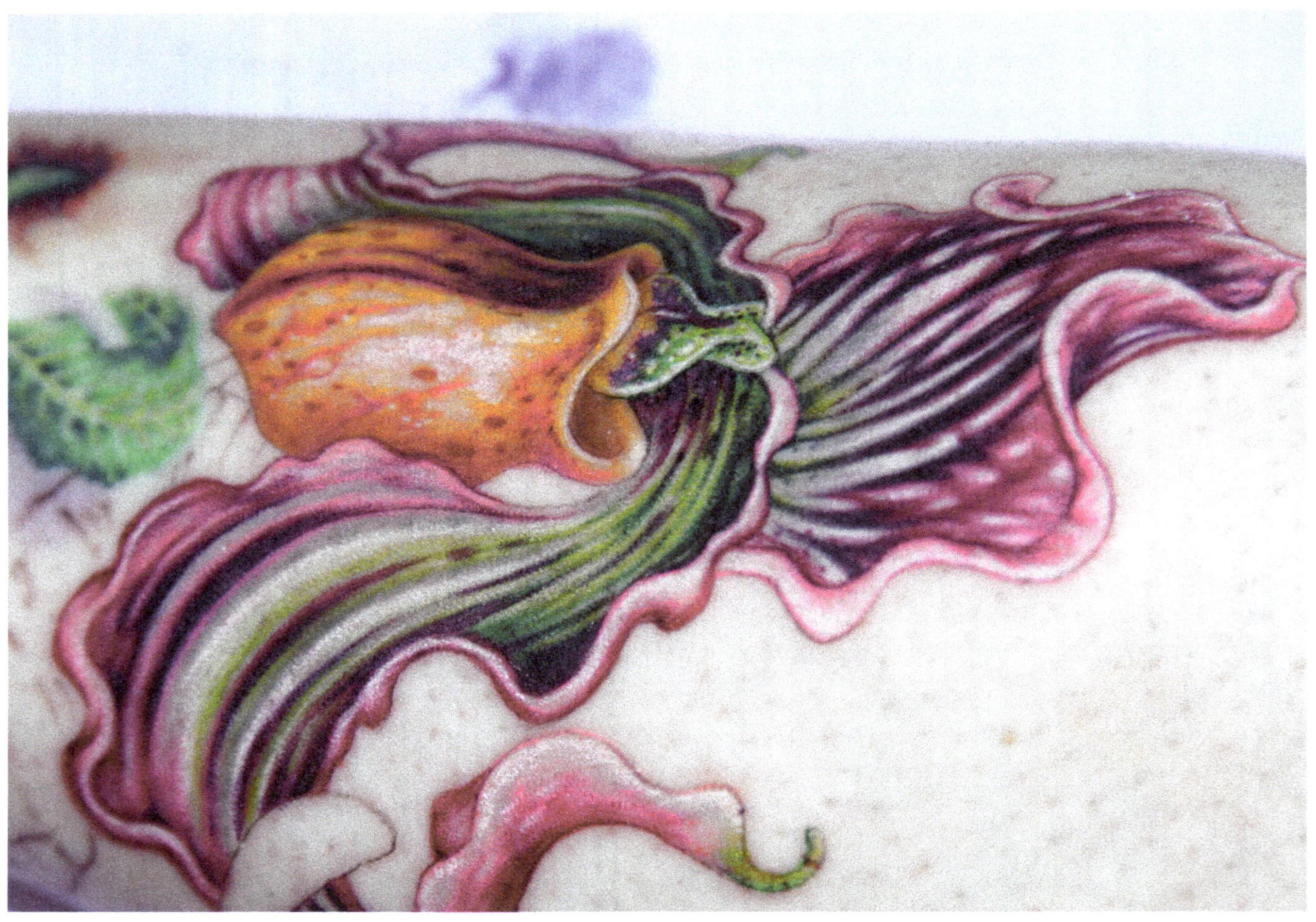

One of the many colorful tattoos you'll see illustrated in this book, this pistol and flower arrangement has been placed in a subtle location.

have been as far back as 12000 BC when the first use of ink on skin was seen. The record books are a bit sketchy that far back, but there is evidence many early civilizations used this technique to mark the flesh. The word tattoo is taken from the Tahitian word "tatu,", which means to mark something, early tattoos were used to indicate a person's status, skill level or availability as a mate. The Egyptian people were some of the first to use inks to mark human flesh, and the practice traveled to China as early as 2000 BC.

Tattoos were used by the Greeks to show the proficiency of their spies, while the Romans illustrated their slaves and criminals. Many times, single women of other races wore ink to indicate their availability to single men and the married women wore ink to do the same. After

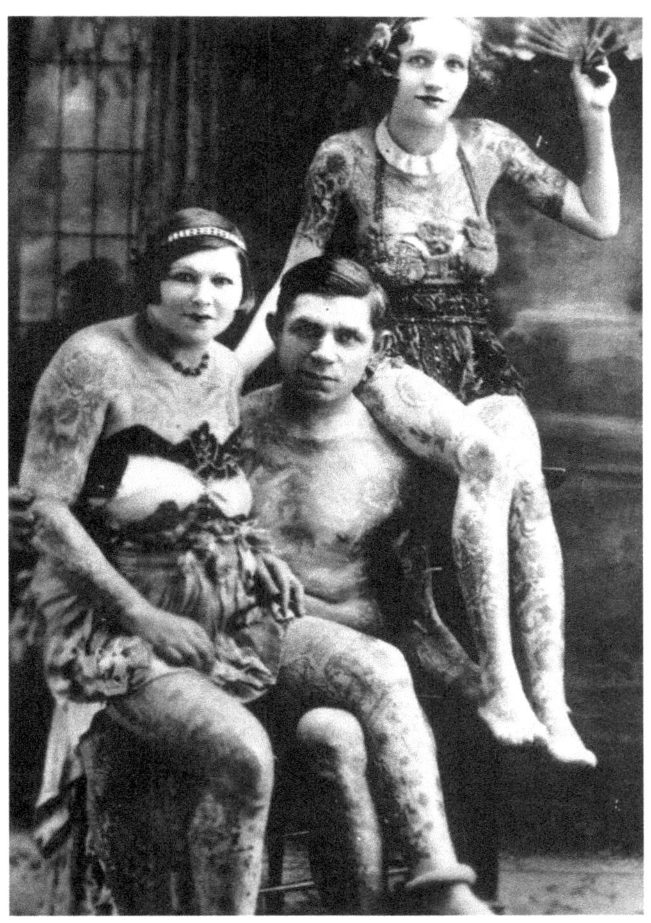

A trio of proud tattoo recipients poses to show off their ink, and having two women wearing tattoos in the same room must have been quite rare. Pollack

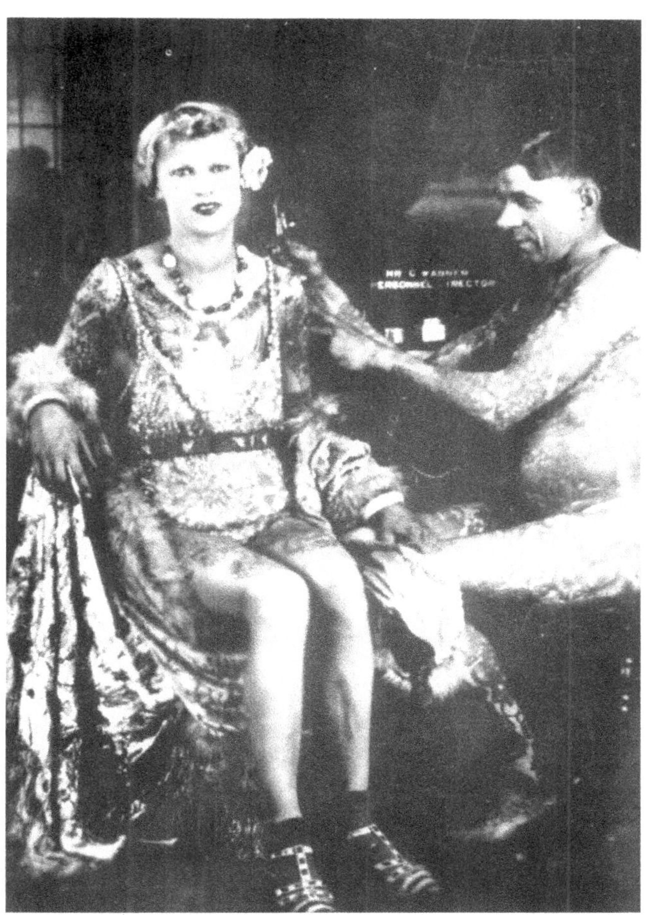

As if getting tattoo work wasn't strange enough in the 1930's, having a naked man do the needle work must have been a real oddity. Rich "Pyro" Pollack

taking the head of an opponent, a Dayak soldier would receive a tattoo on his hand to illustrate his prowess as a warrior. Western culture also used tattoos to highlight a variety of classes, and the Danes and Saxons were among those who had family crests tattooed onto their flesh.

Of course with any popular trend, there will be those who stand against it. 787 AD saw the ban of tattoos hail from Pope Hadrian, and Britain's use would cease after the Norman Invasion of 1066. After existing and thriving for thousands of years, western culture would not see tattoo art again until after the 16th century.

Fast forward to the latter part of the 1700s, and we find Captain Cook making his journeys to the south Pacific, and returning with tales of illustrated people. After one of his sojourns he

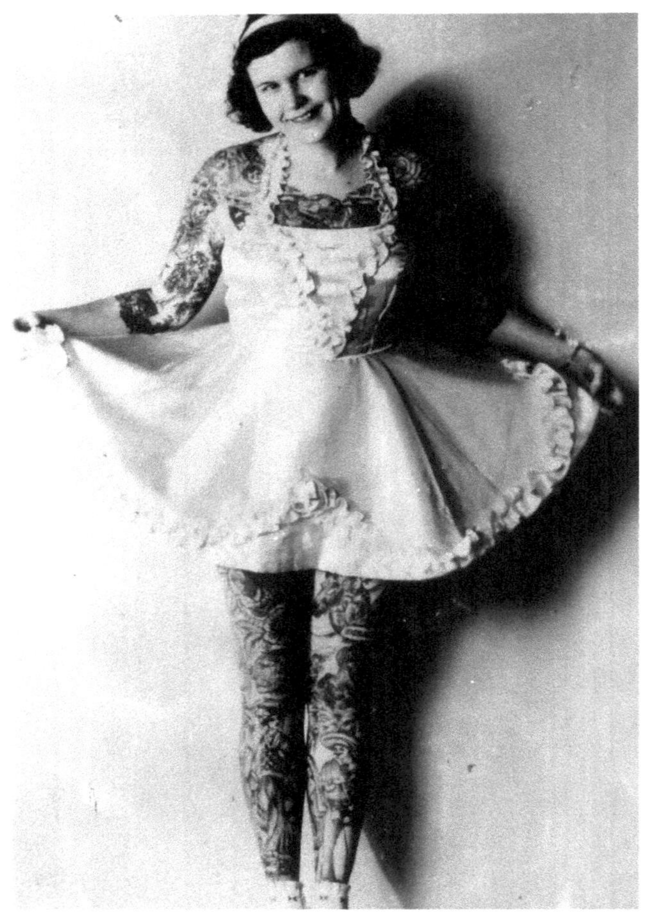

As one of the main attractions in the Ringling Brother's circus, Betty Brodbent earned a place in history during the 1930's. Rich "Pyro" Pollack

brought home a Polynesian native who was heavily tattooed, and this seemed to re-ignite people's desire to get their own. Of course one needed to be discreet when making this decision and even more discreet when having the work done.

As intriguing as having their own tattoo may have been back then, the process was nowhere near as fast or comfortable as today's work. With a hand-formed needle being tapped by hand into the skin, the process was arduous and quite painful. Taking a clue from Thomas Edison's electric pen that was used to mark paper patterns, Samuel O'Reily patented the first electric tattoo machine in 1891. This revelation made the process far less painful as well as providing greater control of the ink when held in skilled hands.

The birth of the 1900s saw tattoos fall into the dark shadows again. People wanting to have one added to their skin needed to travel to the seedy underbelly of the city to find an artist, and overall the art form once again became something of a black art. The only people thought to be desiring such a thing were criminals and thugs. This was not really the case, but the stereotype grew. Betty Brodbent was the "tattooed lady" and made her way through life in the freak show of Ringling Brothers Circus in the 1930s. As popular as her part of the show was, it was hardly considered something for a proper woman to do.

U.S. Soldiers heading overseas to do battle in the Korean, or European, conflict often wore art showing their dedication to a loved one or their combat unit. Although completed in typically

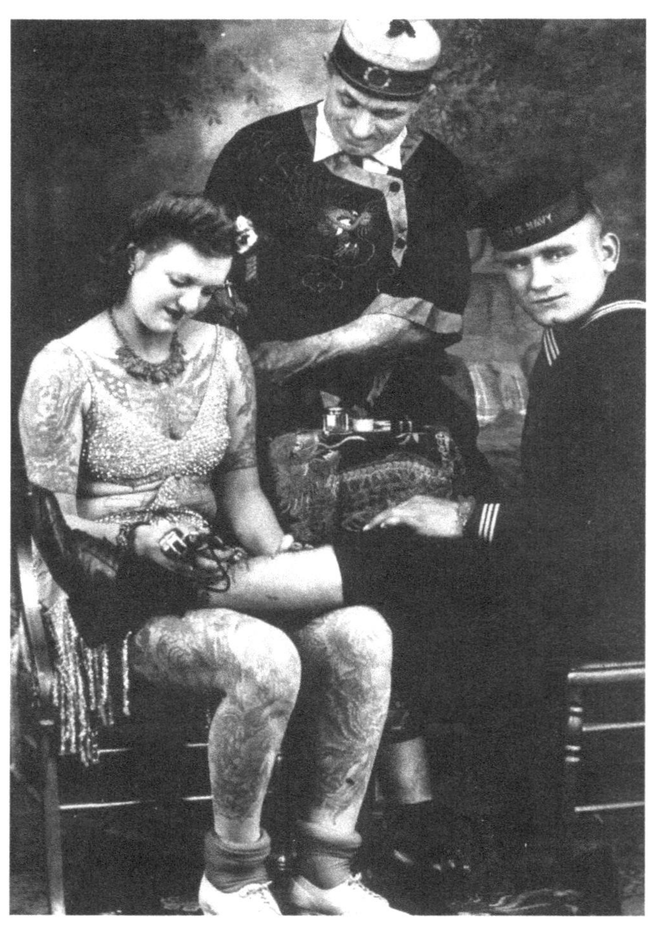

Although sailors getting tattoos was not unusual, having a woman do the work was probably a bit off the beaten path. Rich "Pyro" Pollack

simple form, these bits of hand crafted art provided a daily reminder of what they were proud of.

After the Second World War ended, tattoos once again found themselves being pushed into the dank, dark shadows of American culture. Even though he was known for his reclusive life style, George Fosdick was one of the most celebrated ink masters. Though George died in 1946, his legend lives on today in the history books and tales of yesteryear.

Fast forward to the new millennium, and we find the art of tattoos once again becoming a hugely popular method of displaying your own personal colors. Anyone curious about the process, hoping to learn more about those involved, need only turn on the television, or visit their local news stand. A variety of programs that chronicle some of today's most famous artists can be viewed on any given night of the week. The tattoo art may be somewhat muddled by the required on-screen drama of each episode, but they reveal one level of the modern tattoo arena.

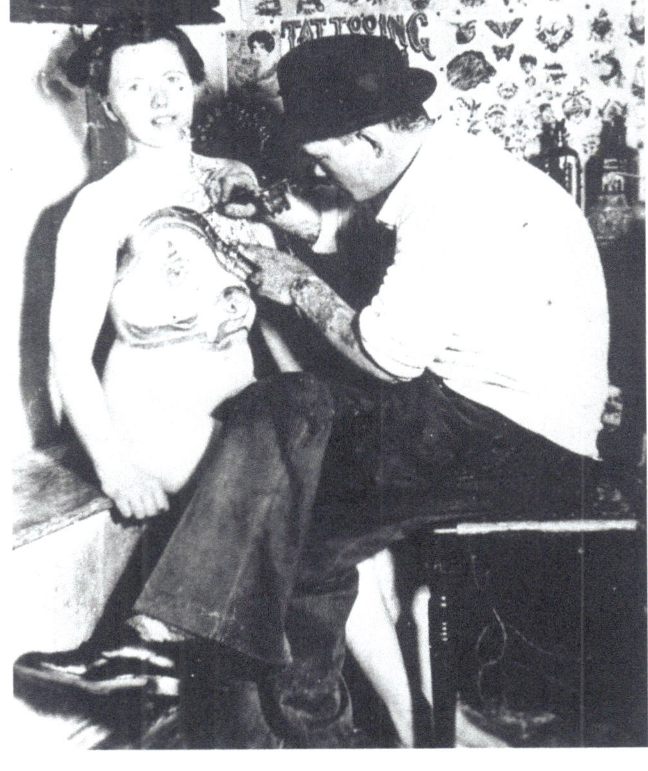

Although he's fully clad for this tattoo, his shop looks to be less than sterile, judging by the dirty sill that woman is seated on. Rich "Pyro" Pollack

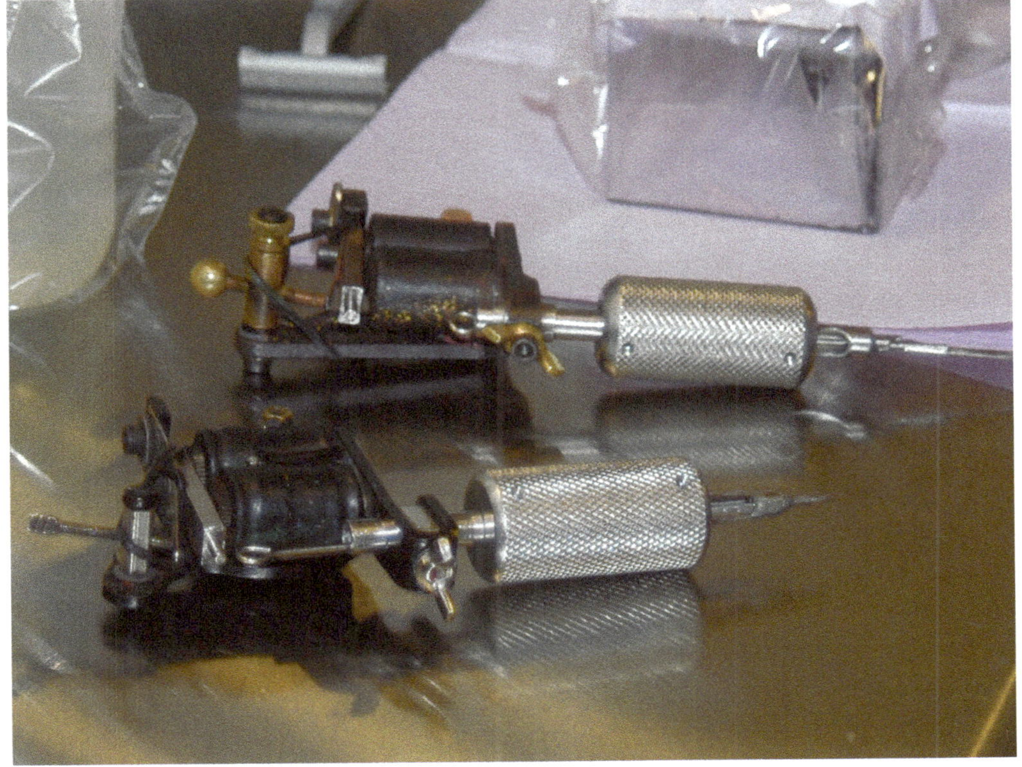

Taking a clue from Thomas Edison's electric pen that was used to mark paper patterns, Samuel O'Reily patented the first electric tattoo machine in 1891.

One of the best and most efficient ways to expose yourself to the universe of tattoo artists is to visit a convention. Of the hundreds that criss-cross the country each year, the Hell City Tattoo Festival is rated as one of the best by critics and tattoo fans alike. The 2006 event was held in Columbus, Ohio and was expected to draw nearly 8000 people through the doors. Once inside, they could visit with almost 60 different tattoo artists from across the country. Many people waited months, or years, for their opportunity to be inked by their favorite out-of-state artist, while others were forced to stand by and watch, as time was limited. Walking the aisles of artists, vendors and related craftsmen gives you a real sense of what can be achieved once you've decided to get some work done. There appears to be no limit to the creativity and, dare I say, depravity of some of the artists. Not everyone is happy with a smiley-face tattoo. Even the decor of the site was taken from carnivals of the past, with colorful banners hawking the circus entertainers in their finest display of oddity. Tattoo contests, educational seminars and multi-media displays are all a part of the show, and make it a worthy event for anyone with curiosity about the craft.

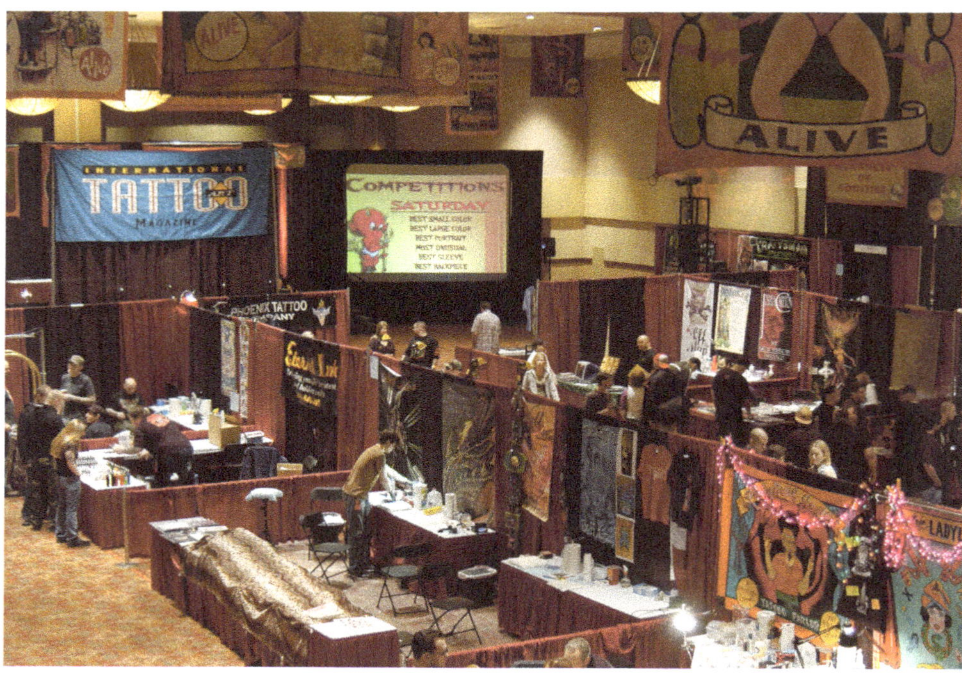

The main floor of the Hell City Tattoo Festival, held in Columbus, Ohio, was action packed with vendors of all stripes.

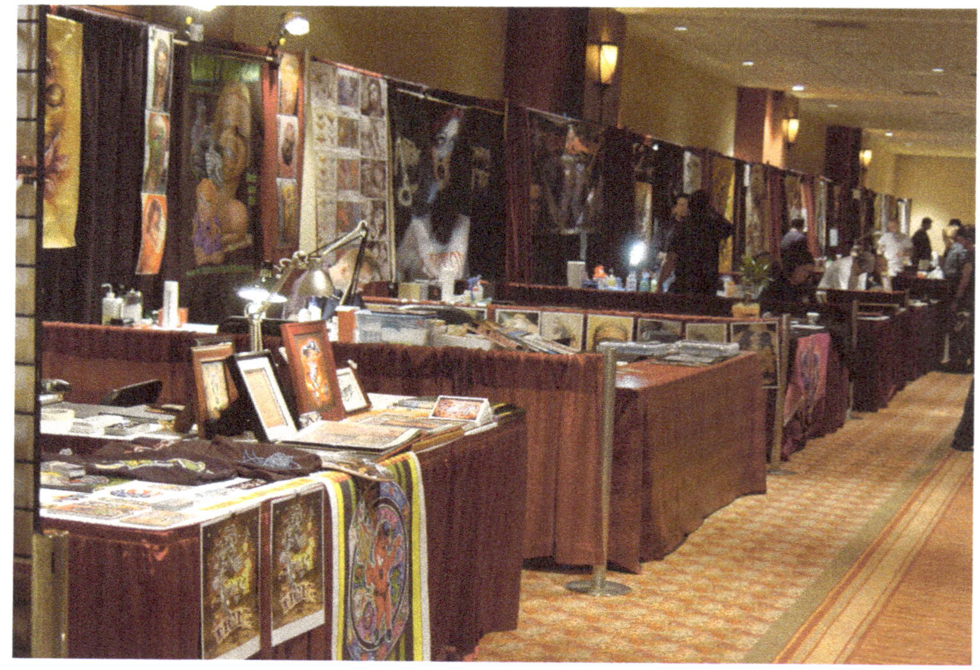

With the main floor packed, additional artists and vendors could be found on the balcony overlooking the main floor.

The three day event includes a variety of things to see and do, including the Heck City section for the kids. Chris Sablone and Durb Morrison are the gentlemen who put on the show, and have their 5th annual spectacular set for August of 2007 in Phoenix, Arizona.

As history has proven, the tattoo has been scorned and adored by many, but remains a popular choice for those wanting to wear their colors permanently.

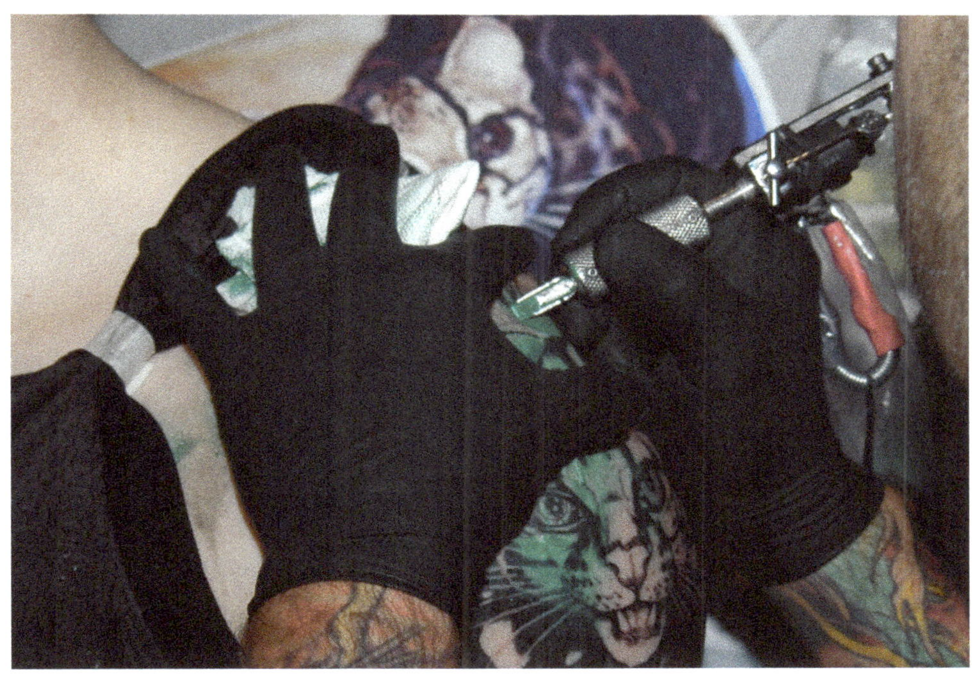

Created on-site at the Hell City Festival was this margay cat artwork.

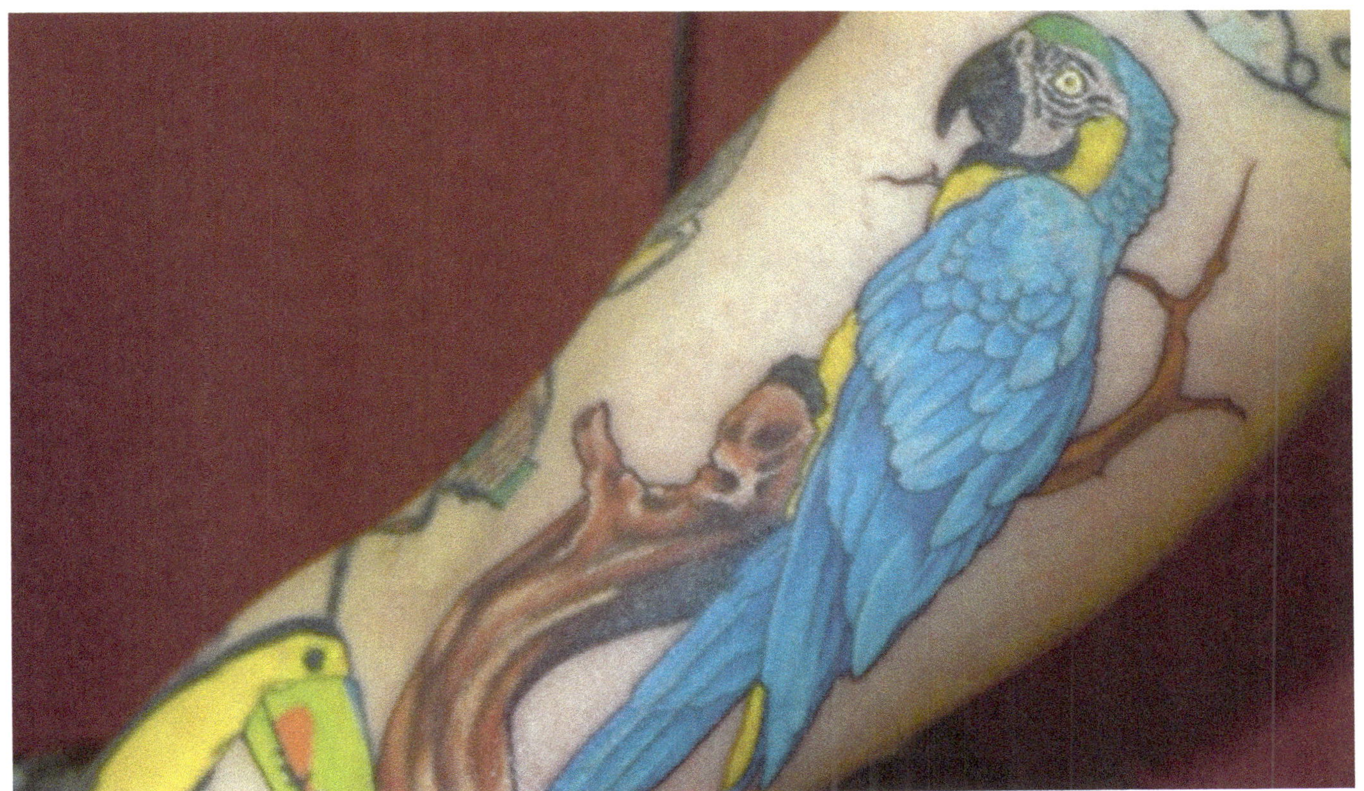

This colorful macaw was created in Florida and is just one of the many styles of ink you'll find in this book.

Chapter One

Stephen Knight

Orchid Tattoo

In my experience capturing the tattoo process for my books, I have witnessed many artists using their own unique style and equipment. Yet, Stephen Knight exhibited tools and techniques that are new to me. This is not to say that all the other artists are wrong in their methods, but simply to illustrate that there's more than one way to tattoo the human canvas.

The first distinction is his choice of linear rotary machines versus the more typical coil-type machines often used. He likes the smoother action and reduced noise of these machines along with

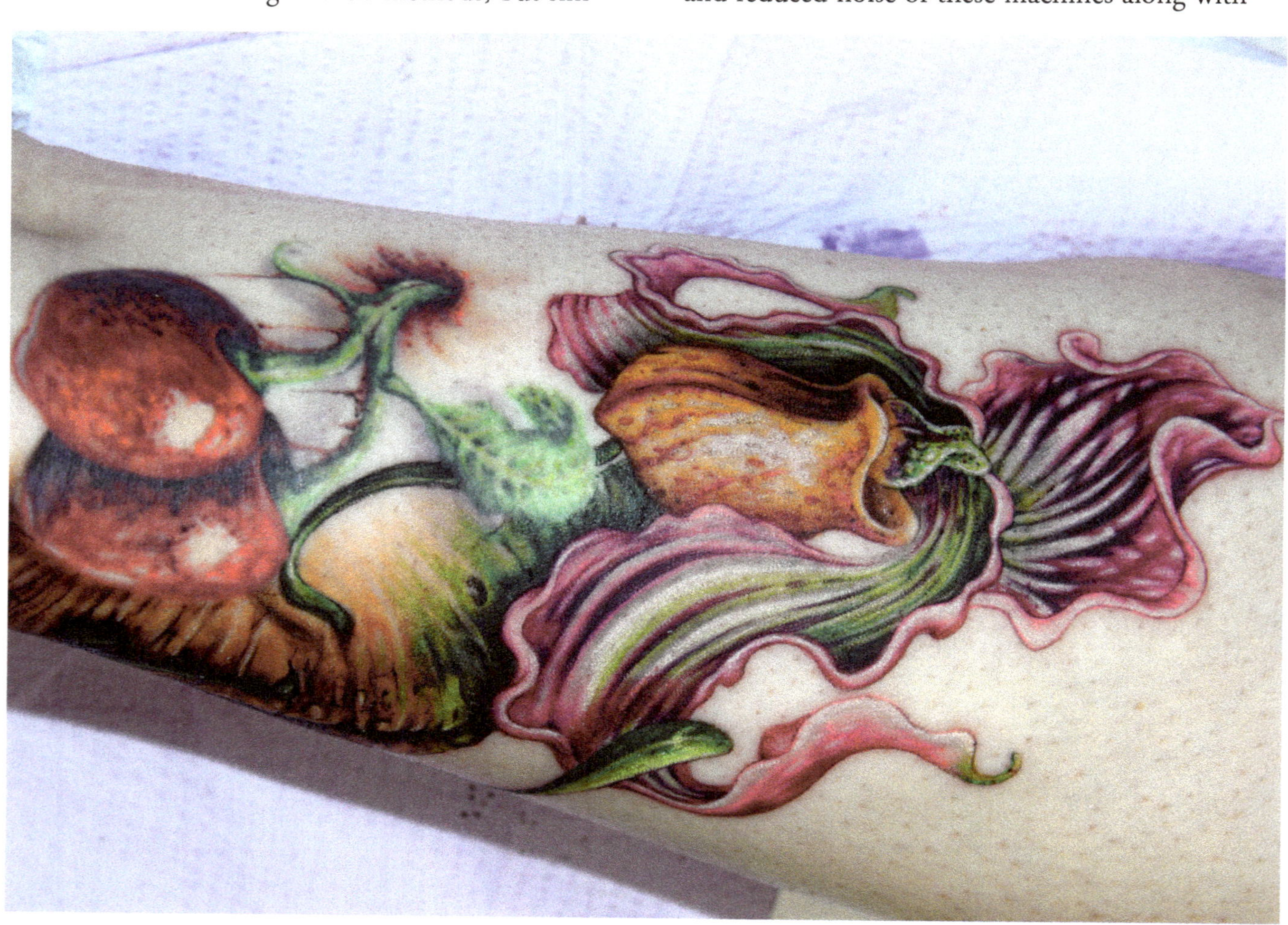

The finished tattoo art shows both intense color and incredible detail.

their lighter weight. His clients experience less discomfort during extended art applications which is always welcome. His personal touch is also considered light or "the touch of an angel" as Alex, the recipient of the slipper orchid tattoo will attest. It is not her first piece from Stephen so she is well aware of the low level of pain he delivers. The fact that very little blood was seen as he moved through the steps is more evidence that the combination of a rotary along with his gentle touch makes for minimal trauma to the skin. In part to compensate for the lighter contact provided by the rotary machine, Stephen uses very rapid yet controlled hand movements to add ink to the art. This doesn't increase pressure but simply allows him to adjust for the machine's reduced impact.

Instead of first outlining the piece in black ink, he prefers "gray lining" which uses a lighter shade of ink to outline the transfer before beginning to fill in the blanks. He feels the less intrusive nature of the gray allows him greater flexibility as he moves forward with the remaining colors being used. A 5-round needle set was chosen for the gray outline on today's piece and is not an uncommon selection as he begins other pieces of his art. Stephen also uses stainless steel bits that are disposable as he feels they offer a more sanitary method of applying ink. Once again he is not saying that others are wrong for using equipment that needs to be sterilized before it can be used again he simply likes the on-time design of his hardware.

One of the most distinctive things I discovered was his method of changing from dark to light and using the colors needed as he saw fit. Most others I have witnessed work from dark to light shades and usually stick with one hue until they move to the next step of the process. Stephen is careful to wash away residue from each color before adding the next to avoid contamination.

My exposure to the tattoo universe has been limited, but when compared to what I have taken in working with other artists in the field these features help to make Stephen's efforts stand out and to distinguish his creations in their depth and intensity while keeping the client as comfortable as possible.

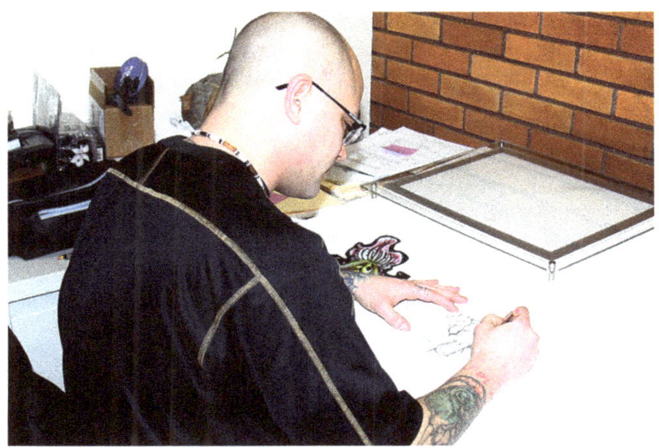

Stephen puts the finishing touches on the drawing that will be used to create the transfer. He is using art created by Alex, the tattoo recipient, as his guide.

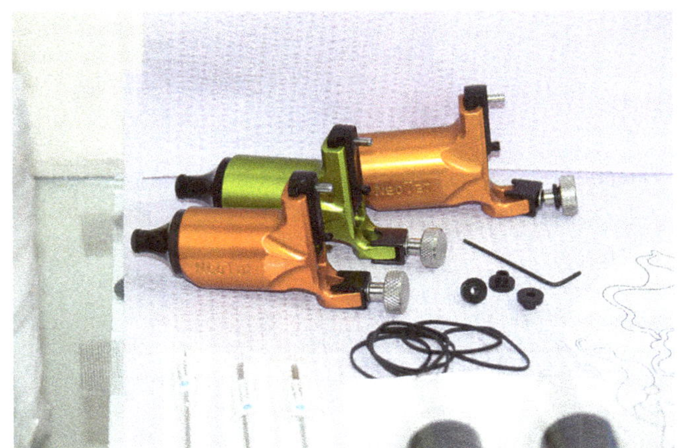

Linear rotary machines from NeoTat are Stephen's choice for their quiet and less painful operation.

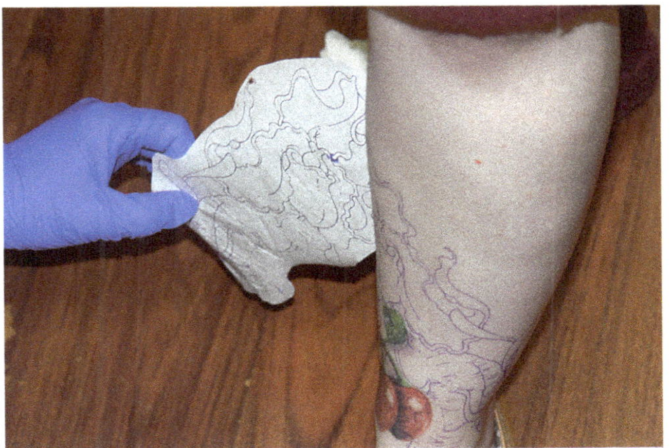

Slowly removing the heat transfer from Alex's skin reveals the outline of the art that will become the slipper orchid tattoo.

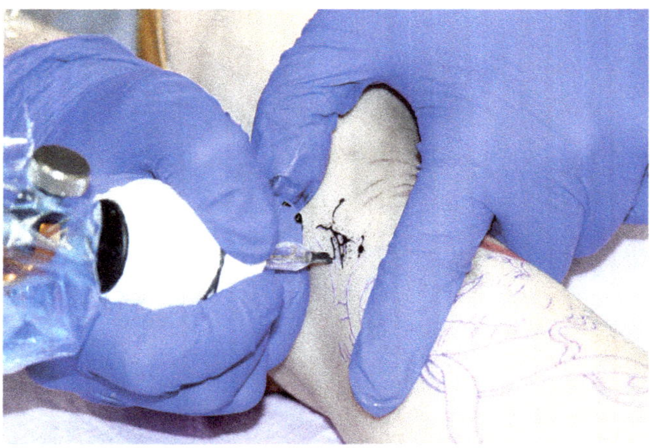

Stephen chooses gray ink to produce the required outline that will allow him to fill in each section of the colorful orchid.

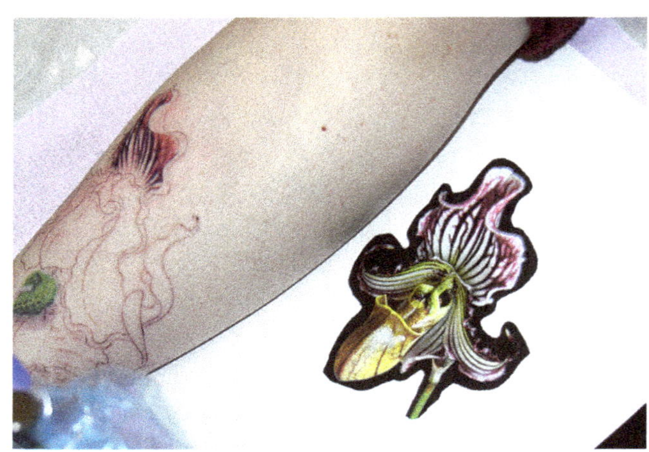

Keeping Alex's original art close at hand gives a better road map for Stephen to follow on his journey.

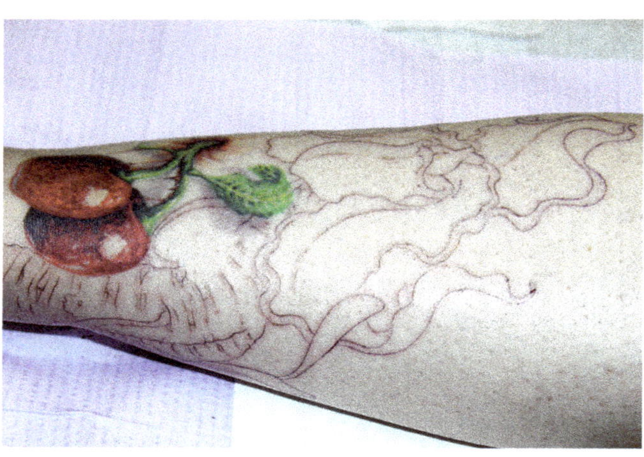

The completed "gray lining" shows us the overall design of the piece and will guide Stephen through the balance of the required steps.

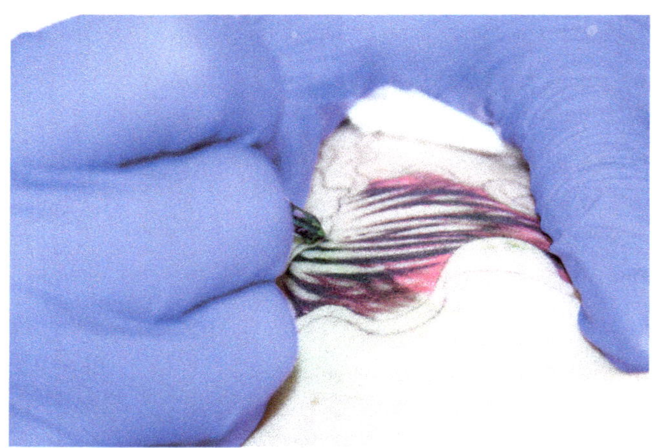

Using an olive colored ink allows him to transition from black as he nears a separate section of the orchid's design.

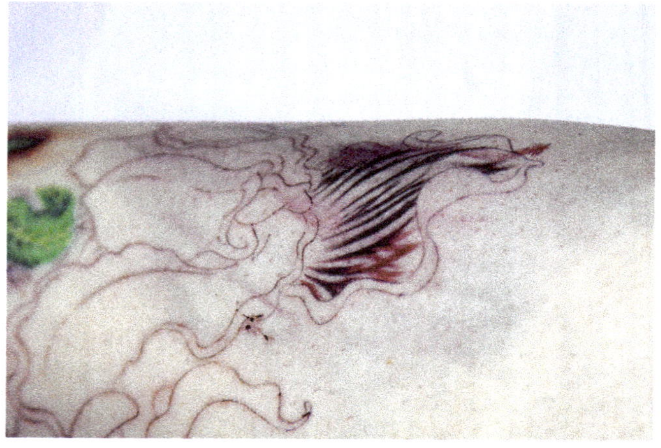

Using dark purple and magenta ink from Intenze shows us the first few results of his movements.

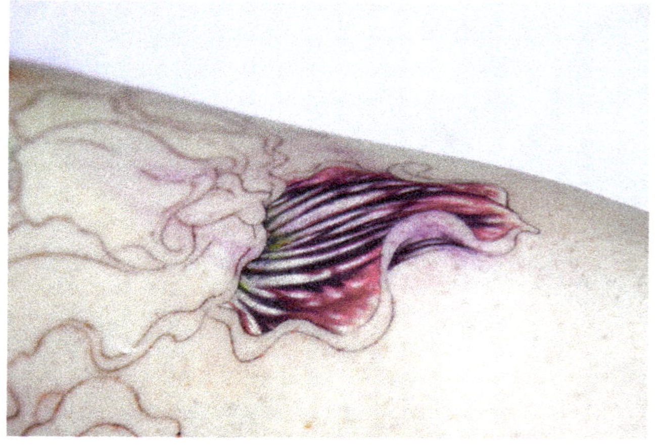

Following small bits of light gray, white, dark and light green, he now moves to a dark purple ink. All can be seen in the intricate details of the art.

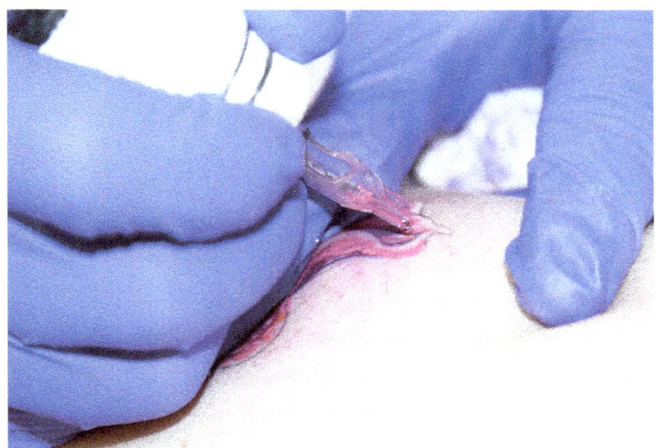

Using a 5 round set of needles he returns to a lighter shade of magenta for the next section.

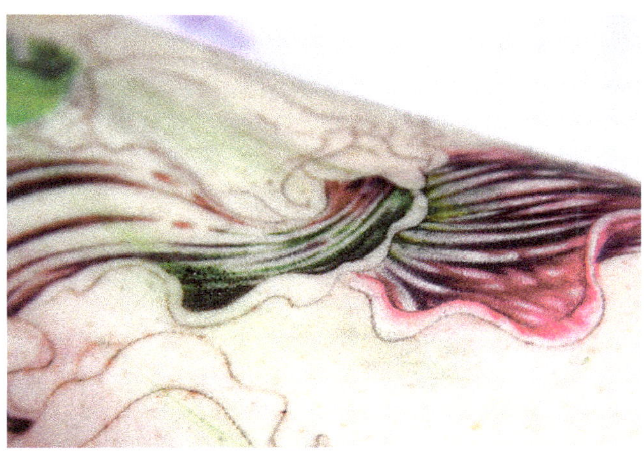

Wiping away the excess ink reveals the section of green that has been added to the piece.

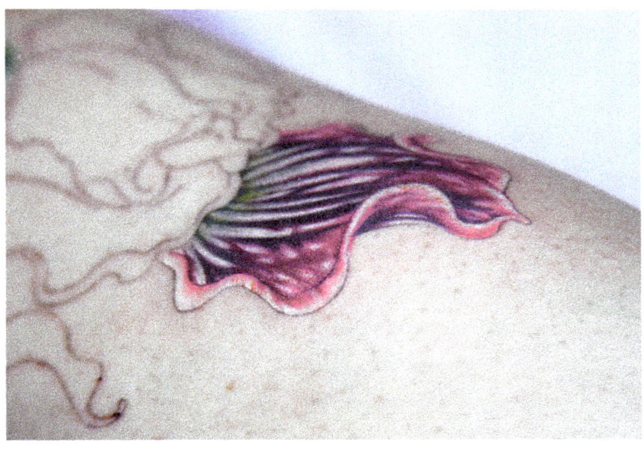

Stepping away from his efforts so far we can see how he builds the intensity and details as he moves ahead with carefully measured steps.

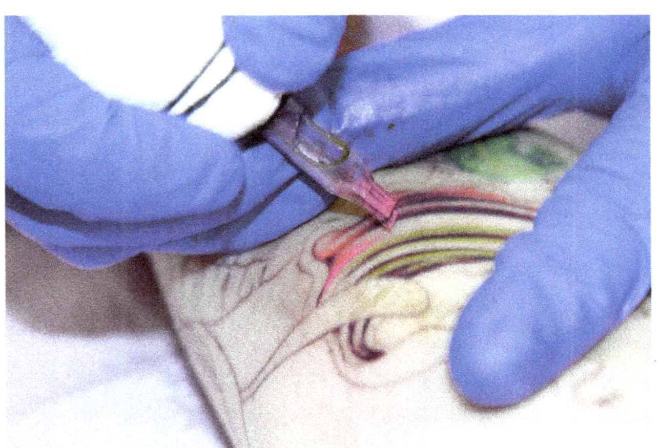

Additional touches of bright magenta are added to small sections as he sees the need.

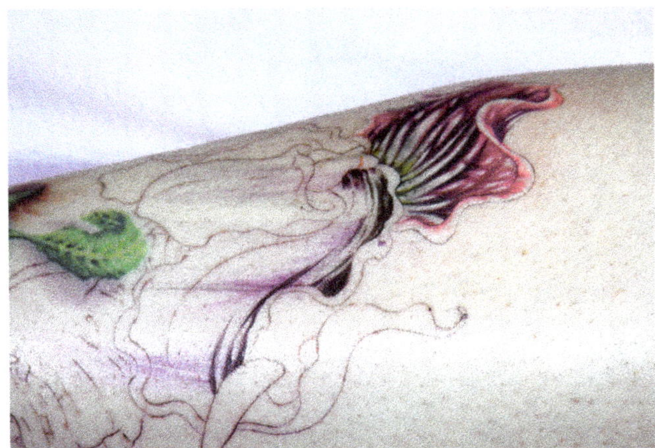

Initial line work begins on the flowing petals of the slipper orchid which flow away from the main body of the flower.

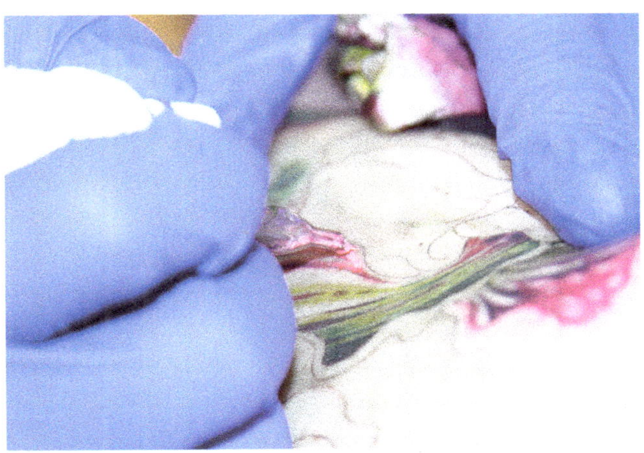

Choosing a shade of light pink he now adds a contrasting line to the darker hues already in place.

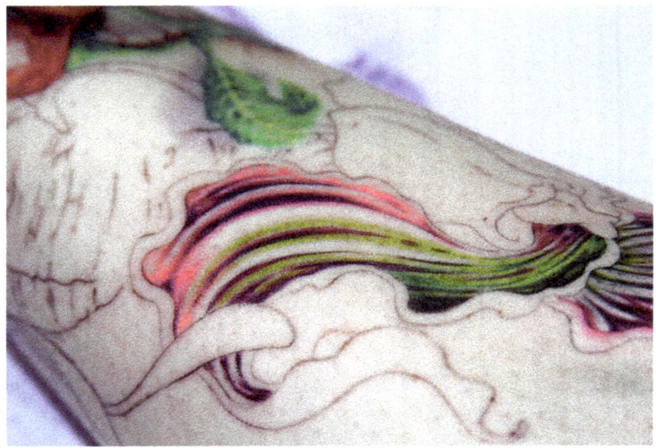

The varied shades of magenta, pink and different intensities of green really add shape and detail to the curving petals of the orchid.

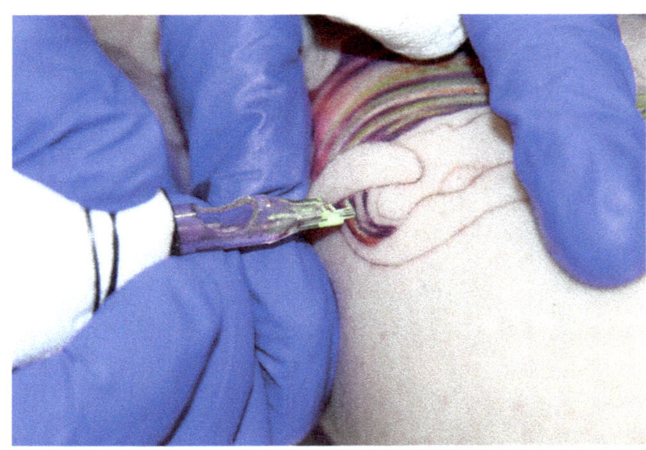

The light shade of green is barely visible but will enhance the overall composition of the finished piece.

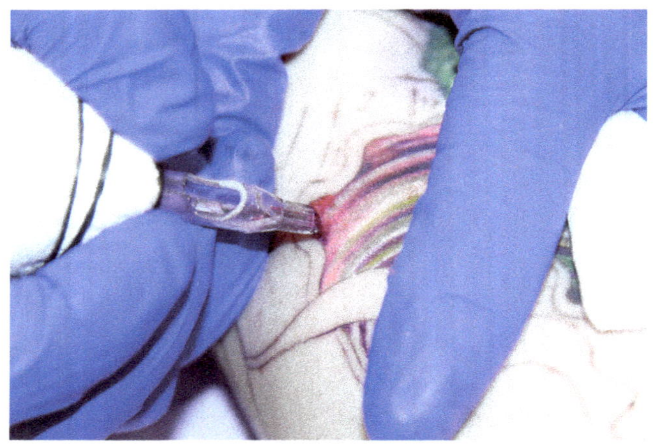

More magenta is used to bring needed changes to the canvas on Alex's leg.

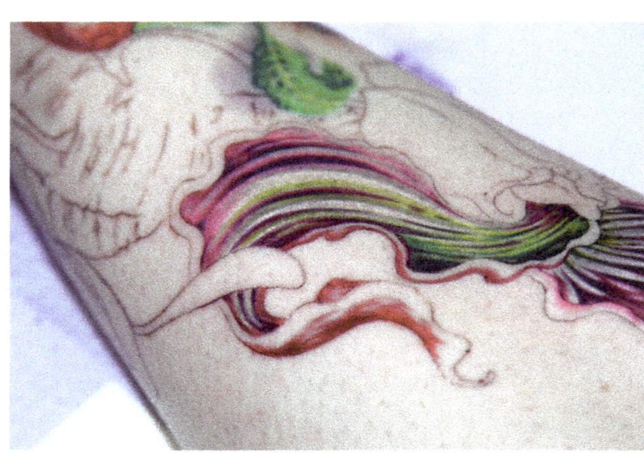

Once again cleaned of stray ink, we can see how Stephen is building the contours and definition of the orchid's petal.

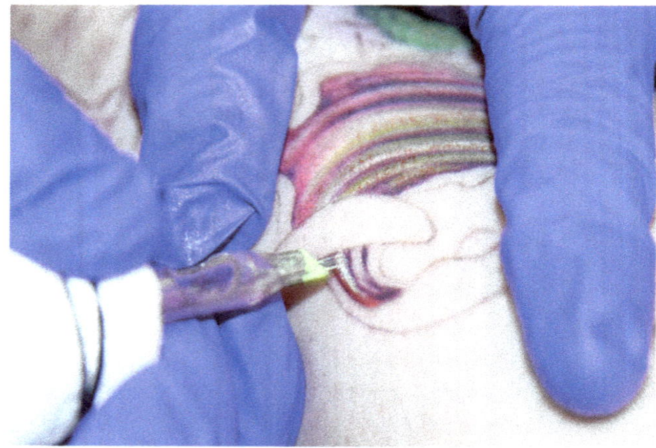

Tiny hints of light green will bring additional detail to the art and are only used in moderation as the piece is assembled.

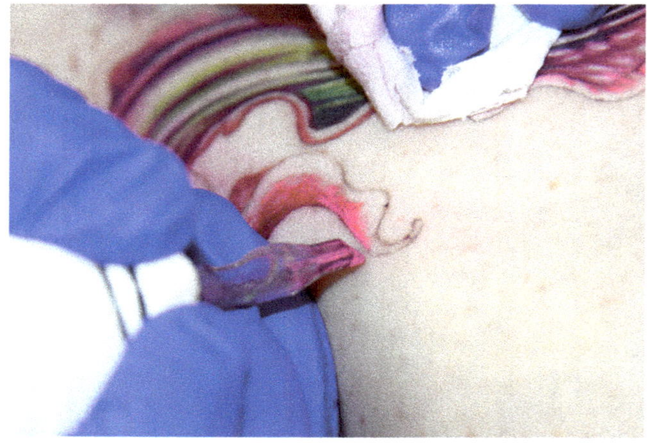

Returning to the bright magenta brings real clarity to the art and will closely mimic nature's design.

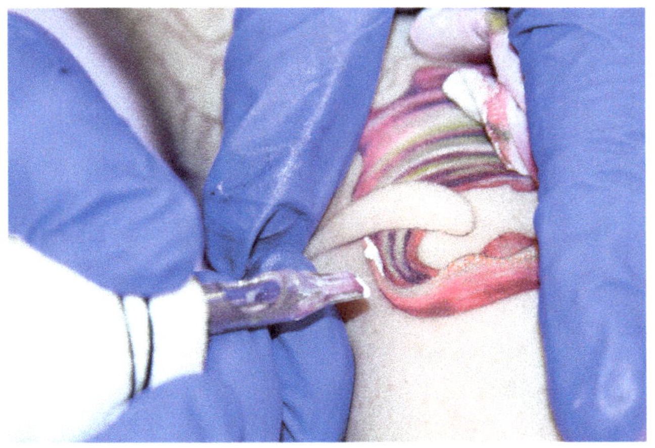

Adding tiny spots of white to bring highlights to the curves of the petal show his attention to detail.

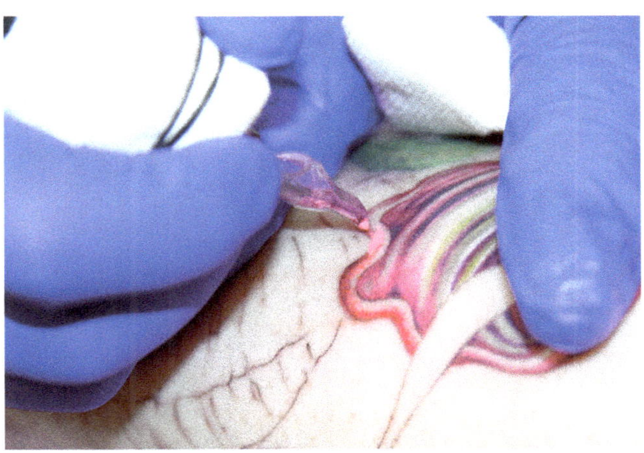

Switching rapidly and often from color to color is a distinct trait of Stephen's methods but the results are clear.

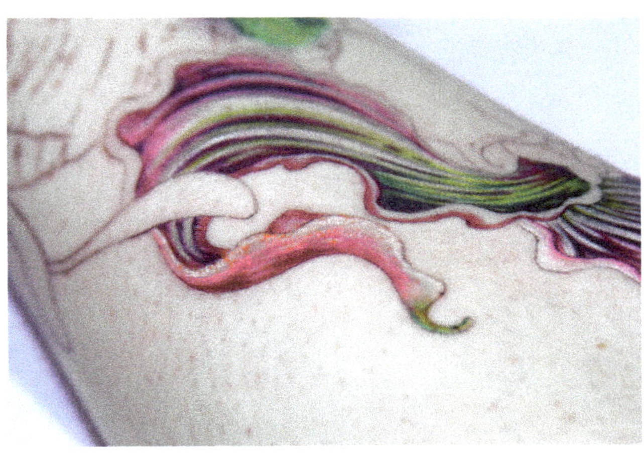

Another clean view shows only the tiniest trace of blood and the growing depth of the art.

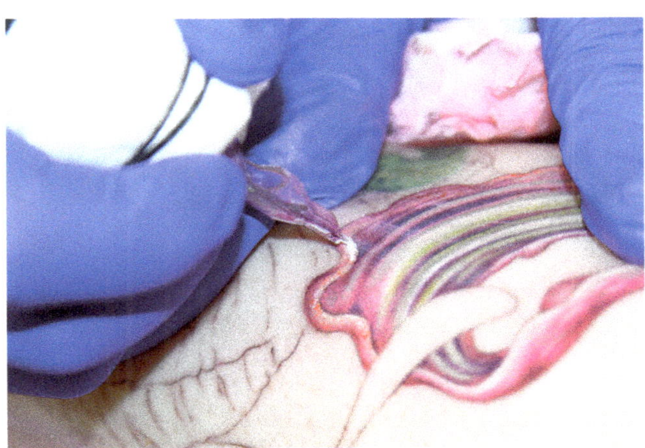

More highlights of white are added where he sees their need to bring added luster to the design.

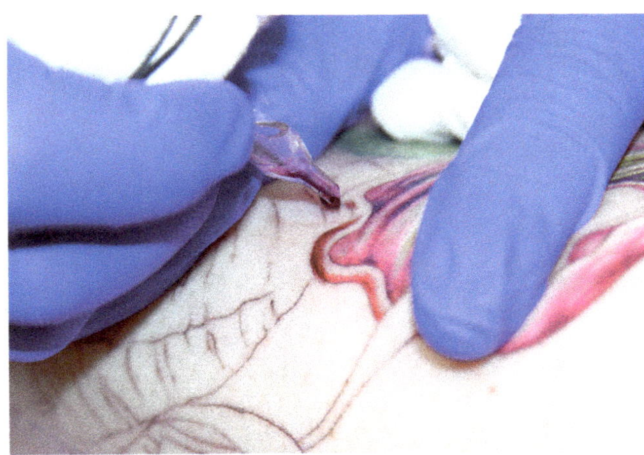

A darker shade of magenta will accent the lighter hues and create realistic contours to the 2-dimensional art.

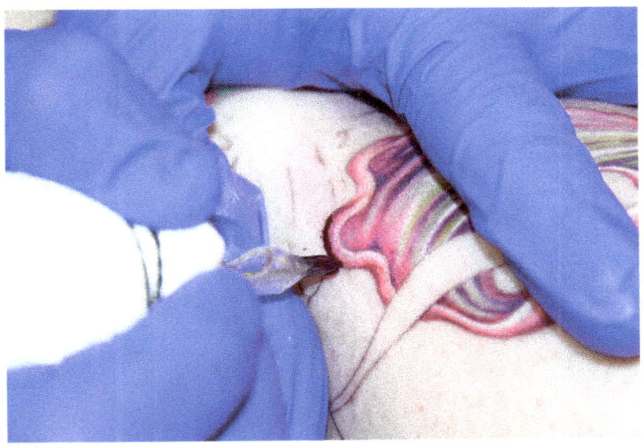

Dark magenta will highlight the edges of the petal and contrast nicely with the lighter colors used.

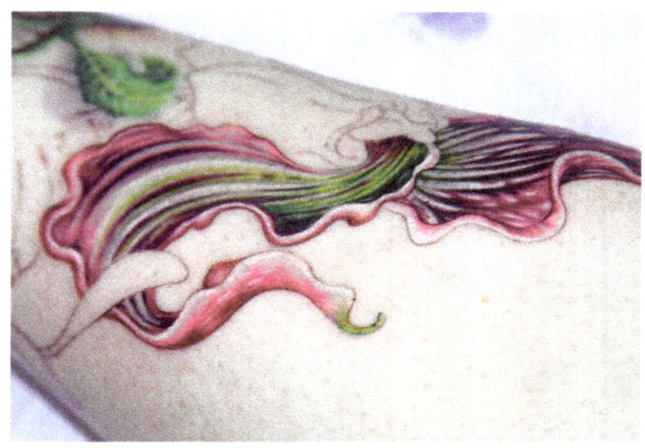

Another look at the work in progress shows us the gentle ways of bringing the piece to life.

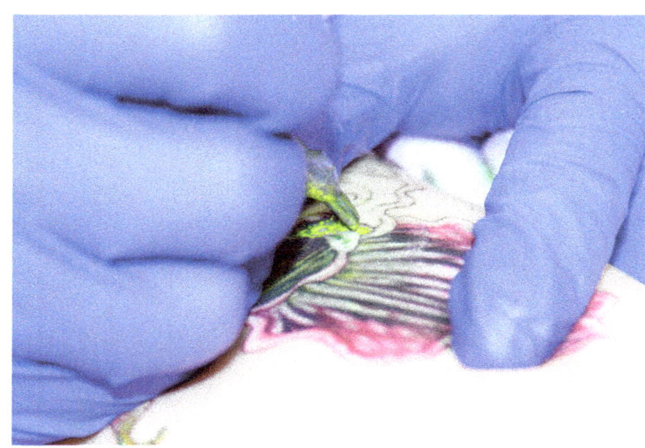

A vivid shade of green will bring added zest to the piece and is used sparingly to avoid the piece looking unnatural in its coloration.

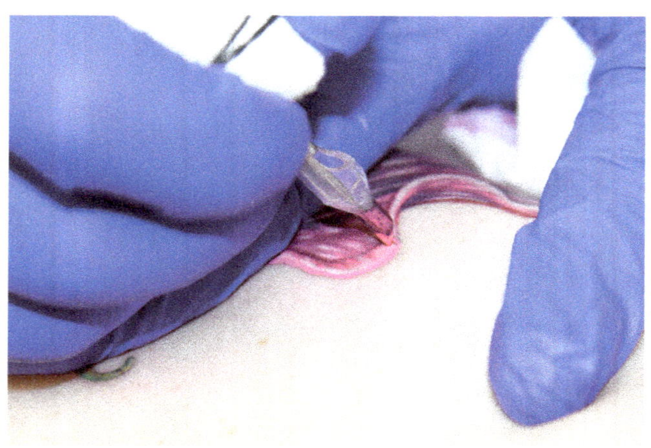

Again selecting a magenta tone to add more detail to the outer edges of the orchid, Stephen chooses carefully as he moves ahead with each step.

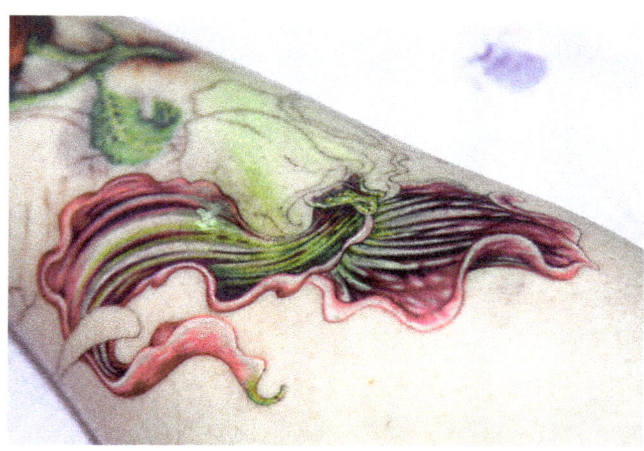

Each group of small steps brings the piece into greater detail and sharpness.

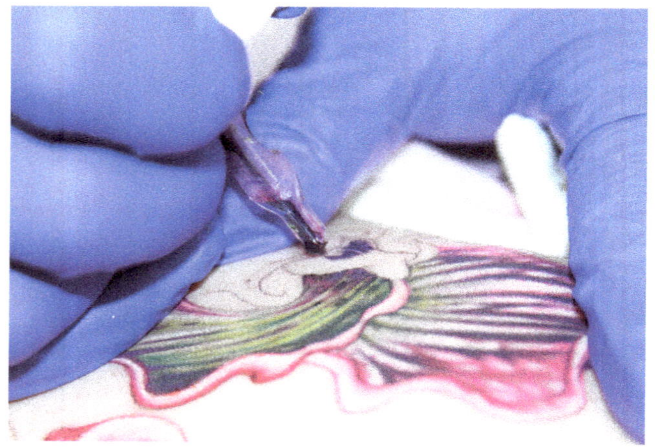

Choosing a dark purple from his array of inks he adds small segments to the lower portion of the body of the flower.

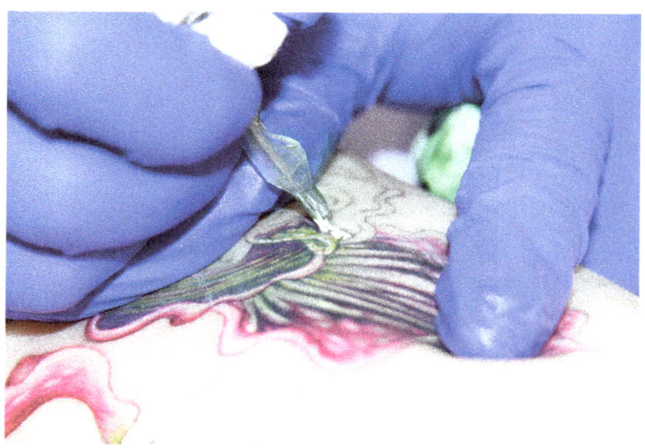

Small segments of bright white ink will bring intensity to some of the darker sections of the flower.

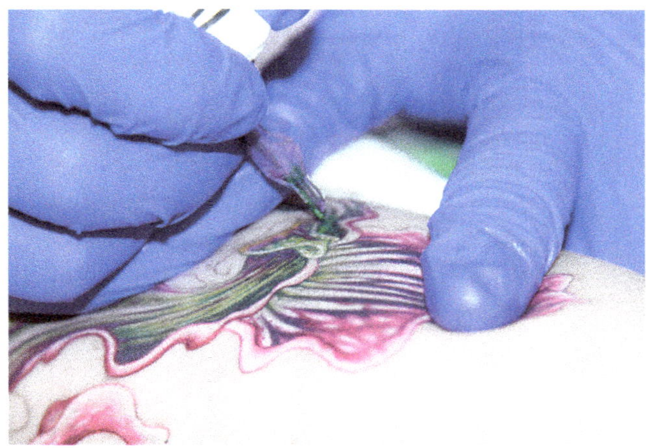

A variety of green inks will be used to ensure the completed piece will have enough hints of nature to compliment the more vivacious hues.

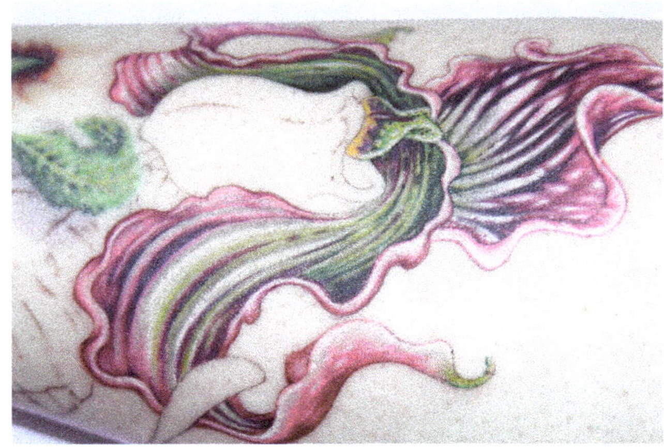

Every time he steps back to remove the excess ink from his art we see the added intensity of colors along with growing detail.

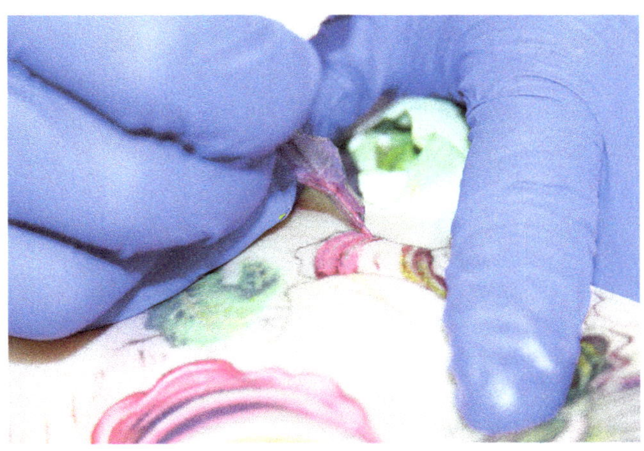

A light magenta ink is again chosen to bring color to the art in a truthful rendition of the orchid.

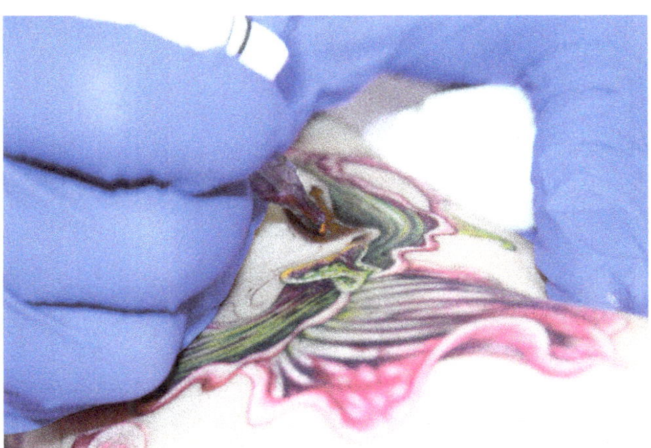

Blending two different hues he creates a shade of raw umber to once again add more subdued colors of nature to the design.

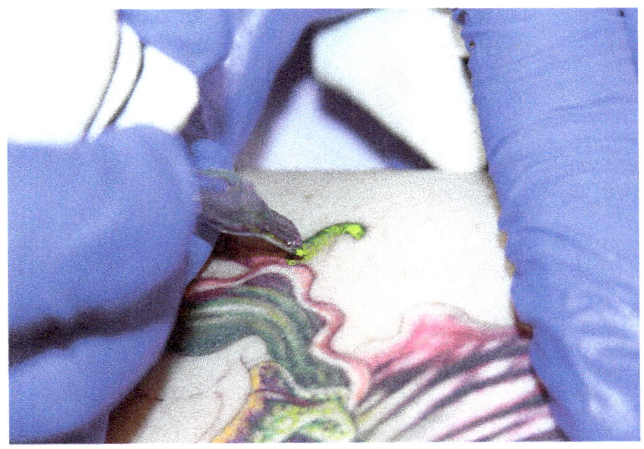

Using a different shade of light green he adds more custom blended hues to the piece.

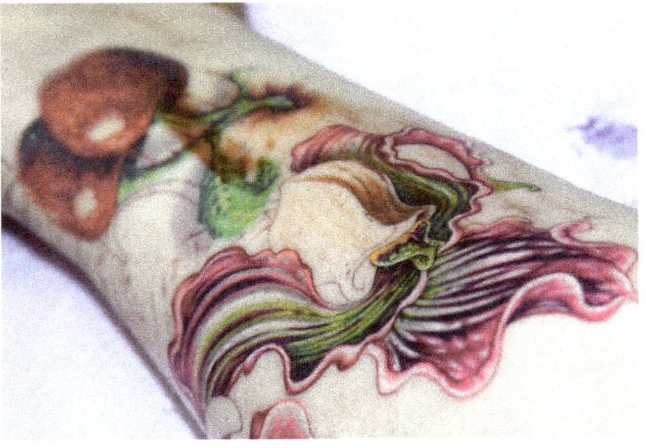

The use of so many colors as he progresses with the piece gives us proof of his unusual methods when creating a tattoo.

Q&A Stephen Knight

What your earliest interest in art discovered?

I began drawing when I was 5 and my parents noticed how well I did at it.

When did you become interested in tattoos?

As a sophomore in high school in 1993, I was a big rebel and saw the tattoo as one of the ways to show the world you were not willing to conform.

Who first taught you tattoo skills?

Jackie Melzner was the mother of my girl friend, who didn't tell me of her mom's ink or talent when we met.

Who became a mentor or inspiration for your work?

One of the biggest was Guy Aitchison who I became aware of in 2000. He was a painter and tattoo artist whose work really appealed to me and drew me to his style of art. Nick Baxter is another influence whose art also gained my attentions when I was younger.

How long have you been creating tattoo art?

1994 was the first year I actually put a needle to skin.

Do you remember who got your first tattoo and what it was?

Yes, Rich Borris got a picture of Mike Meyer from the Halloween movie ripping through the skin on his arm.

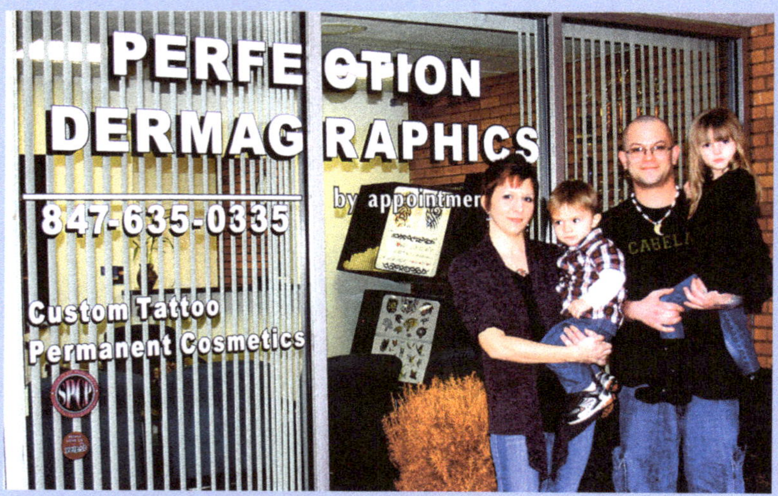

Stephen is seen here with his wife Jenny, his son Damien and his daughter Cordelia, in front of his shop.

When did you first get your shop experience?

In 2000 I spent time at Ageless Arts learning the craft and business of tattoos.

Do you have a favorite style or genre?

I really enjoy working in realism and flowers and natural subjects have always been my favorite pieces to create.

What was your biggest tattoo?

I have done numerous full back pieces, as well as complete legs, arms and chest designs.

What changes have you seen in the tattoo world since you began?

The exposure received on TV shows has altered the way people view a tattoo. They come into the shop wanting to buy a product when I think tattoos are still a form of art. They also think they can get an enormous piece done in an hour because that's what they see on TV. To create a truly high-quality piece it takes far more time and expense than many are willing to accept and I am not really sad to see them choose to walk away.

How long have you been at this location and how many artists do you have on staff?

We've been here since march of 2005. We currently have two full-time traditional artists and one part time. We also have one cosmetic artist who does the permanent-cosmetic style work.

What sort of future plans do you have for the business?

Having been a manager for many years, I hope to spend more time and attention on my art. By being able to focus on that aspect of the craft I can create better art which will show the world how my skills differ from others in the field.

Stephen also wants readers to know that the state of Illinois has passed a law making it illegal to get any tattoo work done outside of a registered shop. This helps to keep people without the needed skills and safety efforts to avoid damaging the reputation of those who spend a lot of time adhering to the guidelines that make tattoo art a safe way of expressing your thoughts in that manner.

He often adds touches of ink that are almost impossible to detect but will result in a highly detailed bit of unique art when done.

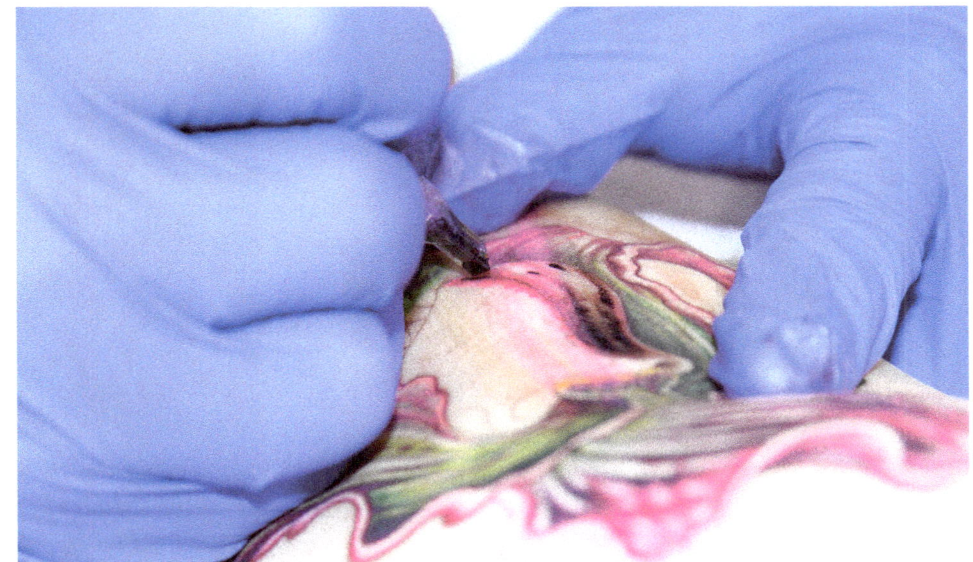

Bright yellow is used for most of the orchid's pouch and brings contrast to the shades of magenta used before.

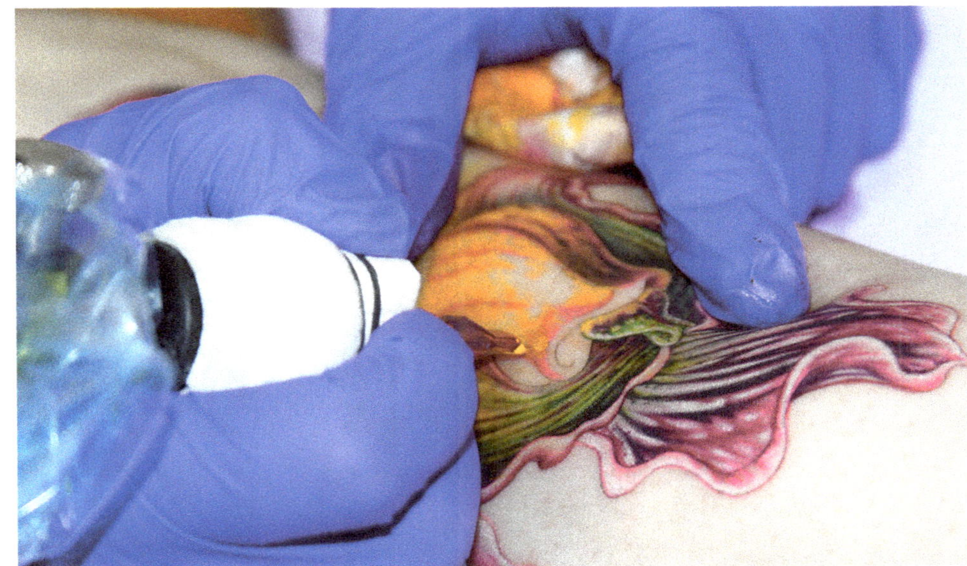

Fine lines of color including yellow are used to create the 3-dimensional shapes seen on the orchid's components.

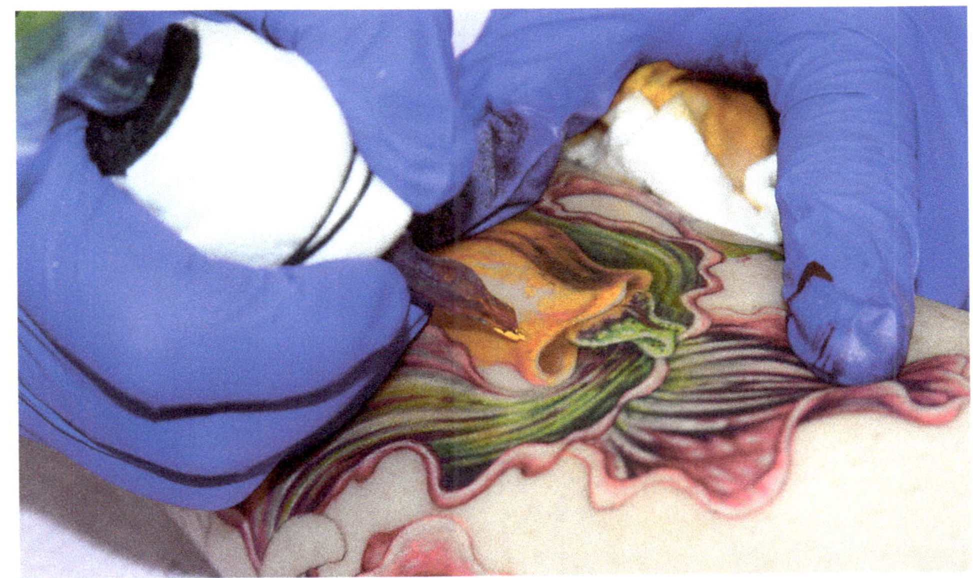

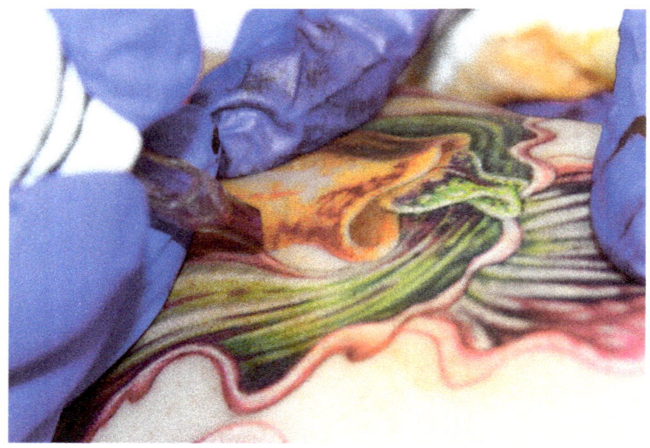

Additional hints of magenta are used to continue the brightly colored theme.

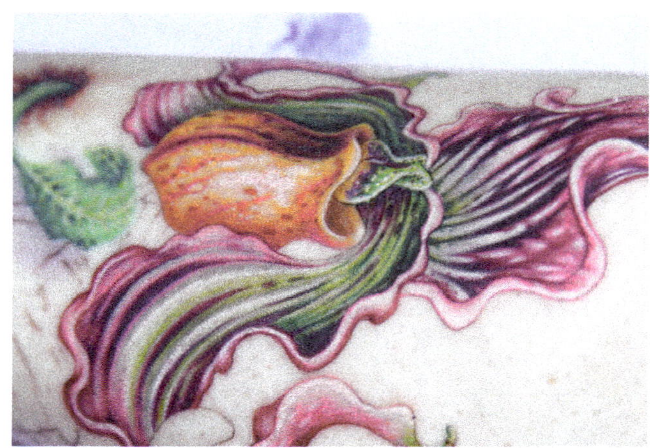

The addition of the glowing yellow pouch at the center of the art highlights the myriad of colors and shapes used on this design.

With the yellow pouch in the background more pink is added to the surrounding foliage.

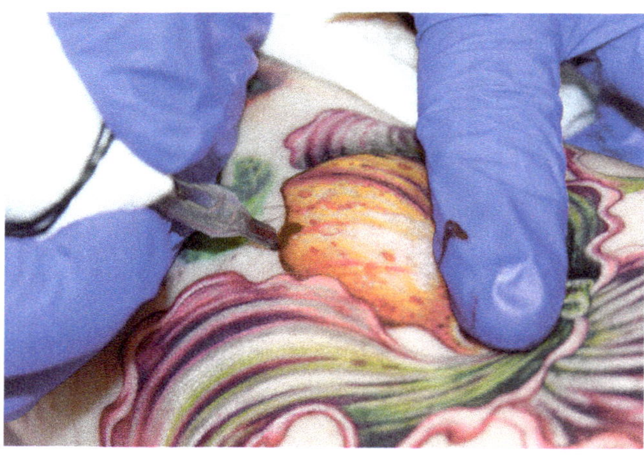

Not satisfied with the earlier use of brown, Stephen returns to the scene to augment the earlier section on the bottom of the pouch.

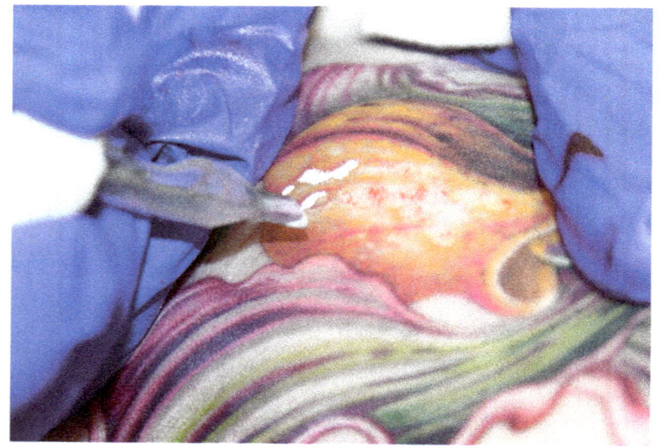

Alternating between a 7 mag and 5 round needle set allows Stephen to change the width of his lines along with the variety of colors.

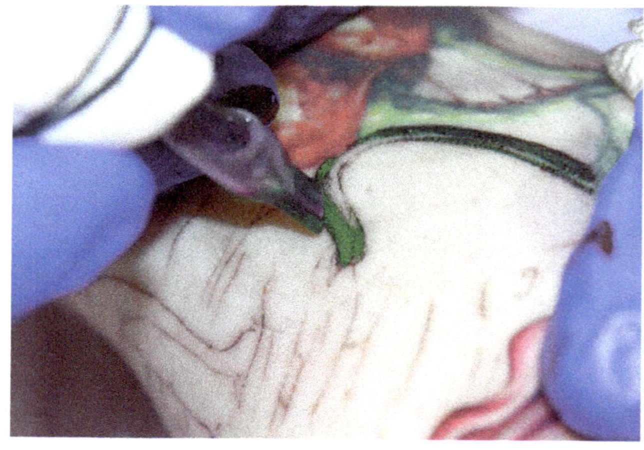

Turning his attention to the vines a green ink is chosen to fill in the curved shapes.

A dark shade of olive green is used to separate the petals from the root that will now become a part of the plan.

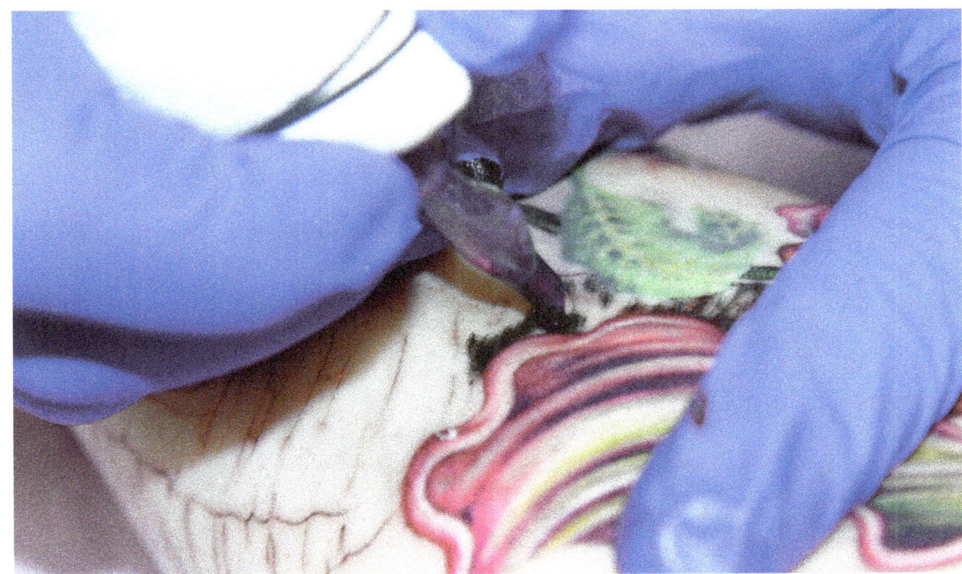

The 7 mag needle set will allow him to add a larger sections of green and brown to the root as desired.

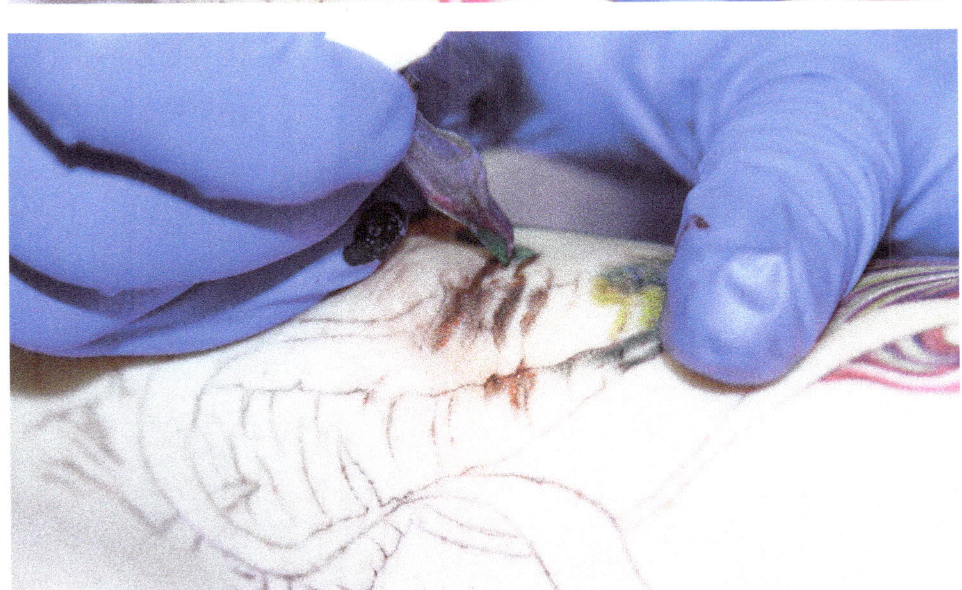

Short, staccato motions allow tiny lines of black to be used to add a drop shadow to the lower portion on the pouch.

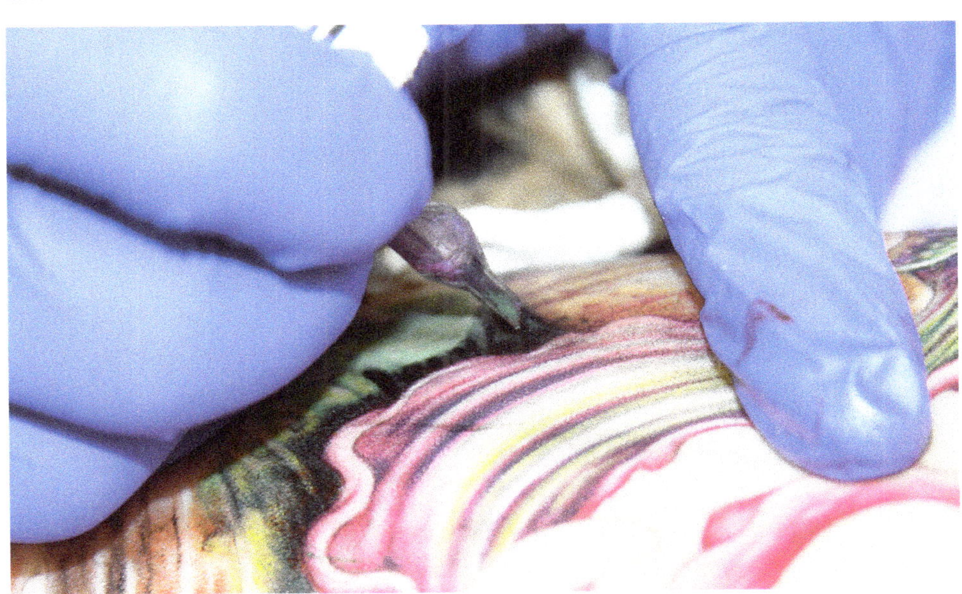

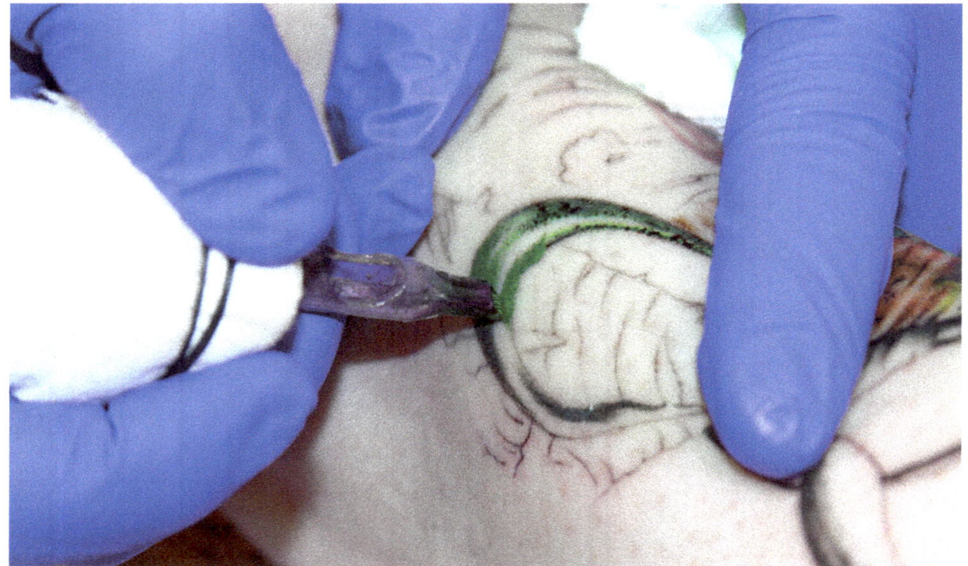

More blended green in used to bring dimension to the accenting vines.

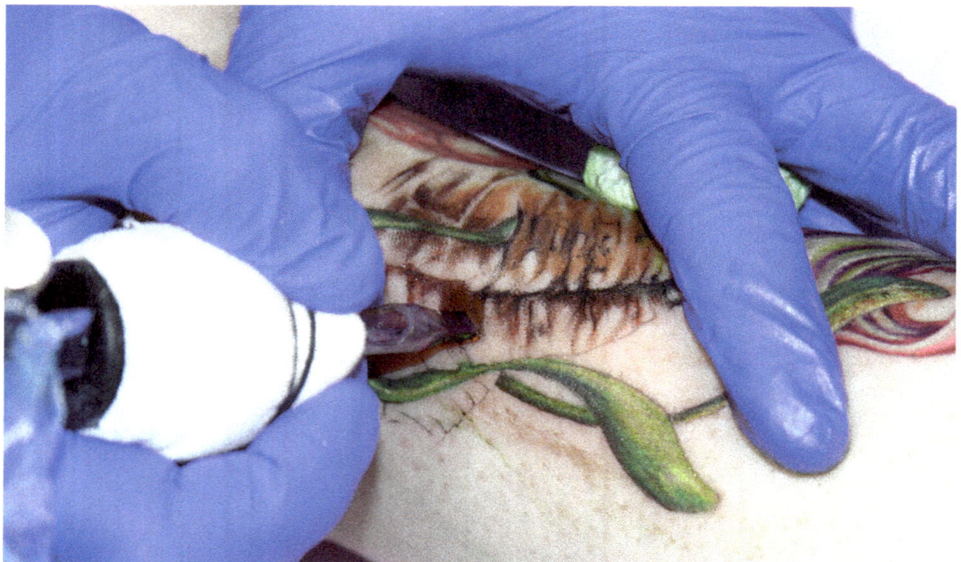

The root will be primarily brown and green as seen in nature.

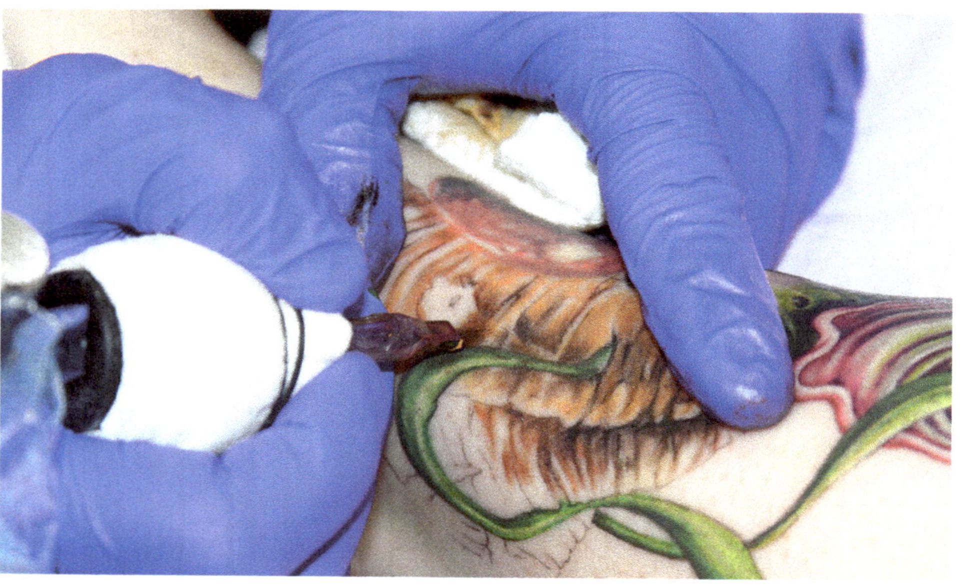

Using a blended shade of tan to bring more natural colors to the root we can see and almost taste the plant.

The root portion of the tattoo is detailed but a bit more subtle than the focus of the piece, the slipper orchid.

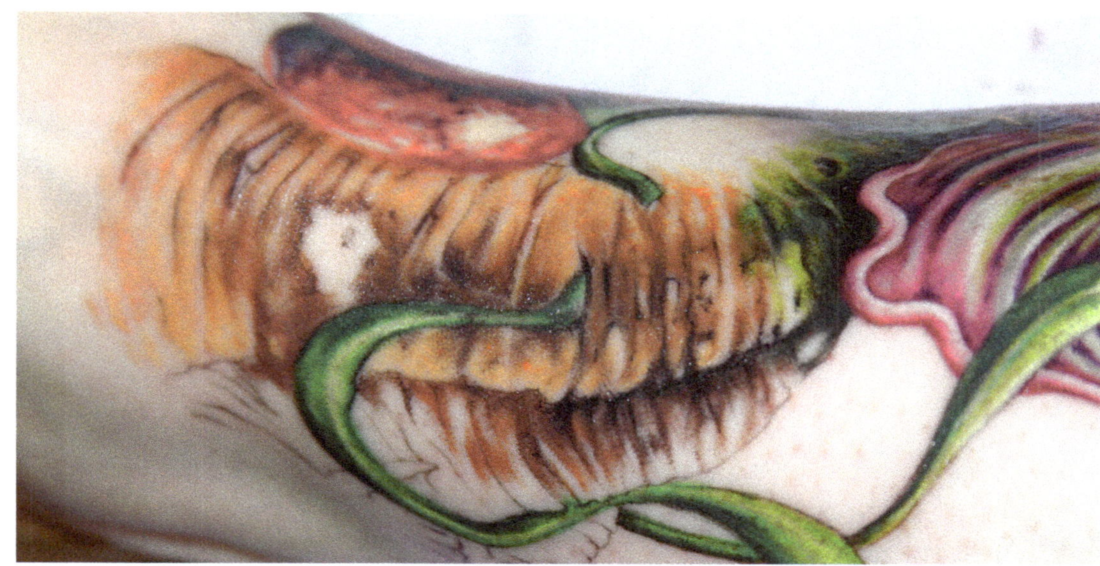

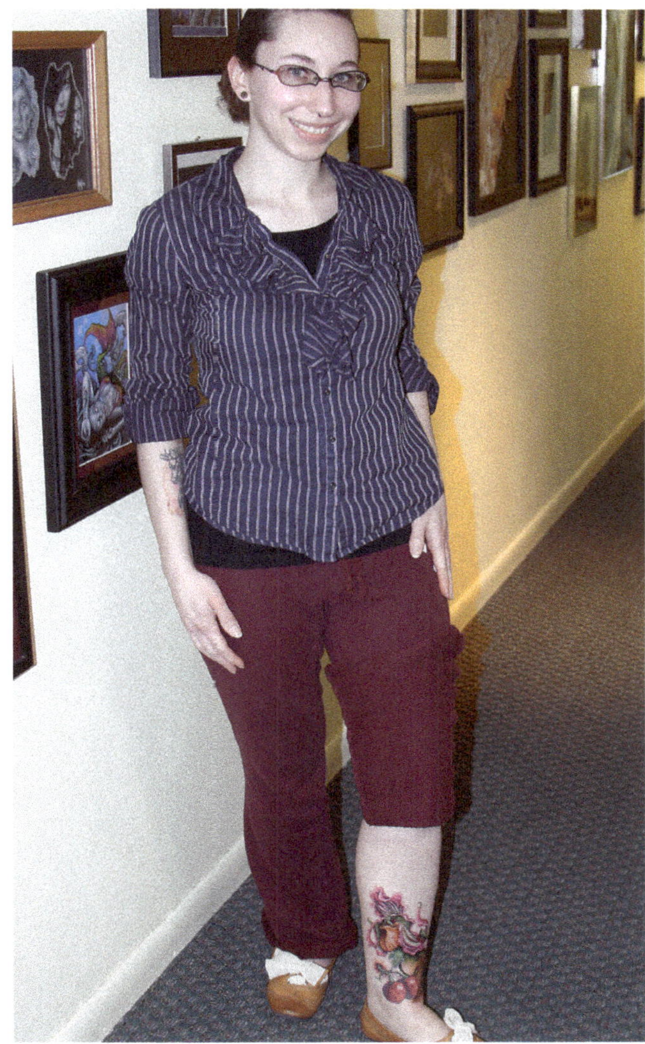

Alex proudly displays her latest tattoo in the hallway of the shop. Her illustration was the genesis of the art, so she can rightly take an added level of pride in the piece.

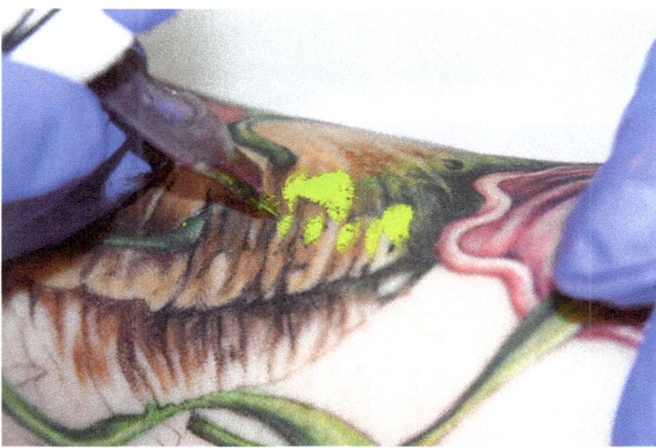

Bringing some levity to the brown root a bright green hue is added for highlights.

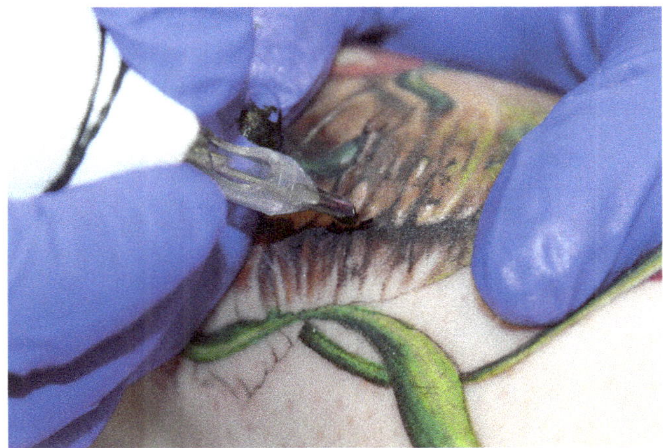

Dark brown ink is added to the root in contrast to the intense green seen a few steps ago.

Chapter One

Larry Brogan

Tattoo City

With his interest in art beginning at a very young age, people knew that Larry Brogan would follow some path in that arena; they just weren't sure which one. He studied art in both high school and college, and went on to begin doing tattoos over 16 years ago. His work has become well respected in the industry, and the walls of his shop, Tattoo City, are covered in trophies, plaques and awards from shows and magazines. While he has his portfolio walking around on the streets, the in-store awards are one way for a person to gauge his success.

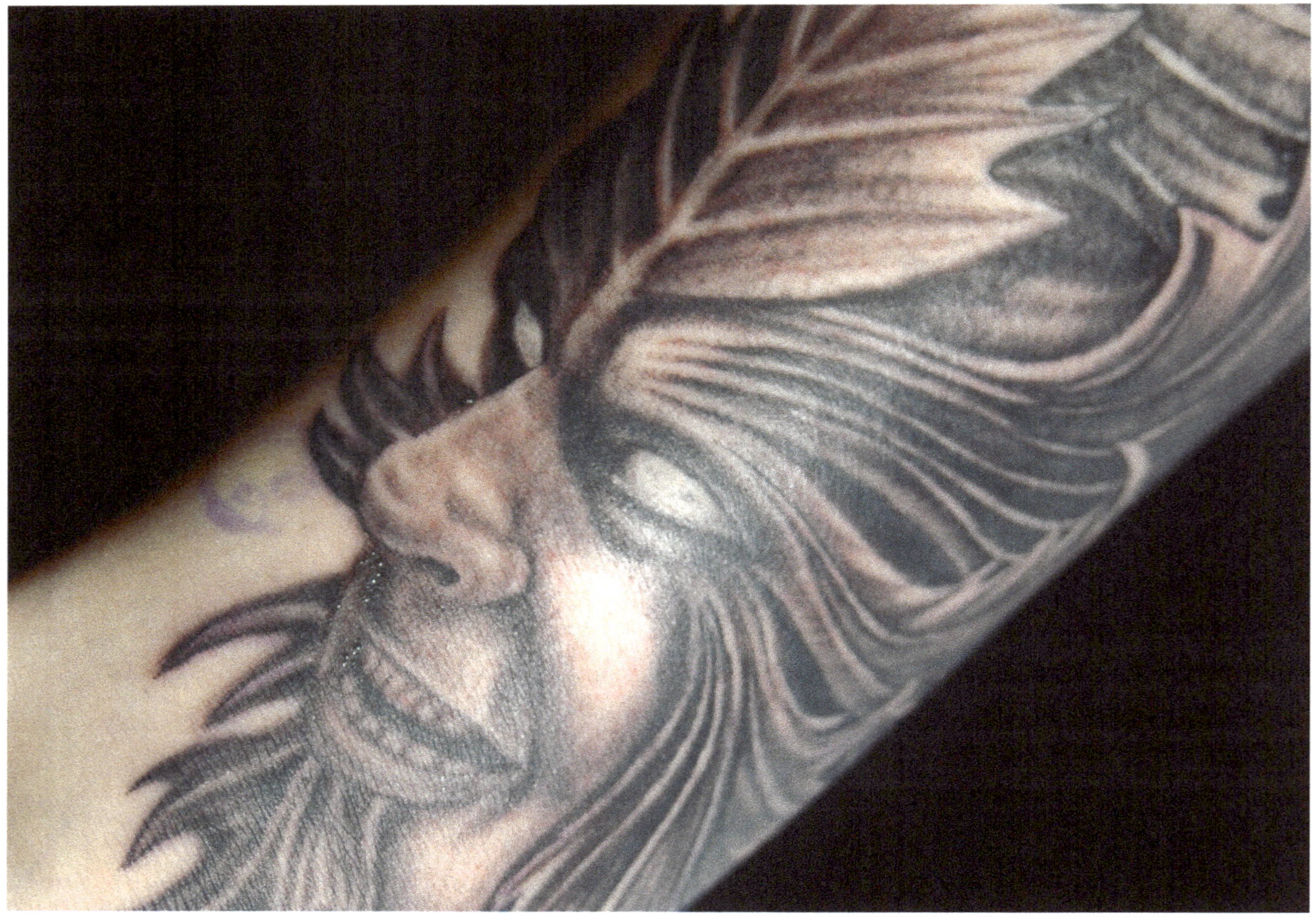

With a well earned reputation as a tattoo artist who works in the horror field, Larry's latest effort was to create a "leaf man" character for his client. With Halloween a strong factor, and an image of Jack Nicholson for inspiration, Larry sketched out then put to skin this highly detailed black and gray piece.

Being a big fan of the Halloween season, Frankie had instructed Larry to create a "leaf man" for his next bit of ink. Working from some reference images, including one taken from a popular horror movie, Larry sketched up the illustration. Even this basic drawing shows us his ability to create art in a one dimensional form, but this is only the tip of the iceberg when it comes to the actual tattoo. Frankie reviewed the drawing, and after a few minor suggestions they selected the proper location on his lower leg for the needle work. It was designed to be a black and gray piece, and I wondered how different the process would be when there were no colors in the finished tattoo.

Once Frankie's leg was prepped and shaved, Larry transferred the image to his skin. A few final lines from a felt tip pen completed the required guide lines and Larry was ready to get to work. Before putting a single needle to the skin, he always checks the sharpness of the hardware through a jeweler's loupe. He says that even the factory-sealed, sterilized needles can have bent or "hooked" tips, causing a lot of pain and resulting in a lower quality piece if art.

Satisfied with the sharpness of the selected 7 and 13 mag needle sets, he loads them into the waiting machines. Larry used a disposable tube for the larger 13 mag needle because he was running short of the steel ones that can carry the bigger set. He often uses these disposable tubes when traveling to shows as a way to keep his flying weight down, and to avoid having to drag home a bunch of used and dirty tubes.

With this being the first black and gray piece I witnessed, I asked what changes in the process would be used. The layered look of the leaf man's foliage would require the facial features to be darker while the uppermost would be a bit lighter for effect. No black outline was used on the face and surrounding illustration, only shading and contours would define that section. A few of the upper leaves were to get an outline, if only to set it apart from the skin in higher definition.

With a copy of his original sketch as well as a print-out of the movie star's grimacing face, Larry set his needles to work. Beginning around the lips, teeth and nose, the shape of the face quickly takes

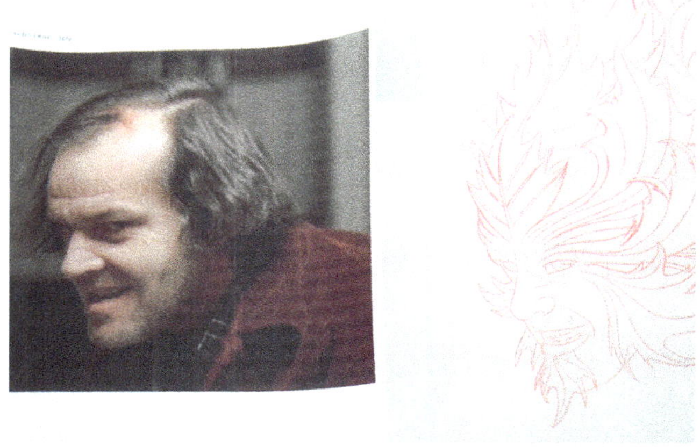

Finding this image on the internet, Larry used the grimacing facial features as a guide when drawing up his own illustration.

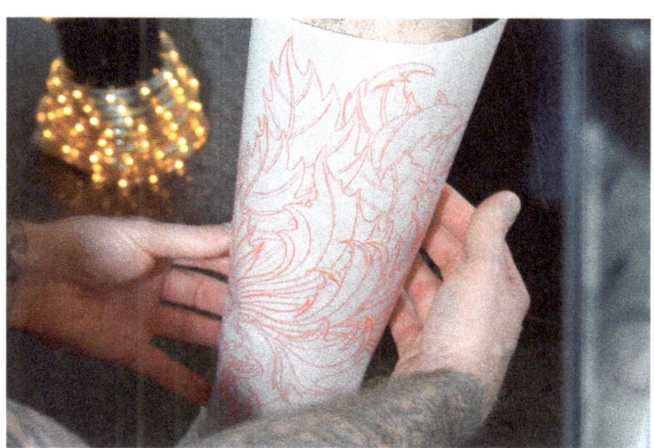

After a few minor changes to the sketch, Larry tests the size and placement on Frankie's leg.

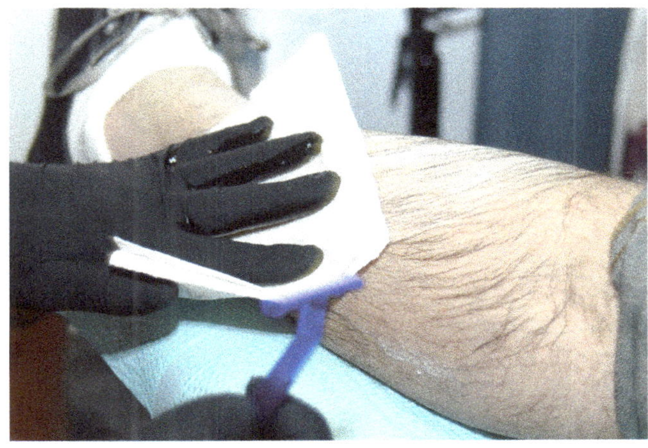

Now seated in the chair, Larry preps the area to be inked by wiping it down with cleansing soap prior to shaving the calf.

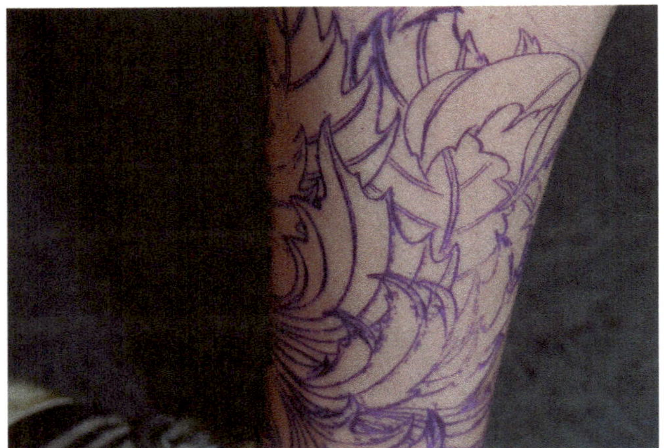

With the transfer paper removed we can see the ink blue lines that will guide Larry through the process.

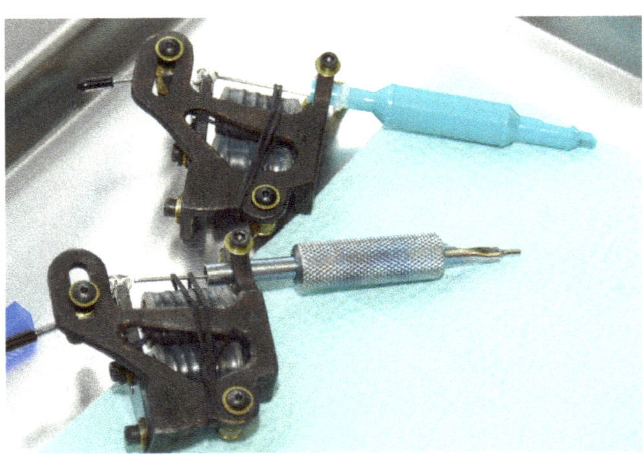

This black and gray tattoo will be produced using only 2 needle sets, and each is pre-loaded into their own machine before the process begins.

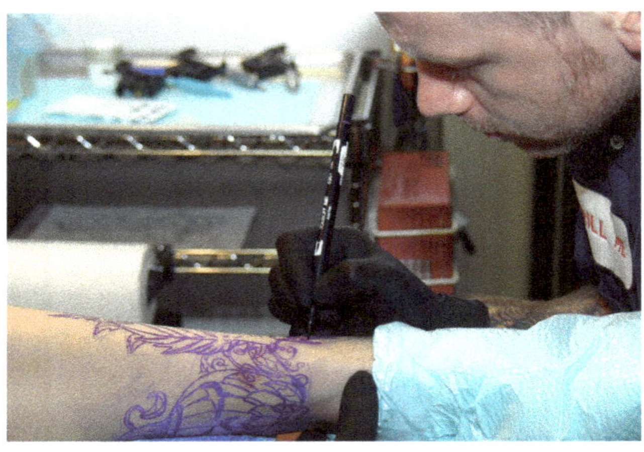

Larry spends a few minutes making sure that every line of the piece is easy to see before getting started and uses a felt tip pen to add missing lengths of line.

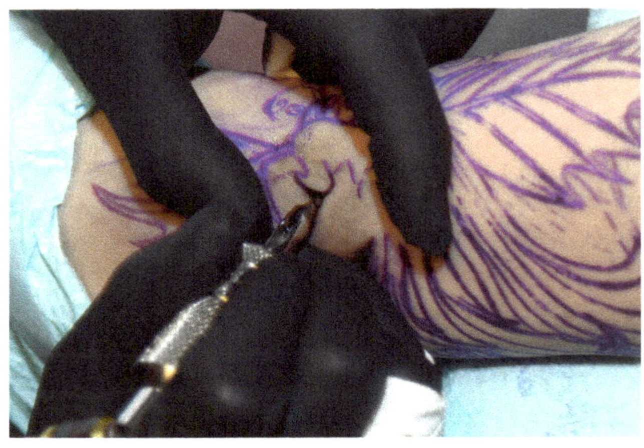

A 7 mag set begins the basic work of the piece, but very little outlining will be done due to the black and gray artwork that is scheduled.

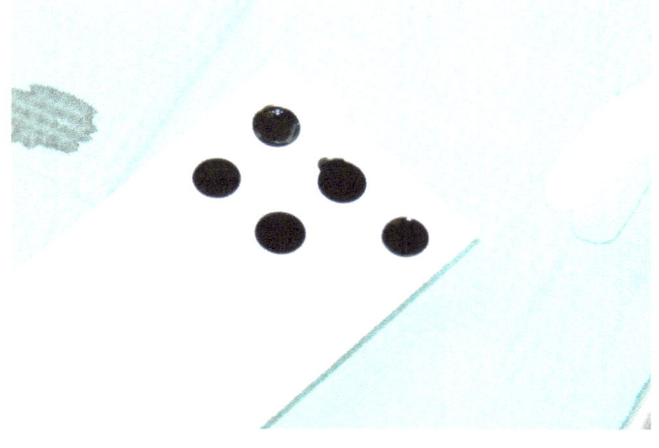

A molded tray holds the black ink in place as well as the thinner shades of gray that will be employed during the work.

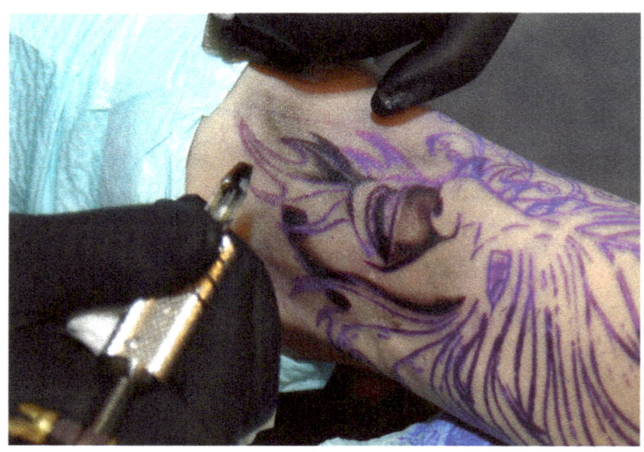

Larry has begun work around the grinning moth of the leaf man and shades each area carefully to build up the shadows and shapes.

shape. When working in the black and gray style, the definition of shape and contour takes place more slowly as to avoid turning any area into a puddle of black. Small sections of ink were installed, leaving behind a subtle shape that would grow into a nearly 3-dimensional form as he progressed. The cups of ink were filled with a pure black, as well as a few that were thinned-out with water for the gray in-between shades. Given this limited range of density, I was surprised to watch as the tattoo came to life in ever-expanding detail. Having learned about eight tattoos ago not to ask questions of why something was being done, it was amazing to see Larry work his magic using only shades of black.

To achieve the depth and definition he required, Larry also filled in several well placed areas with nearly pure black to make them appear as shadowy areas among the highly detailed. As I told him during the work I'd be happy to be able to draw with such clarity and detail, let alone translate it into a tattoo. As they say on TV, don't try this at home.

A few breaks were taken during the process, but the needle work still progressed quickly and the tattoo took on more life with every passing sting of the needles. Frankie's discomfort seemed to be highly tolerable for about 95% of the work, only squirming when certain sections of the calf were darkened. Not being a beginner at getting new ink, he had been ready for whatever level of pain might occur. All in all he said that other pieces he wears were far worse.

Larry worked steadily, and the piece grew in intensity as he continued to fill the needles, place the ink and wipe away the excess. Every once in awhile he would wipe the work clean to reveal his progress, and that would tell him more clearly what needed to be addressed. His eye for detail was astounding as he saw and added small bits that didn't even seem to be required. The size of the art and the placement on Frankie's calf required him to change his position often so Larry could reach every corner of the guide lines. When placing the transfer onto his leg, Larry left room for the next installation, which will be an evil jack-o-lantern that will nestle between the leaves of this mythical creature.

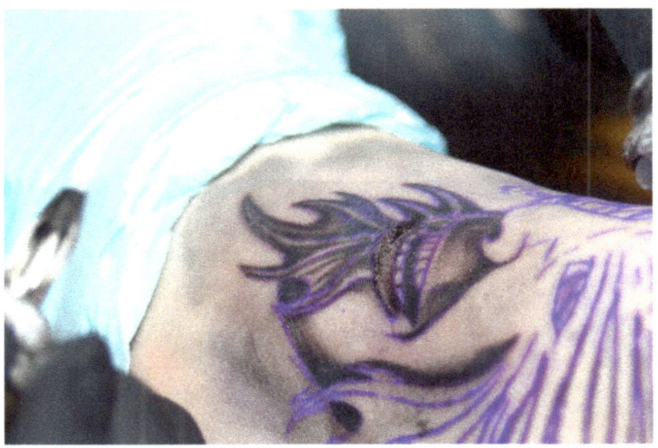

Even lacking the usual black outline we can quickly see the 3-dimension effects of Larry's ink work.

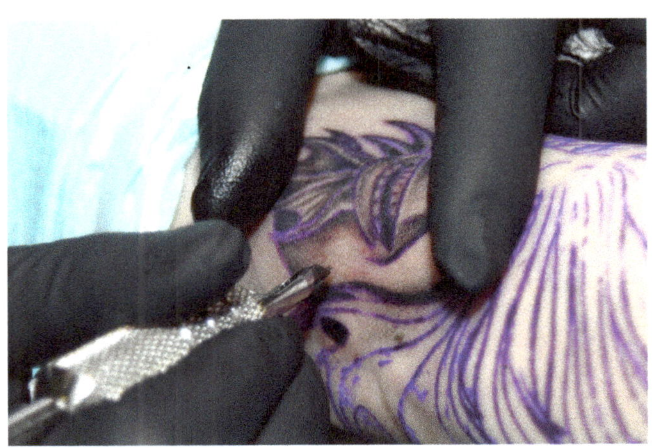

Holding the leg meat of Frankie taught, Larry continues to apply small sections of black and gray ink.

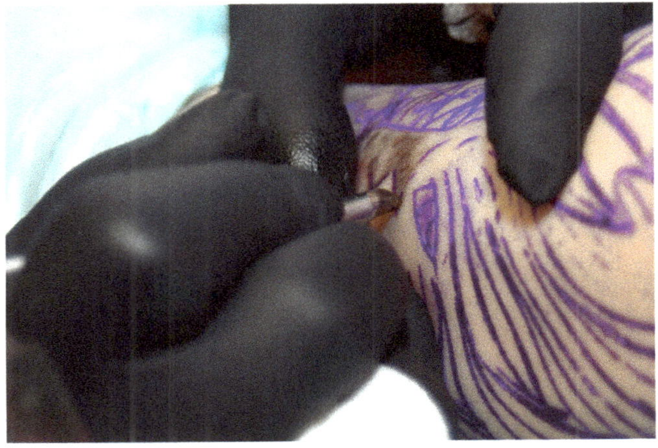

Small details are added as the tedious process moves along, exposing more and more of the epidural engraving.

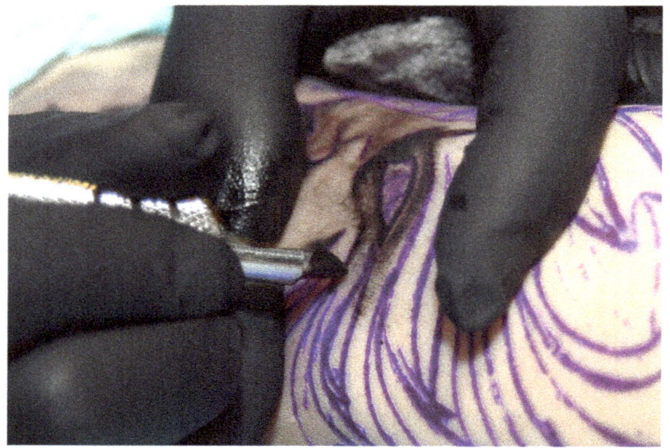

Shading around the eyes will enhance the vacant orbs that will be highlighted in a later step.

The tattoo required nearly seven hours in the chair, but in the end all parties were very satisfied with the results. It would take another week to ten days for the piece to heal completely, but the immediate effects of Larry's talented hands were obvious. During the creation of this tattoo, several people came into, or called the shop inquiring about getting work done. Sadly for them, Larry had to explain that he was booked for nearly 2 months in advance. This long lead time is only one more way to gauge the talents of a gifted artist from those who may still be learning the craft. Between the awards in his shop, and the amount of eager clients waiting to receive his work it was obvious to me that Larry has earned a top spot in the crowded world of tattoo artists.

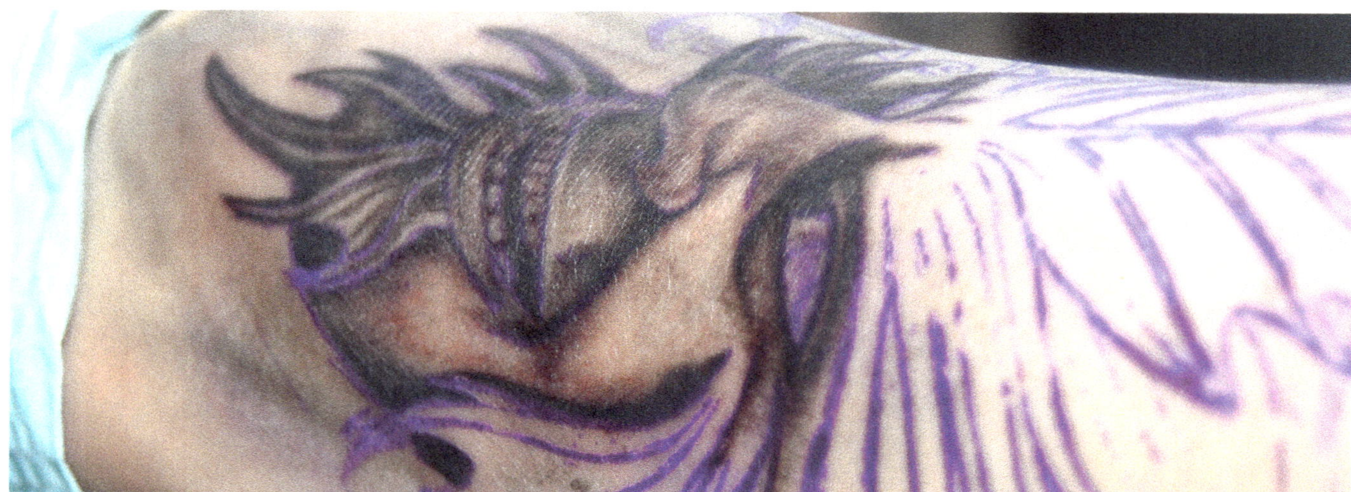

The evil grimace of the piece begins to take shape as Larry steps back to review his work so far.

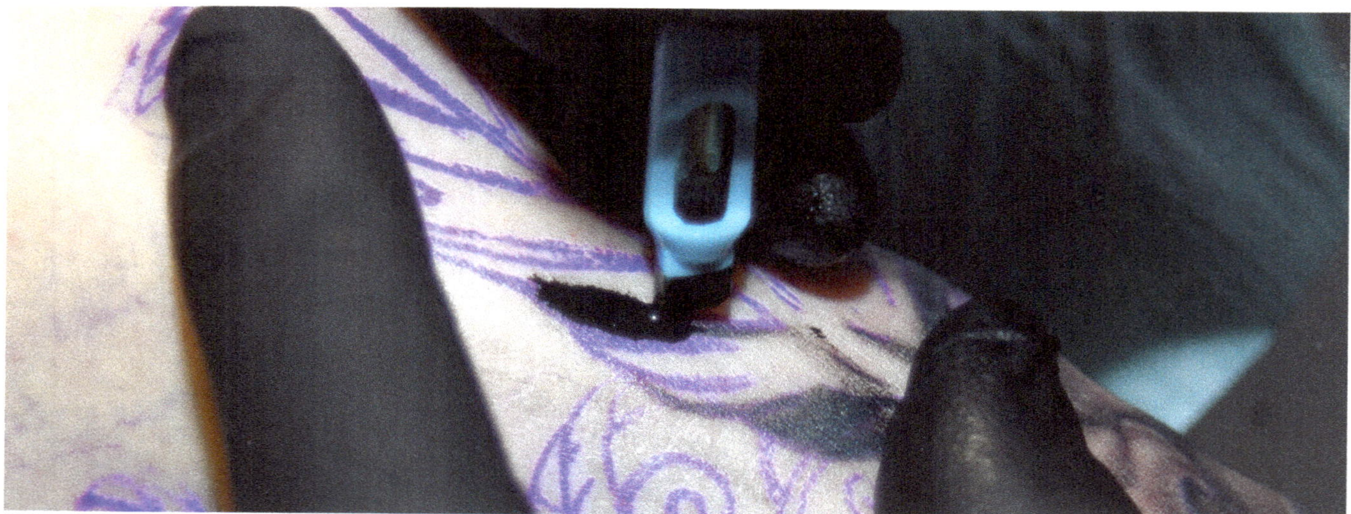

Turning his attentions to some of facial leaves for now, Larry begins to fill and shade their shapes.

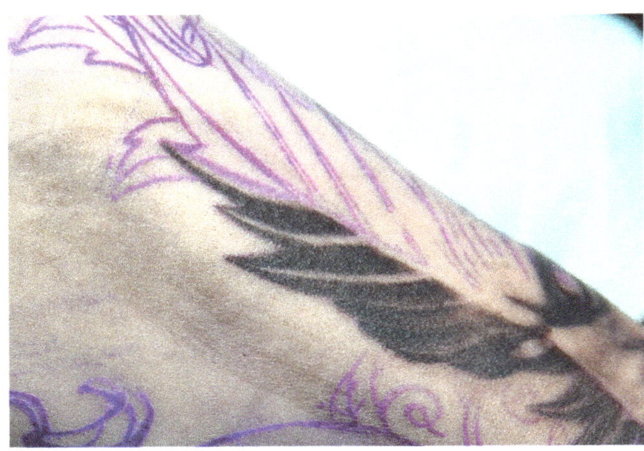

The leaves near the face will be done in darker shades of black and gray while those toward the top of the piece will recede into lighter levels.

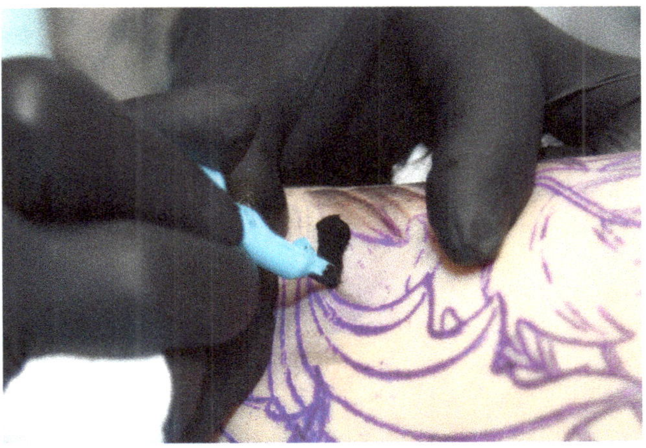

An area in between some of the leaves will be much darker to enhance the depth of the piece.

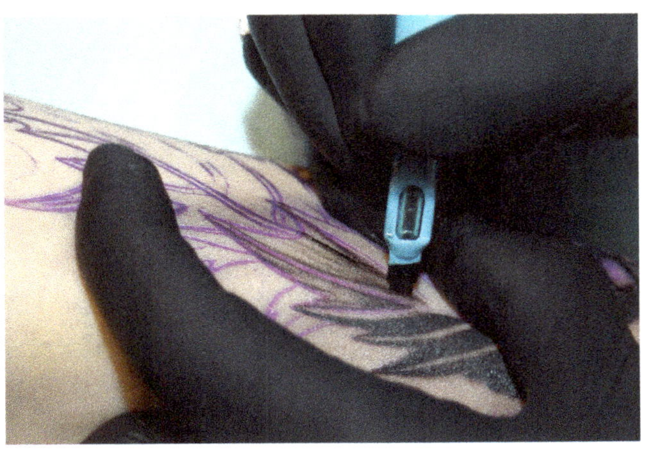

Subtle contours of each leaf must be built-up slowly to avoid turning too dark and appearing only as black clumps.

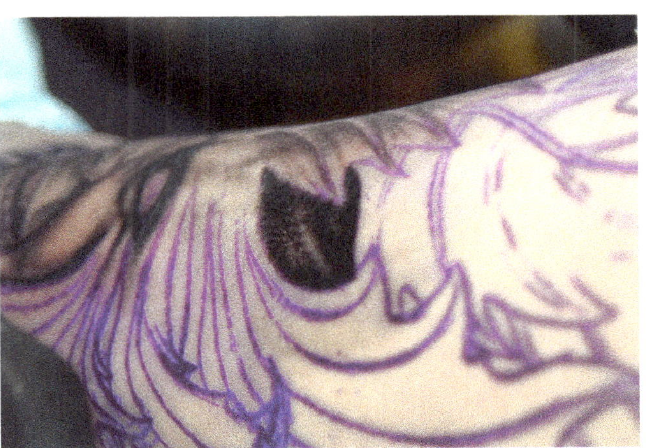

The shadowy area behind some of the frontal leaves will create more life when the tattoo is complete.

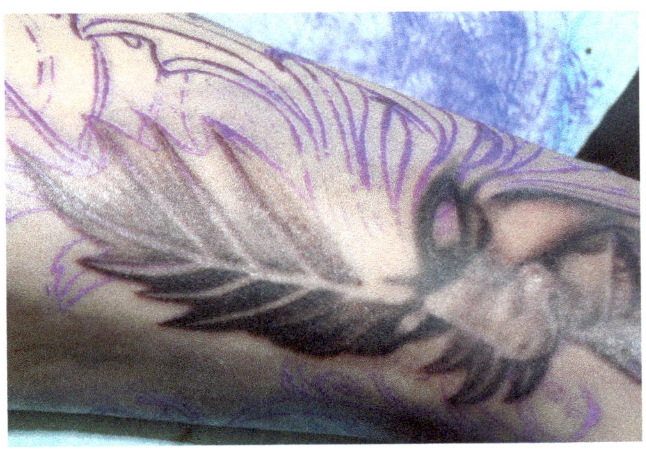

Another step back from the work so far reveals Larry's progress and gives Frankie a brief respite from the stinging needles.

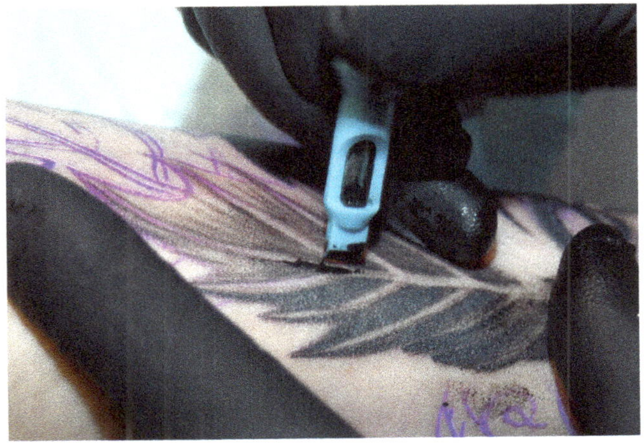

Using the wider 13 mag needles, Larry turns the machine sideways to create a thin detail with the bigger instrument.

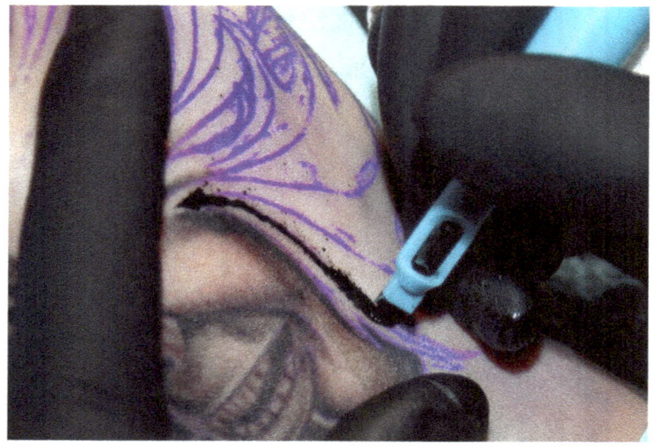

Not sure if they are leaves or sideburns, but Larry turns his attention to the flowing lines that surround the mouth.

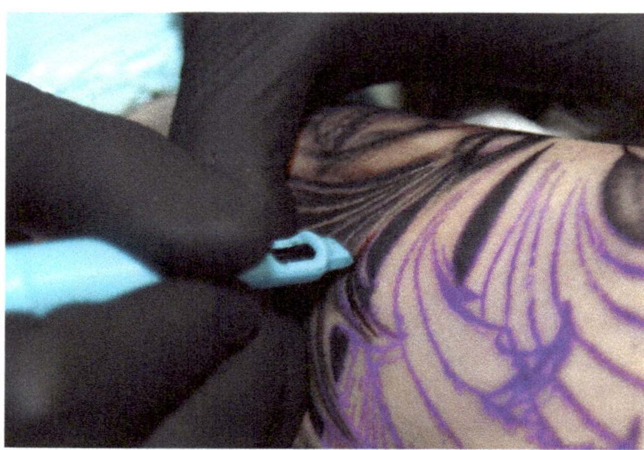

The areas of pure black will contrast nicely against the lighter, more detailed sections of the work.

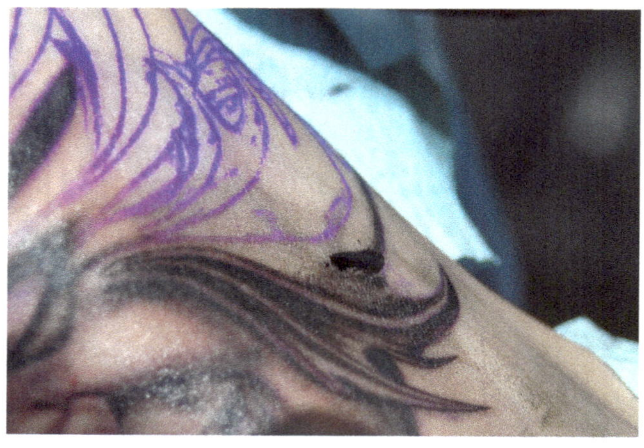

Smudges of black ink soon turn into amazing details under the control of Larry's talented hands.

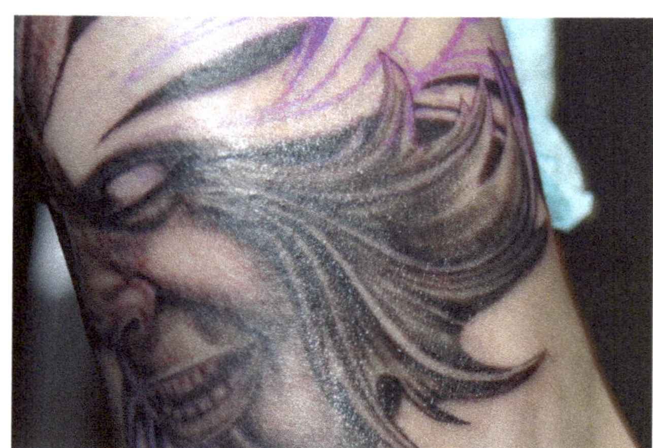

Larry's efforts are rewarded with a section of the face that seems to be almost photographic in its detail.

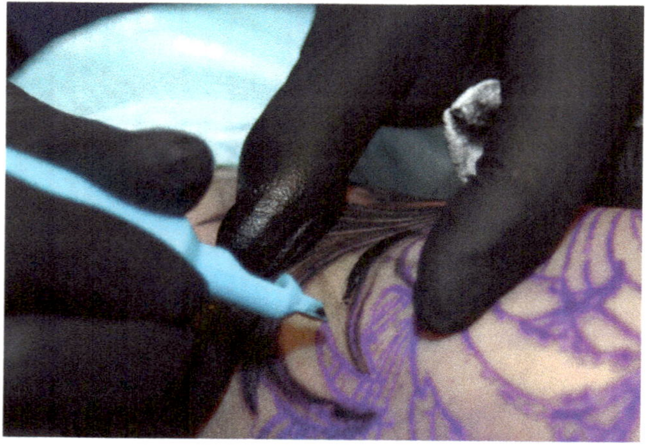

Certain areas of the tattoo are completed with long sweeps of the needles while some require smaller movements.

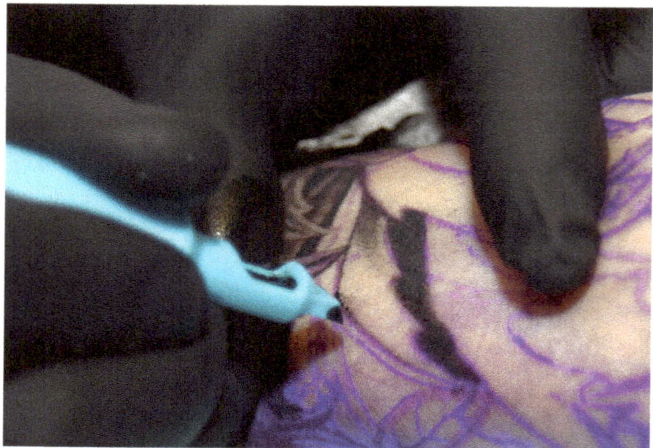

Again, the larger 13 mag needle is used to fill in a bigger segment of the art.

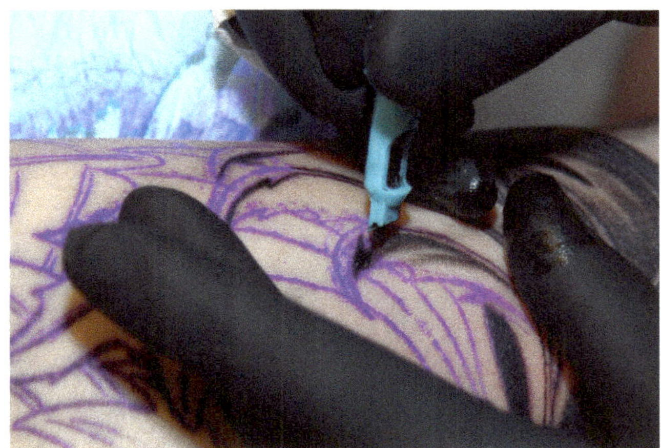

Moving towards the central region of the tattoo, Larry continues to create each leaf in small steps for the greatest realism.

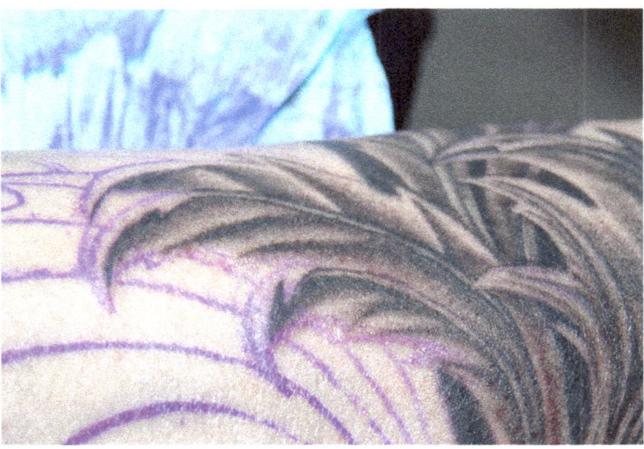

The ongoing detail work on the leafy face continues and we can see how Larry's careful steps have created a layered look on the flat surface.

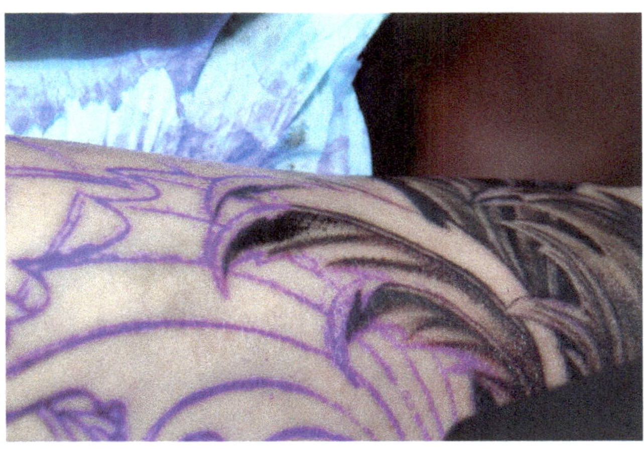

To my untrained eyes, the initial steps always look fairly crude, but will quickly develop into terrific detail.

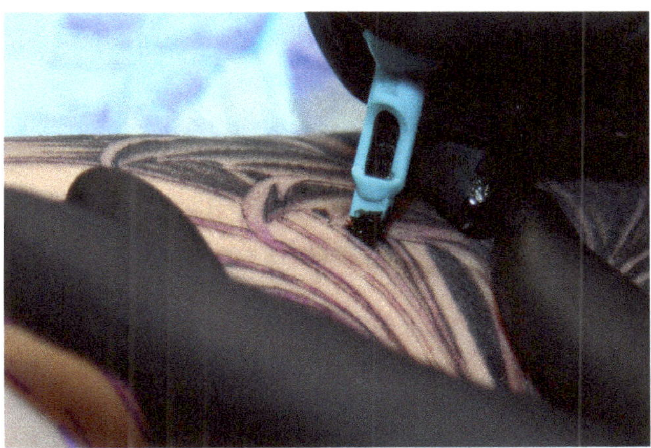

Once again, the edge of the larger 13 mag needle is used to create a thin line of ink.

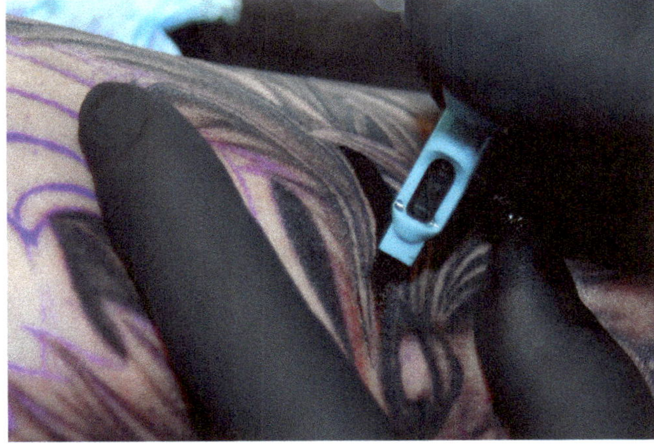

Turning the width of the 13 mag needles one way or another allows Larry to create a variety of line widths.

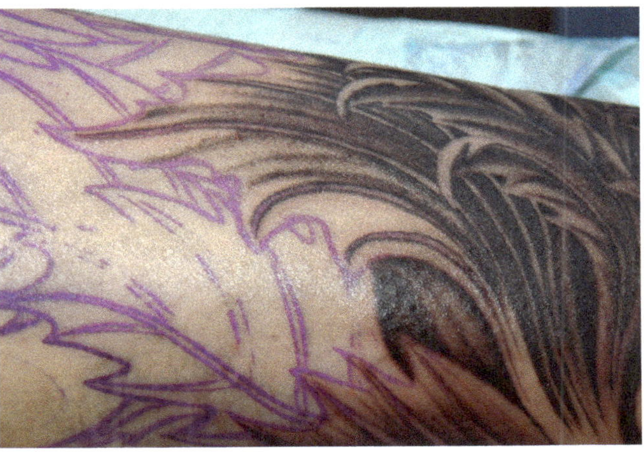

We can now see the beginning of Larry's efforts to go from dark to light leaves as he moves upwards on the tattoo.

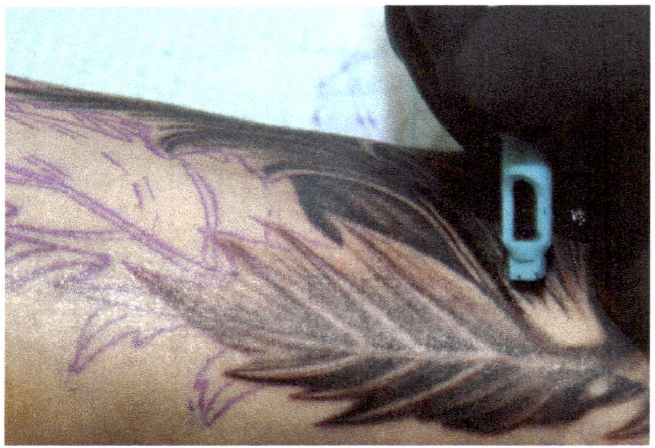

To augment and accentuate the lower sections, more black ink is used to define the shadows.

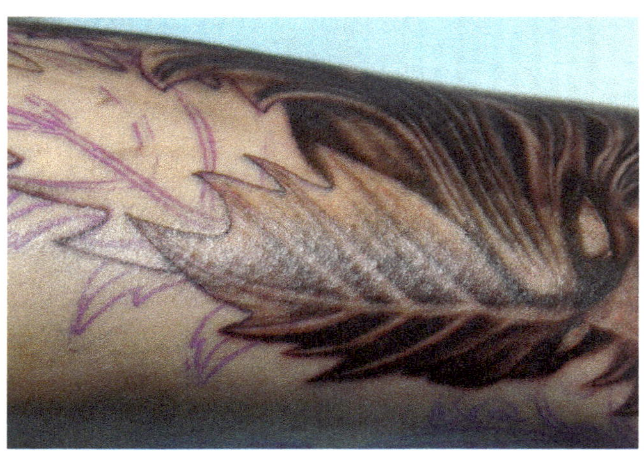

Using both shading and outlining ensures that the upper leaves are set apart from those lower on the piece.

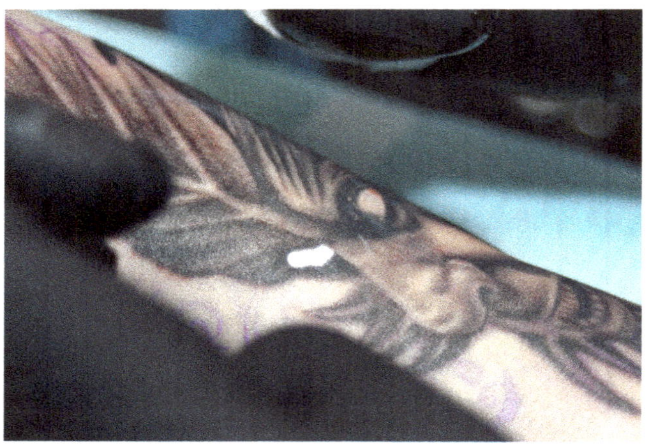

Making sure that the eyes of the leaf man stand out, a layer of white ink is used to highlight the vacant orbs.

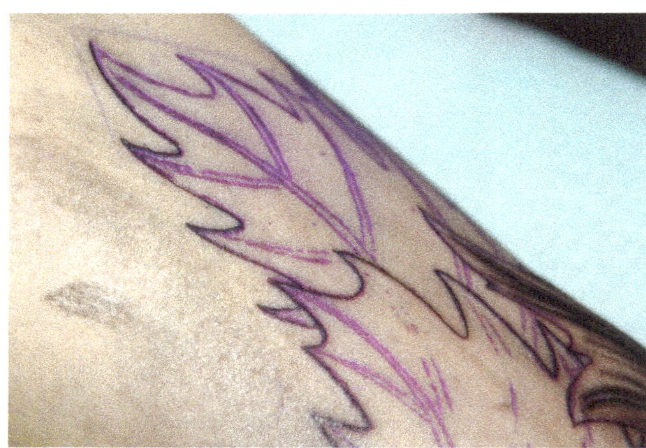

The leaves that will be seen against the empty skin are to be outlined as well for better definition.

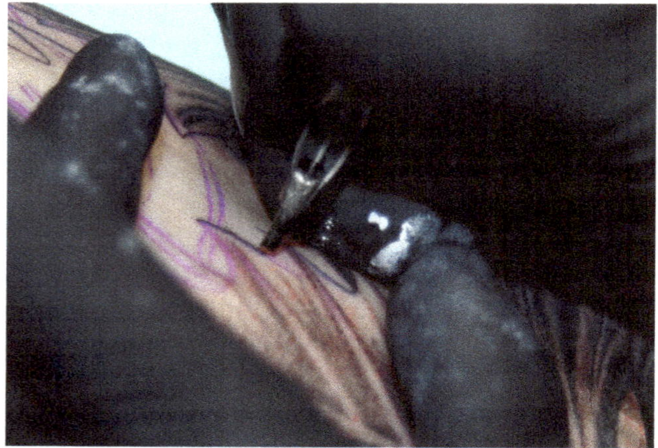

Unlike the lower leaves, the upper bits will be outlined in black to compensate for their lighter shade when filled in.

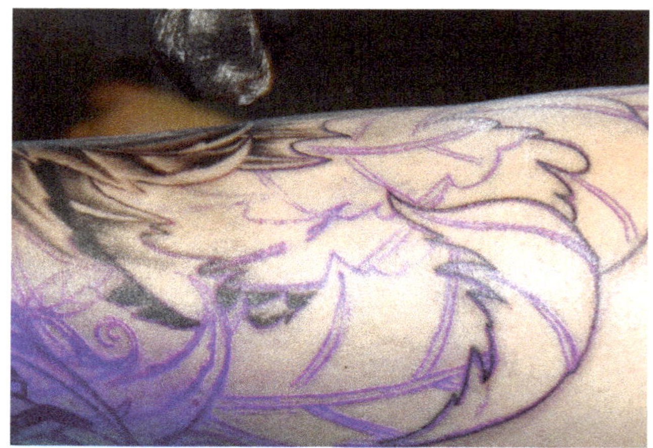

Slowly we see the blue guide lines being replaced by the permanent ink.

Q&A: Larry Brogan

How long have you been doing tattoos?

It has been about 16 years now, and I never did a formal apprenticeship, but I did get some great training in the early days.

What was the first piece you did ?

I did a skull with crossed wrenches on a friend's arm that measured about 4"x 6", in color.

Do you have a favorite style of work?

I like doing all kinds of tattoos, but the pin-up stuff is the most fun. I have done lots of monsters too, and try to use realism in a lot of my work.

Any person of particular inspiration?

Lots of guys in the tattoo industry, but outside of that, Frank Frazetta is probably the guy I admire the most. I have done lots of tatts of his illustrations, and presented his family with a scrapbook of those images.

Do you have one piece that you are well known for?

I just finished a full set of sleeves that feature images of the famous Route 66. It was hundreds of hours to do. I also did a full back piece featuring two women kissing while they straddle a machine gun.

What improvements do you see coming in the tattoo industry?

The machines themselves are only glorified door bells, and I don't see much changing in that regard. Fresh, and really talented artists, are making a big difference though, as they improve the way people see our form of art as just that.

Tell us about Tattoo City.

Four years after starting, I wanted to open my own shop. I found this location for rent, and we began in 1994. This second section of the business opened in 2004, and caters more to the custom designed and created ink. We have 3 other artists working here, 2 for tattoos and one for piercings.

What kind of art background do you have?

I was drawing things even as a kid and took a ton of art classes in high school and college. I never got a formal degree, but still create paintings and illustrations outside of the tattoo world.

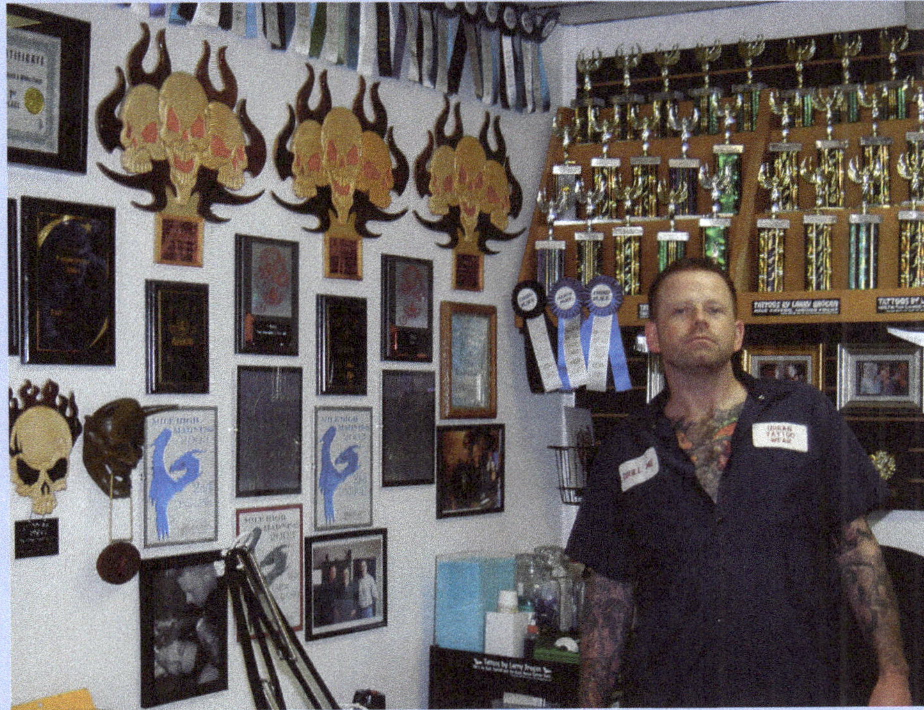

The walls and shelves in Larry's custom show room are covered with the trophies and awards he has won for his tattoo efforts, and set him apart from many other artists.

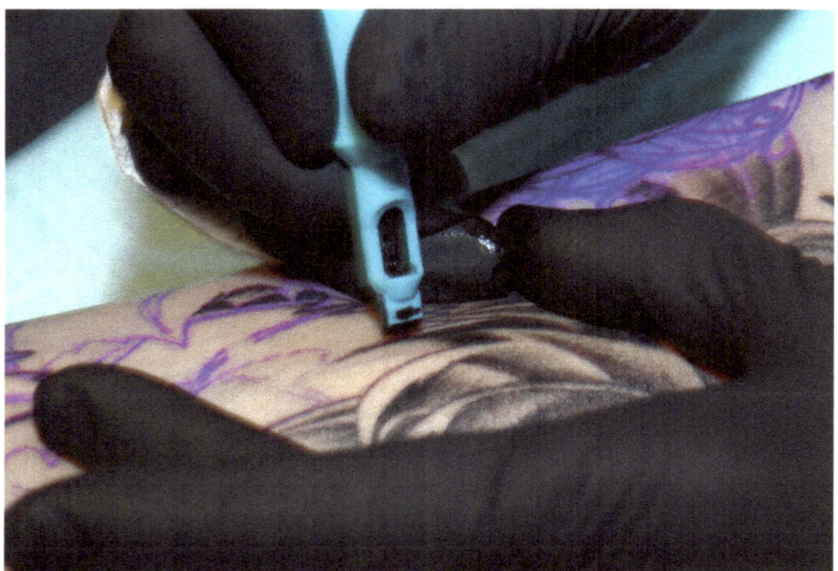

Some of the shading is quickly accomplished using the full width of the 13 mag needle set.

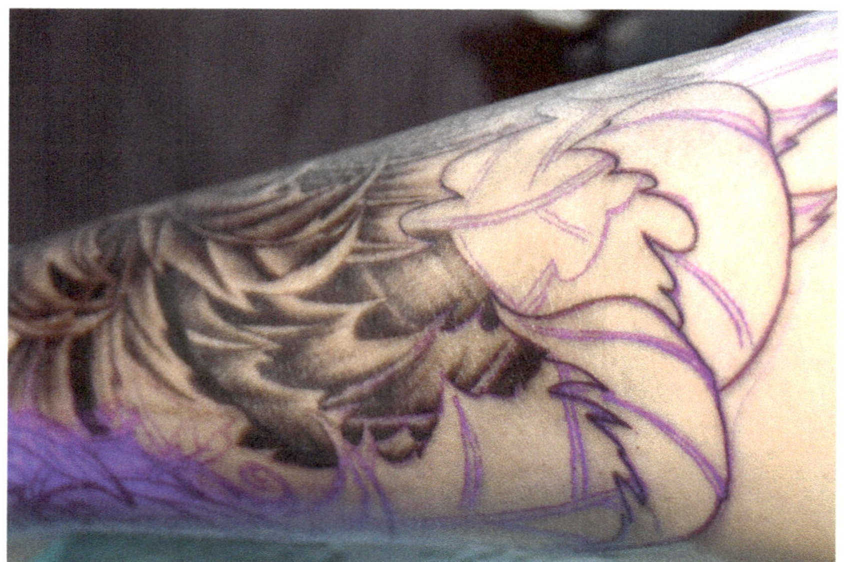

Progress has been steady, but most of the upper leaves have yet to be filled in with the black and gray ink.

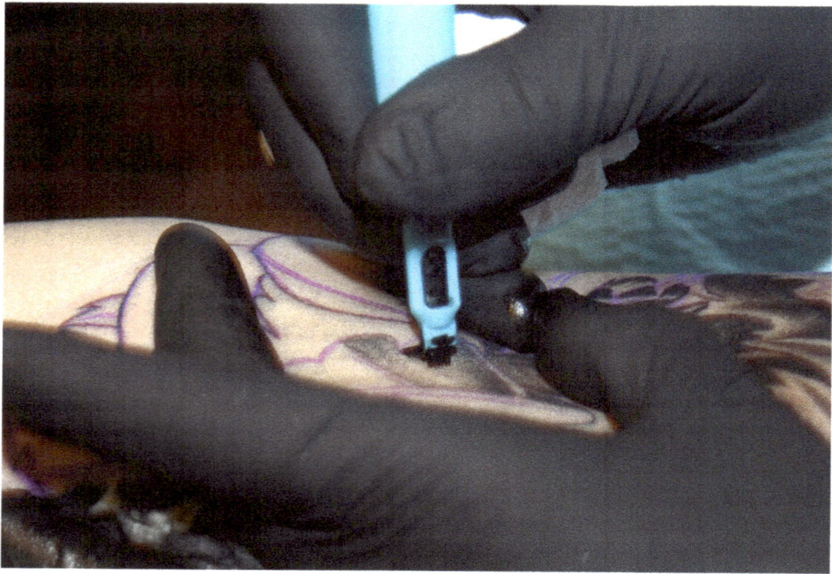

Some fairly large portions of the leaves are now addressed as Larry continues the steps, nearing completion.

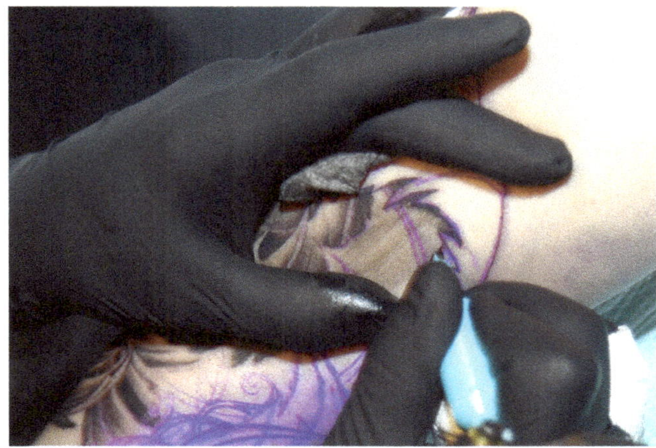

A heavier outline is now applied to the upper edges of the leaf man's foliage for added distinction.

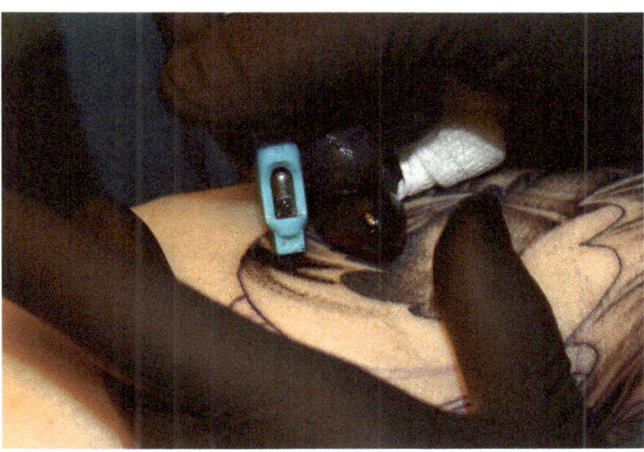

The uppermost sections of the leaves are now filled in with contours and shadows.

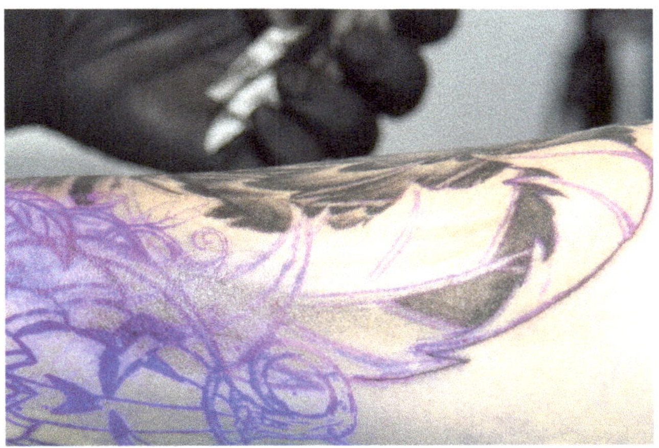

Shading of the upper greenery takes shape as Larry moves from place to place, making subtle additions at every stop.

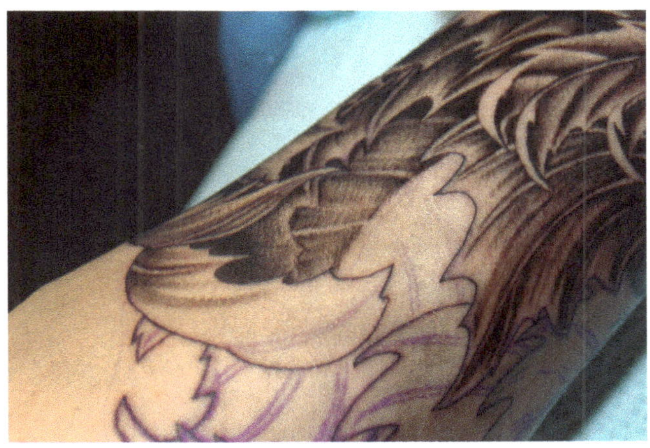

Only a few more leaves remain to be filled in, and will require less time and attention than the rest due to their lighter density.

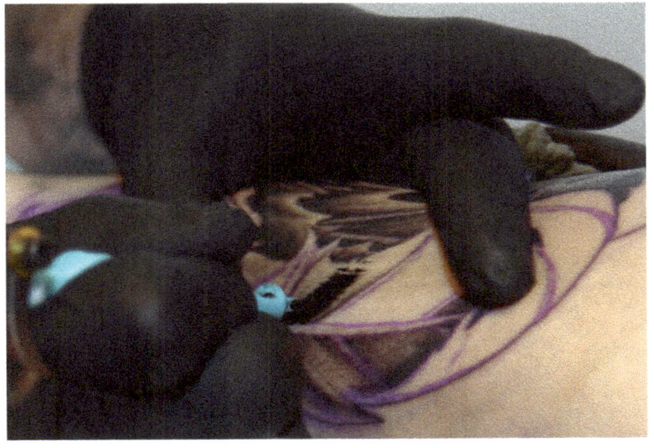

Another large blotch of ink is thrown into the blend, with the tattoo's completion drawing near.

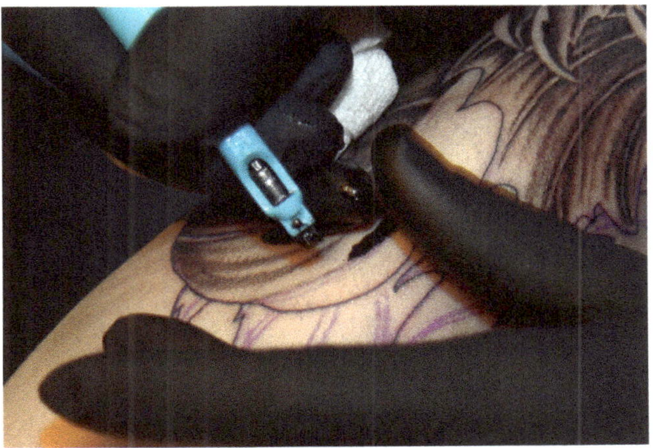

Bold use of the black ink will be wiped away leaving behind a gentle curve that accents the shape.

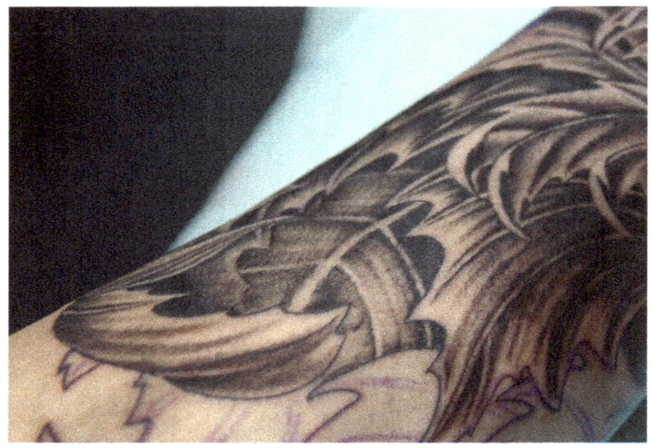

Although subtle, each step taken by Larry leaves behind another whiff of the finished piece.

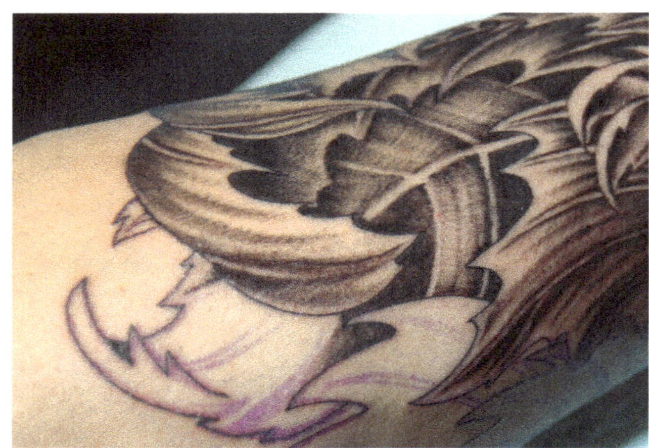

The contours of each leaf differ, bringing added dimension and realism to the overall tattoo.

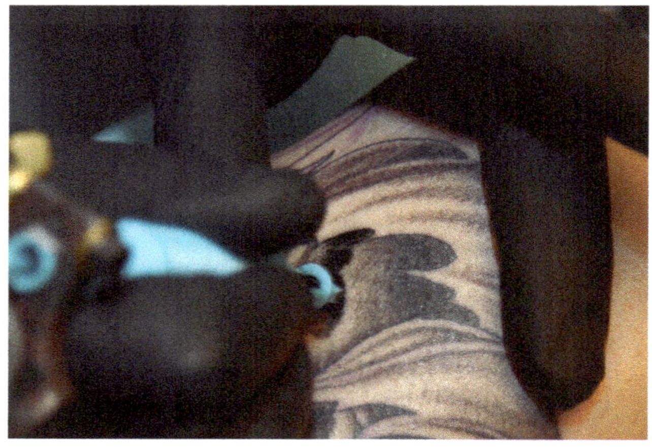

The curving edges of the leaves are darkened with additional ink, building their intensity.

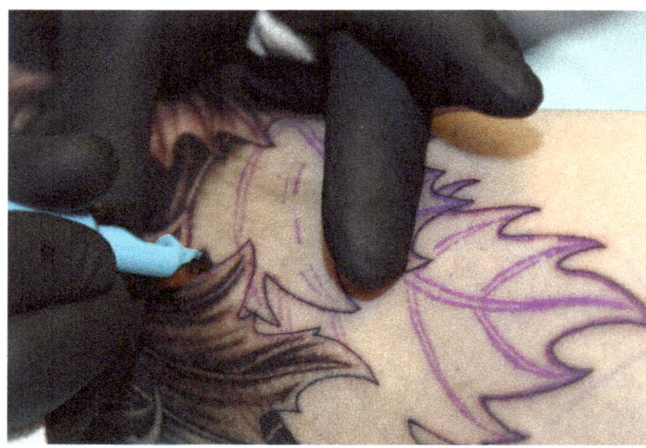

With only 2 or 3 leaves left to be filled in, we are getting excited to view the completed work.

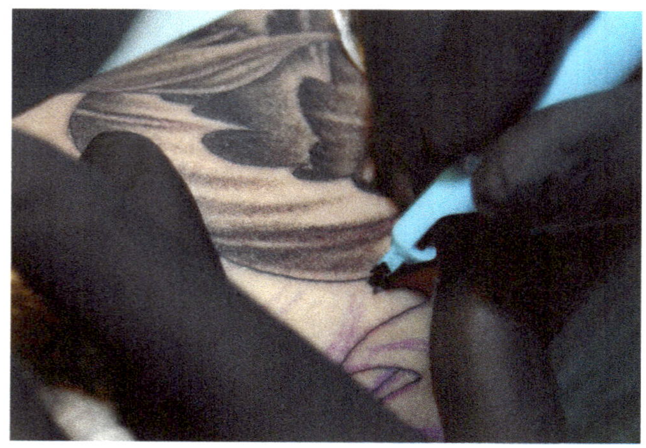

Work begins on the last of the leaf man's facial foliage.

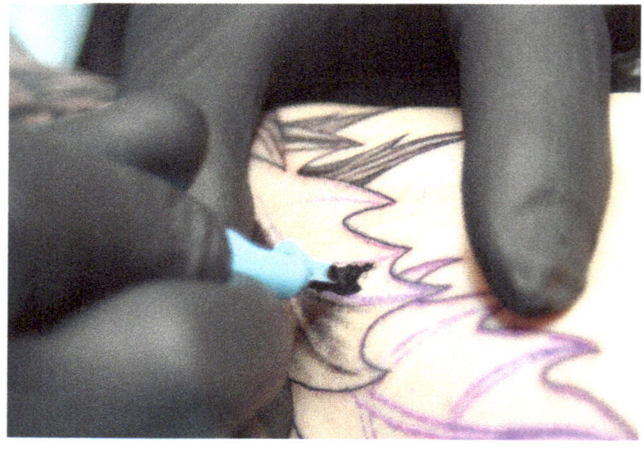

The previously outlined leaf designs are now getting their share of shadowy detail.

With the upper section now complete, Larry stands back to look for any additional details he feels need to be added.

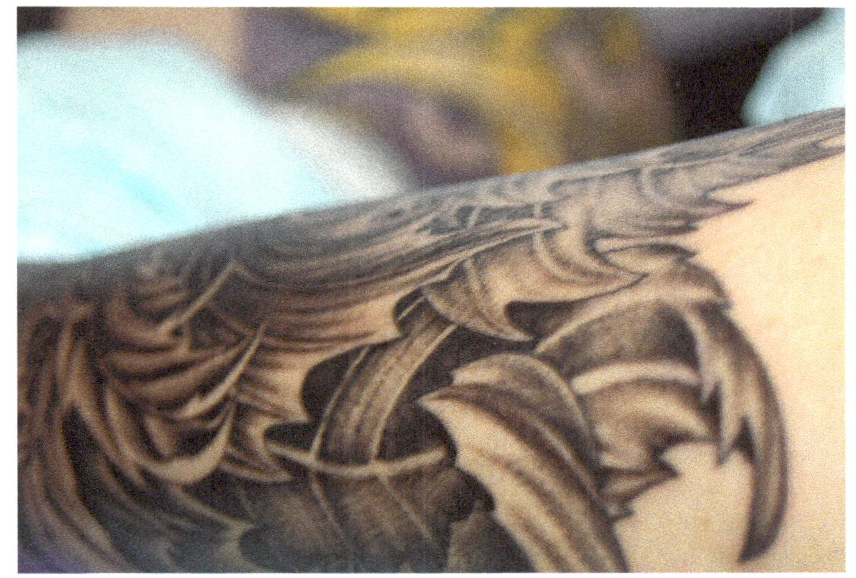

Here we can see most of the front section, revealing the details, contours and shading that have created a realistic tattoo, even though it lacks any form of color.

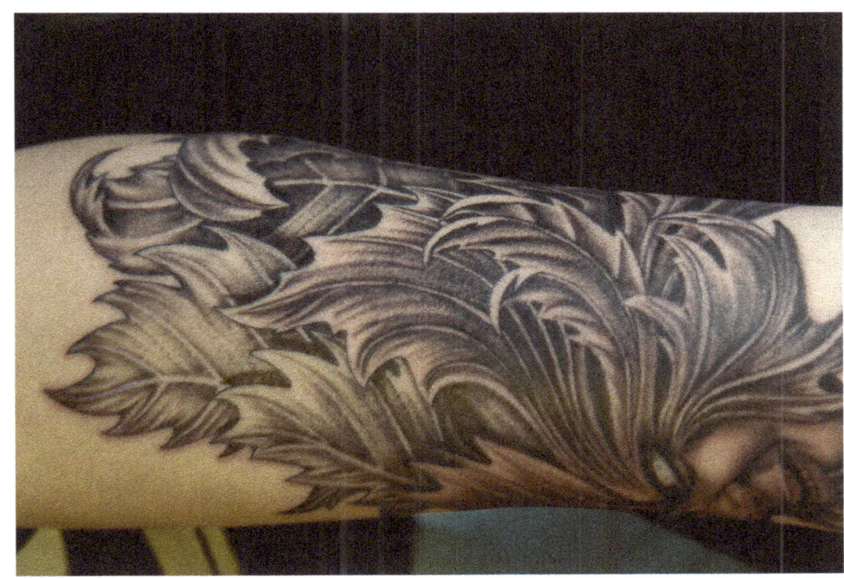

The backside of the piece is equally detailed, and will soon be joined by an evil jack-o-lantern that Larry has already drawn up and integrated into the layout of the leaf man piece.

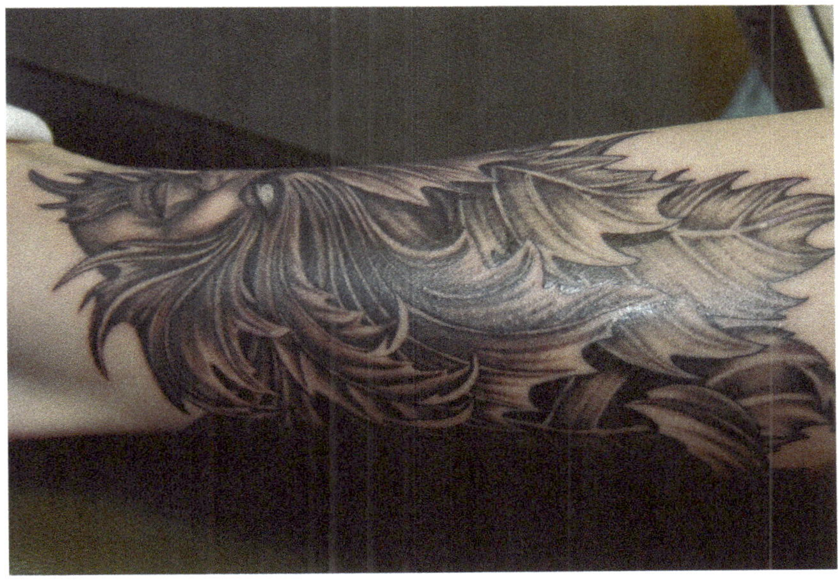

Chapter Three

Lance Norris

Adrenaline Tattoo

Like most talented tattoo artists, Lance prefers doing custom ink. Some customers will still choose a bit of safe, factory art for their images. The more adventuresome, however, understand that a truly individual bit of design sets a tattoo apart from all the rest. Having no limits as to what kind of images he'll do, Lance is fairly fearless in that arena. "The darker and more evil, the better", claims Lance when asked about his favorite style of tattoo. "Gruesome, ghoulish, macabre stuff is the

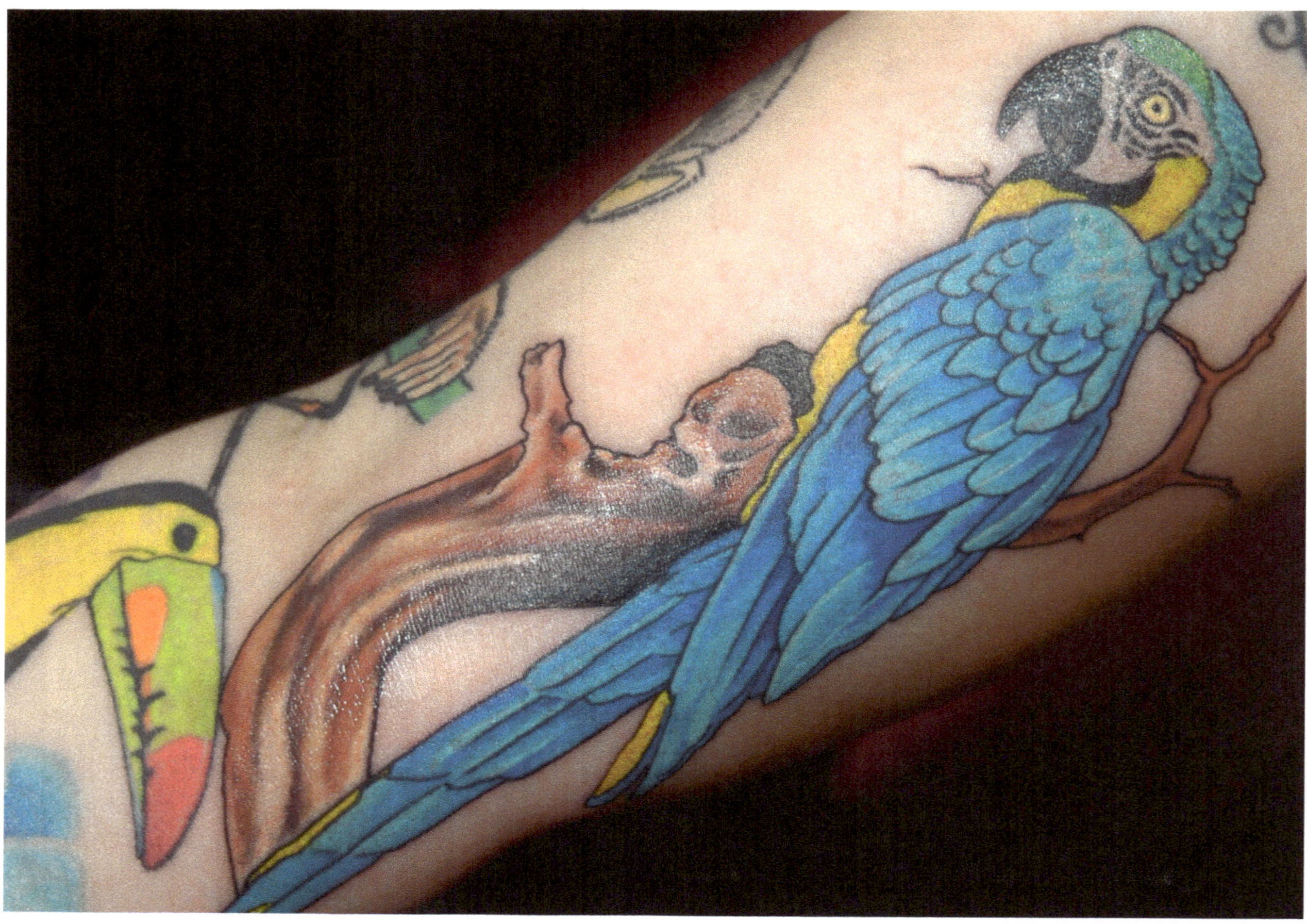

While requesting the safety of anonymity, Lisa happily agreed to have her latest bit of ink created by Lance Norris. Her existing veldt of jungle foliage and creatures made the perfect backdrop for her latest parrot art, and closely resembles one of her own at-home pets.

most fun, especially when the person getting the ink sets me free."

From what I have seen so far, the majority of tattoo shops are kept as clean as they can be. The front showrooms may appear to be a bit dodgy, but the actual tattoo booths are antiseptically clean. Lance is no different, and strives to make and keep his area as neat as a pin. In his case the pin may be sticking through an illustrated eyeball, but you get the idea.

For this blue and gold Macaw tatt, Lance began with a simple outline of the bird in question, and then added his own personal flair to the piece. Often times, additional details will be added to the piece as it progresses. Lance says that he can see the finished tattoo in his mind long before touching needle to skin. This level of creativity is rare, but makes for a terrific ink-master. Given his druthers the bird would have been sporting a skull of some sort, but he was able to behave himself this time around. The next guy may not be as lucky.

The procedure for creating any tattoo begins with the transfer of an image to skin. Once this guideline has been positioned the real work begins. The basic black outline will determine the overall image as well as creating boundaries for the soon to be applied colors. Any areas to be shaded in black are completed next so that the colors can be laid on top, creating the shapely contours in the finished art.

Having seen several other tattoos being created by now, Lance's methods were fairly typical while his attention to detail was top-shelf. He targeted one area at a time then moved to another. This process keeps the discomfort level to a tolerable threshold for the tattooee. Not being a fan of the aviary world, it was something to watch him turn blank skin into a highly detailed bird, with an incredible amount of contour in the feathers covering the body. The tiny spots on the bird's face were another highlight that a lesser artist may have overlooked.

The pain threshold and sensitivity of each recipient is different, and the needle didn't seem to bother Lisa too badly, but wiping away the excess

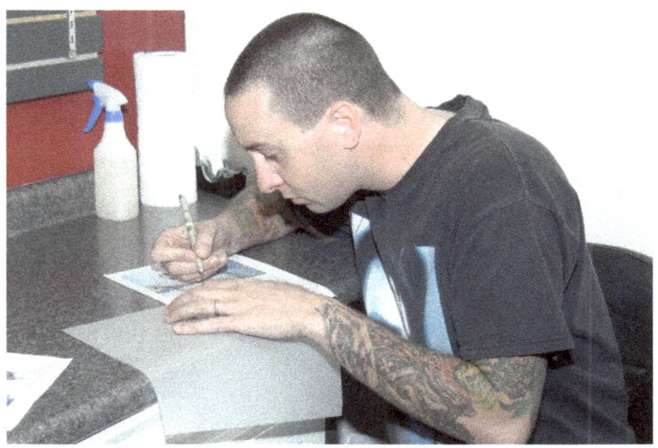

Working with an existing piece of art, Lance traces the desired form to fit the client's request.

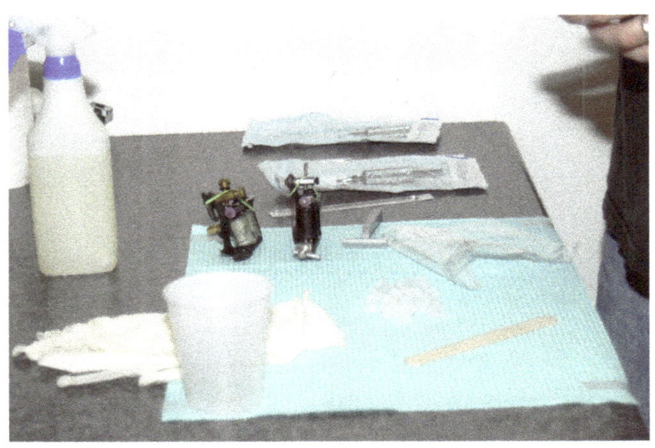

A clean sheet of material is placed on the work surface and the basic needs are set out.

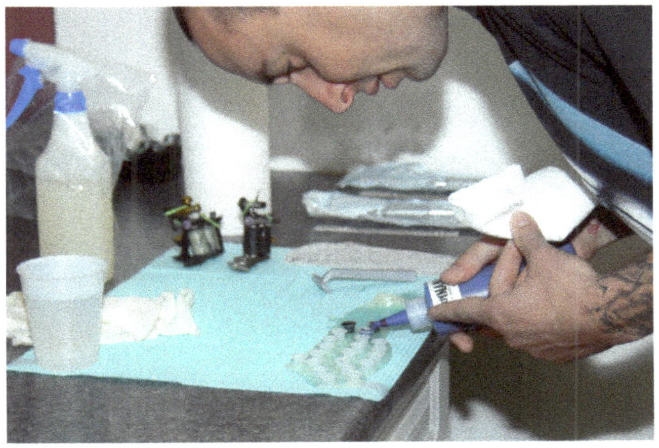

Black and blue ink will be used in the first steps, and the colors are squeezed into the waiting cups.

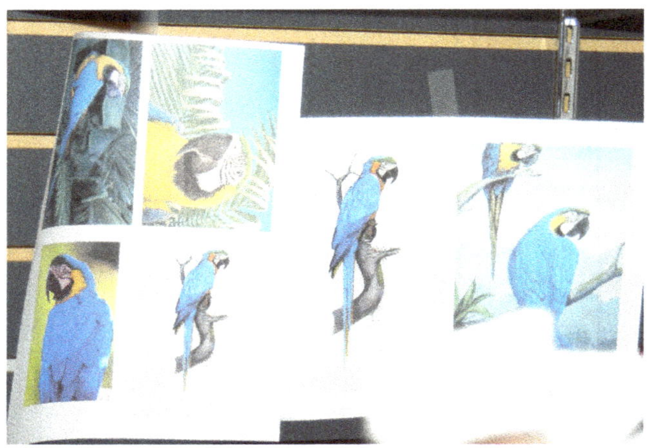

A series of additional art will help to guide Lance through the maze of details to be used on the tattoo.

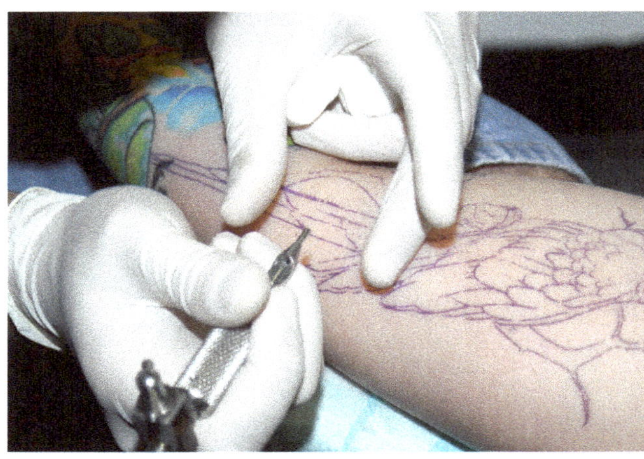

In typical fashion, the work begins by outlining the tattoo in black.

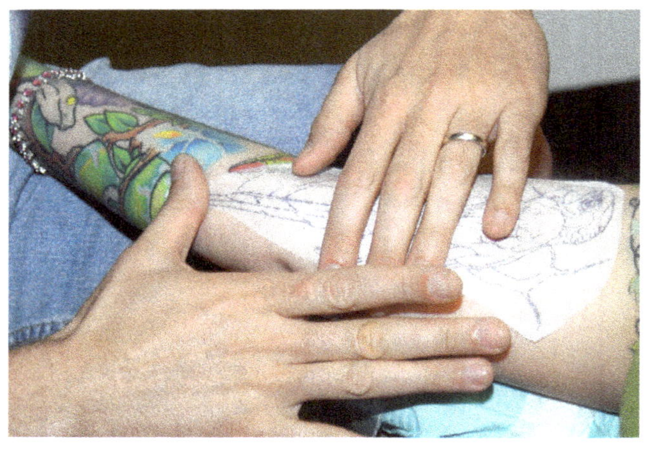

A slight amount of pressure transfers the image from the paper to the skin.

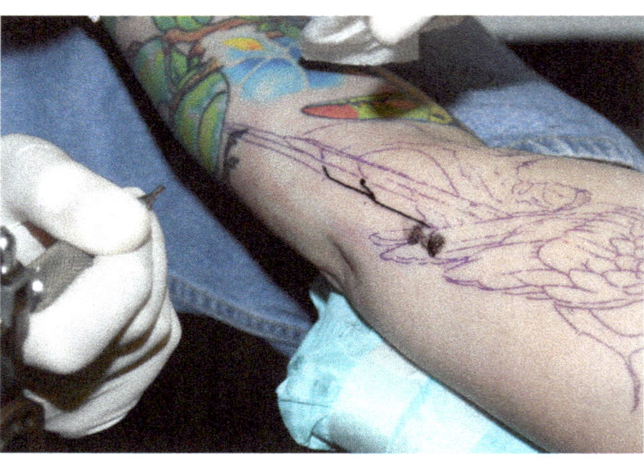

Staying within the lines is a key ingredient to a finely detailed piece, although the task is tedious.

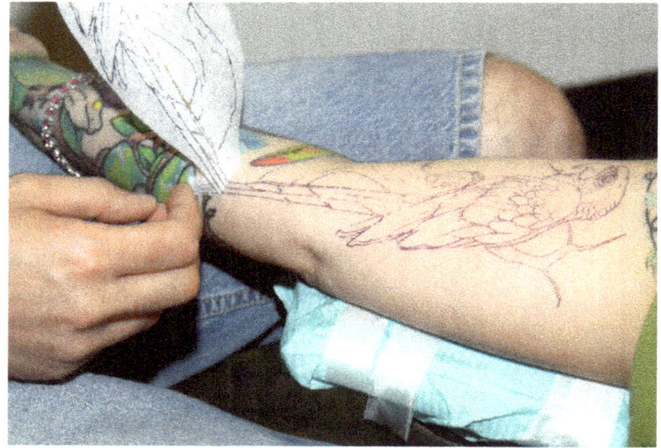

After lifting the backing paper, a clear image of the tattoo is left behind, providing Lance with a map to the finished piece.

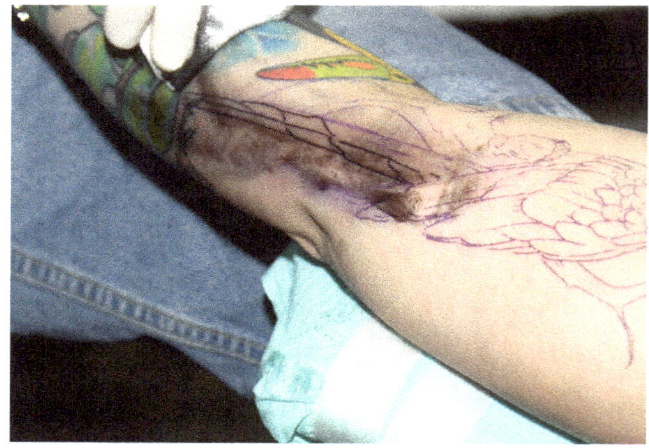

As the black outline progresses, excess ink smears the area until wiped clean.

ink was avoided when possible. Other tattoos are wiped clean more often as the artist gauges his progress and checks for needed details. Attempting to keep Lisa's discomfort level under control, Lance was forced to skip that step a few times.

Personally, I have a tough time talking and doing much of anything else at the same time. Lance on the other hand was able to chat with Lisa, her husband and I without a hitch as the needle buzzed away on Lisa's skin. Our topics of conversation seemed to center around gruesome motion pictures and other related subjects. Lance has two kids, one of which already has a large tattoo featuring an angel holding its own heart, having been recently torn from its chest cavity. Not the happiest of images, but right up Lance's alley. He told us that his son has a nice collection of sharp edged weapons in his bedroom, and was a point of pride for Lance. Some kids collect trading cards for fun, but that wouldn't seem right being an offspring of Lance.

Before beginning work on the parrot, Lance guessed an elapsed time of about two hours to complete the work. It ended up being slightly more than that, but the constant chattering between the people in the room may have been the cause for the extension. In the end, Lisa was pleased with her new art, nestled amongst the virtual jungle she has growing on her arm already. Monkeys, tropical plants and other assorted animals have been inked onto her arm so far, with more additions to follow. "In about 6 months" she claimed. As with other pieces I have seen, the artist will usually ask the client if they intend on adding more to the area in the future. This allows them the ability to plan ahead, leaving space for fresh ink as the client requests. This small gesture makes life far easier for the artist and avoids the need to work around an existing piece or to cover it completely with fresh color.

As we mentioned earlier, a parrot is hardly what Lance typically applies to a customer, but he is fully capable of creating a finished piece that is worthy of his talents.

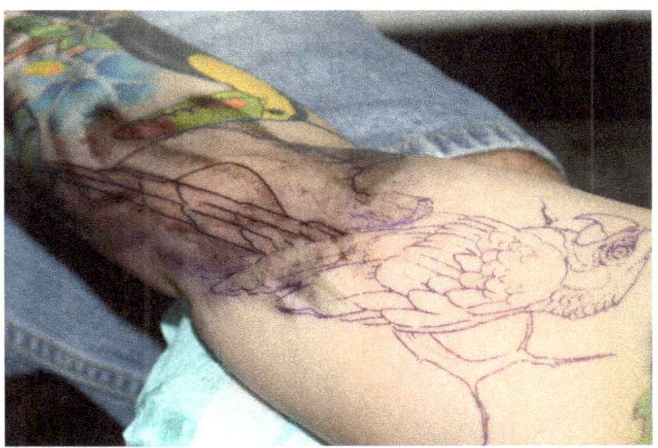

Beneath the smudged area we can see the completed outline of the bird's tail feathers.

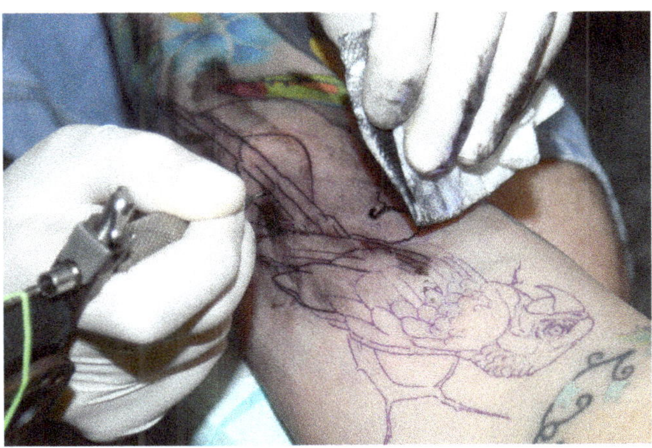

Continuing upwards, outlining the body of the parrot is now in process.

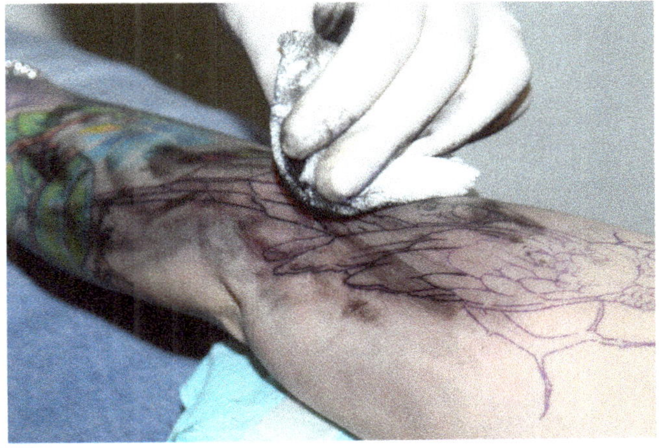

The ink continues to smear over the affected region, but will soon be cleaned off to reveal the work so far.

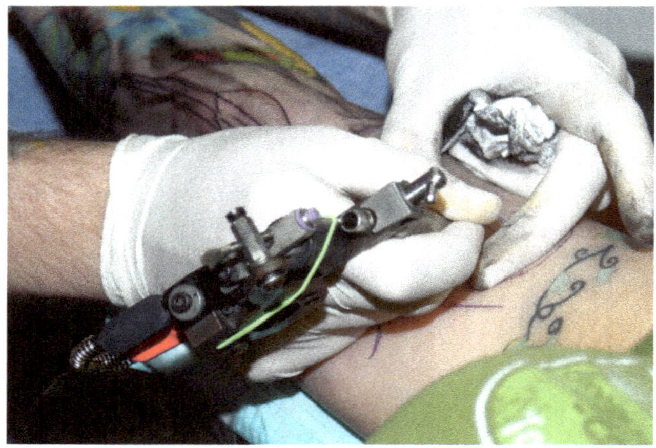

Returning to the scene of the crime, more details are added to the body of the bird.

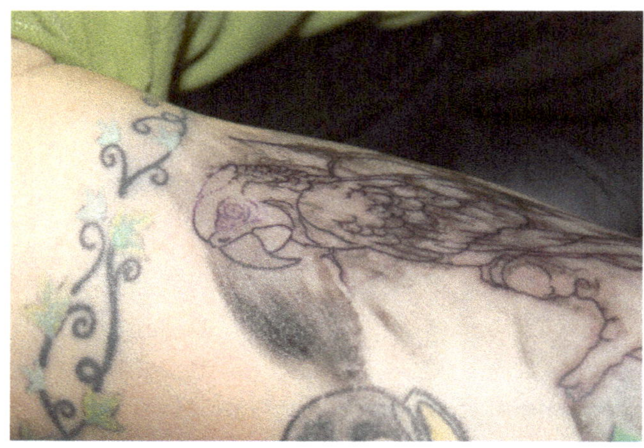

The parrot's head is the last thing to be outlined, leading us to the more exciting application of colored inks.

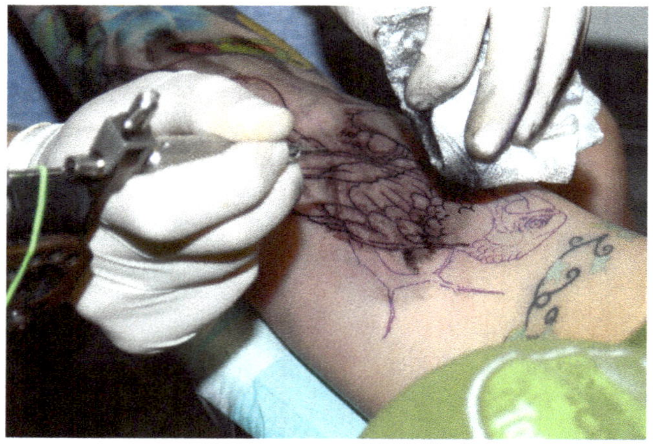

The body of the bird contains more detail than the tail, and requires more attention.

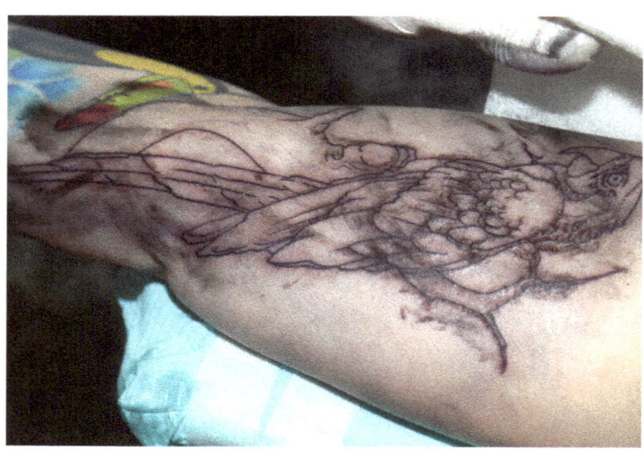

The outline complete, but has yet to be wiped clean of the smudged refuse.

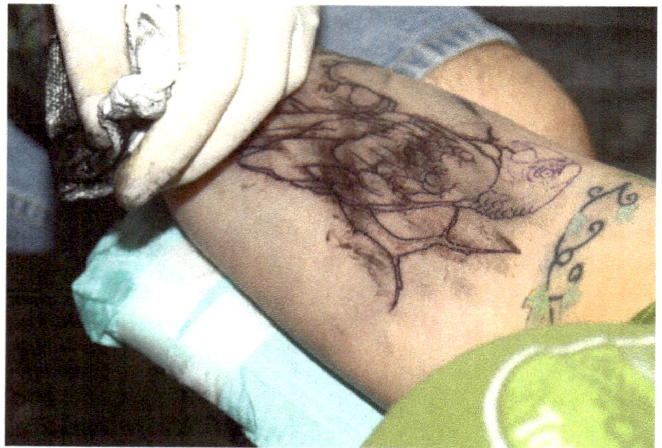

With most of the Macaw's body done, additional outline work is done on the tree branch.

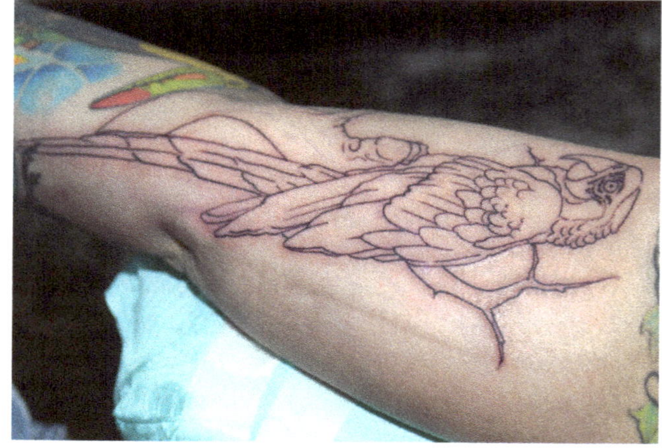

After being cleaned, we can see the clear outline of the tattoo awaiting the first dabs of blue.

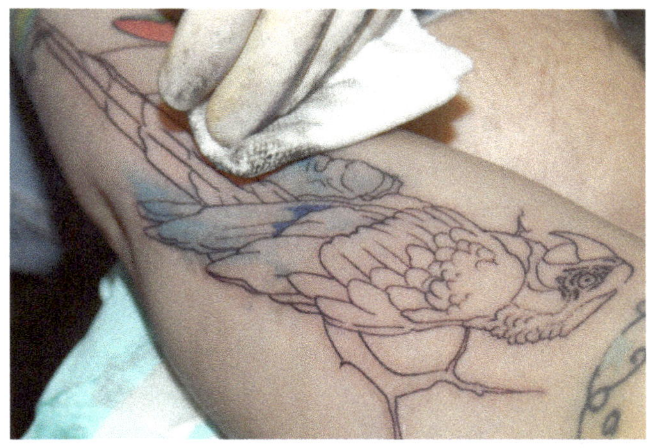

Returning to the tail feathers, the first bits of blue ink are now being applied.

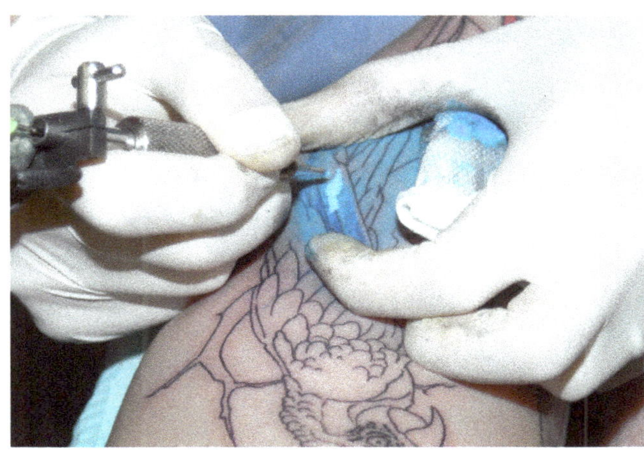

Contours and shading are achieved by using different shades of blue, going from dark to light.

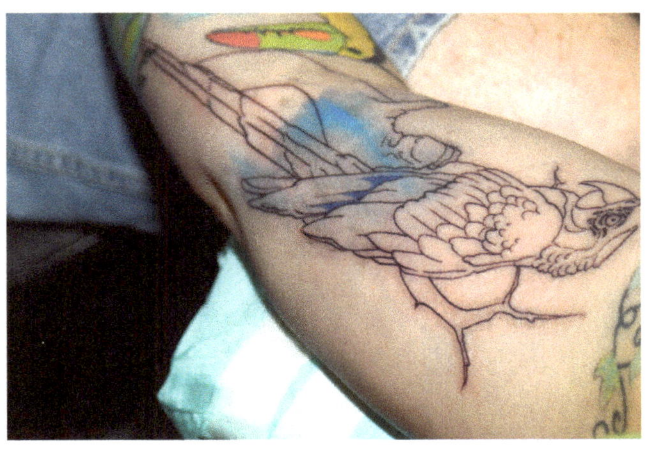

Methodical movements reveal details that only Lance can see in his mind.

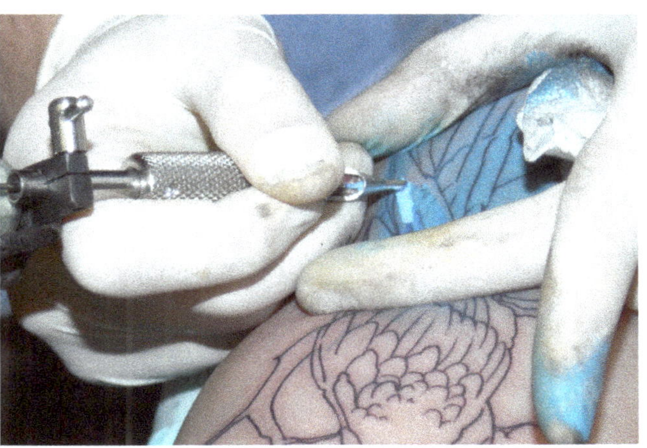

Completed in small sections, the ink will slowly be built up to become a finished bit of art.

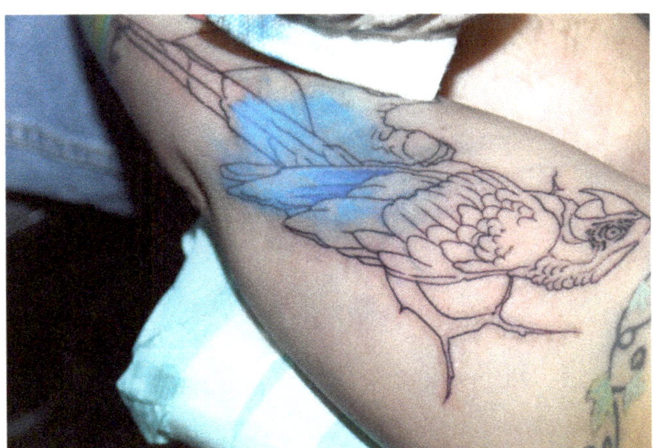

Even the earliest applications begin to show us the shading and contours that will make the finished piece appear to be 3-dimensional.

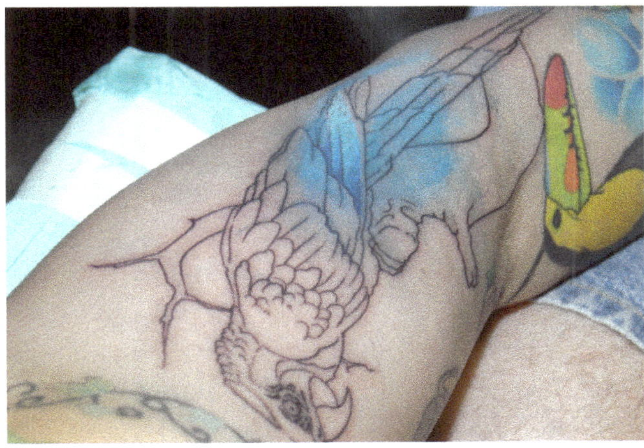

Despite the clutter of excess ink, we can begin to see the contours of the feathers taking shape.

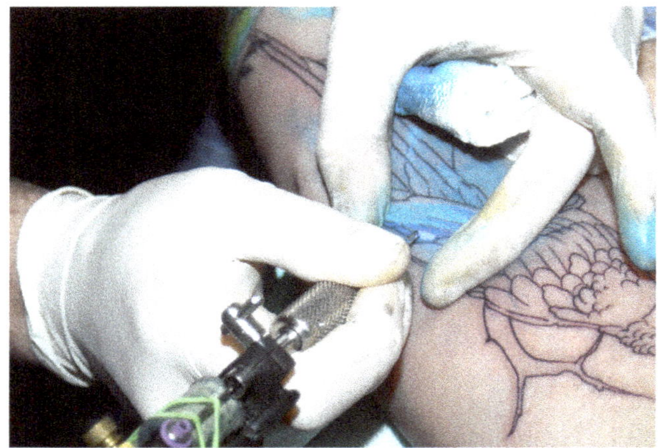

Small sections of lighter blue are used to add dimension.

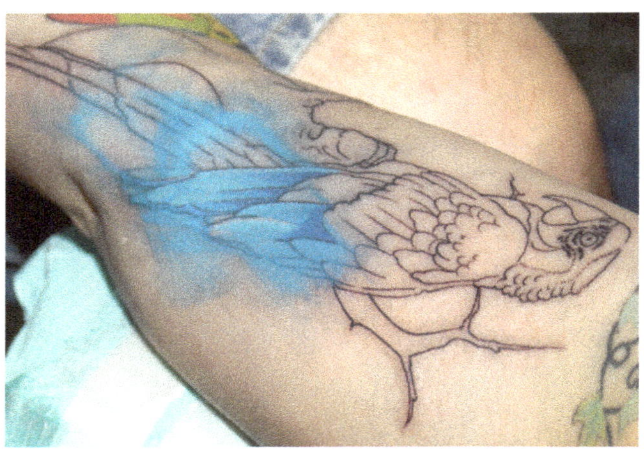

Moving to the body feathers, the Macaw is starting to appear shapelier.

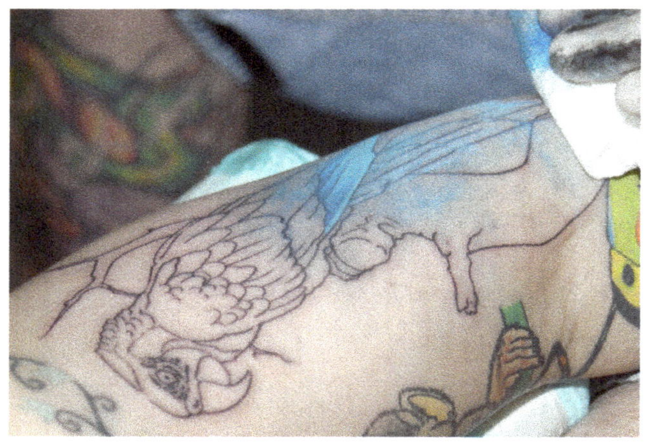

Every step shows us additional detail and clarity of the finished piece.

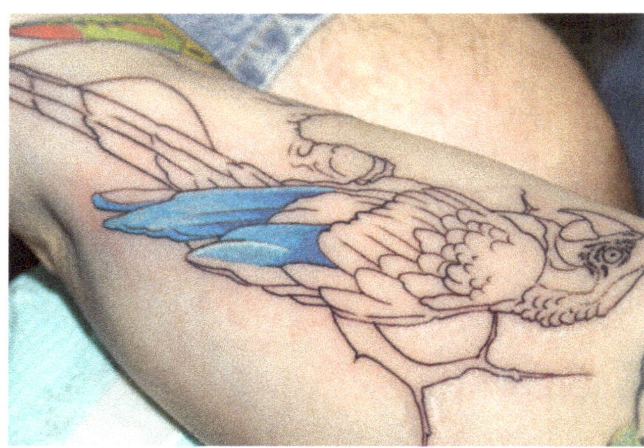

With the unused ink wiped clean, we can see the results of the basic color application.

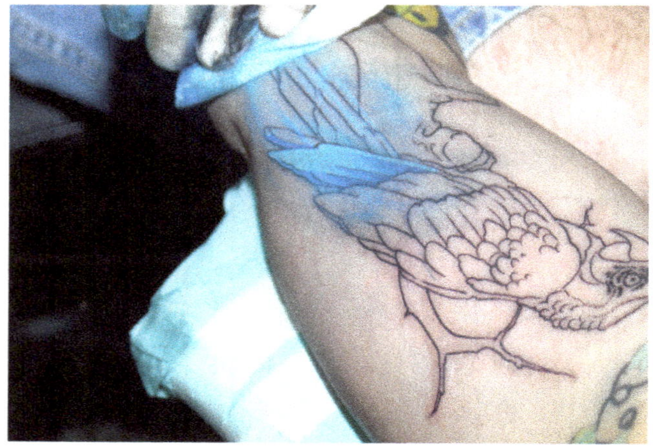

With many steps to follow, we can already begin to see the bird coming to life.

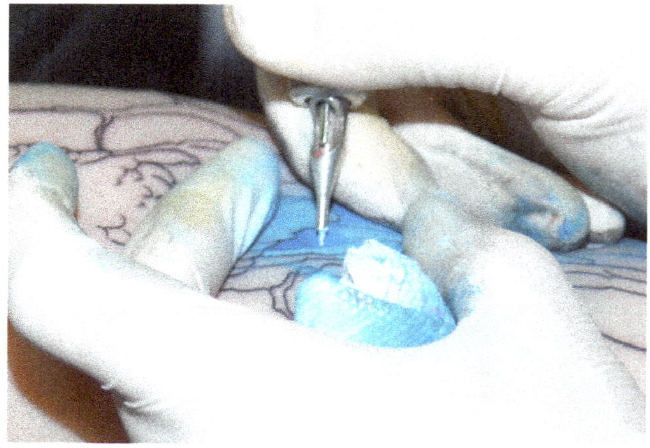

As the piece continues, smaller details are added that will enhance the completed art.

Q&A: Lance Norris

How long have you been doing tattoos?

12 years in total, four of them at Adrenaline

What kind of art background do you have?

Always had friends asking me to draw them images that they wanted as tattoos and that led to my apprenticeship in the world of tattooing others.

What was the first tattoo you did for someone?

I was still an apprentice, but did a skull wearing a top hat.

Any people in the tattoo world that inspire you?

I get most of my inspiration from my brother's art, and taught myself how to draw the things people see in their minds.

Do you have a specific genre or favorite style?

A combination of dark, evil, corrupted subjects like zombie children is probably my best known subject. I like using bright colors with ghoulish characters.

What's your best known or largest work?

I did a huge mutated elephant that began as a full back tattoo. It was later extended to reach all the way around the front to encompass the entire chest region.

What changes do you see happening in the industry?

I think the tools of the trade have reached a pinnacle, but the inks continue to improve. The colors last longer and a wider variety are available.

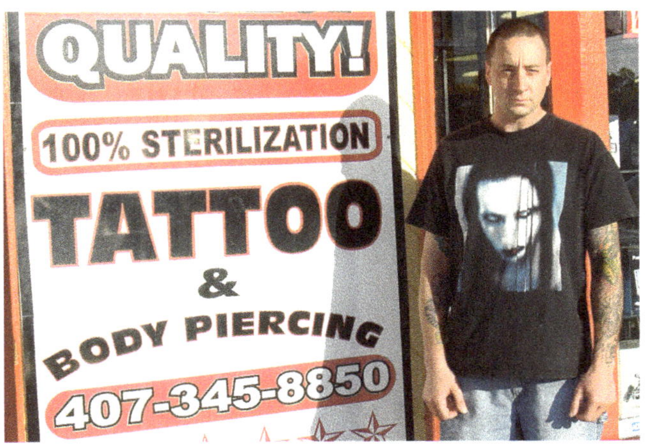

Lance Norris was the artist selected for this tattoo, and he plies his craft at Adrenaline Tattoo in Orlando, Florida.

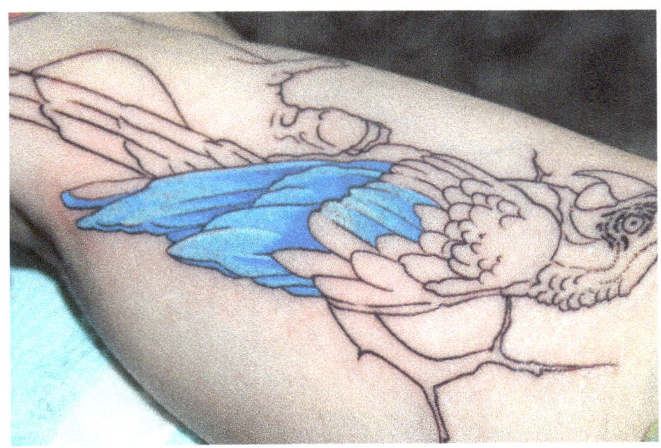

Again wiped clean, the body of the Macaw is taking shape.

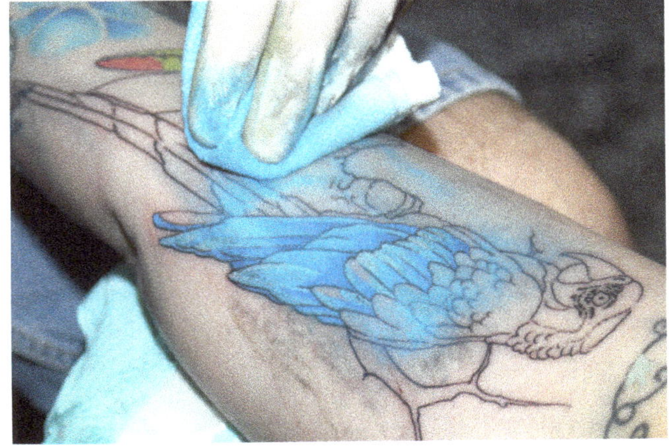

Section by section we can see how the application of the blue ink turns blank skin into a finished bird.

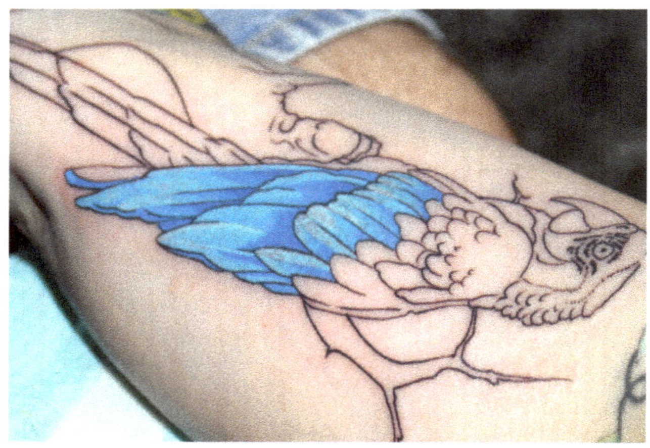

More frequent cleaning of the area is required to keep tabs on progress and required contours.

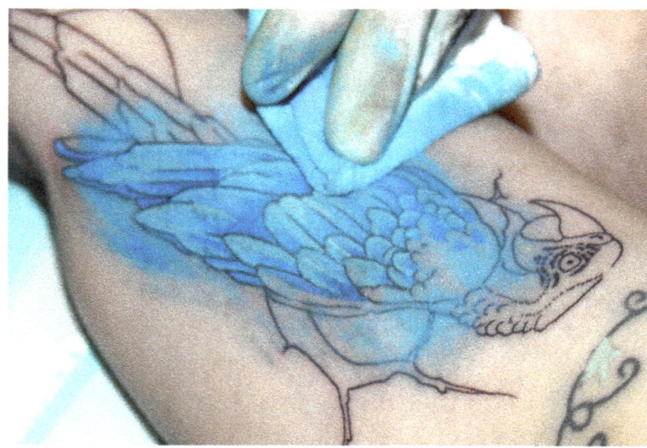

The tiny steps being taken are now adding up as the body of the parrot gets closer to being finished.

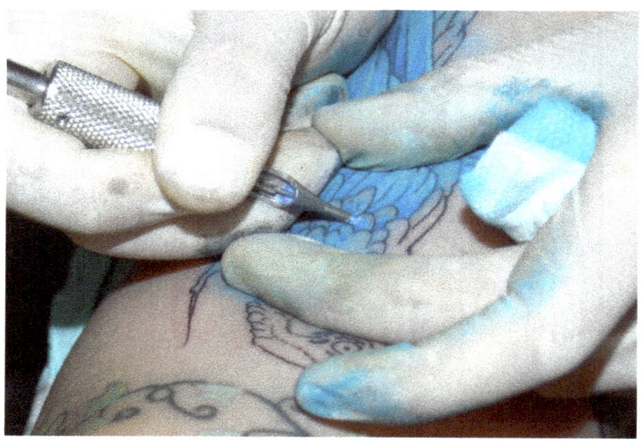

The intricate efforts will set this tattoo apart from those done without the same attention to detail.

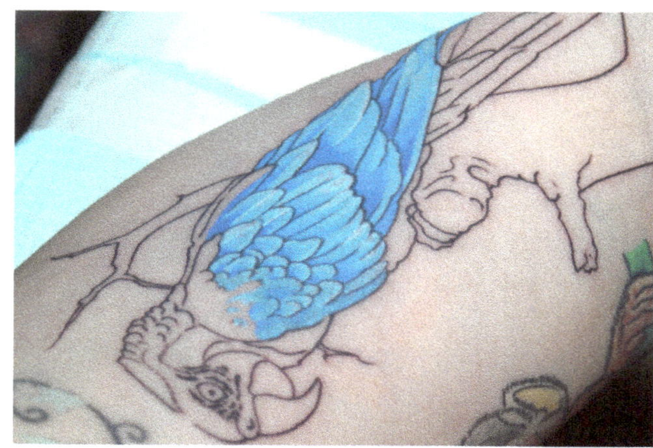

Another view cleared of the excess ink shows us a nearly complete body.

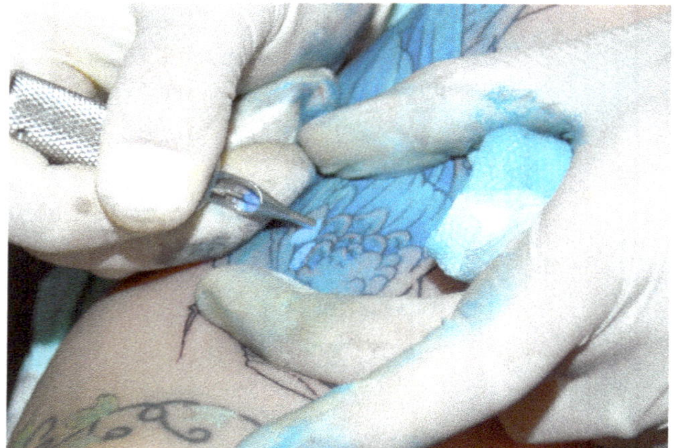

Feather by feather we can see the work coming to life.

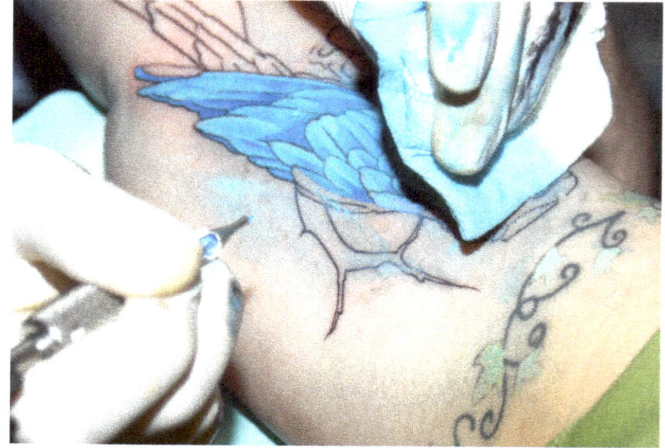

Lighter shades of blue, laid over the darker base colors, gives the art its extra dimension.

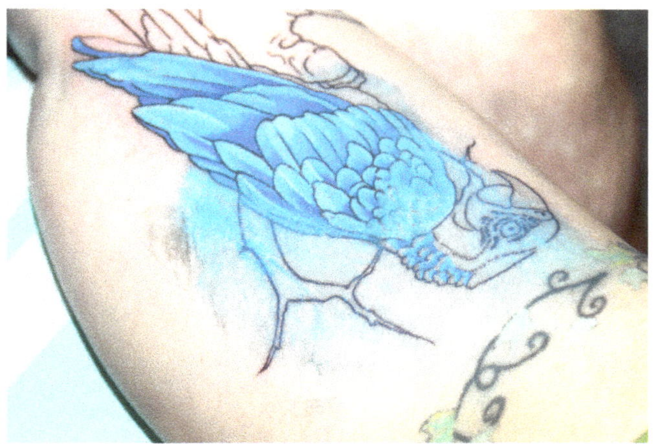

With the body complete, work begins on the finely detailed head of the parrot.

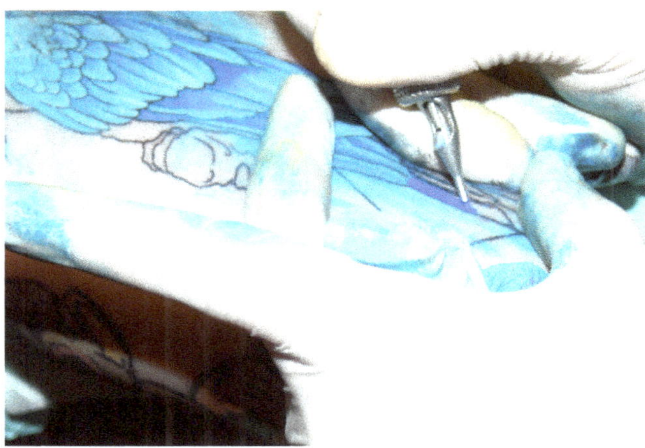

Longer tail feathers are filled-in individually before lighter shades are placed on top.

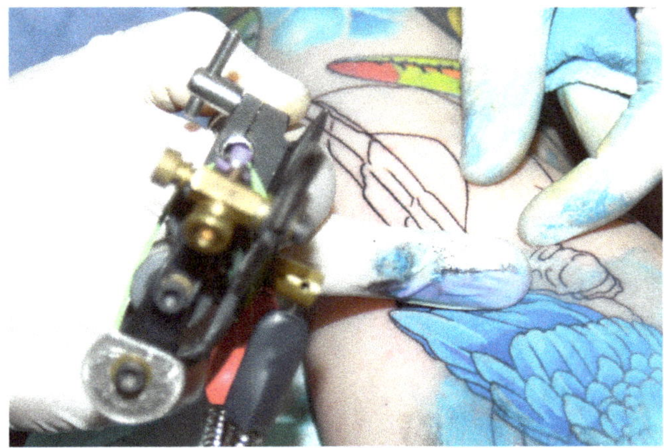

Moving from the head to the tail, ink can now be applied to that region of the piece.

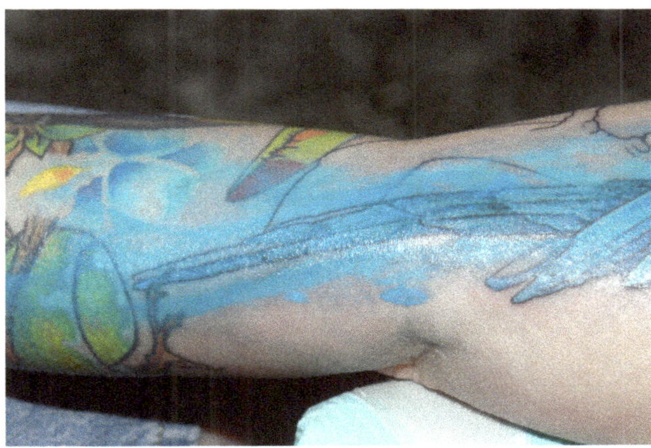

Although not yet cleaned, we can see that the basic blues of the tail feathers are now complete.

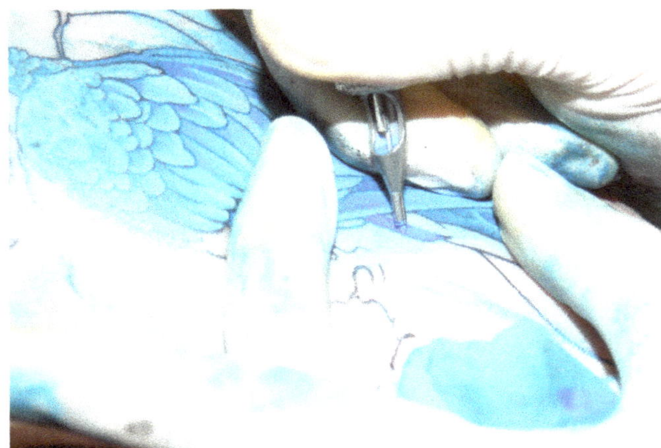

Additional shades of blue are introduced to the canvas, adding a new level of realism.

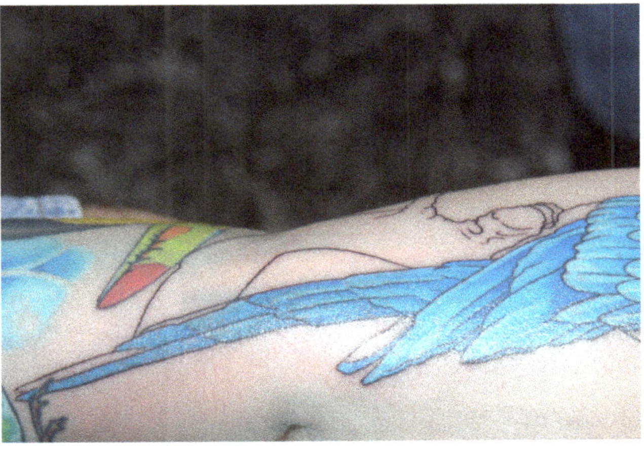

Before moving on to the lighter colors, we now get a glimpse at the completed blue segments.

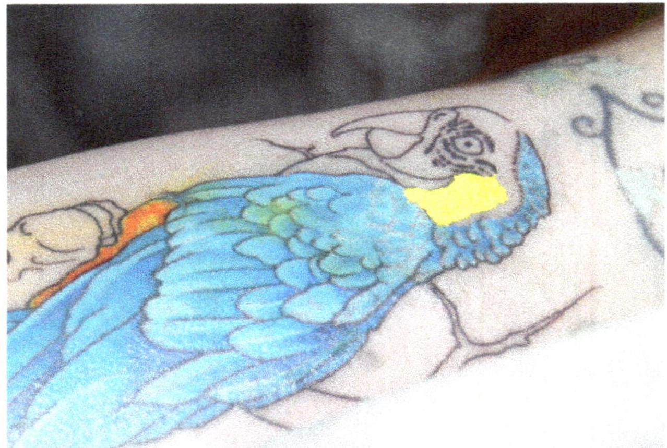

Being a blue and gold Macaw, it's time to begin adding some of the brighter ink to the head.

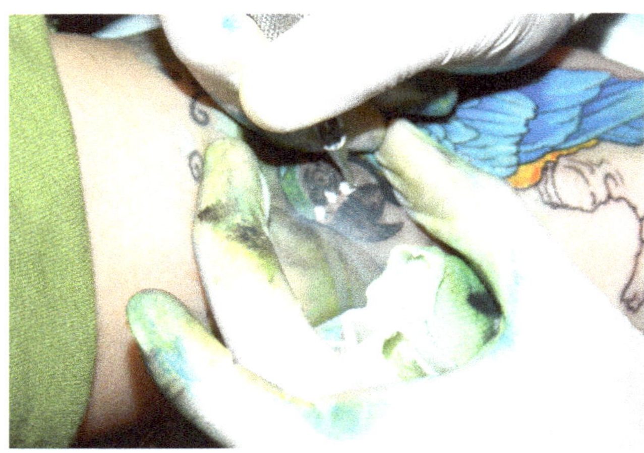

Highlights of white are drawn onto the face, bringing new levels of detail to the piece.

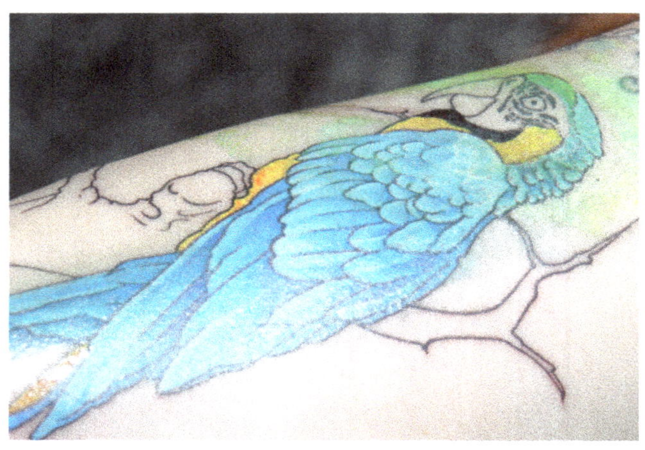

Areas of gold have also been added to the chest and tail to bring more realism to the art.

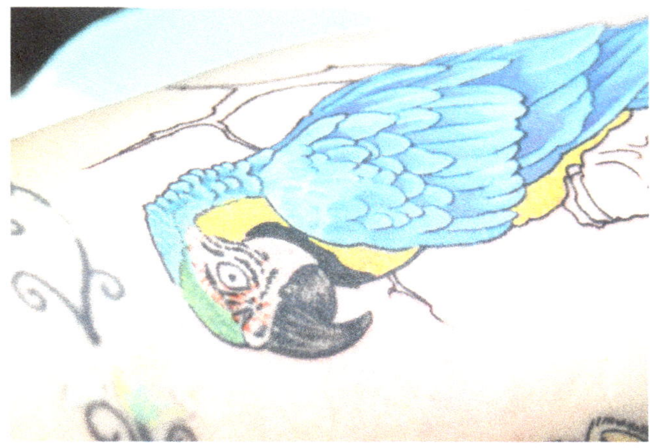

A hint of green is added to the top of the head just as we see on the actual bird used as our model.

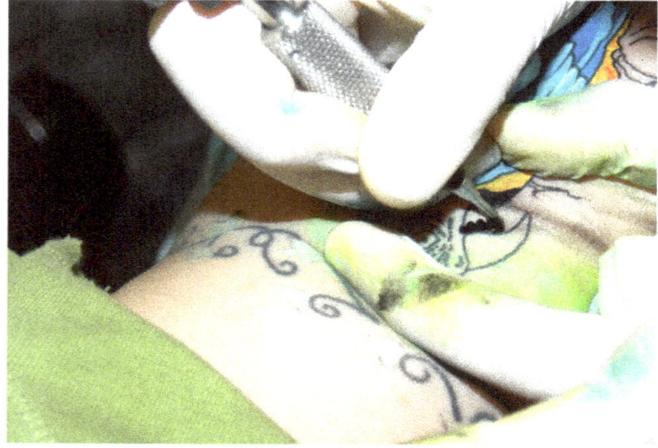

Shading on the pointed beak comes next and is also done to show shape and dimension.

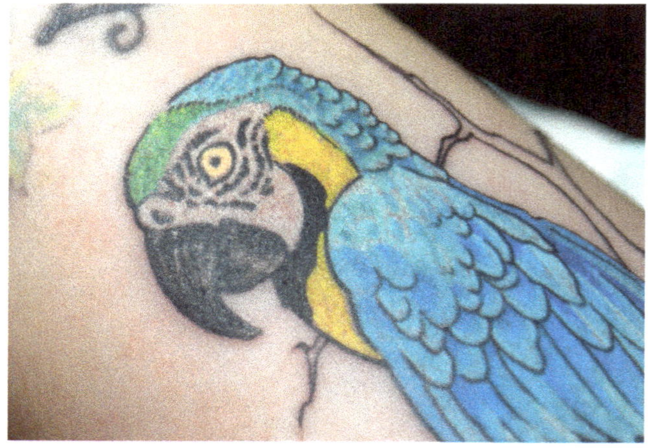

A yellow eye glares at us after being filled in with the appropriate hue.

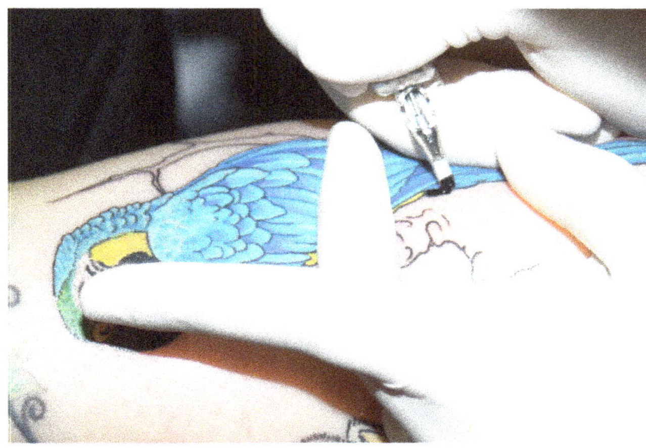

The tree limb gets its first bit of color, and is begun using a wider 7 mag needle.

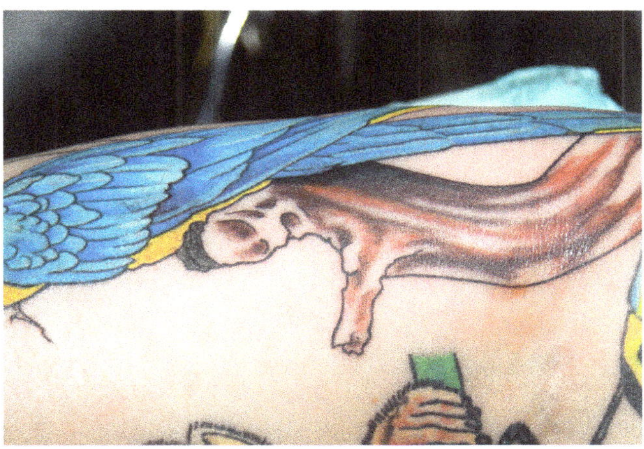

Gently shaded curves define the branch but don't take away from the primary focus.

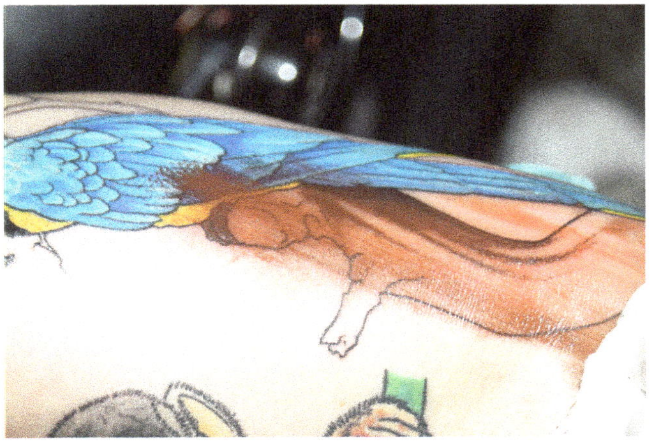

Large sections are first filled in before shades of brown are added to the branch.

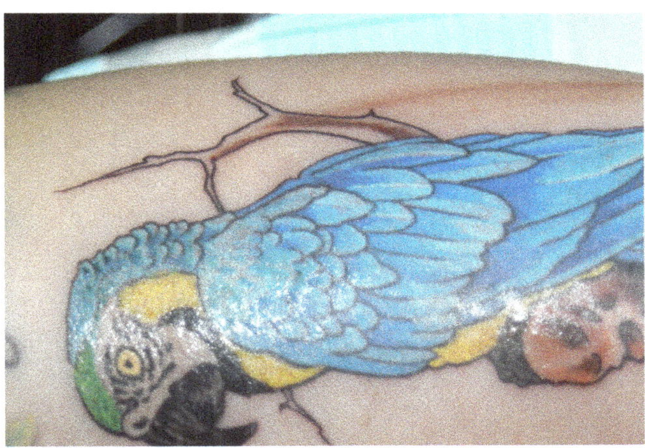

The upper segment of the branch is now addressed with the first touches of brown.

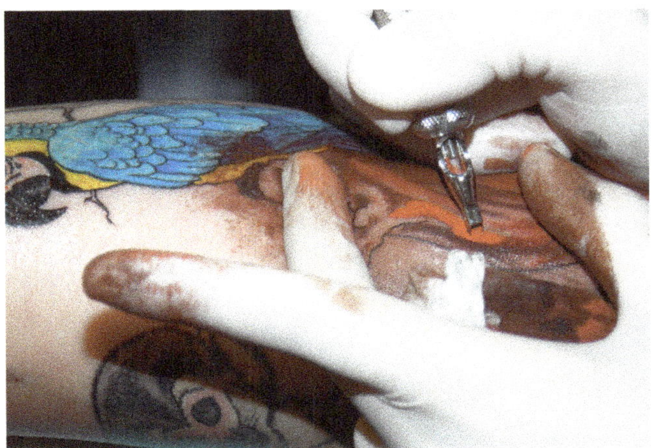

A reddish-brown is now thrown into the mix to bring life to the perch.

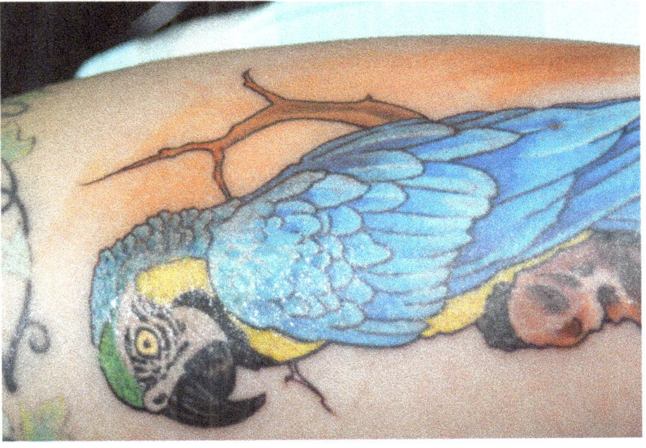

The last area to be finished, the twig is completed by using other shades of the same color.

Chapter Four

U.D.

Art With Atattooed

Having spent the better part of New Year's Eve in the shop documenting the process for this tattoo, I found it difficult to put a finger on U.D.'s energy level. Somewhere between a Japanese bullet train and the space shuttle at lift-off is about right. The man moves with a nervous, yet highly focused, action. In addition to the tattoo shop, he delivers packages for a prominent carrier. "If I didn't have kids, I'd do tattoos full-time," claims Dale. The benefits that are

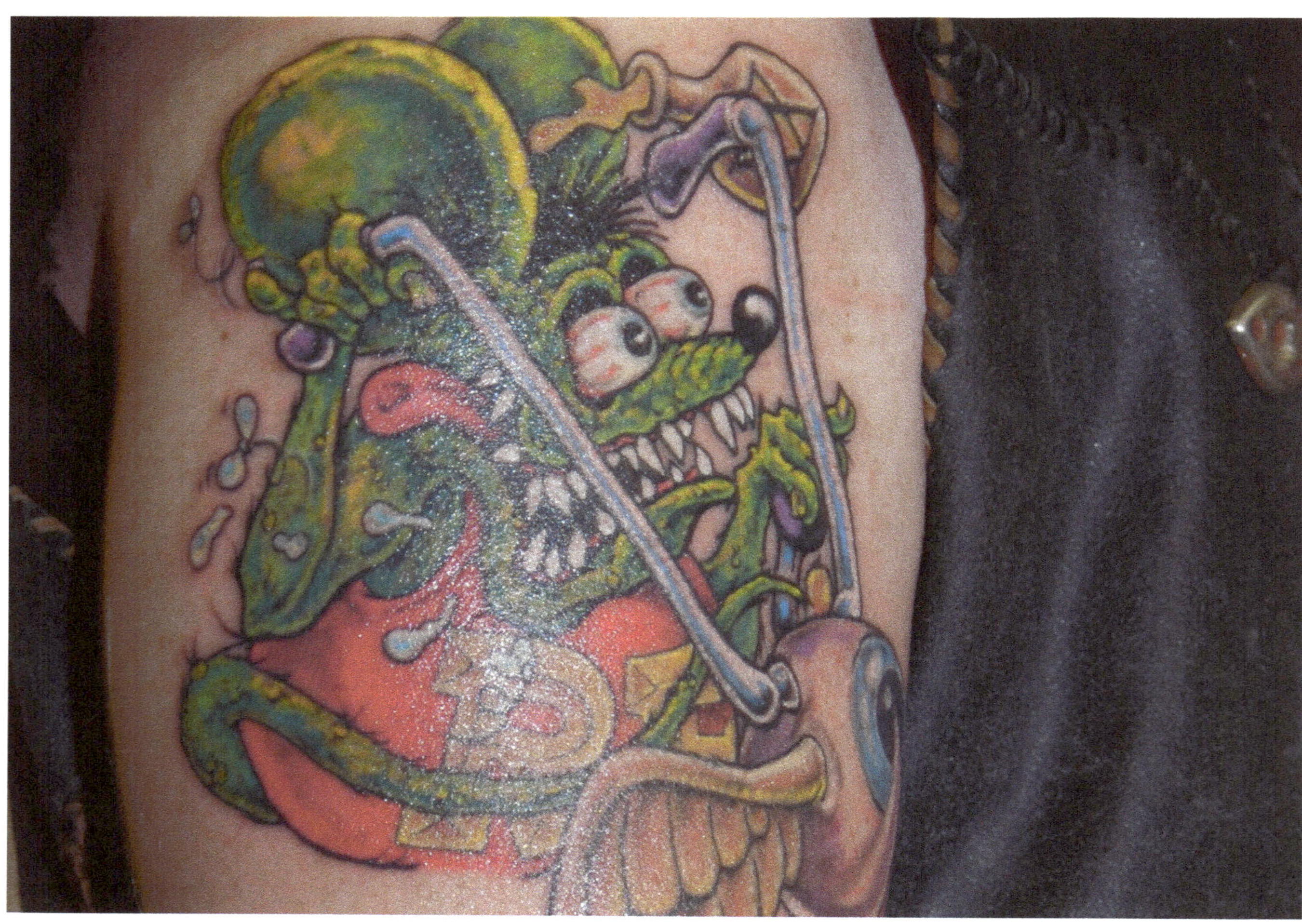

Returning to the chair for a second round, "Pyro" chose "U.D." of Art with Atattooed for his newest ink. Borrowing heavily from the art of Ed "Rat Fink" Roth, the new art features a drooling rat grasping a high set of handlebars, complete with the flying eye ball of Von Dutch.

afforded him through his full-time job provide security for his family, thus making it a difficult path to stray from.

As with all tattoo artists I've met, Dale does his best to communicate with the customer before touching a needle to skin. Along with the usual conversations and comparing notes, Dale tries to incorporate the person's attitude into the work being done. "I have sent a few people home to think more deeply about their desired tatts before allowing them to take a seat in my chair." This level of personal input makes for a happier client, and keeps both new and old customers coming back for more. The shop offers a wall full of standard art to choose from, but most clients prefer a one-of-a-kind bit of art. Some will bring in rough sketches of what they'd like, and the artists create a more finely honed illustration before the work begins.

Once the chosen design has been confirmed, Dale will start with either a heat transfer or scribe the outline directly onto the skin. Additional details can also be added to a heat transfer before the actual process begins. The better the road transfer, the better the end results will be.

In his earlier days, Dale actually designed and built his own tattoo power supply, based on what he found missing on existing units. Using a variety of electronic components, his machine delivered supper-smooth flow of power and allowed almost anyone to create high-quality ink work. This fact posed a problem for experienced artists, thus forcing Dale's machine into the shadows before wreaking havoc in the open market. Nothing like providing amateurs with gear that can produce professional results to mess up the works.

Dale considers tattoos to be "The last form of freestyle art" known to man. With the many variations and derivations I have witnessed so far, I'd have to say he's correct. There may be genres, styles and formats that can be put into groups, but it appears that many of the tattoos being done today fall into categories that refuse to be labeled. How could a person define a cartoon mouse that was wielding an assault rifle and a bloody head?

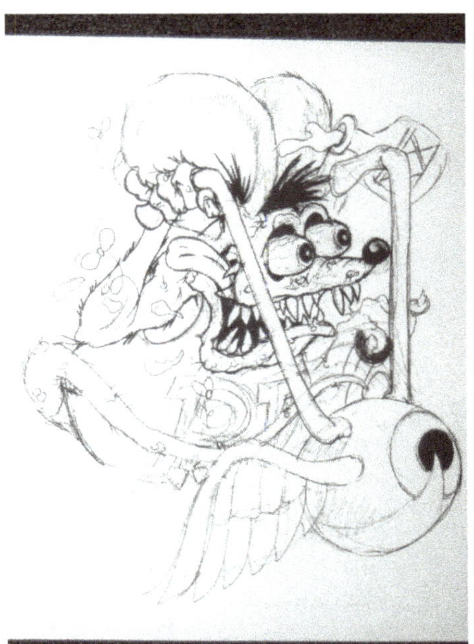

After many communications between U.D and Pyro, the final sketch is ready to be transferred to the skin.

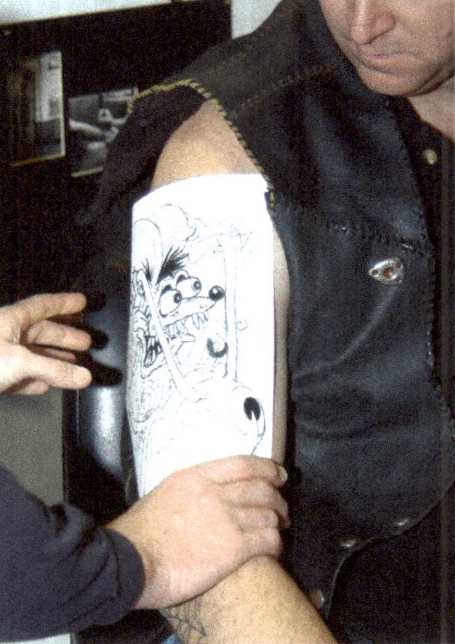

Placing the finalized sketch on the target area assures both parties that size and location are correct.

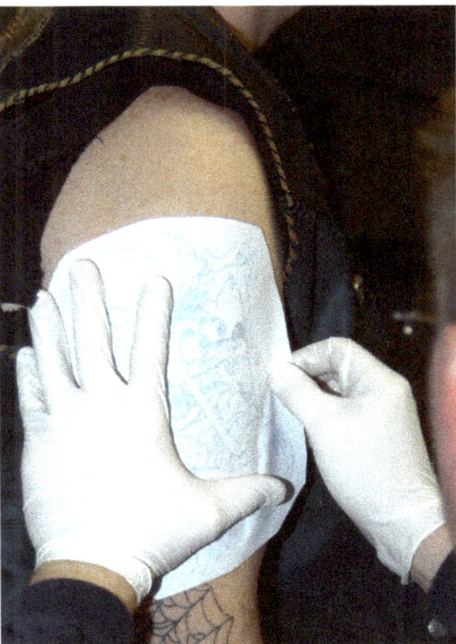

The heat transfer art is now applied to the flesh, then pealed away leaving the blue lines behind.

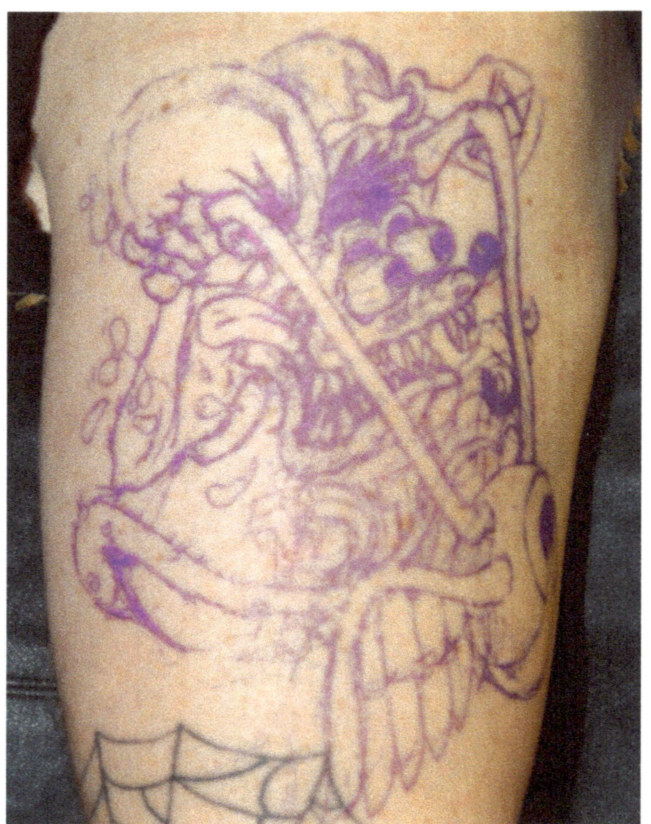

One final check of the placement and size before the needle gets put to use.

Cleanliness is again the dominant feature of the shop and the process. Numerous efforts are taken to ensure that no fluids are transferred from the client to anyone else. Repeated use of the ultrasonic machine keeps the tattoo machine in tip-top form as well as keeping colors from blending until needed. Surfaces of the work station are wiped clean before any other steps are taken, and individual containment of the required tools help to safeguard the client.

Being a bit of a maverick, Dale used to make his own needles for use in the machine. Although they did the job, current production units are of far better quality and deliver a consistent flow of ink. Despite his old world talents, some new-fangled hardware really helps his cause.

Art with Atattooed employs about six artists although they are seldom all on duty at the same time. Early morning appointments are not an option as most shops in the arena don't even open before noon. You can't force creativity out of bed too soon. Even though we were working on New Year's Eve, the flow of people into the shop was steady and many had to wait for over an hour for the chance to get their work done. No complaints were heard as the eager customers sat and awaited their number to be called.

Although his life is divided into the roles of family man and working man, Dale still has plenty of passion and energy to create his own form of art on the clients lucky enough to get an appointment with him. Maybe one day his other responsibilities will allow for more time behind the machine, but for now he's happy to create what he can, when he can.

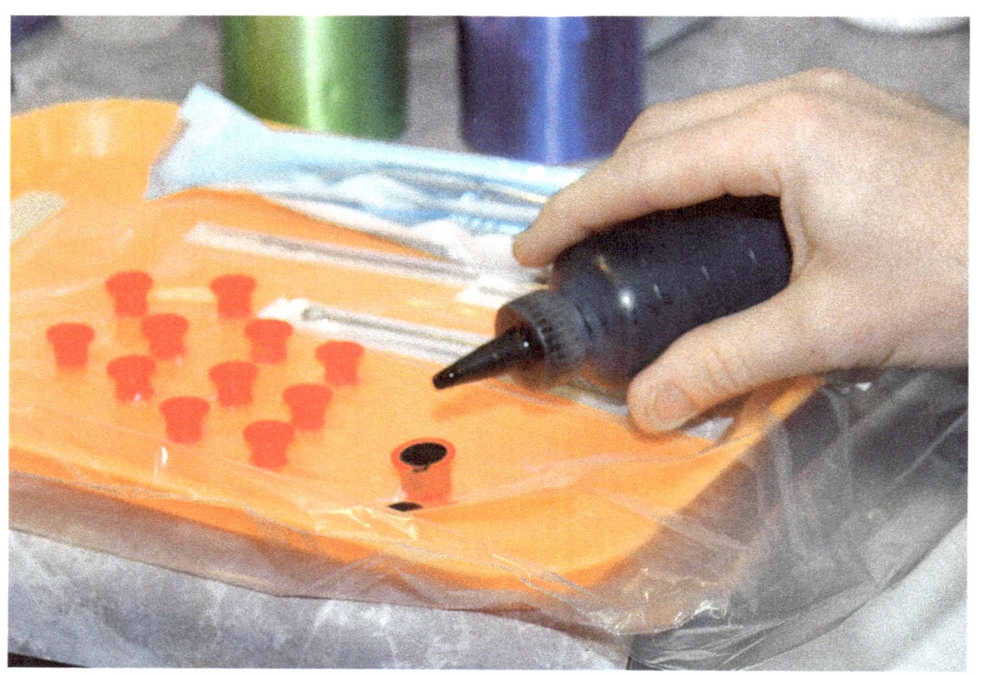

With black being the first color required, the small cup is filled with ink.

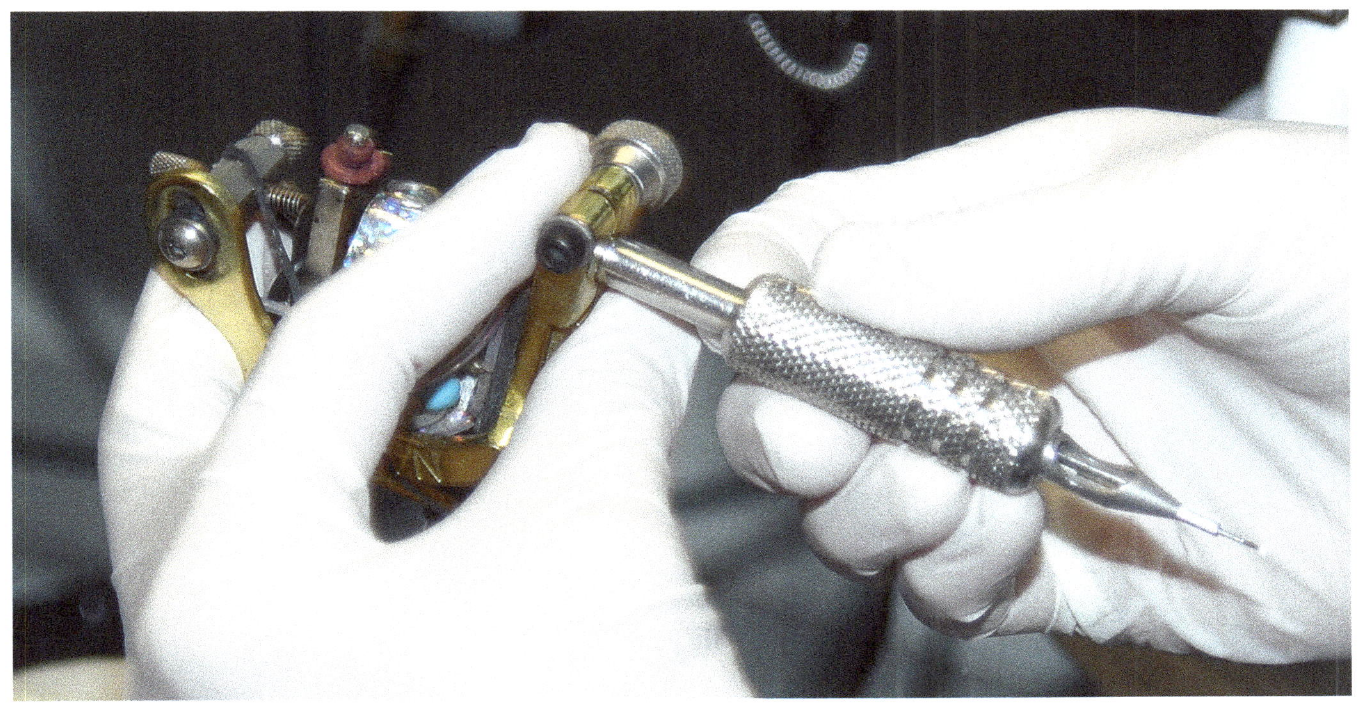

The appropriate needle is now loaded into the machine and strapped into place.

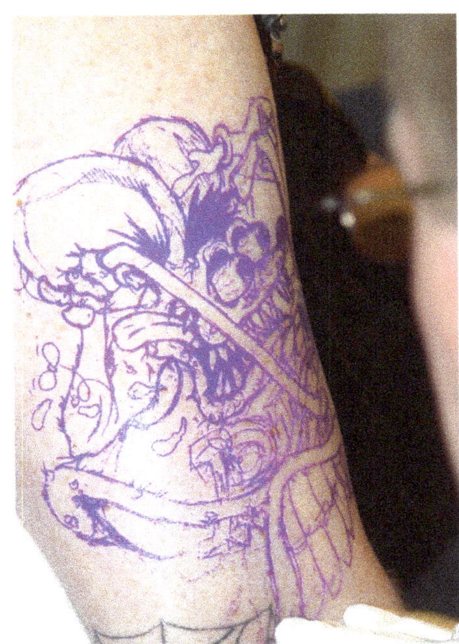

A moment is taken to chart his strategy before beginning the needle work.

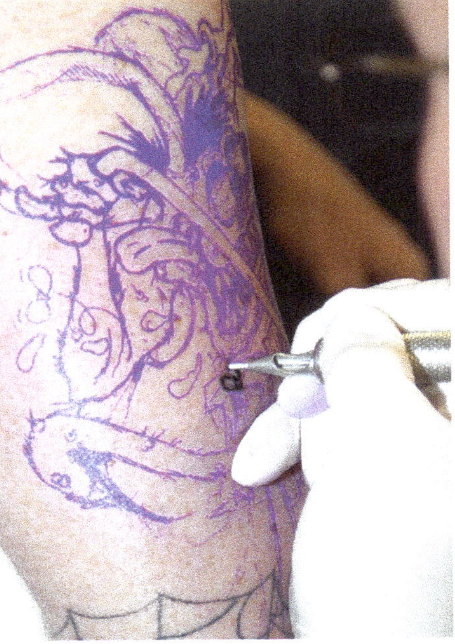

Starting at the bottom of the piece will keep the stencil fresher, providing a clear map as work moves along.

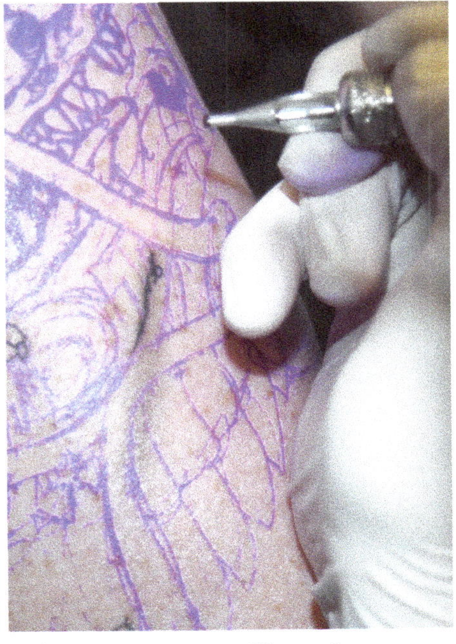

The intricate art will require many stages of work to achieve the final results, and even the curly-cues of tail hair are addressed early on.

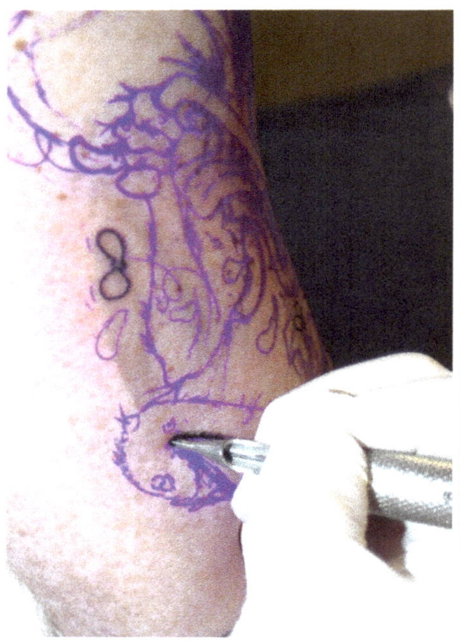

Details on the elongated tail are numerous and will make for a terrific piece when complete.

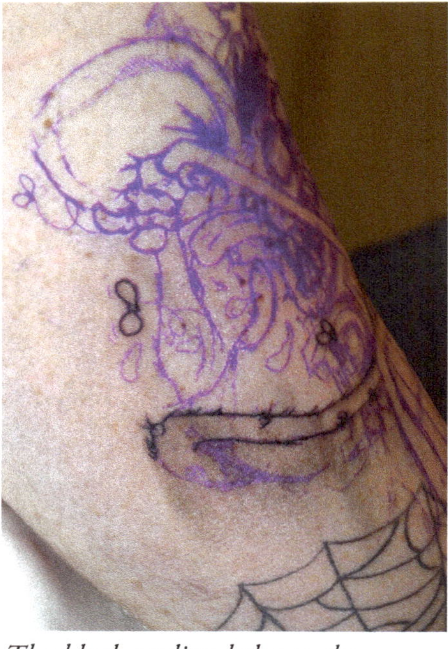

The black outline helps to show U.D. the way as he continues laying the ground work for the rest of the work.

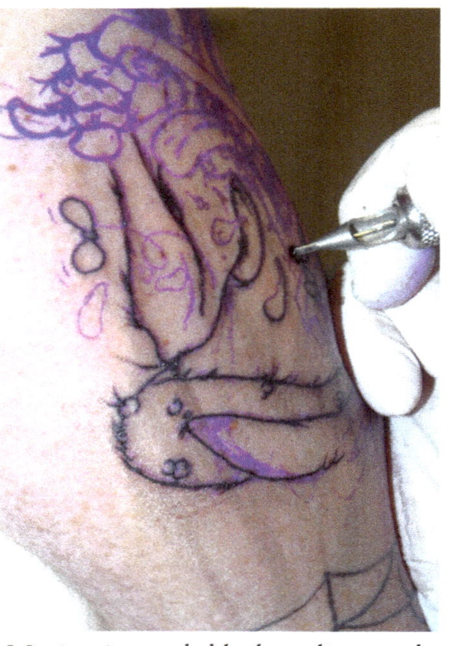

Moving inward, black outlines and minor details are made in tiny increments.

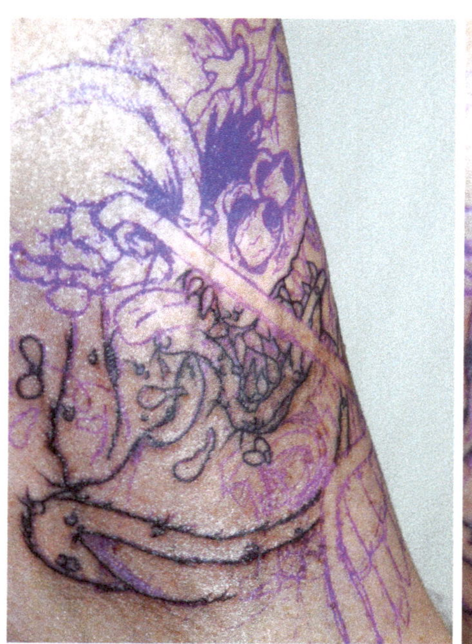

Teeth, tail and part of the forearm are now outlined in black and await additional color.

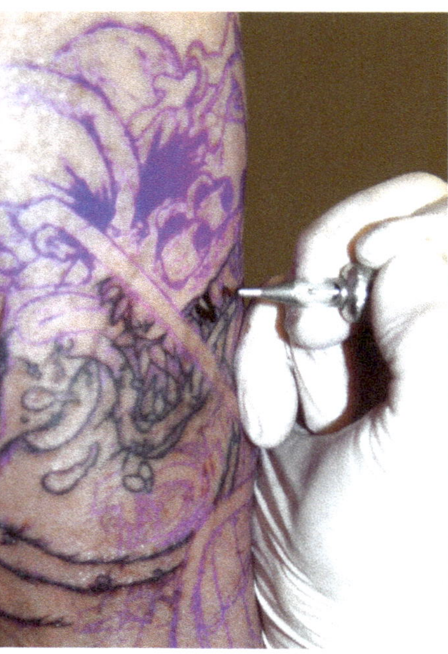

Filling in some areas around the pointed teeth adds to the dimension of the art.

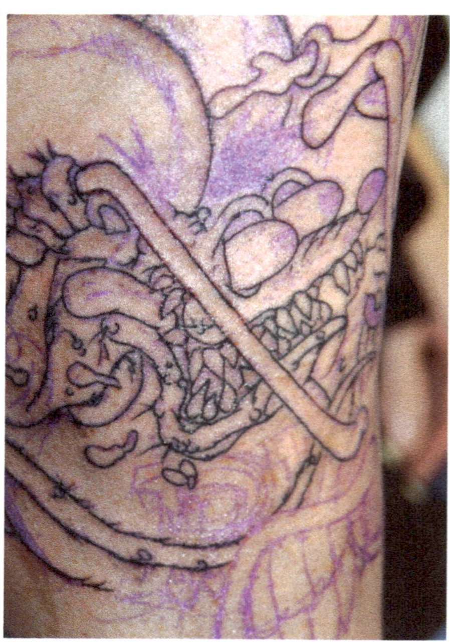

Black ink has now been applied to most of the upper portion of the transfer and we can begin to see the creature come to life.

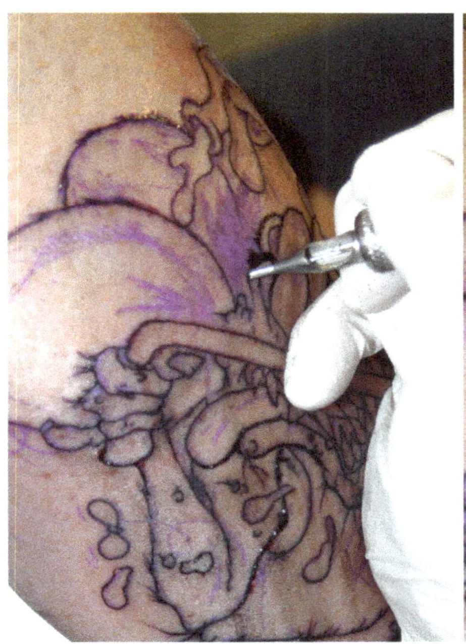

Small areas of heavier concentration will complete the black work before moving on to the use of colors.

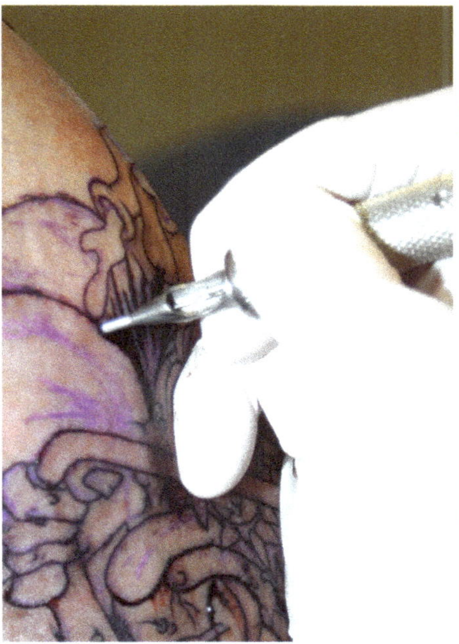

The large ears are now approached and are given their share of shading.

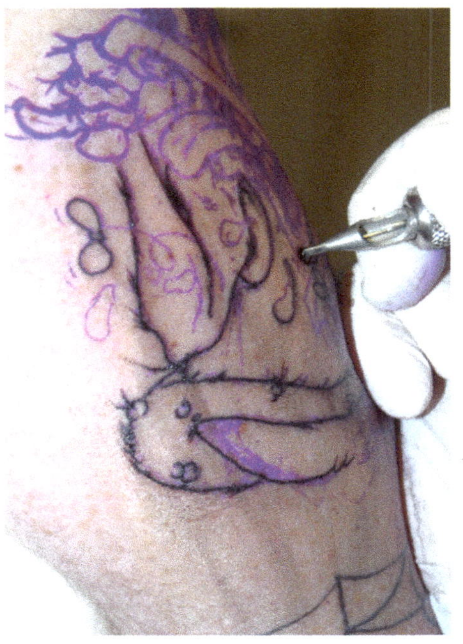

Even having the smallest spaces filled in with black helps to illuminate the direction of the work.

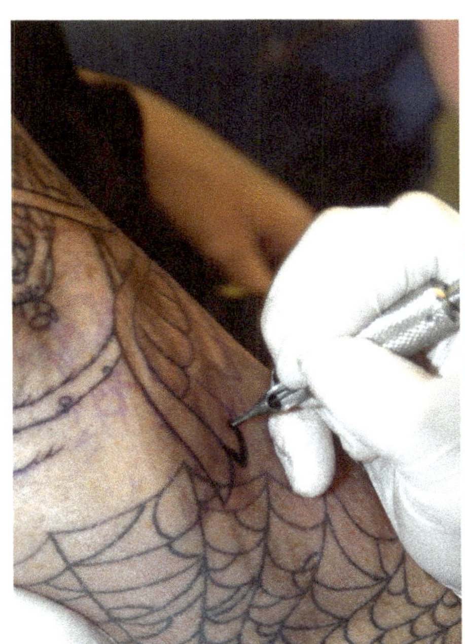

Outlining on the flying eyeball now begins.

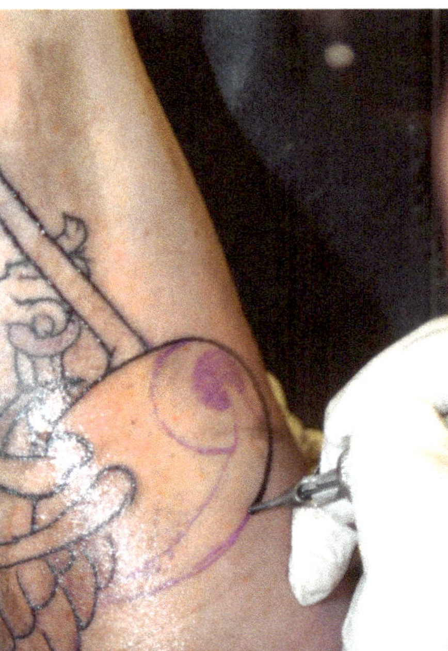

Most of the steps required seem to achieve little until we see those that follow.

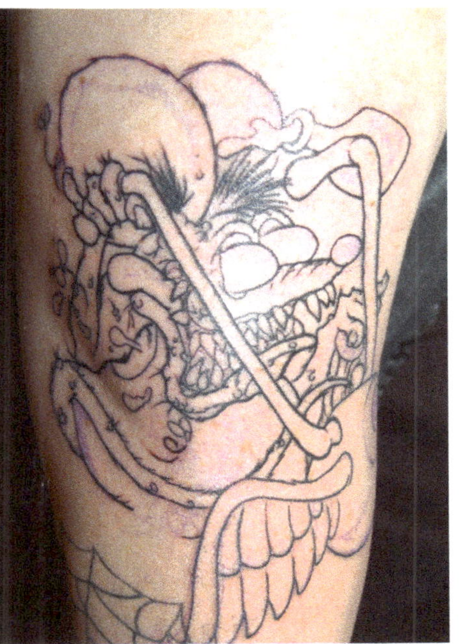

A majority of the black outline is now complete and awaits further detail efforts.

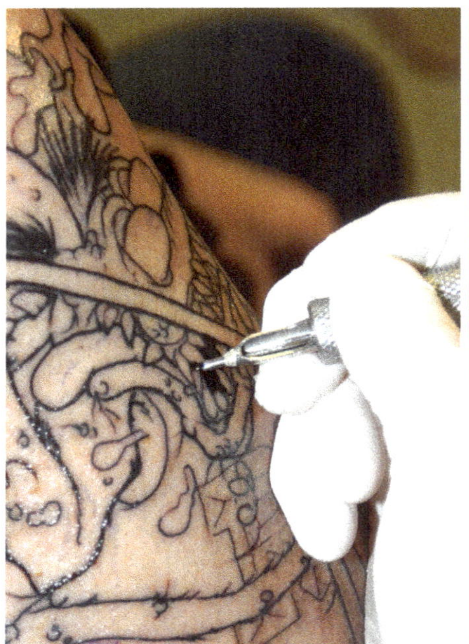

Returning to the mouth, shading will help to define the jagged teeth that lie within.

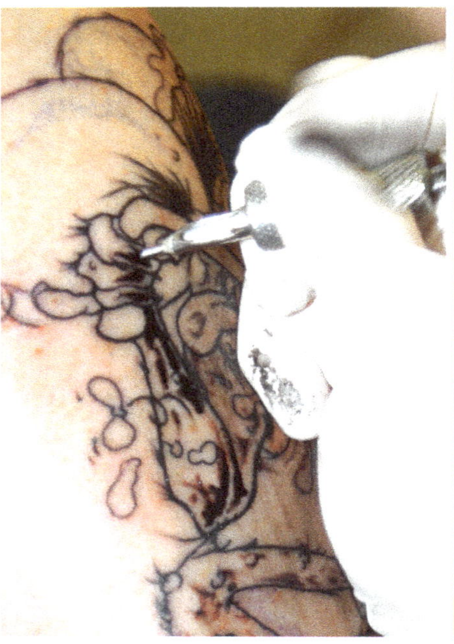

Additional detailing on the finger-tips will later show us the results of these minor touches.

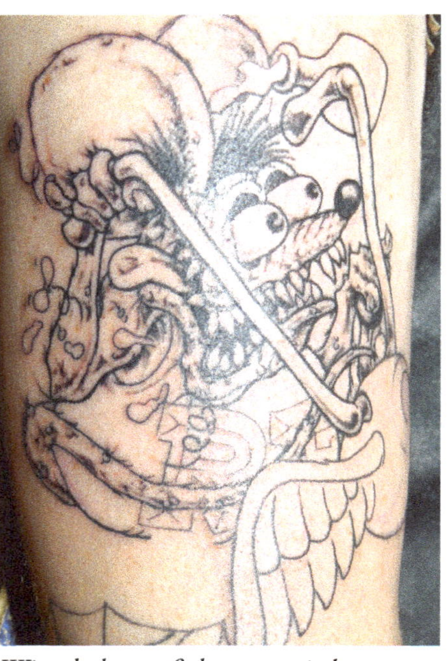

Wiped clean of the excess ink, we can now begin to see the three-dimensional form taking shape.

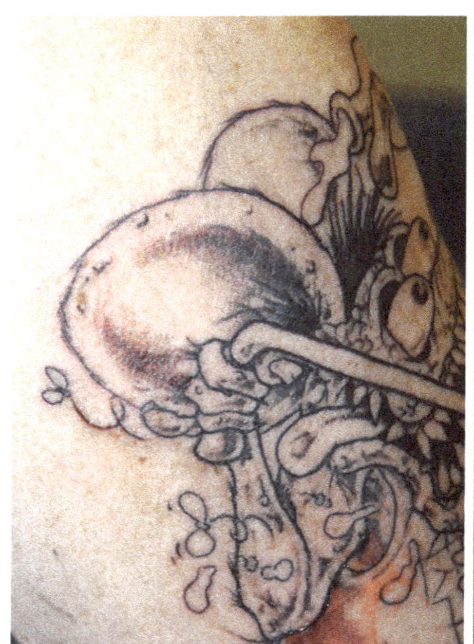

Subtle shading in the ears helps to bring depth to the work and sets U.D.'s tattoos apart from the rest

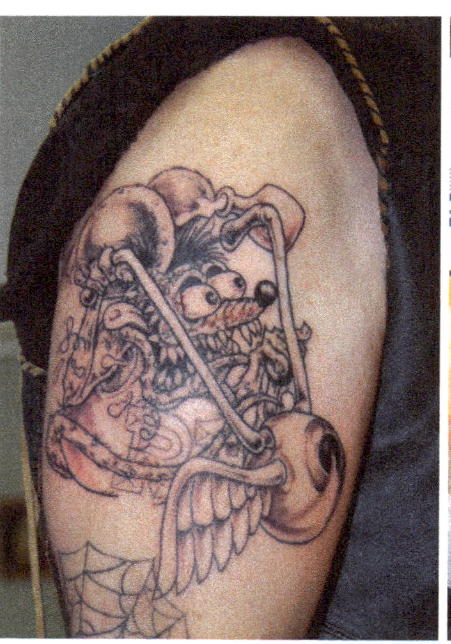

With the black ink work now complete we all look forward to the installation of the many hues that will be used.

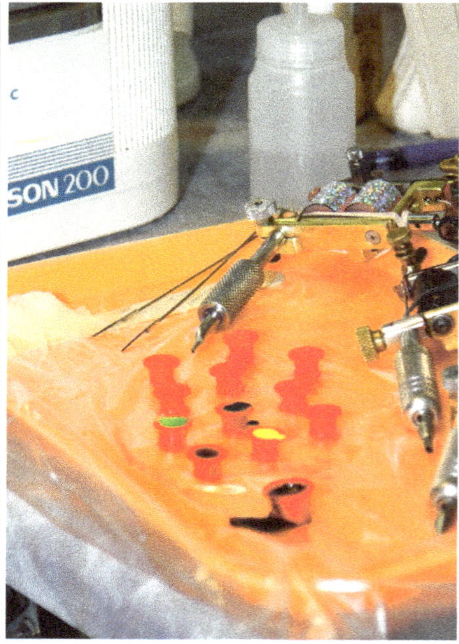

A variety of colored inks will be used to complete the piece and small amounts are meted out into the waiting cups.

Q&A: U.D.

How long have you been doing tattoos?

About 18 or 19 years.

What was the first tattoo you did?

Created from a sketch of my own creation, we did a four inch, three-dimensional sword with an eyeball. It was black and gray and applied to a forearm.

Do you have a favorite genre you prefer?

Of course the bigger pieces are easier and give me more room to create, and abstract textures done in black and gray rank high on my list.

Do you find inspiration from any particular source?

There are so many great artists out there, both old and new-school, it would be hard to select just one.

Are you best known for any tattoo?

Years ago I did and old school, punk rock Old Style beer label on the top of someone's head. The location and detail kind of made me a name.

Do you see any big changes in the world of tattoos?

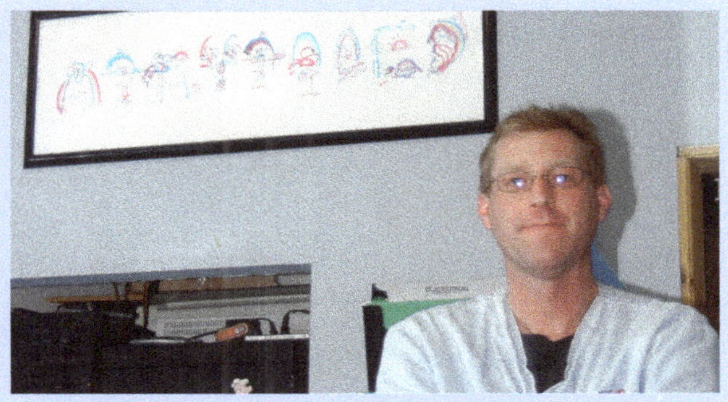

Improvements in the pigments have made for longer lasting colors and better gear makes it easier to do the job.

How long has this shop been in operation?

We opened up in August of 1998.

Any background you'd care to share with us?

I began working as a graphic artist and slid into camera work and screen printing. The Marines made me one their own between 1985 and 1991, and I served in the Desert Storm campaign. My apprenticeship began right around then and my work continued to improve with every passing day. After working at a few other shops we decided to open our own.

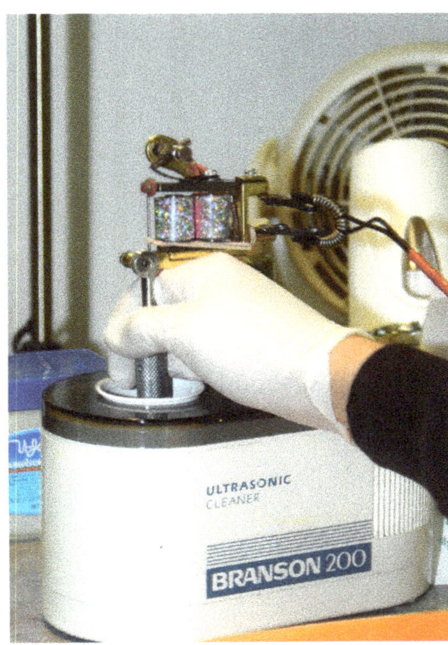

The ultrasonic cleaner continues to keep things clean as we prepare for the first use of color.

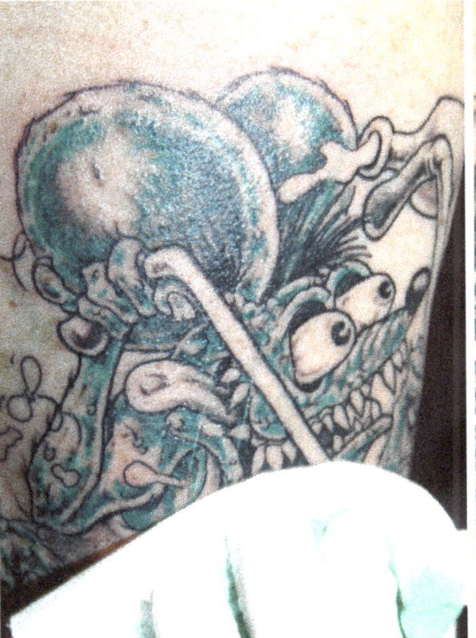

Dark green is the first color applied as U.D. works from dark to light colors.

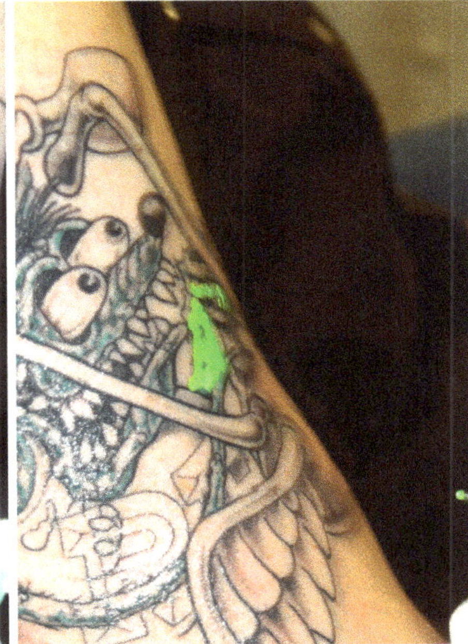

Smaller segments of a brighter green are now completed as the transformation continues.

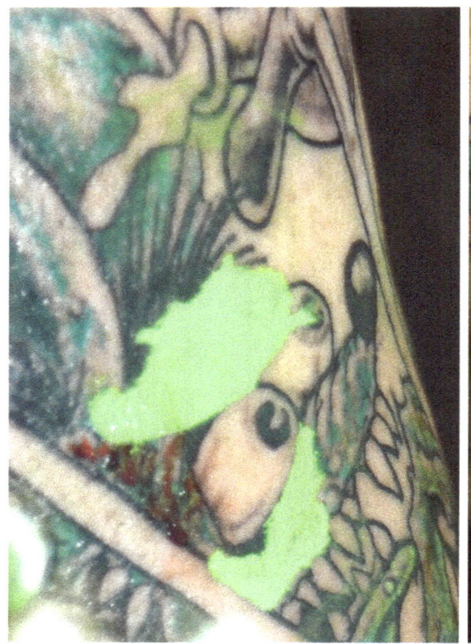

The needle places the ink into place, leaving excess color that will be wiped clean to reveal the next bit of shading.

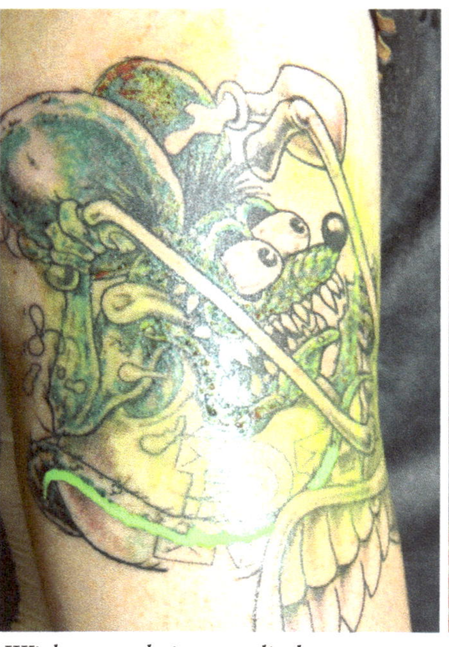

With green being applied over much of the piece, we can see more and more of the details revealed

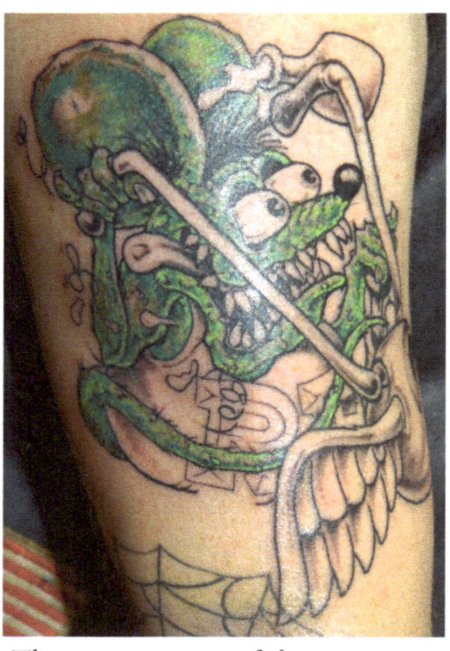

The green portions of the piece are now complete and the extra ink has been wiped clean

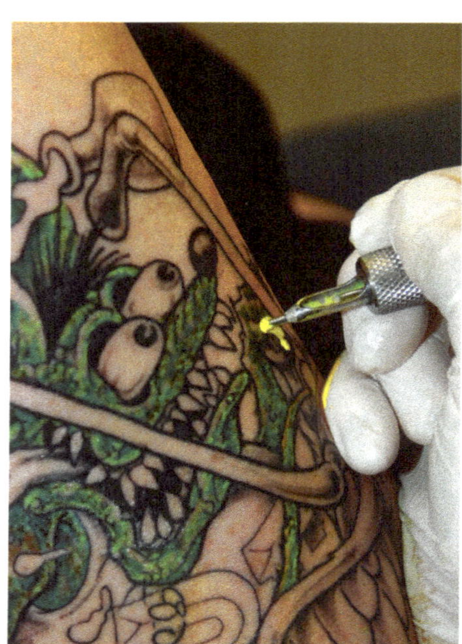

Moving into a range of lighter colors, bits of yellow are now added to the equation.

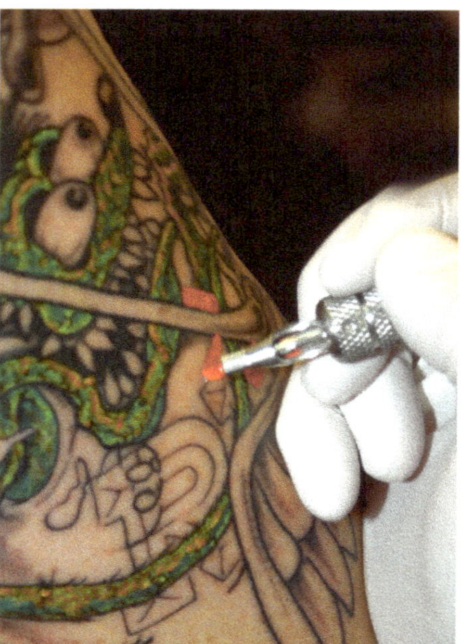

Bright red will bring some additional brilliance to the finished piece.

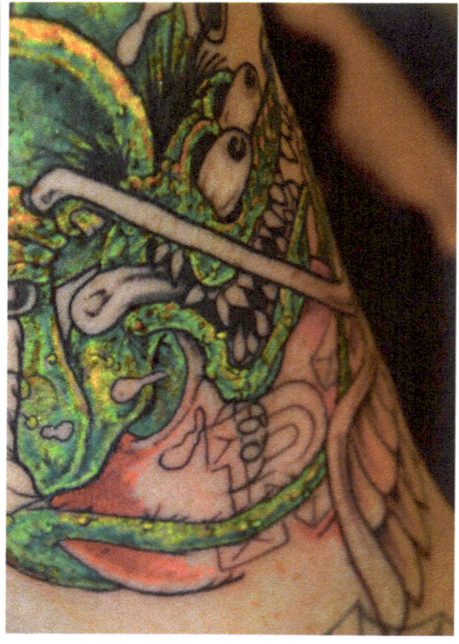

Large areas of the belly need to be filled in with red, but is done so in small sections.

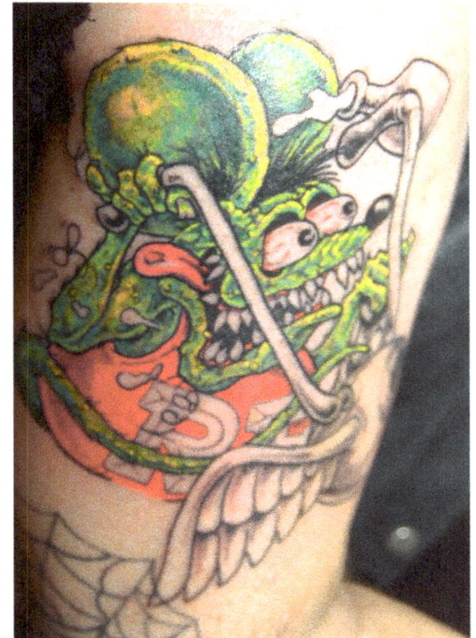

Red can be seen in the eyes, tongue, belly and gums of the mouth, showing the level of detail being attained.

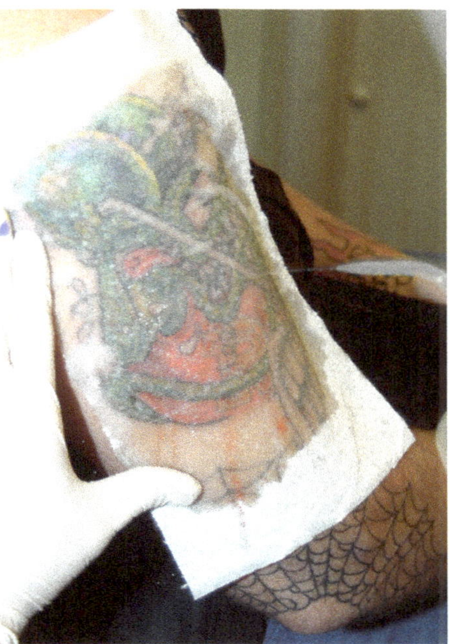

Periodically, the area is washed down with diluted green soap, covered with a soft paper towel and cleaned.

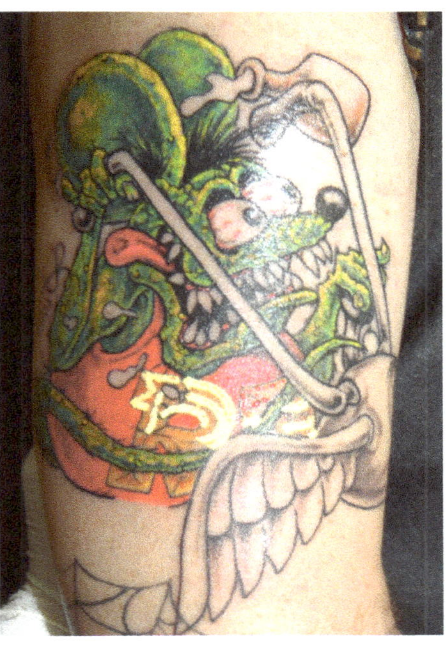

Work now begins on the letters of the shirt with yellow as the dominant hue.

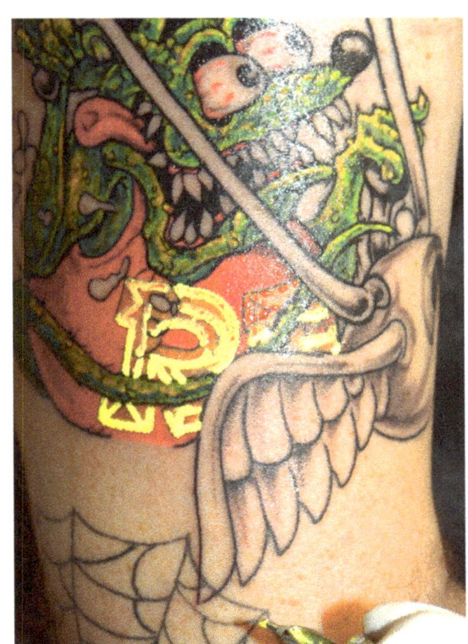

Each letter is outlined first, to be followed by additional colors for shape and detail

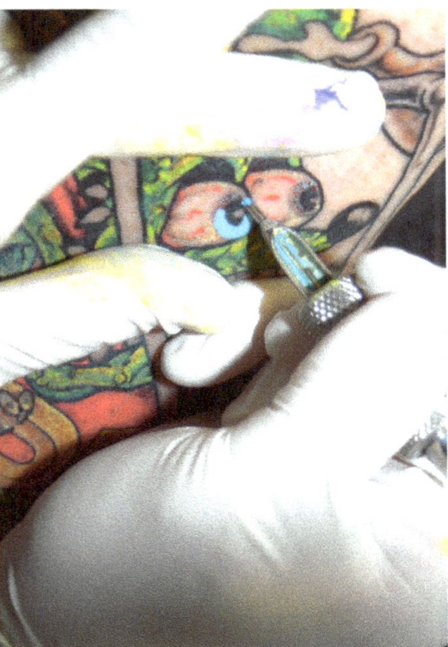

Bright blue is selected to bring the eyes to life.

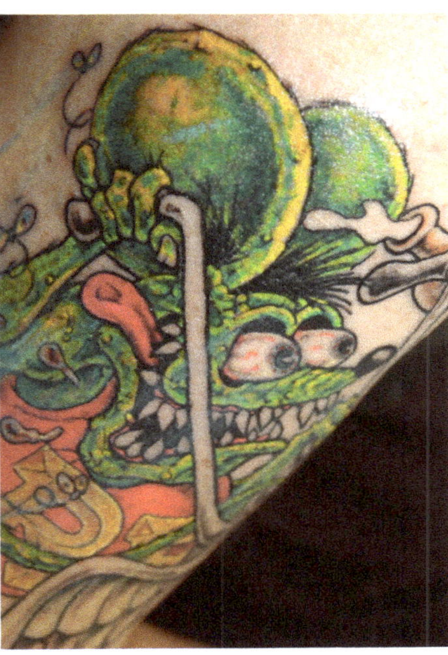

The canvas of Pyro's flesh is taking on a new life as details and contours continue to be added.

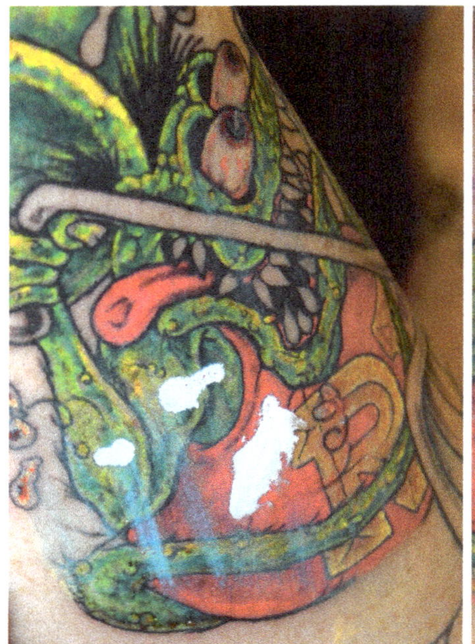

Pale blue highlights will do their part in bringing depth to the effort.

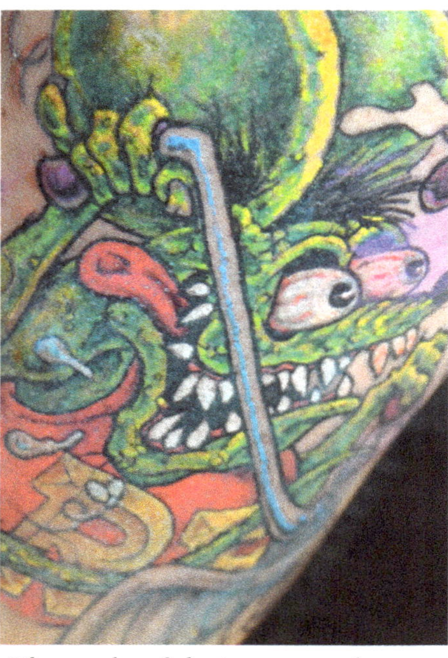

The results of the incremental steps are becoming more apparent as we approach the final steps.

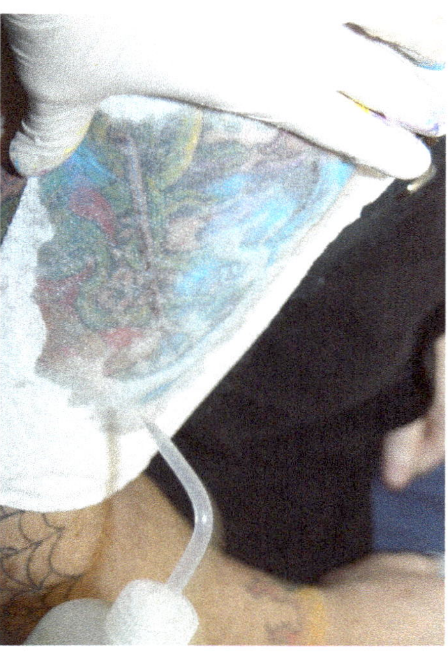

Another cleansing of the piece will show U.D. where the last bits of detail will be required.

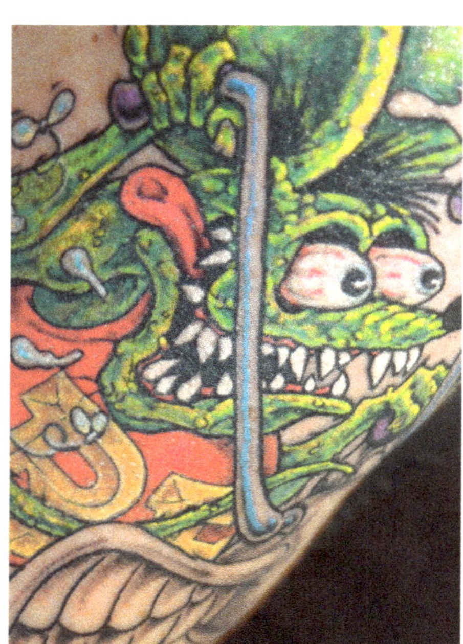

The high-rise handlebars are given their own bit of contour by using a bright blue detail.

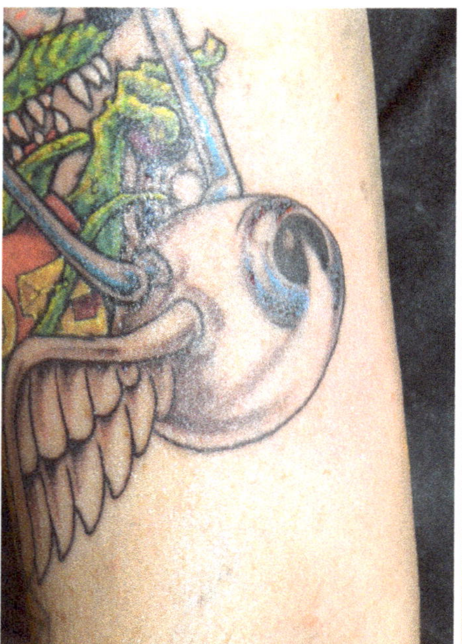

A few subtle shapes help to define the flying orb.

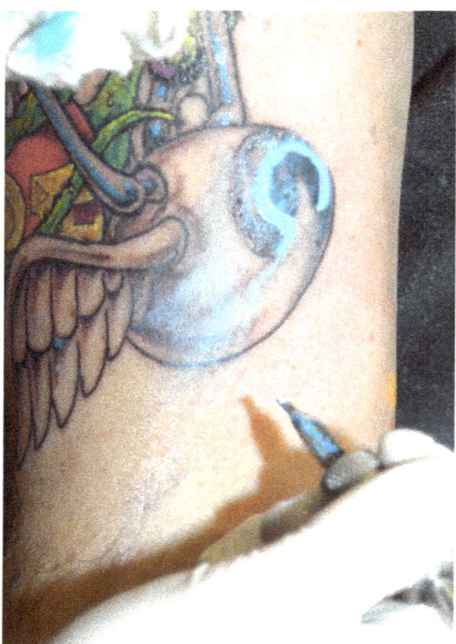

Areas of bright color will give a life-like appearance to the completed eye-ball.

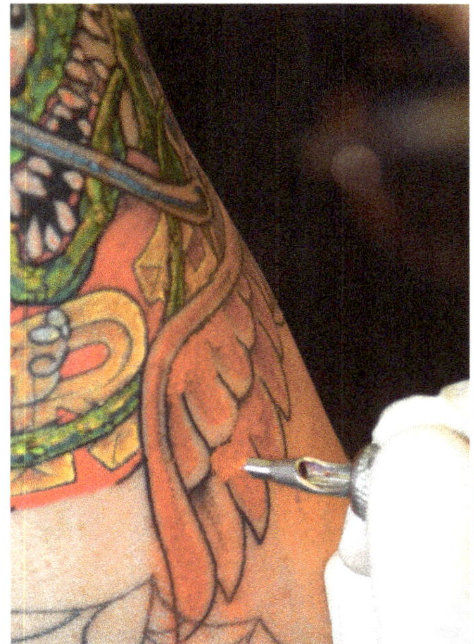

Carrying the flying eye through the night skies will be a pair of red wings.

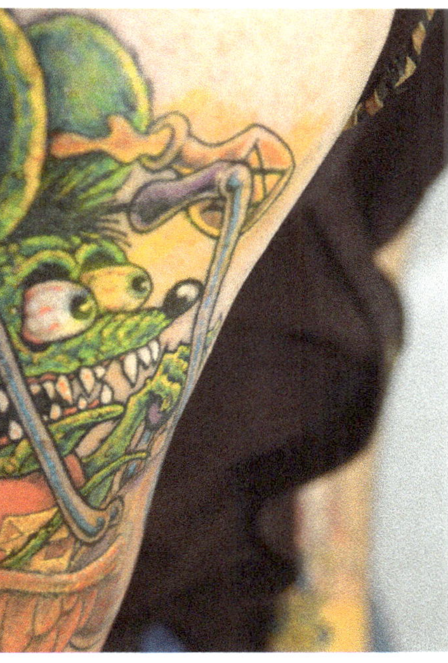

Anyone with an eye for detail will discover the tiny bottle of XXX potion at the top of the art.

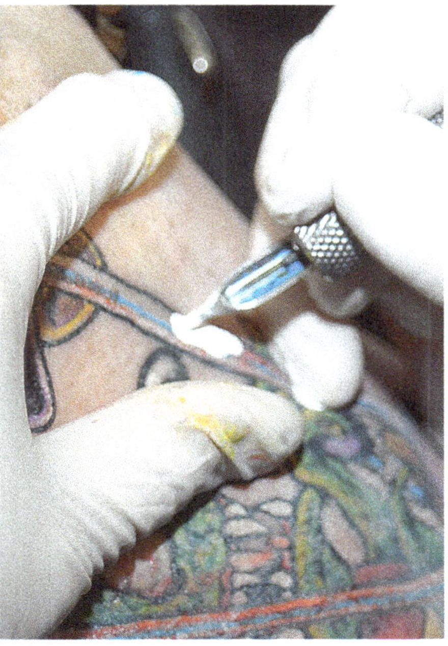

The blue line applied to the handlebars is now highlighted with a brighter shade to provide a tubular look.

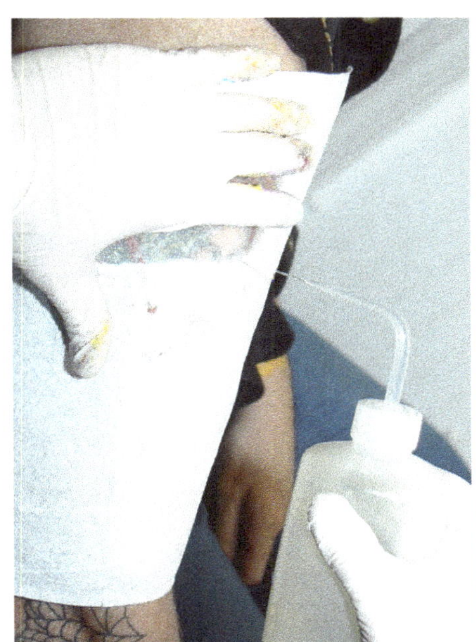

A final bath of green soap will reveal the completed tattoo.

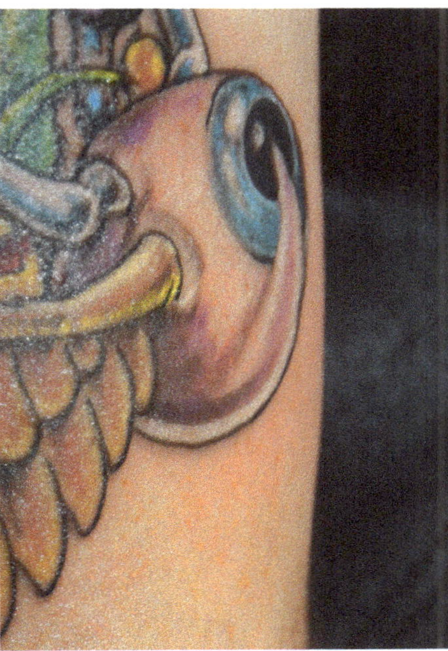

Details seen in every square inch of the piece are a testament to the ability of U.D. and his many years of experience in the field.

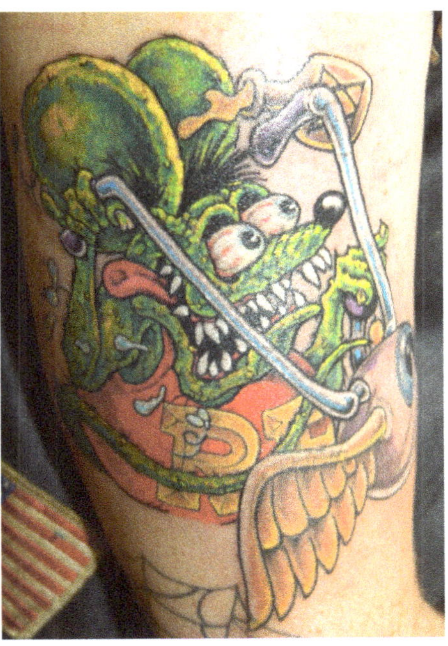

Shown here in all of its final glory is the latest addition to Pyro's collection of body art.

Chapter Five

Little Frank

It's Just A Little Prick

Unlike most, if not all, of the remaining artists in this book, Frank has no formal training in the world of art, drawing or illustration. His intrigue with the craft began with some ink on his grandfather's arm, and his interest grew from that single exposure. At the tender age of 9 he knew he wanted to get tattoos, and probably go on to become a tattoo artist himself. Many of us are still dreaming of being astronauts or some other unrealistic career choice at that stage in life, so we can see how in

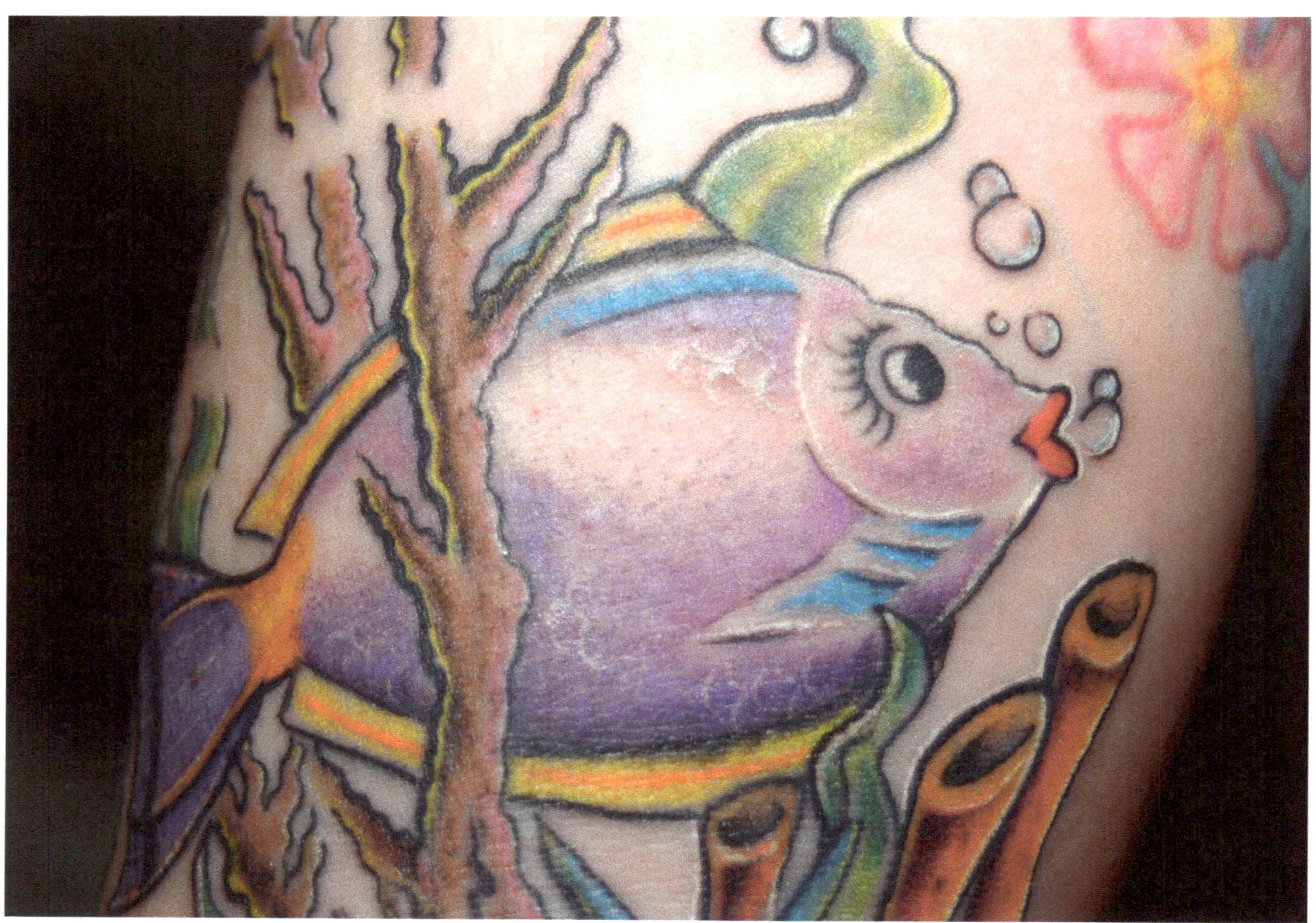

With their pending nuptials on the horizon, Autumn was eager to have her husband apply her next batch of skin art. She is no stranger to the craft and her fiancé has been in the racket for many years himself. The fish was only one piece in a long series of planned pieces.

this case, a person's persistence can pay off.

Like the rest of the artists here, Little Frank takes pride in the cleanliness of his shop. His new location in Decatur, Illinois used to be a dentists office, so the layout of the spot was perfect. Nice waiting room and reception area, with several small suites that have been converted into tattoo booths. Plenty of shelf space and terrific lighting make for a friendly environment. Frank himself is an affable guy who is easy to get along with right from the get-go.

Before setting up for the tattoo, he cleans an already spotless work surface and wraps the required gear in disposable plastic sheathing. These efforts will prevent cross contamination between clients, and keep infections at bay. Several waiting tattoo machines hang at the ready on hand made racks, and can be put into service at a moment's notice. Frank and a partner designed a machine of their own years ago. By drawing the body on Autocad first, then laser cutting the steel into shape, they had a machine to call their very own. Combing their initials, the "Duf" tattoo machine came to be.

His willing participant, Autumn Star, is also his fiancé, and has received many bits of tattoo work from Frank over the years. Frank has even created a major back piece on Autumn's mom, so we know her family is OK with his appearance and career choice. Not everyone in his position can say the same.

While on vacation in Las Vegas recently, Autumn and Frank viewed an enormous fish tank at a chain restaurant. Enamored of the colors and shapes of the fish and their surroundings, it was then decided to be her next bit of ink. Upon returning home, Frank sketched out a small diorama of sea life before continuing. The combination of the fish and the related undersea life captured the essence of what they saw on vacation. Frank's vision had lots of bright colors to really bring the ink to life.

While many shops use a copy machine to move their sketch to the transfer paper, Little Frank prefers to do the work by hand. Additional changes can be made to the art this way, providing one last opportunity to improve the work.

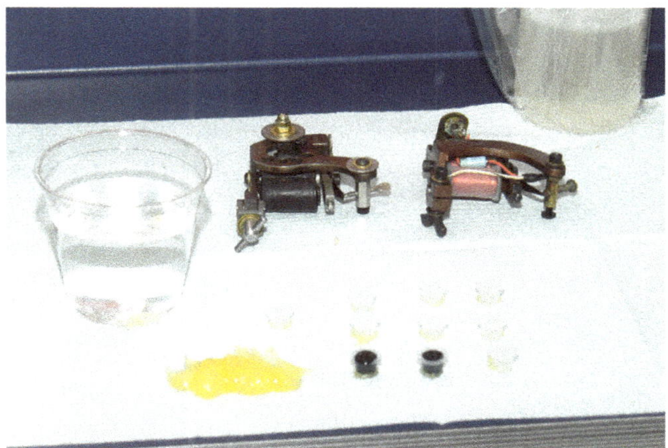

Two of the cups get filled with black ink, and the machines are loaded for action. The water cup will be used to rinse out the needles between steps.

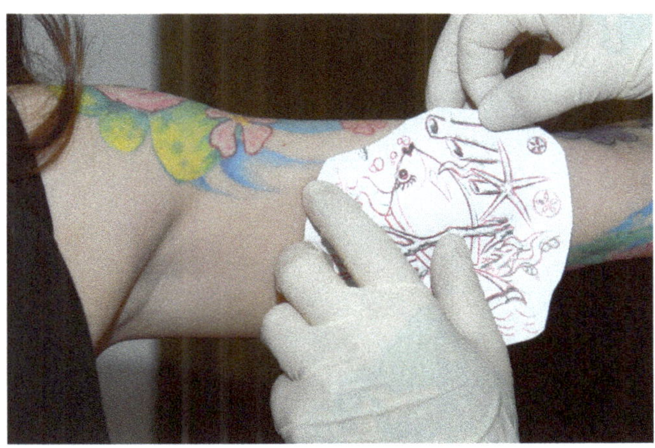

After conferring with another artist in the shop, final location for the new piece is decided on and the transfer is put in place.

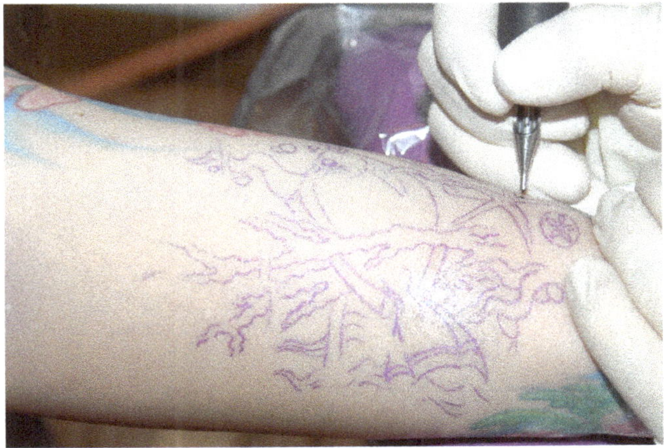

A 3 round, otherwise known as a 3-liner needle, will be used to begin the basic outline of the tattoo. The starfish is the first to get attention.

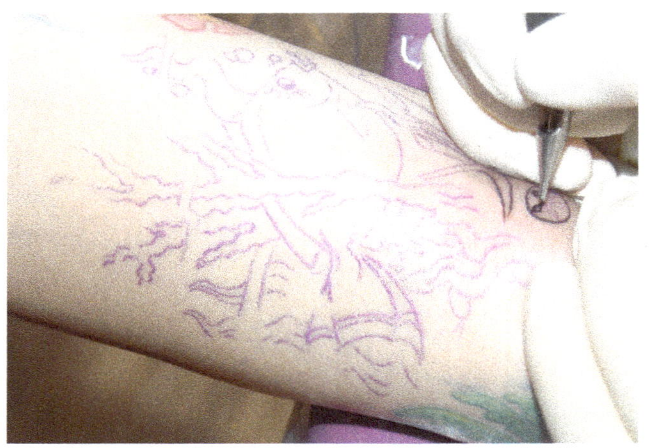

Before completing the outline of the starfish, Little Frank moves to the sand dollar below it to continue with the outline.

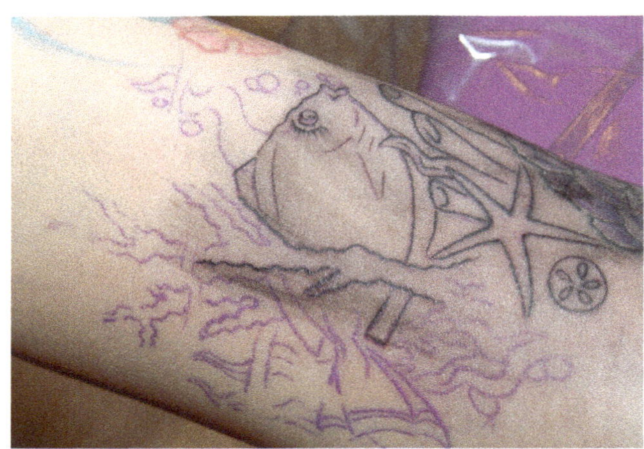

The coral, fish and seaweed are receiving their basic outlines with color inks to follow.

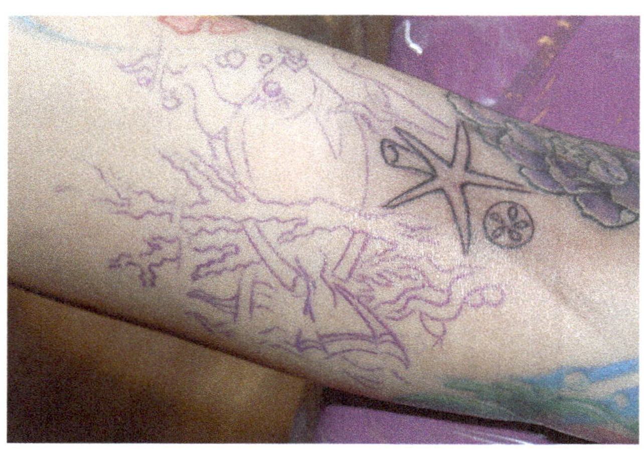

The basic black outline moves along swiftly as other bits of undersea life are completed.

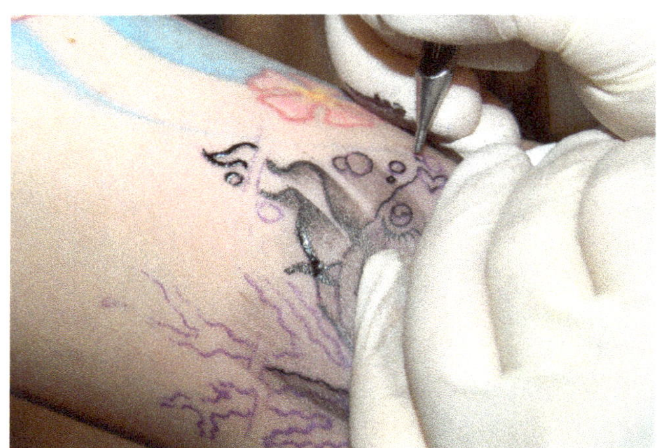

Tiny bubbles and sea weed are all a part of this undersea vision and when completed will make for a great setting.

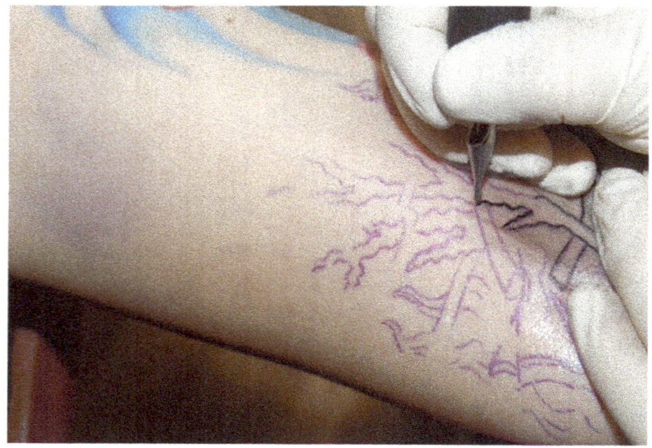

Moving to another section of the skin, the coral is now given its first bit of outlining.

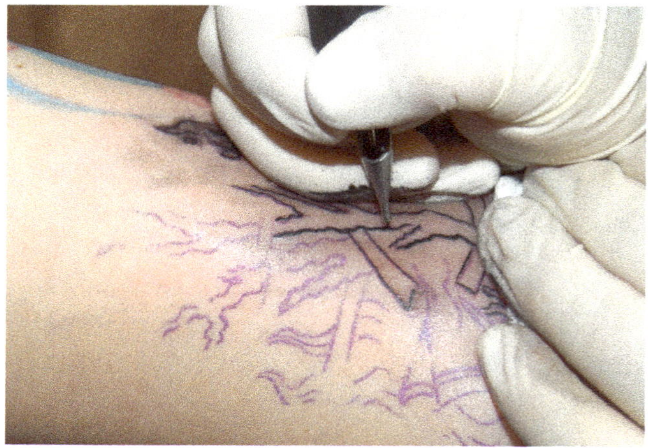

To aid in the illusion of being 3-dimensional, heavier outlining on the coral is now added.

Once the art has been moved to the transfer paper, final decisions on the location are made. Another tattoo artist in the shop gives his opinion on the chosen spot, and all parties agree. Wetting the already shaved region, Frank places the transfer in place and peels away the backing. The blue line art left behind will be his guide for the rest of the tattoo process.

As we have learned by now, the black outline is the first step in any tattoo. Choosing a small, 3-round set of needles for the task, the buzzing of the machine begins. Frank adjusts the power supply to meet the needs of the skin in question before setting the needles to the skin. This is done by sound, and his experience seldom leads him astray. The outlining process moves along quickly as Frank traces the path of the transfer ink. Moving from place to place provides some respite from discomfort for Autumn, although the work doesn't seem to bother her. She already has many tattoos on her person, some in far more delicate locations.

Once the basic outline is complete, Frank chooses a slightly larger 5-round set of needles to accentuate some of the lines already in place. These darker lines will bring more dimension to the piece and add shape to the curves of the scene being created. Once the black lining and shading are complete, Frank refers to a few photos for the application of the color ink on the tattoo. Although the photos were taken of an aquarium, and lack any really specific details, they provide Frank with enough information to make his choices.

The first color ink is applied to the starfish and sand dollar at the bottom of the design. Shades of blue are used to complete the starfish along with highlights of bright green. The sand dollar is done in a peach shade that has been mixed from several inks at his disposal. Each buzz of the machine exposes us to more detail and an expanding array of hues. The shading and accent colors help to make the illustration seem real.

Moving to the coral and sea weed next, Little Frank weaves his magic as the related sea life are filled in with varying hues. The most amazing part

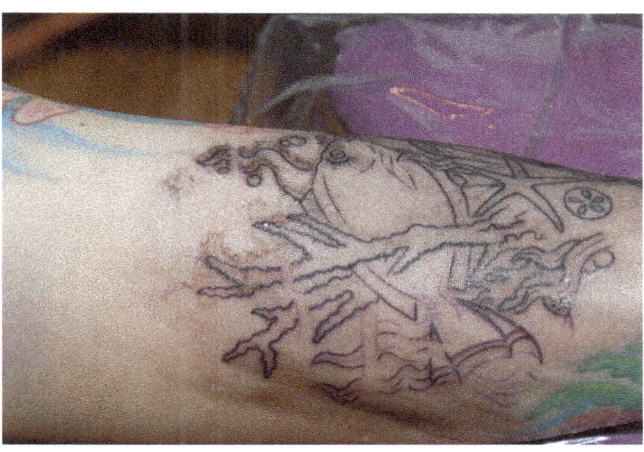

With a majority of the basic outline complete, work will now progress to shading and contours before color can be delivered.

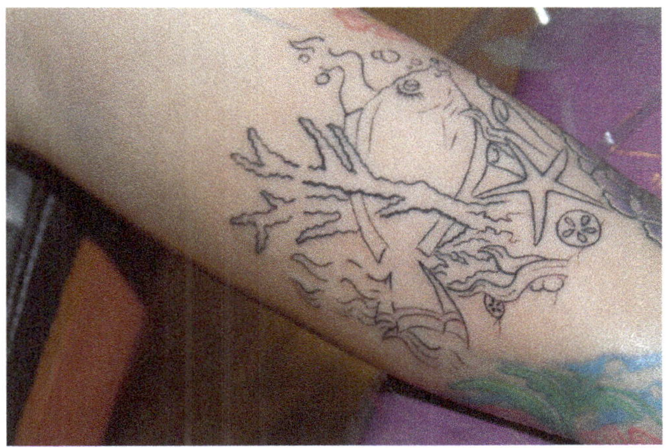

With the smudged ink wiped clean we get a good look at the piece that now awaits details and a rainbow of hues.

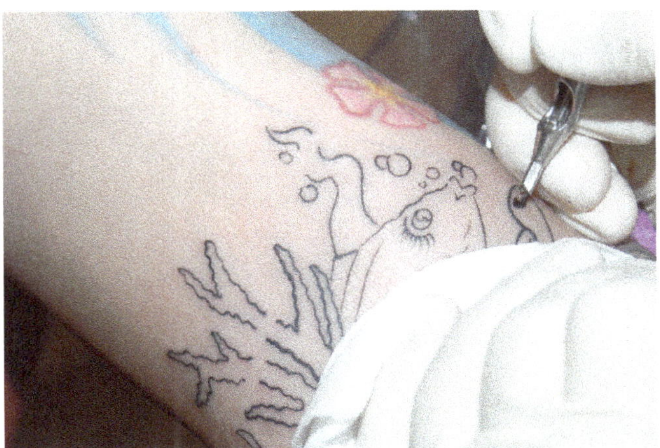

Changing to a 5-round setup, sections of the shape will now be powerlined for additional drama.

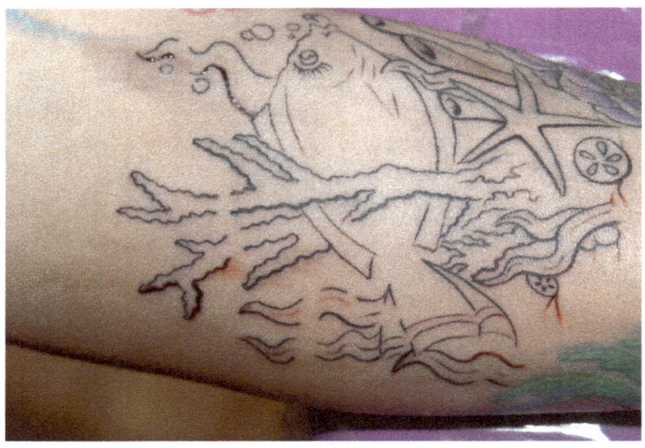

We can see the subtle changes occurring in the coral and other aquatic life depicted.

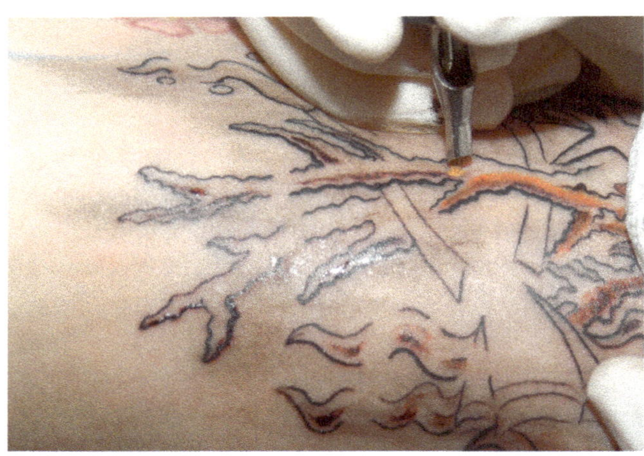

Adding some warmer tones to coral will play a small part in the colorization of the tattoo.

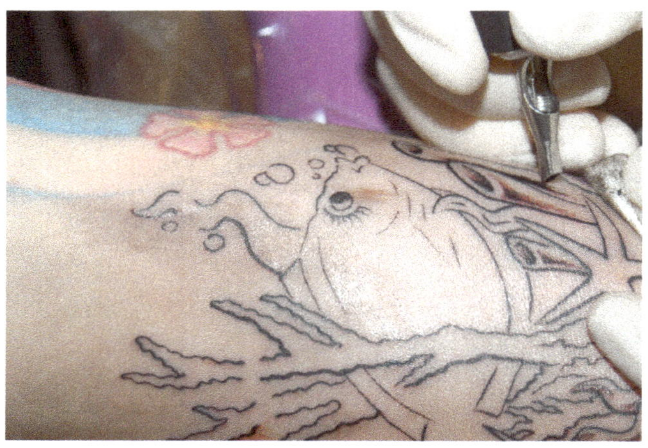

The tubular anemone now get some attention to define their shape.

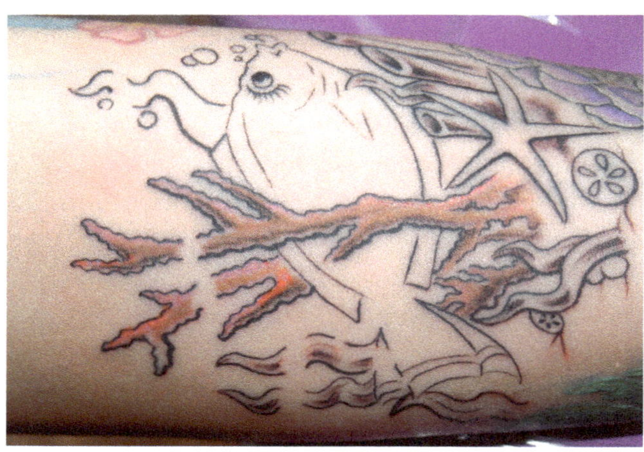

Most of the coral is now shaded with the basic color, but more details will be added later.

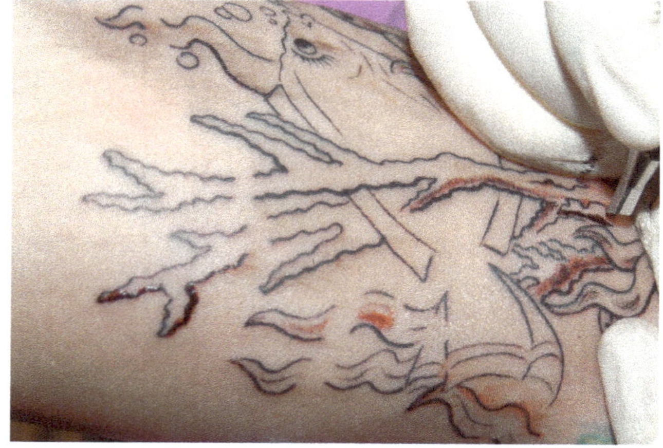

Moving to another spot on the arm, Little Frank heads to the bottom of the sea to add a bit of shading.

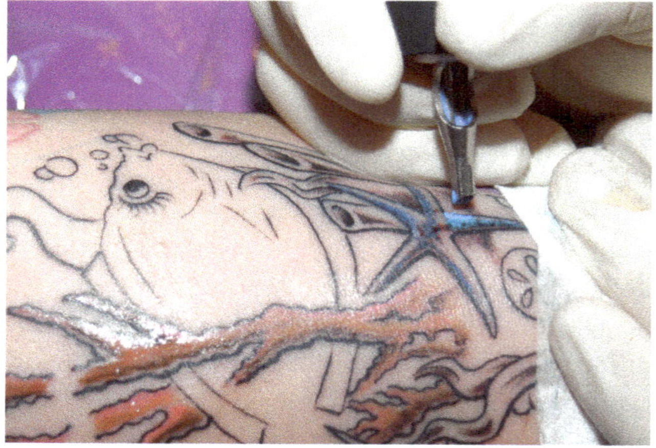

Each leg receives attention as the colored ink process continues.

of this process (to me anyway) is the way the subtle touches of the needles leave behind such intricate details. At first all you see is a blotch of some colored ink being laid down, then voila, we have a new bit of contour to experience. Working again from dark to light keeps the colors true. Once the skin has been broken by the stinging needle it is far more receptive to other colors seeping in where they don't belong. By working up to the lighter shades, the artist can keep the whites and yellows from becoming polluted by the more intense shades being used.

While being fairly realistic, Frank has chosen a few whimsical details for the fish. A set of bright red lips are applied, as are a set of delicate eye lashes. I'm not Jacques Cousteau but I am betting that those two features would be hard to find in the actual undersea world. The fun of any form of art is the ability to play with nature and make her fit your own needs. Since this illustration isn't being used in a school text book, some creative license can be used without fear.

As he approaches the final steps of the illustration, Frank adds tiny bits of white to several of the existing components. Almost imperceptible are the miniscule scales he places on the body of the fish. This step seems to be hardly necessary, but brings a new level of accuracy to the piece. Finally satisfied with the coloration and details, Frank sets aside his machine and reviews his work. Autumn also gives her new piece the once-over and nods in approval. Taking nearly three hours, she is happy to be done with her new art, but has plans to add additional sections in the coming months.

Lacking any education in the world of art, Frank has shown us that schooling isn't a prerequisite to becoming a successful tattoo artist. It has taken him some time, but experience and drive has helped him to overcome any lack of formal training that other artists have been given.

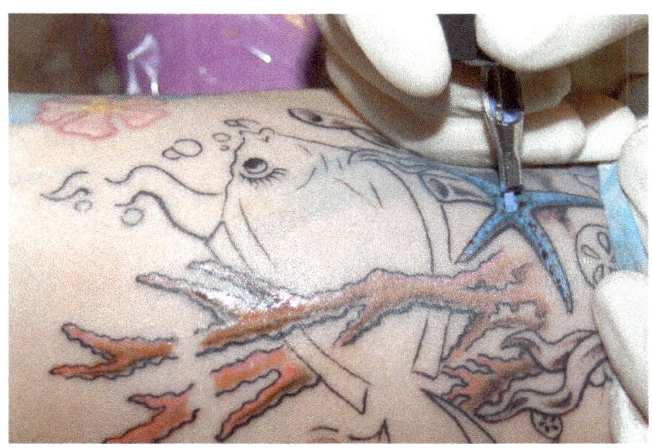

The bulk of the starfish has now been filled in and smaller details can be added as the final steps are growing near.

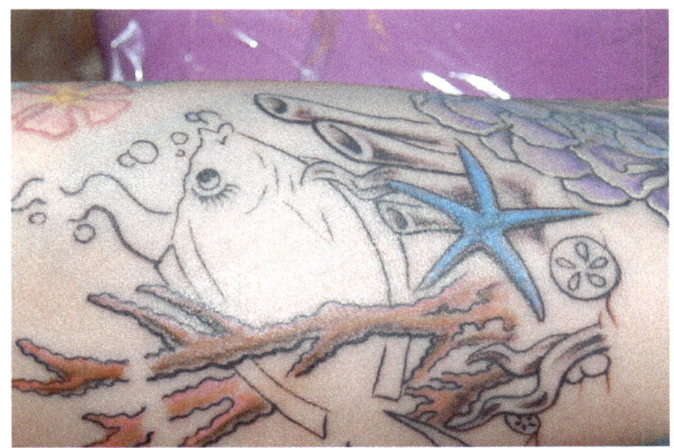

We can now see the results of all the minute steps taken to color in the starfish, which lies nestled among other colorful sea life.

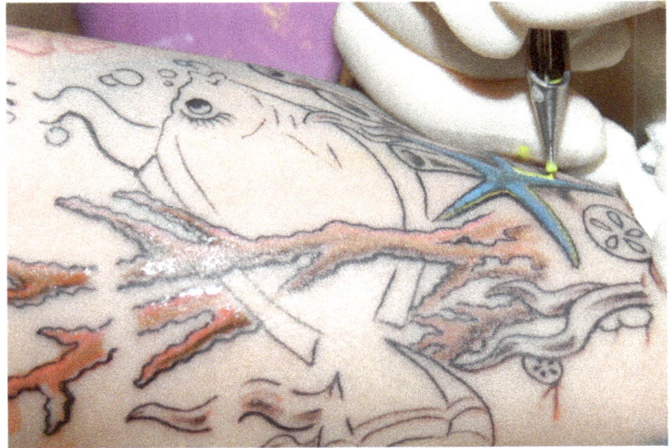

Not satisfied with the blue, Little Frank adds some bright green ink to the edges of each leg.

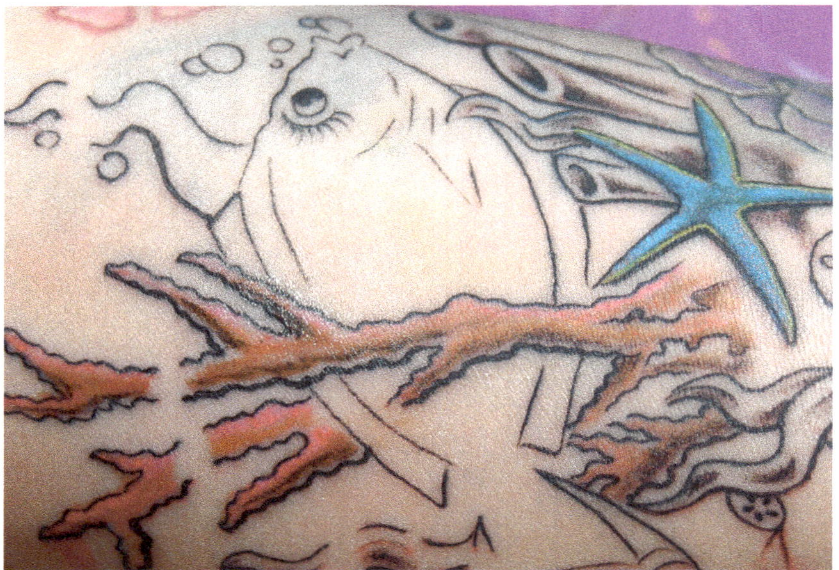

Pleased with the amount of color and detail, Frank can now move on to another segment of the tattoo.

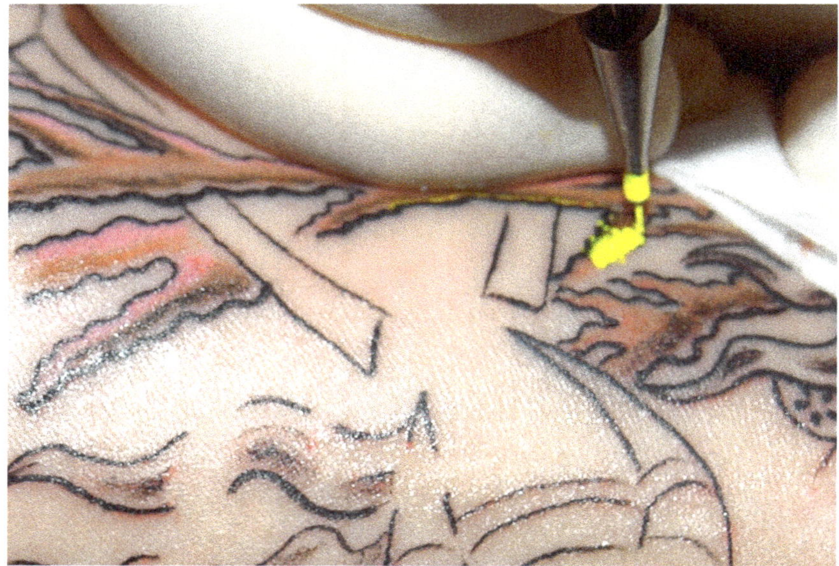

Bright yellow ink will bring some luster to the lower section of this undersea image adding to the overall appeal and intensity

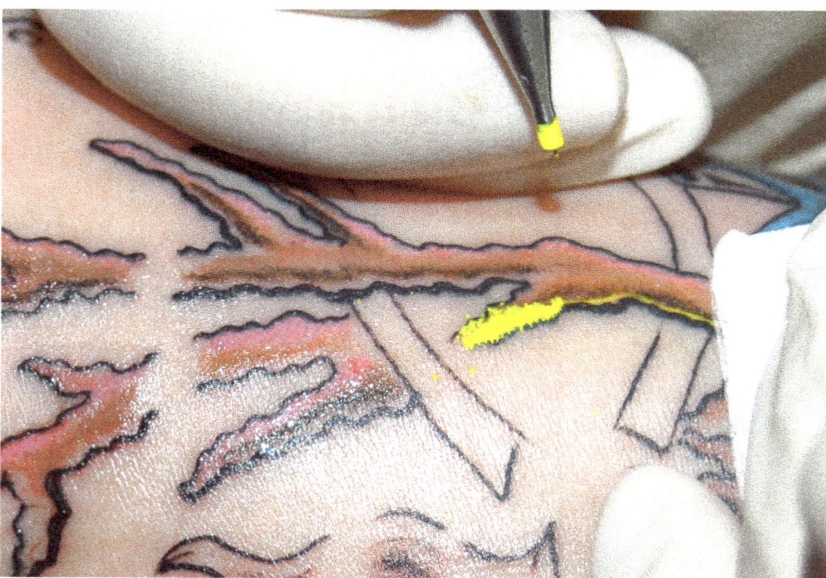

Highlights of the same bright yellow are now added to the edges of the coral to bring the shape into sharper focus.

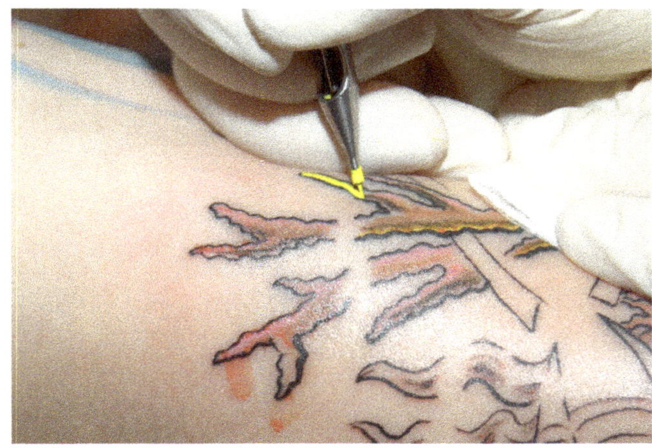

Long sections of the coral are detailed using the light yellow ink to add depth.

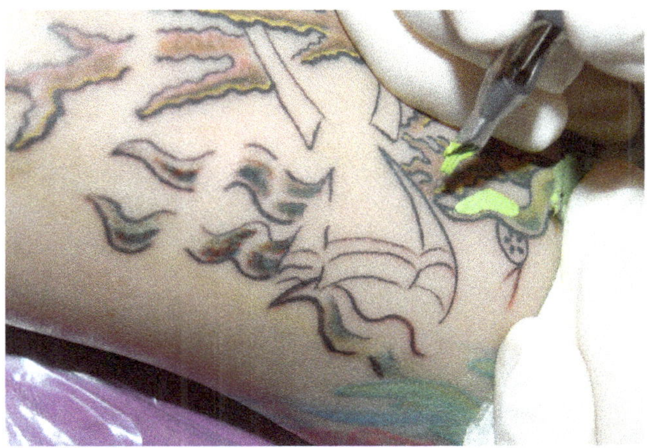

A lighter shade of green is now added to the sea weed to create a 3-dimensional effect to the waving foliage.

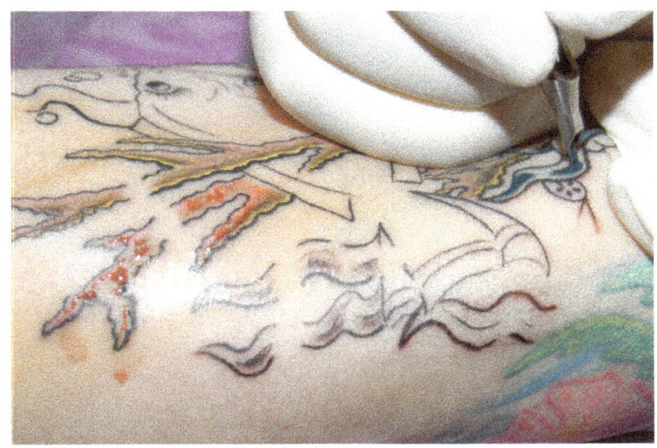

Moving to the sea weed, a dark green ink will begin the multiple stages needed to fill in the affected areas.

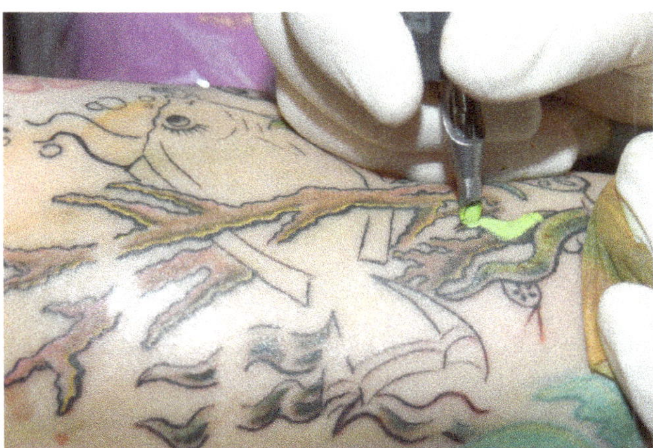

Even the otherwise orange coral gets a bit of bright green ink to add some flair.

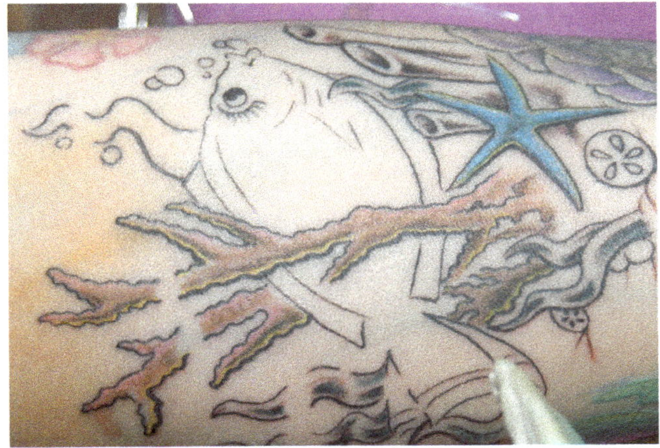

Overall, we can see the tiny bits of color adding to the entire piece, each in their own small measure.

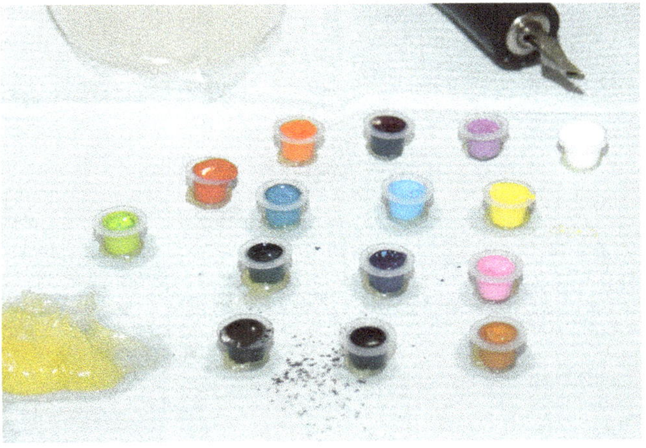

As Little Frank ramps up for the final stretch, a vast palette of colors are put into the waiting ink cups.

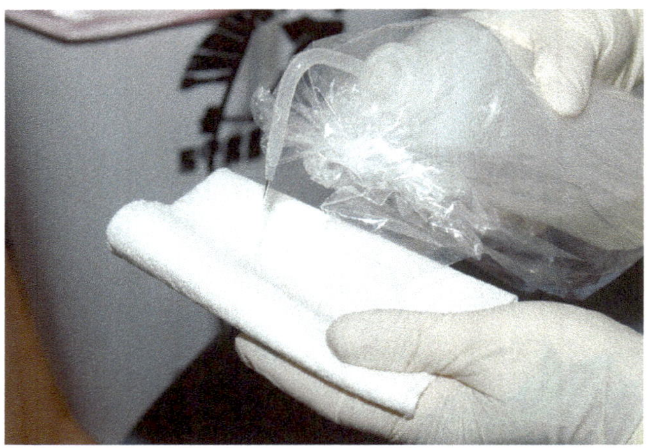

Wetting a paper towel with solution will allow Frank to clean off the stray ink so he can view his work completed so far.

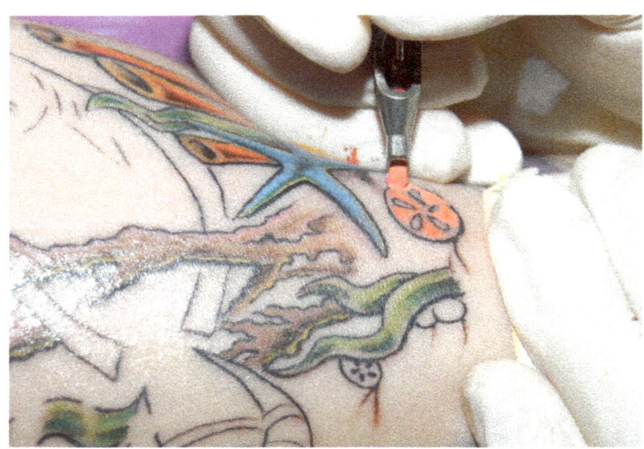

The small sand dollar at the bottom now gets some illuminating coral-colored ink to bring it to life.

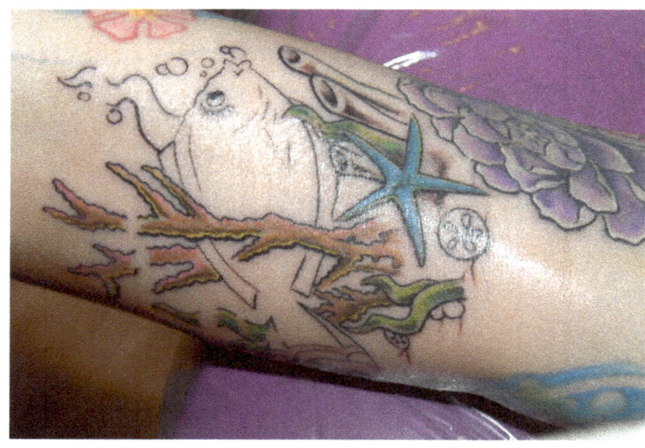

We get a quick glimpse at progress made so far before Frank returns to the skin with his loaded needles of color.

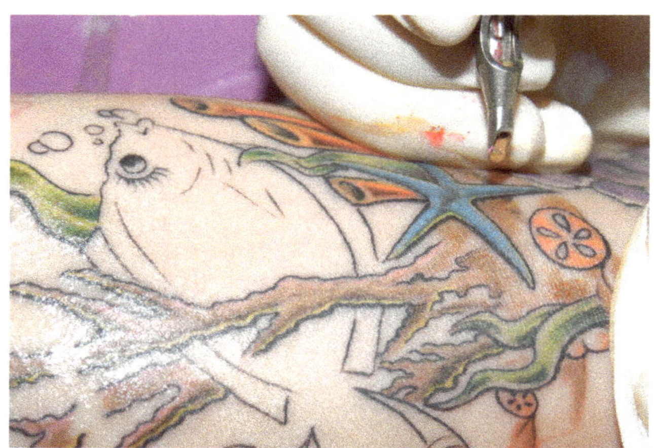

Background shading will help to set off the brighter colors used on the variety of plant life seen on this flesh canvas.

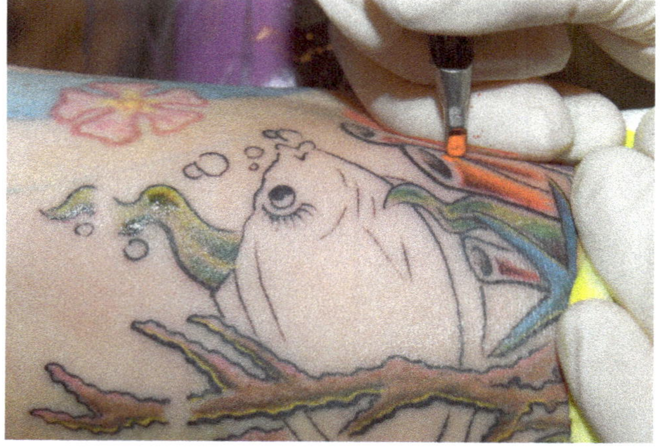

Returning to the anemone with some vivid red ink really adds some "pop" to the tattoo.

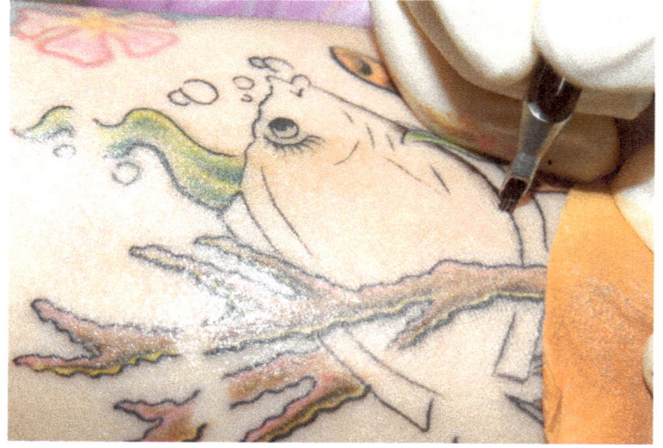

Subtle lavender shading on the body of the fish can now begin, and will be the first of many steps taken.

A saturated periwinkle ink is now added to the body of the fish and will be among many colors utilized.

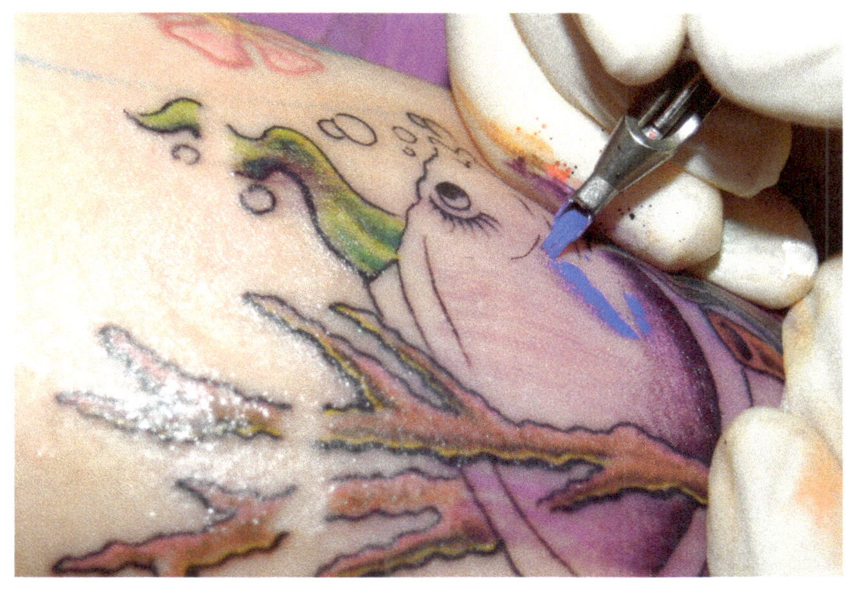

Returning with the lavender ink, Frank works on the top section of the brightly colored fish.

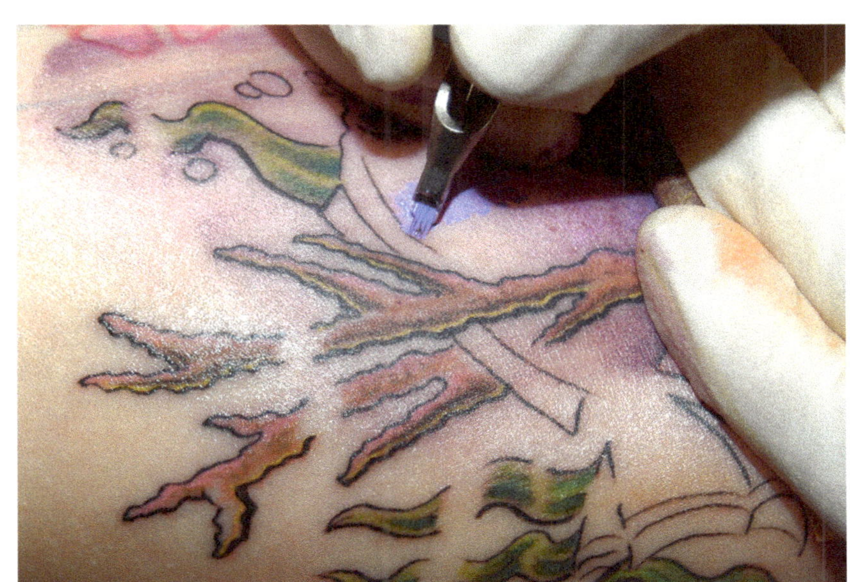

Stepping back from his work, Little Frank sizes up what needs to be done next.

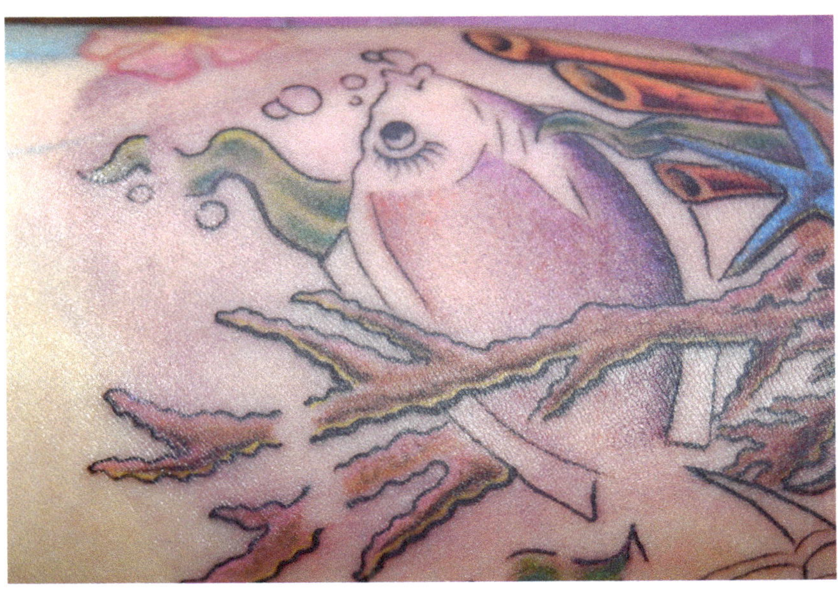

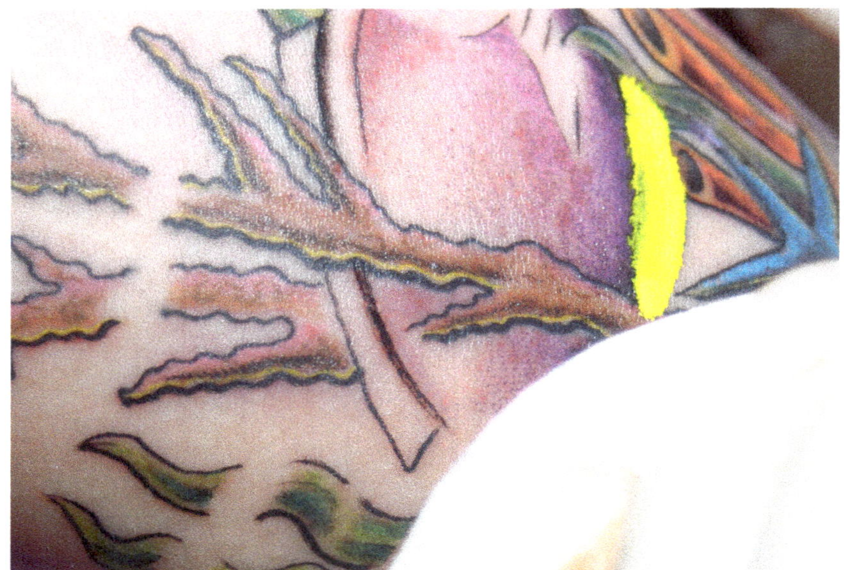

The lower fin receives a large section of light yellow ink to separate it from the blue and purple body.

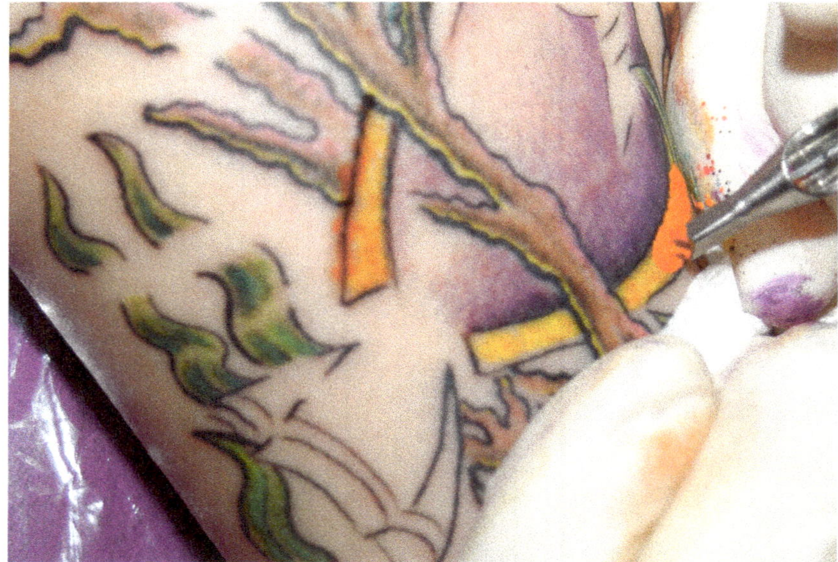

Adding a stripe of orange to the yellow fin will further aid in the decorative nature of this piece.

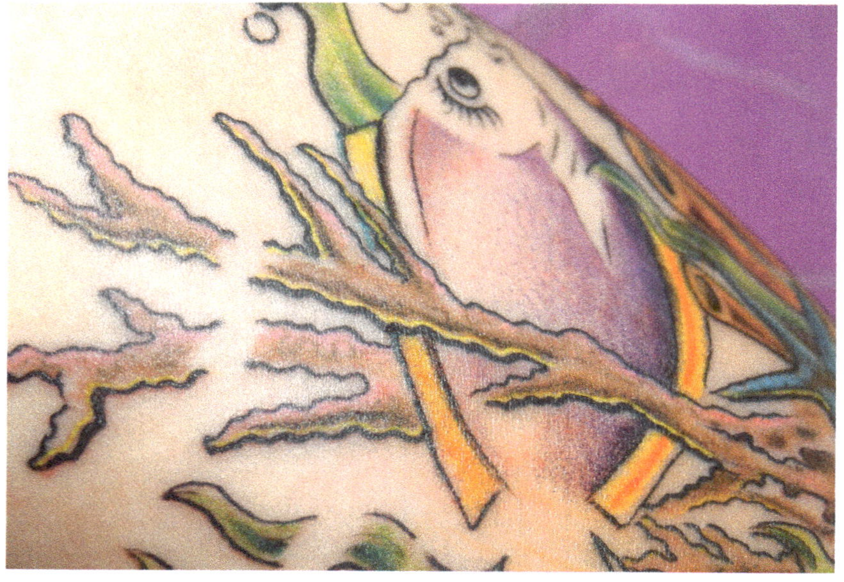

The dorsal fin now gets its own dose of yellow and orange to match the lower fin.

Q&A: Little Frank

How long have you been doing Tattoos?

Three years now.

What was the first tattoo you gave another person?

I put a small butterfly on Autumn's ankle.

Do you have a favorite style or genre you like to work in?

I like doing realistic pieces with lots of color. Of course if the client wants black and white, we can do that as well.

Are there any artists out there who inspire you?

There are several pieces done by Scott Winske in the lobby, and his style and way of using colors are some of my favorites.

What was your largest or best known piece?

My largest piece is my best known right now. Using black, gray and colors we did a full-back piece in an oriental theme.

See any changes in the tattoo world coming down the pike?

I see improved regulations on sterility in the field, as well as more education being offered and taken to comply and expand. The less people fear about infections the more eager they'll be to get some ink of their own.

Tell us about your history before opening this shop.

I actually worked in the home health care industry before doing tattoos. I began body piercing in 1999, then headed into the ink arena in 2003. That's when I opened my first shop, although we moved to this building only three months ago.

What can you tell us about your art background?

I actually have no formal training in the art world. Never took classes in school or after. My grandfather had a tattoo and it always fascinated me. I began wanting to get and do tattoos when I was only nine.

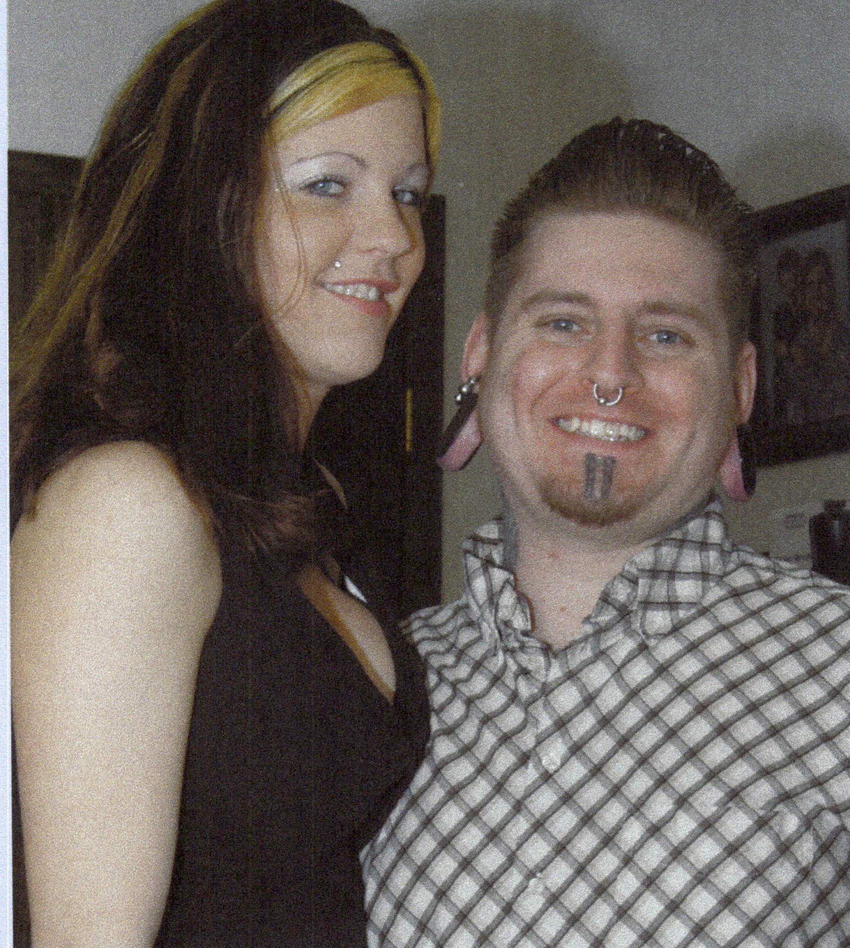

The couple that works together stays together, and Little Frank and Autumn are engaged to be married in the Summer of 2006. How convenient to have a partner capable of adding new pieces to your canvas anytime the mood strikes.

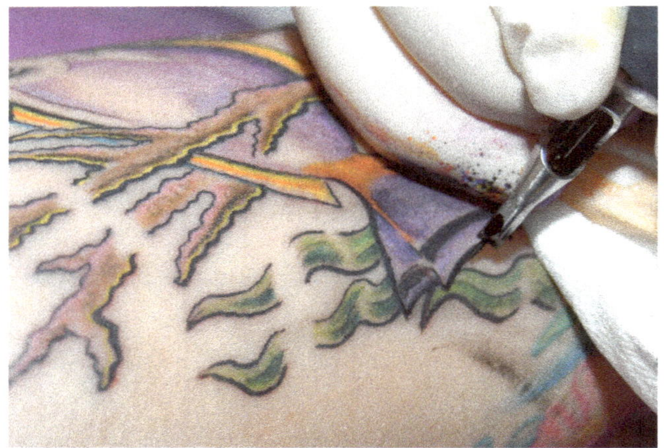

A black outline will help to define the edges of the colorful tail fin.

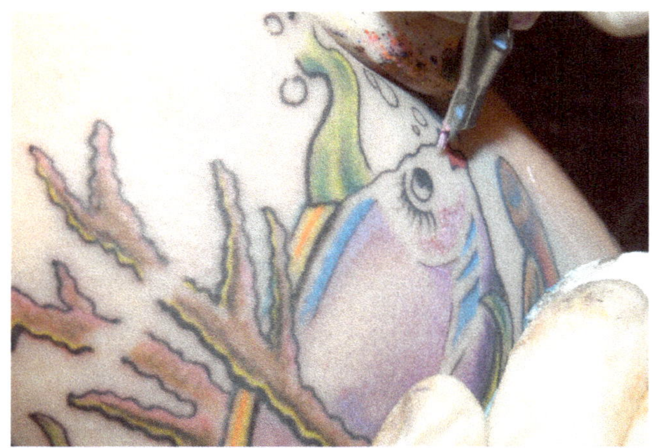

We can now see the shading added to the gills as well as the lavender ink being used to color the face.

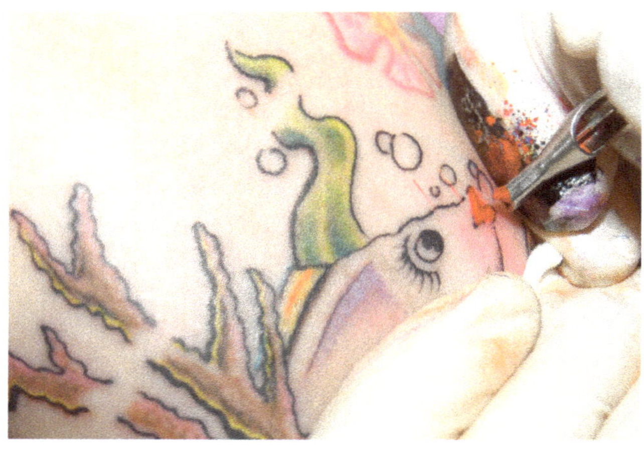

What undersea creature wouldn't like a set of bright red lips? The entertaining nature of this tattoo allows for some creative license.

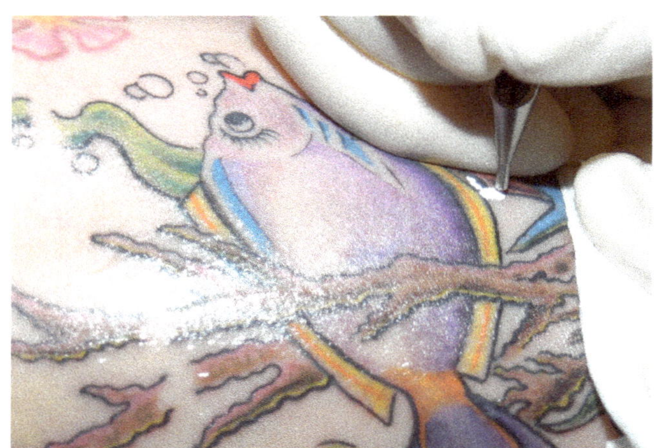

White ink is now applied to the background to be sure to keep the colors segregated from the natural skin tone.

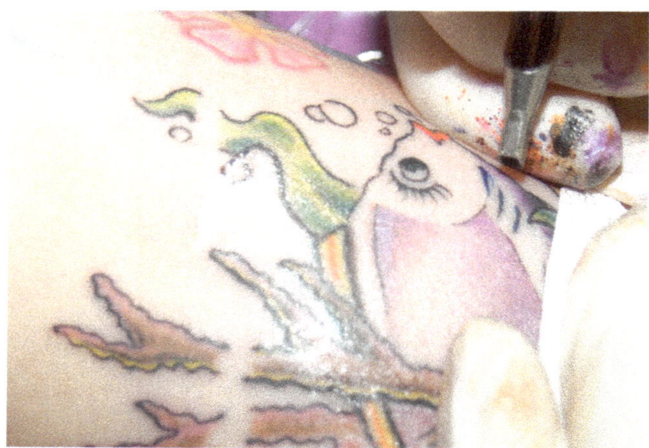

The first slashes that represent the gills of the fish are now added. Ever see a fish with eye lashes before?

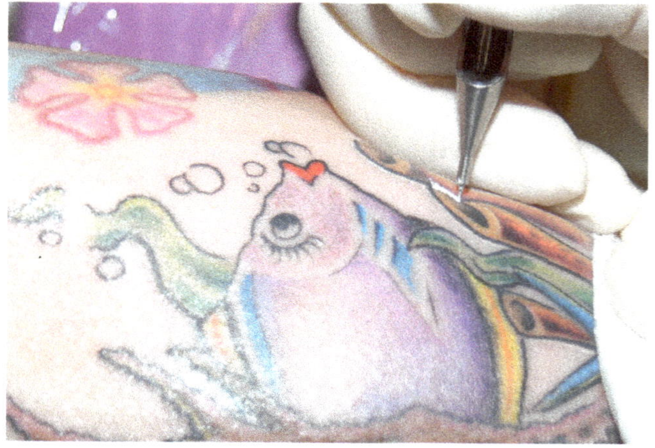

Returning once again to the tubular anemone, Frank creates small sections of white ink to add some finishing touches to the life-like creatures.

The sea weed also receives a bit of white to help define its edges and contours.

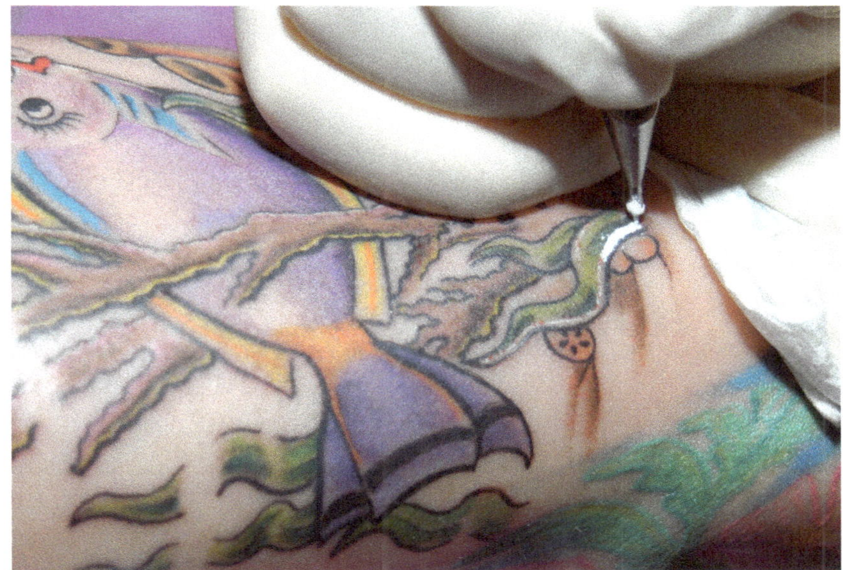

Using white ink, Little Frank adds some tiny and almost invisible scales to the body of the fish. It is details like this that make for a terrific tattoo.

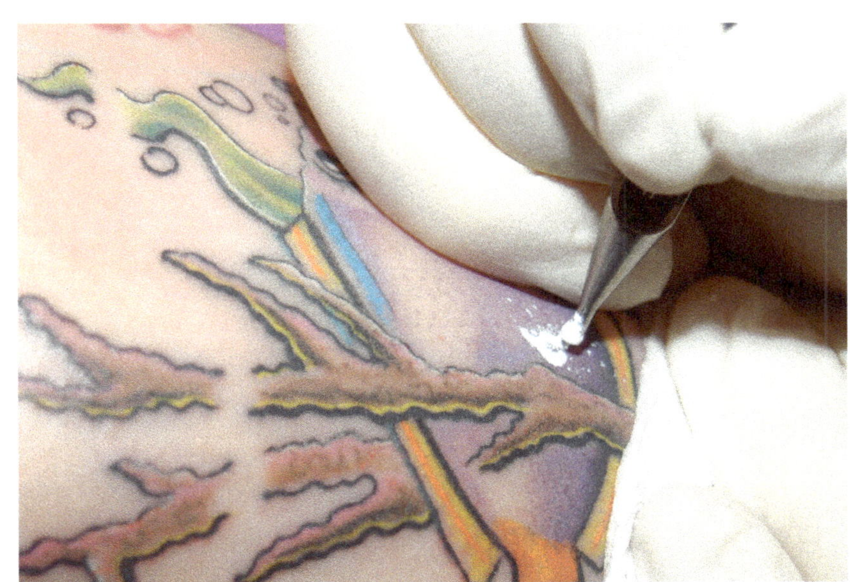

Here we see the completed piece before being wrapped up for take out. Once the art heals the colors will remain true for many years to come.

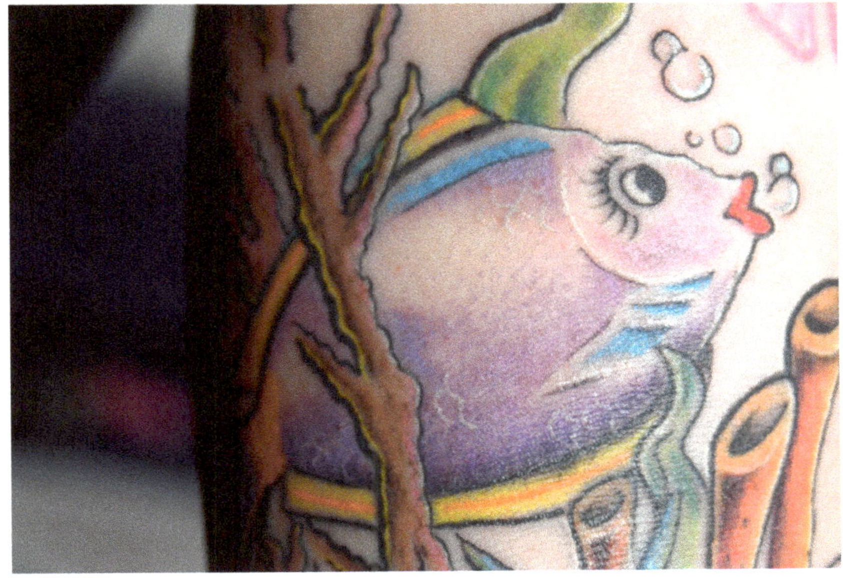

Chapter Six

Ben Esken

The Truth Lies Within

After viewing a large selection of Ben's work it becomes obvious that he really is capable of creating a tattoo in nearly any format or style requested. Some of his pieces are fairly simple, but as with most artists, he prefers dialing-up the intensity and detail of the design to new levels as needed.

Today's art is the result of one of his favorite clients. Missy has had 16 other pieces either created from scratch or modified by Ben over the years. The phrase is borrowed from a popular TV show and she wanted the text to be done in a style that mirrored graffiti found on any city wall. The colors

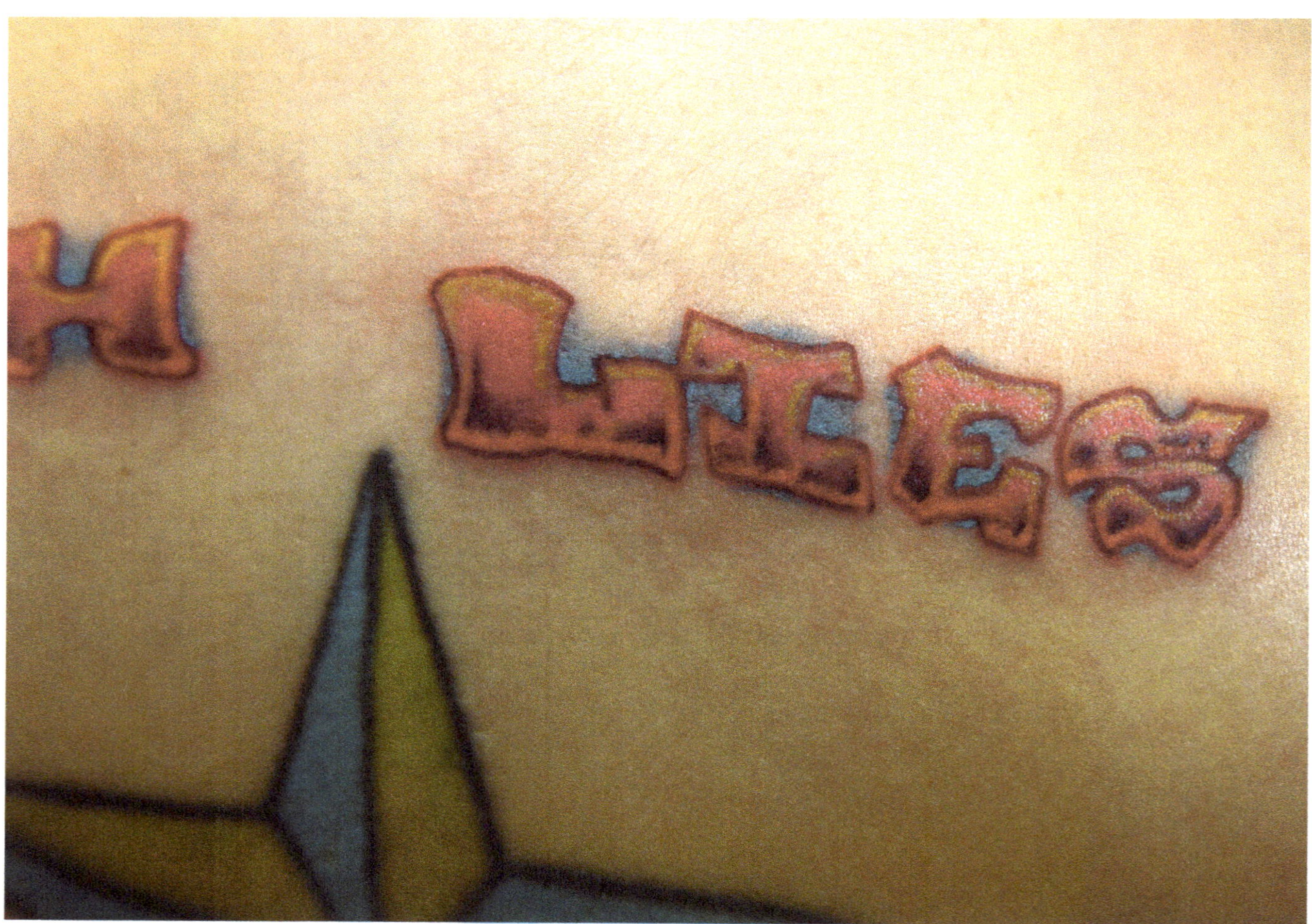

At long last we get to see the entire piece of art cleansed of the ink that's no longer needed for the design.

were left up to Ben's imagination and in keeping with much graffiti found, bright hues were selected to make the piece stand out. The middle of Missy's upper back already has a two-tone star that Ben cleaned up at a previous session and they wanted the new phrase to work with the star, not conflict with it in any way.

While Ben's techniques may be seen as traditional his methods of creating the design and transfer include a high degree of technology. A 32 inch monitor allows him to search for design input and in today's piece he located a font that reminded him of graffiti. He places a small monitor flat on his desk to begin the process as he traces small sections of art that will grow to become the complete layout. Sizing the piece to fit Missy's upper back requires a few attempts until the art is deemed proper and won't overtake the existing star tattoo.

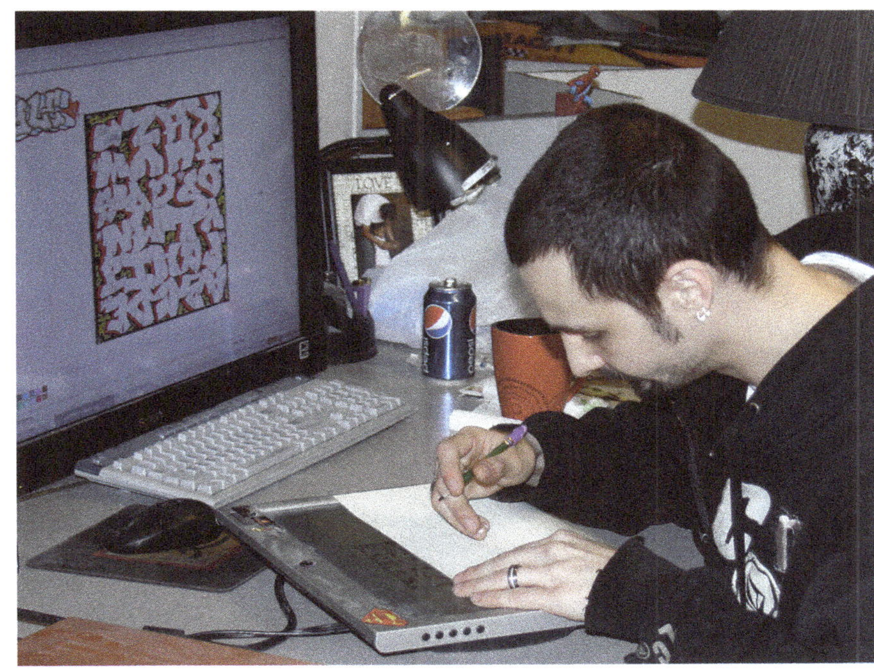

Ben's workstation is a blend of high-tech and old school techniques as he creates the line art that will guide his ink application.

Using traditional carbon paper he is able to copy the completed design to transfer paper, the final step prior to working on skin.

Ben uses several different machines but tends to customize any style chosen regardless of its power supply and function. He has used rotary and pneumatic as well as electric, which is his choice for today's project. Beginning with an Iron Workhorse he modified the springs and control screws to better suit his personal needs and dexterity. A Mastech power supply allows Ben plenty of control and adjustability to fit with the wide array of projects he embarks upon. His needles are often a product of the Precision Needle company and his ink selections are from any number of suppliers. Today's art will utilize product from Intenze, Mom's, and Skin Candy, chosen depending on the intensity of the color he'll need.

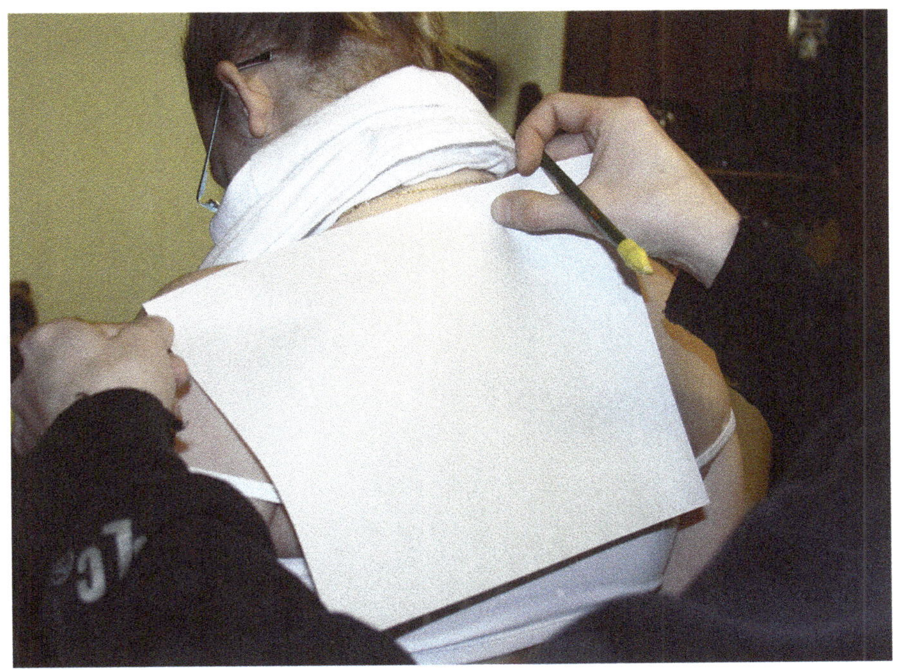

Holding the first draft of the layout to Missy's shoulders guides Ben as he determines the size and location for the art.

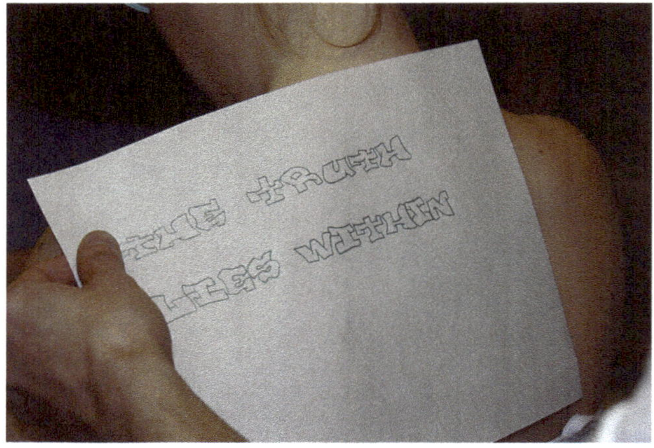

The completed text meets with approval from both parties and requires one last check for location before the lines are transfered to the skin.

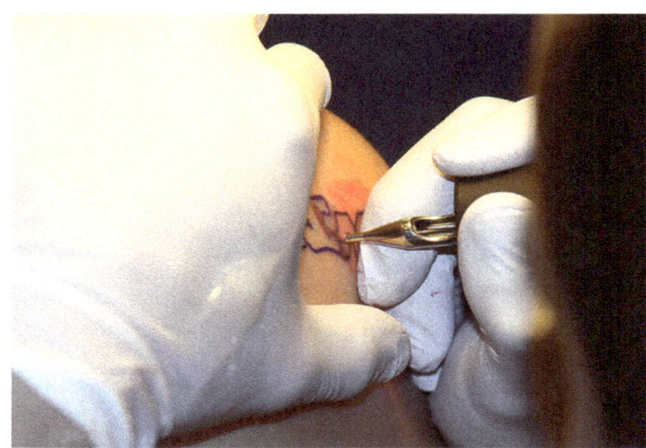

The first needle set is a 7 super-tight round liner that will deliver a finely focused line of color.

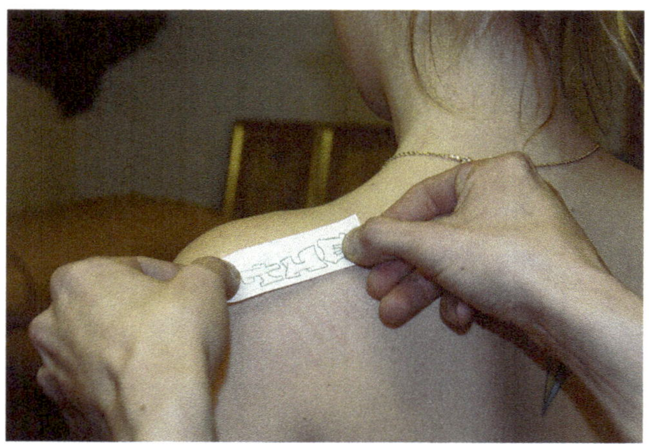

Each of the four words are positioned independently to ensure the correct balance regarding Missy's shoulders and the existing ink.

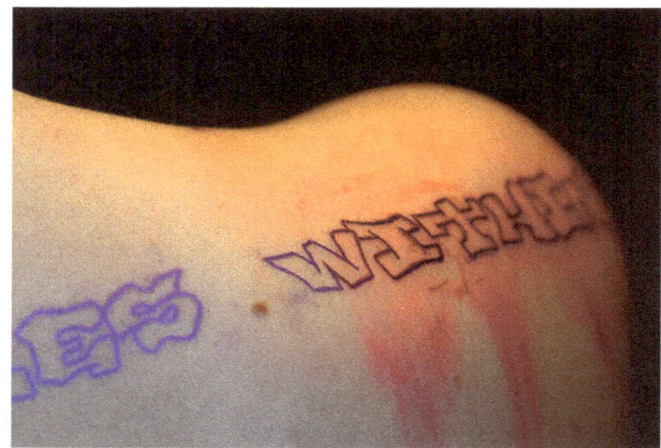

His choice of Mom's Red Rum ink for the outline will add some color to the design versus using a traditional black ink.

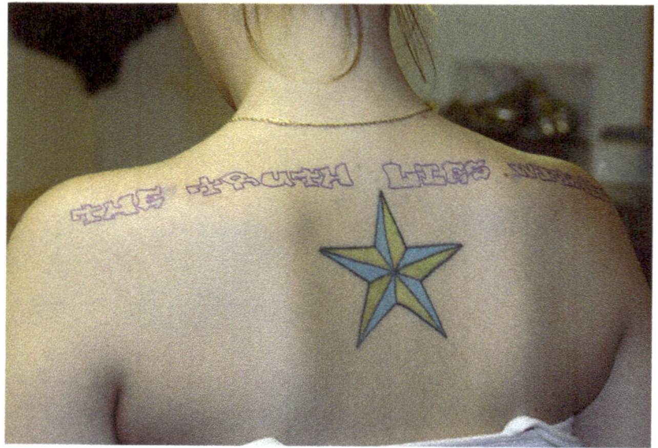

With the words transferred to her skin a final visual inspection makes sure of the position prior to adding ink.

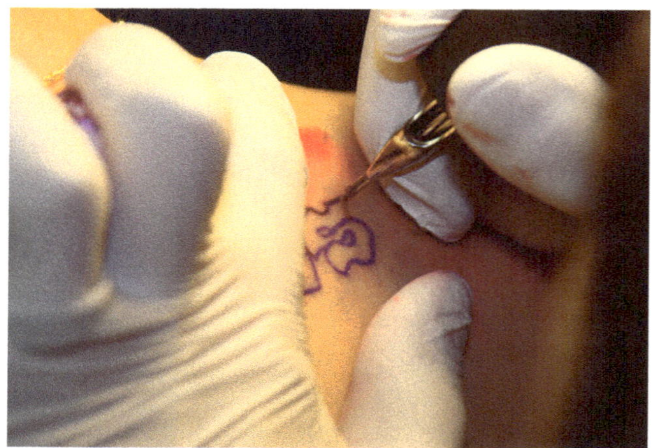

The first portion of the process involves covering the lines of the transfer with the Red Rum ink and requires a steady hand and plenty of control.

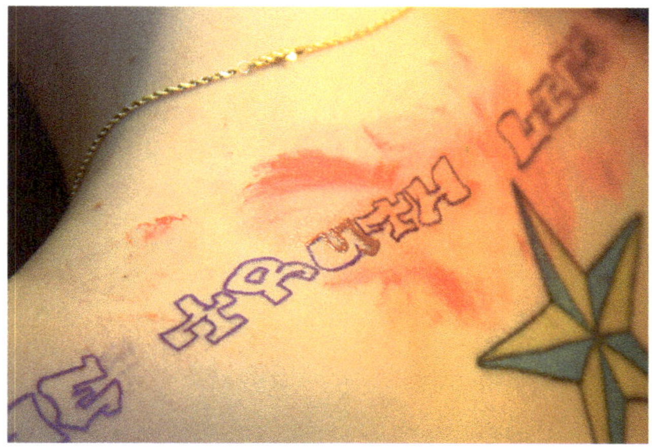

With the first section of outlining complete, Ben can review his efforts before continuing.

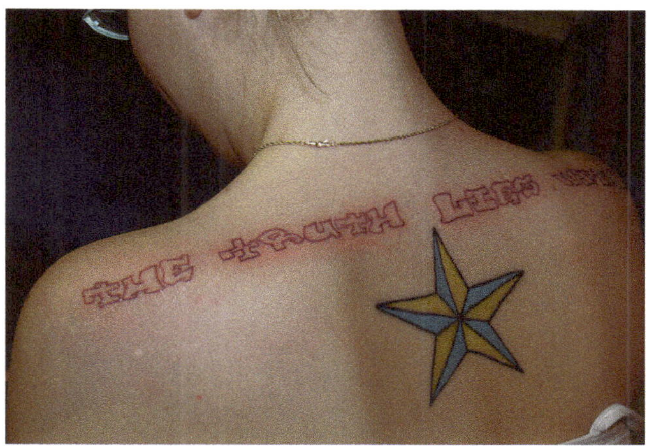

With the excess ink removed, Ben gets an unrestricted view of his efforts so far.

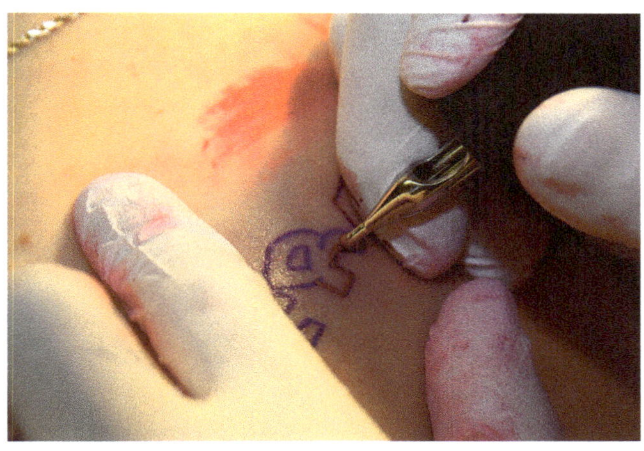

The chosen font was selected to mimic a graffiti style and will be a great showcase for the colors added later.

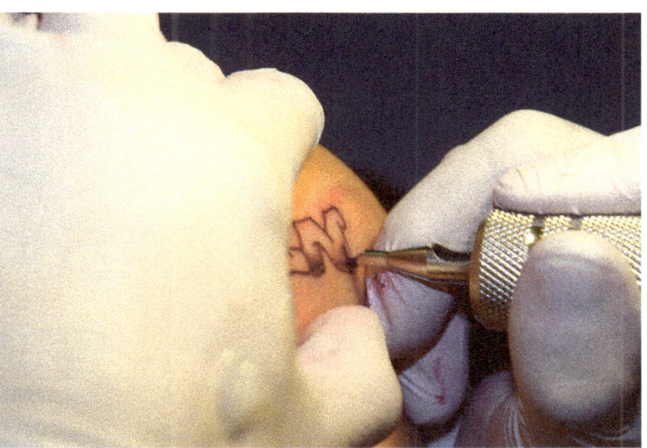

To add segments of shading, Ben has switched to a needle set of 7 double stack mag to provide a wider touch of ink at every touch to skin.

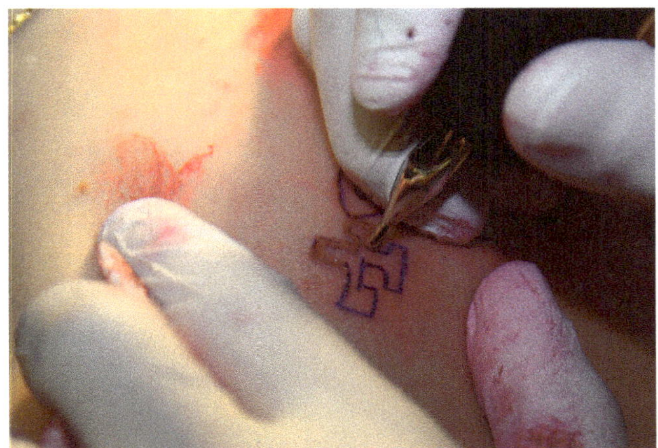

The outer edge of each individual letter needs to be covered in Red Rum ink before moving to the next step.

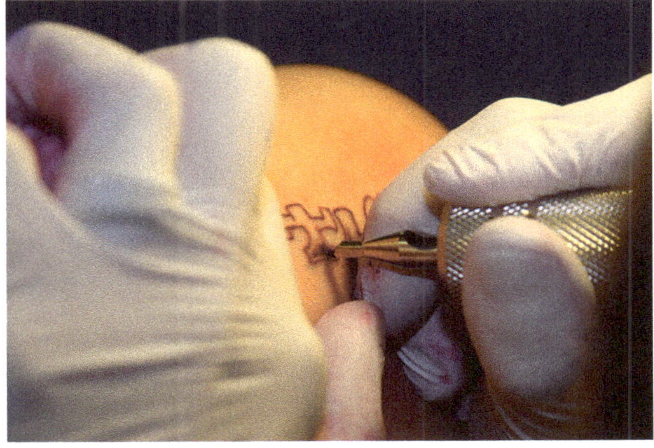

Eternal brand Wild Orchid is the next color being added and will provide a shaded contour to each letter.

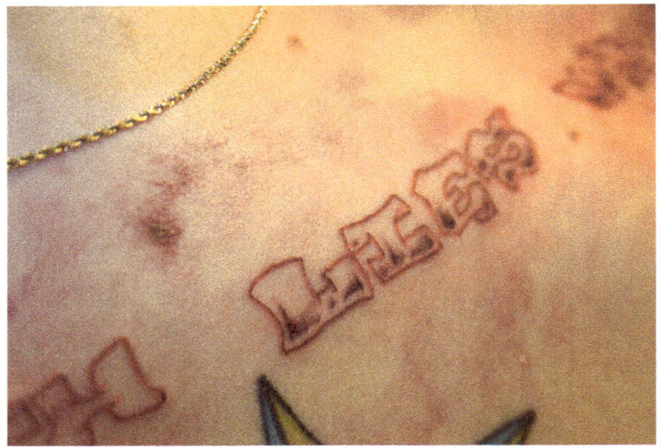

The subtle application of the darker orchid hue can be seen even before Ben wipes away the stray ink.

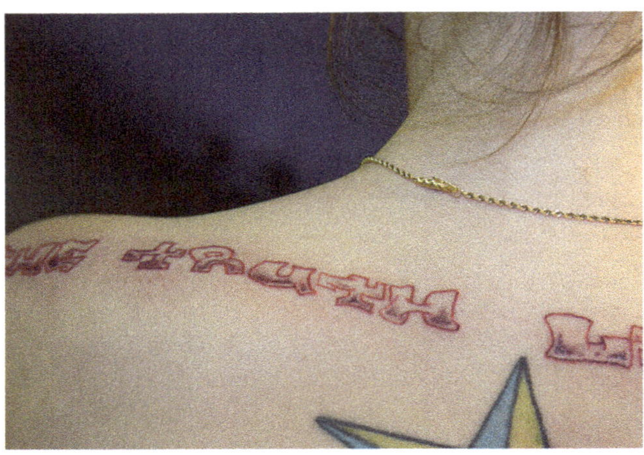

After another cleansing with green soap we can see the results of adding orchid shading to the letters.

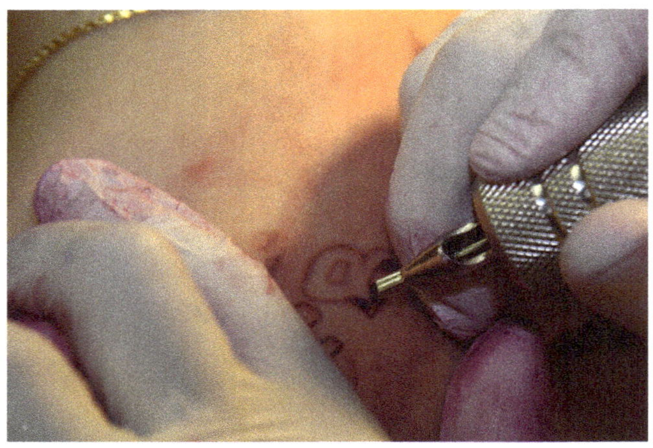

Ben exercises extra care when using the set of larger needles due to the vast amount of ink they can deliver with every contact.

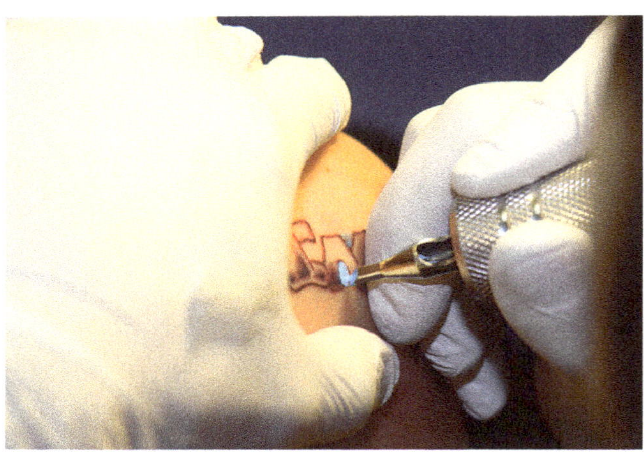

To add some background color, Ben has selected Bell Bottom Blue from Skin Candy.

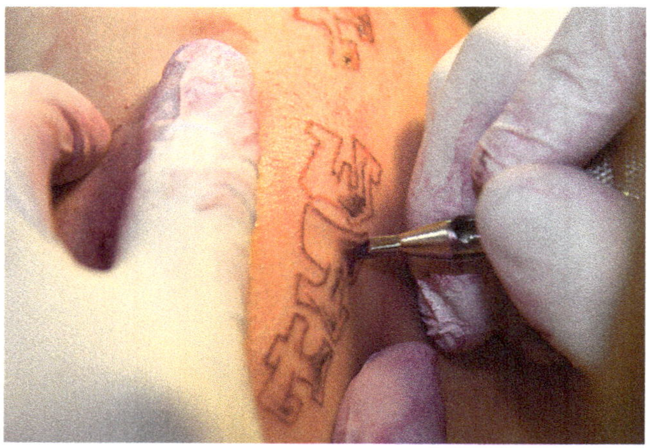

Each letter in the phrase will receive some of the same shading for greater continuity.

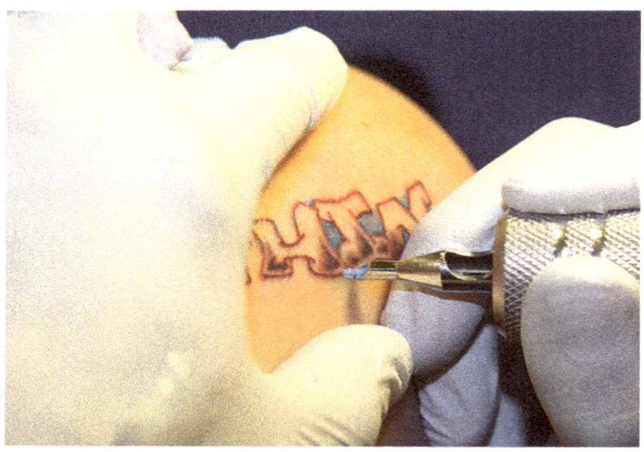

The set of mag needles allows Ben to fill in larger areas behind each letter with the brilliant blue ink.

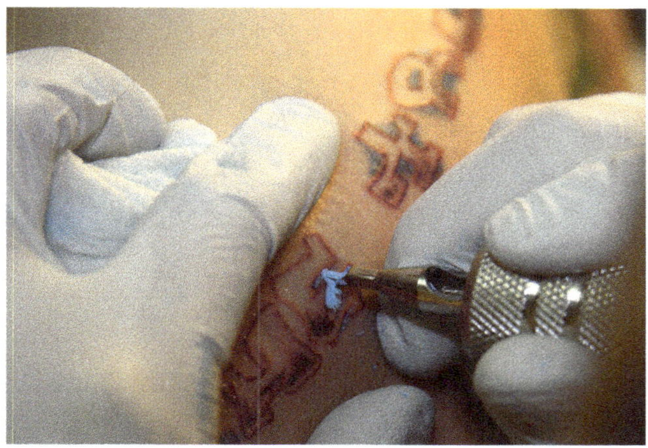

Being used as a background color, the blue ink gets applied in larger quantities to cover the selected area completely.

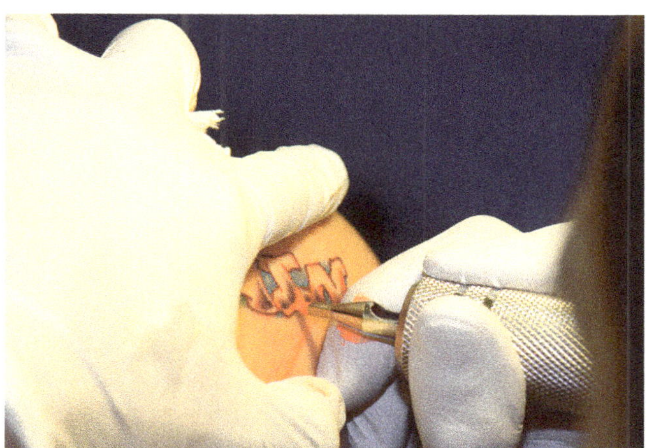

To accent the Wild Orchid shading, the Tokyo Orange makes a strong statement.

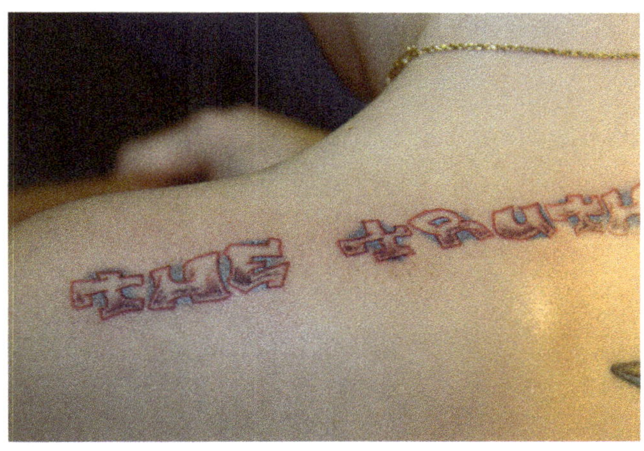

Another cleansing reveals the next step of the process illustrating the blue as a contrasting background color.

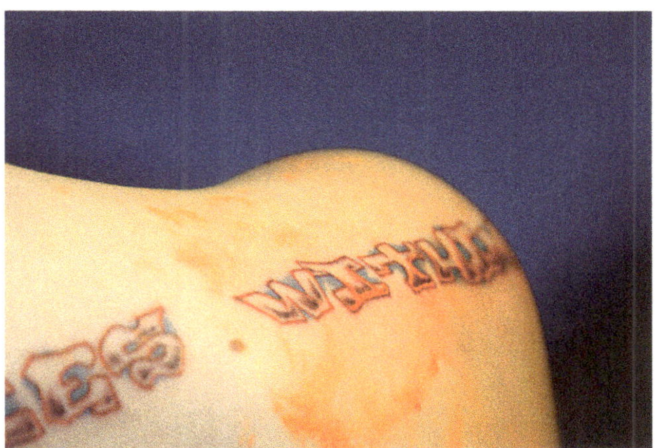

Before he has wiped the area clean of excess ink we can already see the result of adding the vivid orange.

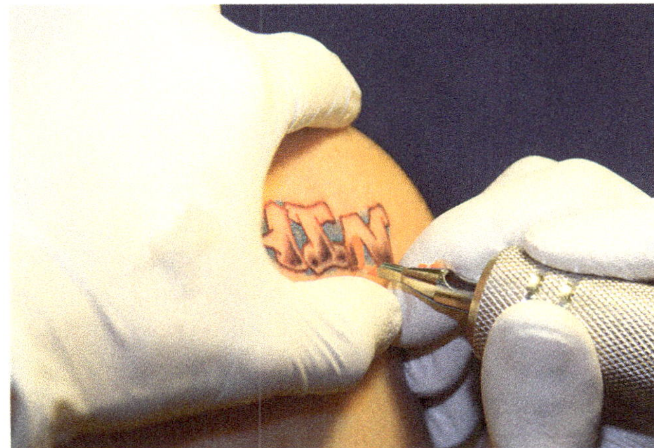

With the needle set cleaned of the previous color, Ben has now loaded the machine with Tokyo Orange, also from Skin Candy.

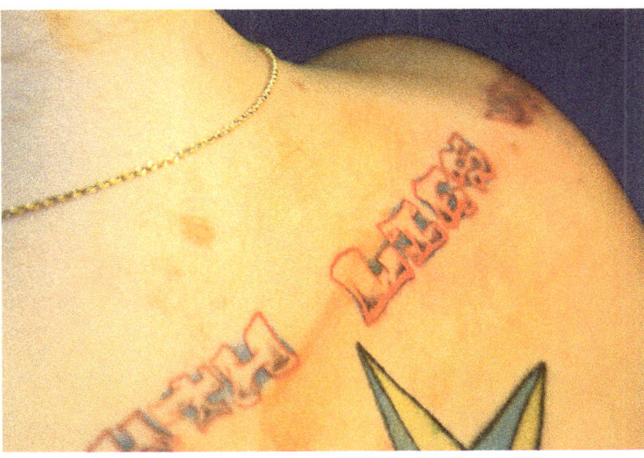

Ben's choice of colors are chosen for their dramatic effect when used in close proximity to each other.

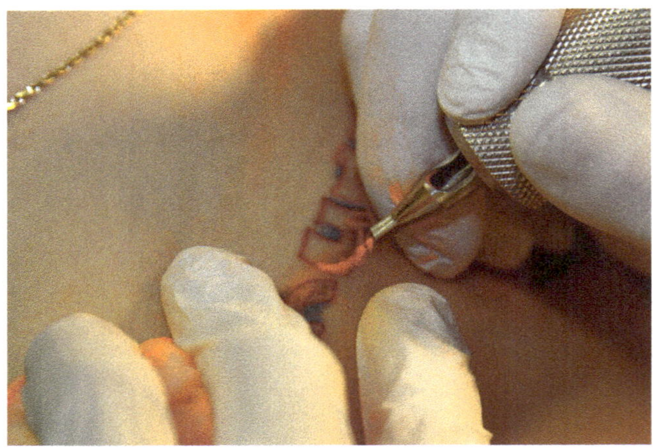

By applying the orange on top of the prior orchid Ben creates a pleasant contrast of hues.

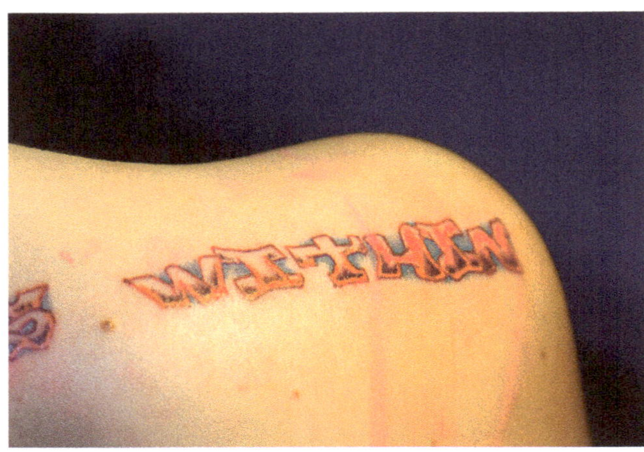

Using the bright pink Lolly Pop ink to fill each letter we can immediately see the bright results.

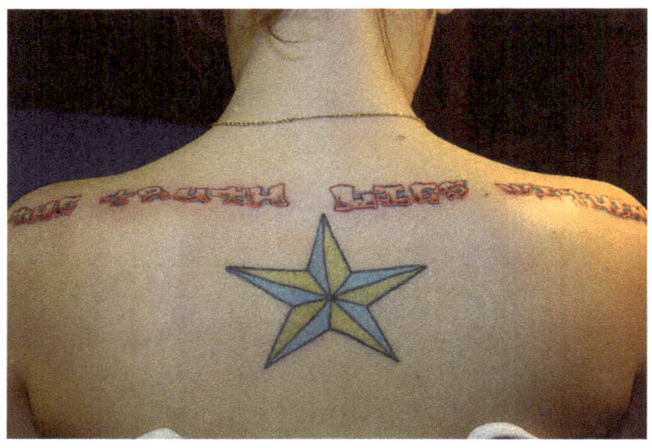

With the excess orange now cleaned from the flesh we can view the latest step in the process, as Ben plans his next step.

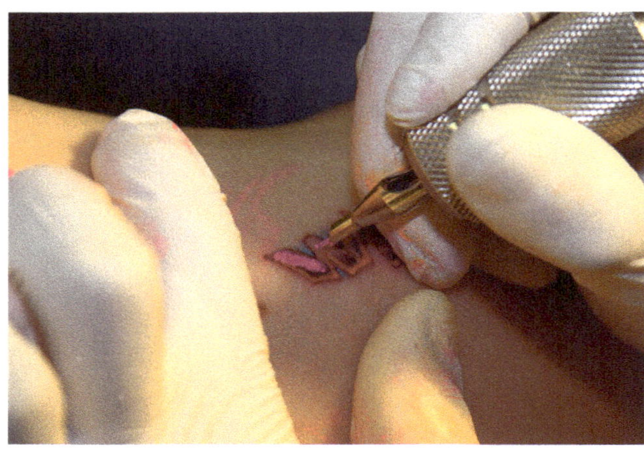

The 7 mag needle set continues to be used as large sections of ink are applied.

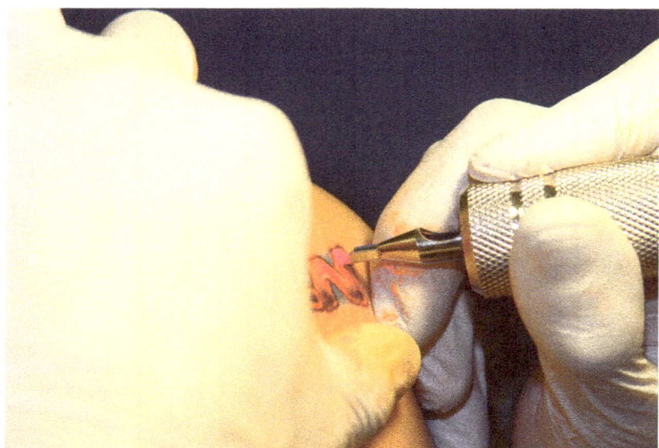

The next color being applied is Lolly Pop from Intenze.

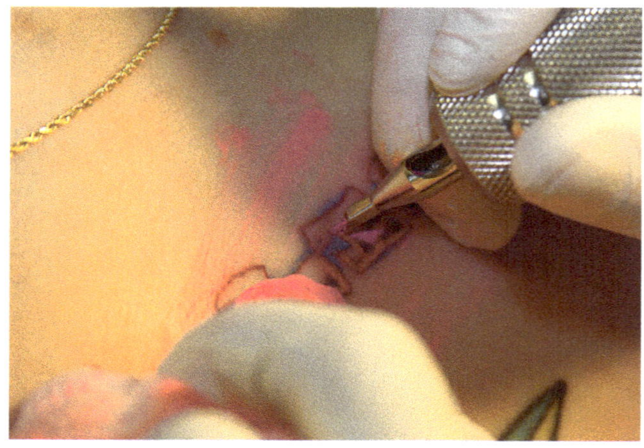

Using care to avoid filling in each space too completely requires a trained hand and watchful eye.

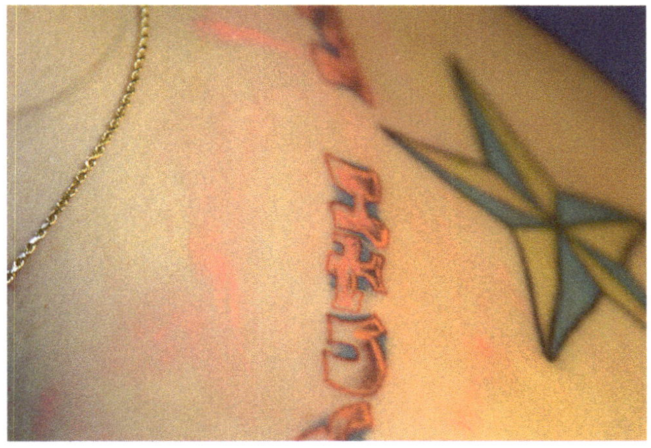

With the existing star looming in the background we can see the results of the addition of Lolly Pop to the new tattoo.

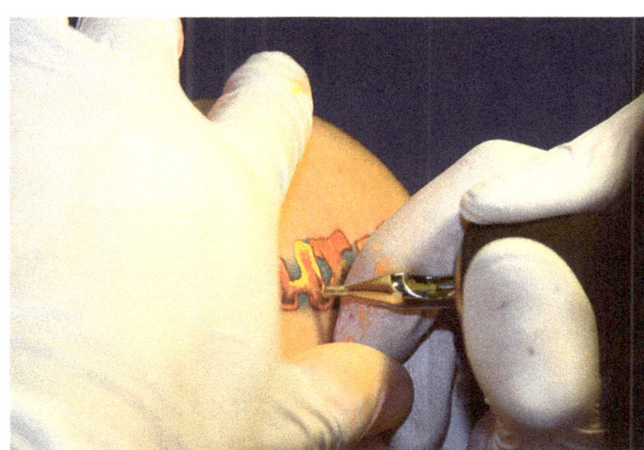

Switching back to the 7 super tight round liner needle set, Ben has also chosen Sunflower ink from Eternal for the final highlights.

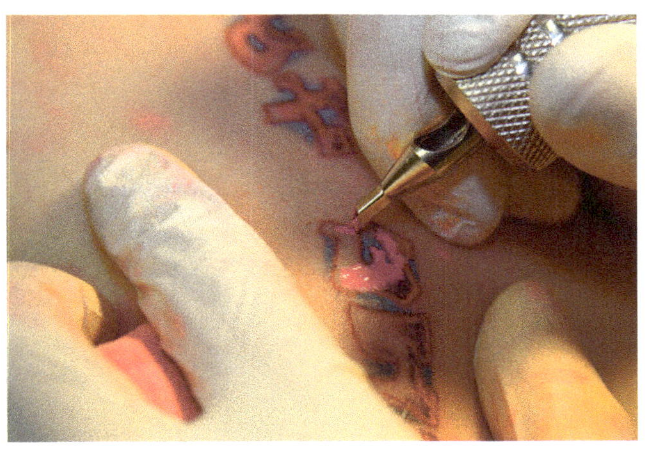

Nearly finished with the Lolly Pop color, Ben is sure that the color is complete before moving to the next hue.

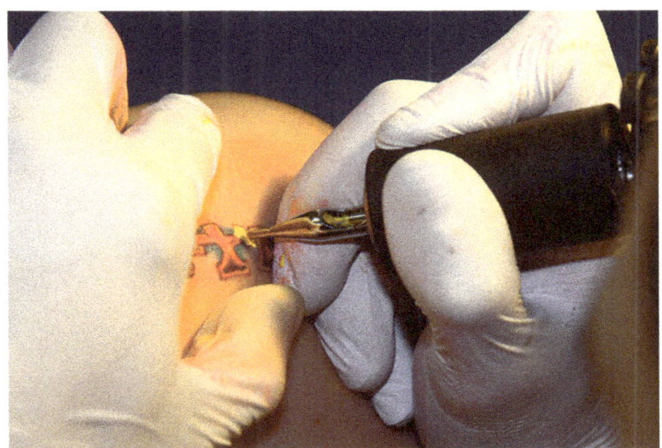

The bright shade of yellow is being used anywhere there is no other color.

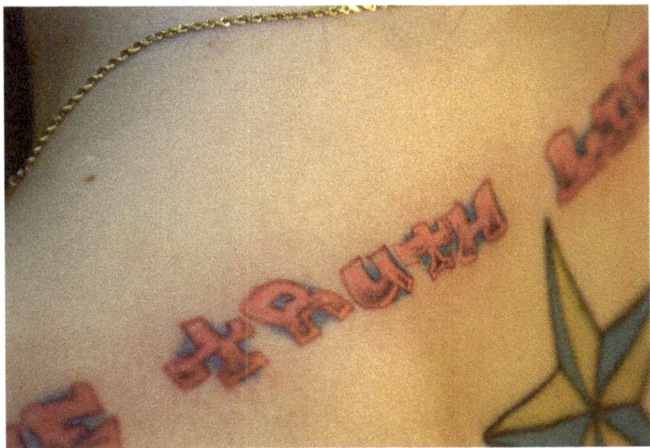

Despite the lilting type face, it takes a great deal of control to create a tattoo that looks random.

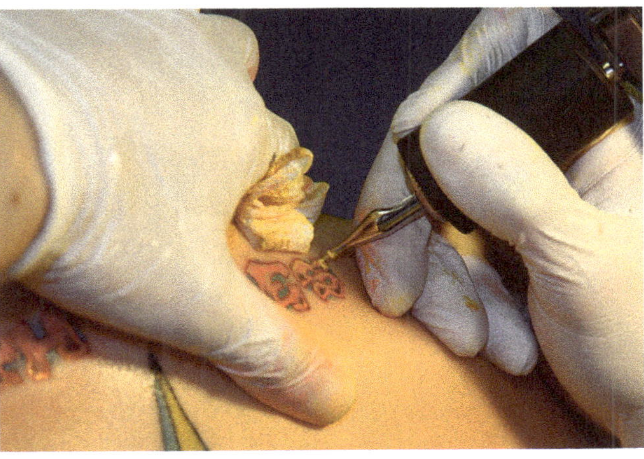

The smaller profile of the 7 round liner allows Ben to place the tiny highlights of yellow where ever needed to complete the design.

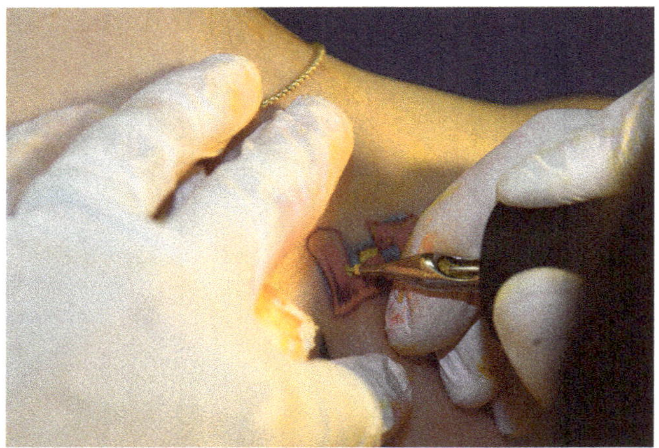

Each letter in the phrase will receive a few finely focused bits of the bright yellow to add brilliance to the overall color scheme.

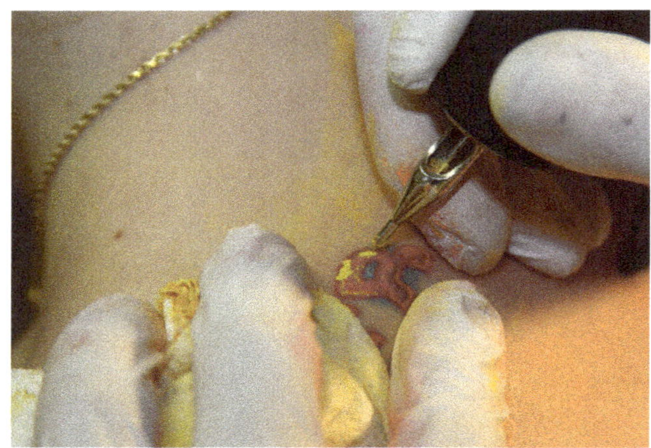

Each swab of color will soon be wiped clean of any excess, revealing the true color.

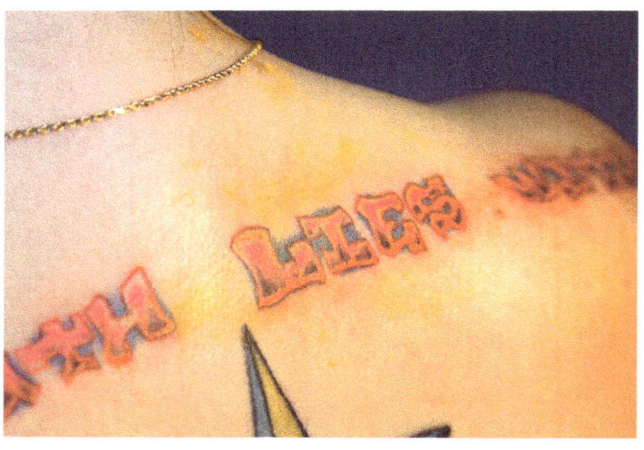

Although not completely cleaned of the excess ink we can still easily see how the letters without yellow differ from those that have the highlights.

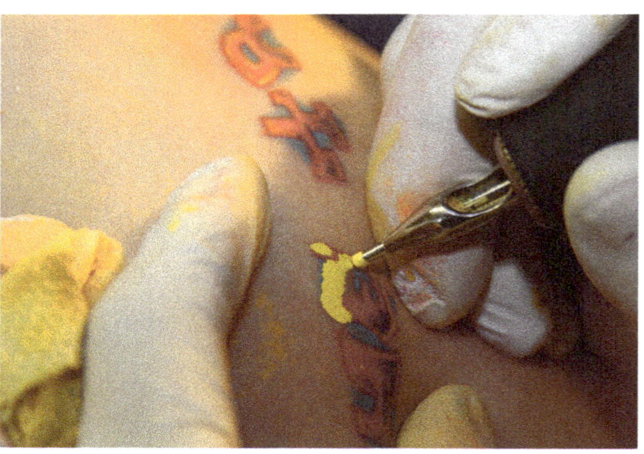

Large applications of the Sunflower ink leaves excess that needs to be wiped.

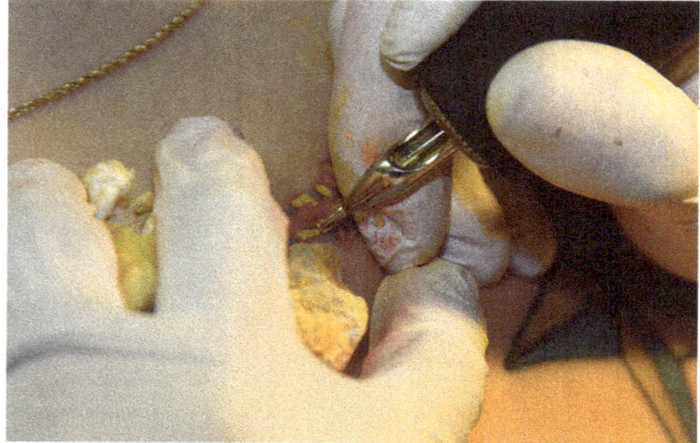

As with most of the tattoos I've seen being created, the dabs of color often seem random to the untrained eye, but the artist knows exactly where each hint of color will go long before touching needles to flesh.

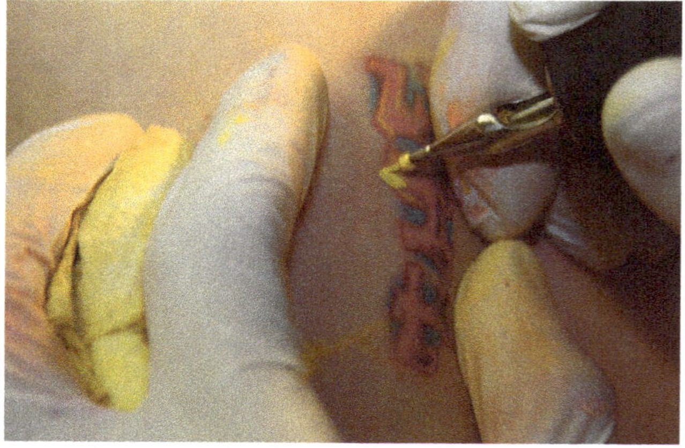

In contrast to the larger sections of ink, the hints of yellow are subtle yet very effective as highlights.

Ben Esken Q&A

How young were you when your skills as an artist became evident?
I was in kindergarten when three other classmates and I were supposed to be practicing our penmanship. I chose to flip my paper over and drew a Mutant Ninja Turtle and another superhero. The other three began doing the same thing. The teacher was not pleased but was surprised at the quality of my drawings.
When did you first get interested in tattoos?
In high school I saw it as a way to be a rebel which was more appealing to me than other groups.
Who taught you your first skills in tattooing?
We had taken a vacation to Mardi Gras and I met an artist doing tattoos and was amazed at his abilities. He showed me a few basics while there and it triggered my desire to follow that path.
Do you have any mentors or people who inspire you?
I actually get excited by studying the early masters like DaVinci and other painters of that period. Their ability to create art that seems to be three-dimensional gives me great inspiration to create ink at that level. If nothing else I am always looking for ways to expand my skills and improve my technique.
How long have you been doing tattoos?
It's been about six years now.
Who got your first tattoo and what was the art?
It was a leprechaun sitting on a spilled pot of gold and Mike Kady was the recipient.
Where did you get your first experience in a tattoo shop?
It was in 2005 at a local place named Sinful Flesh in Peoria, IL.
Do you have a favorite style or genre?
I am usually put under the "Dragon Style" category which means I can produce nearly any style tattoo requested.
What was your biggest tattoo?
I have done several full back pieces as well as complete leg and arm designs.
What changes have you seen in the tattoo world?
When I started out I expected there to be far more sharing of ideas, techniques and input among tattoo artists, but it remains a fairly tight-lipped group of people.
How long have you been at your current shop?
I've been at Mad Tattoo in Peoria for about four years.
What plans do you have for the future?
We hope to begin holding classes for people who want to learn how to do tattoos at Mad Tattoo within the next year if all goes as planned. Maybe open my own shop down the line, but nothing in the immediate future.

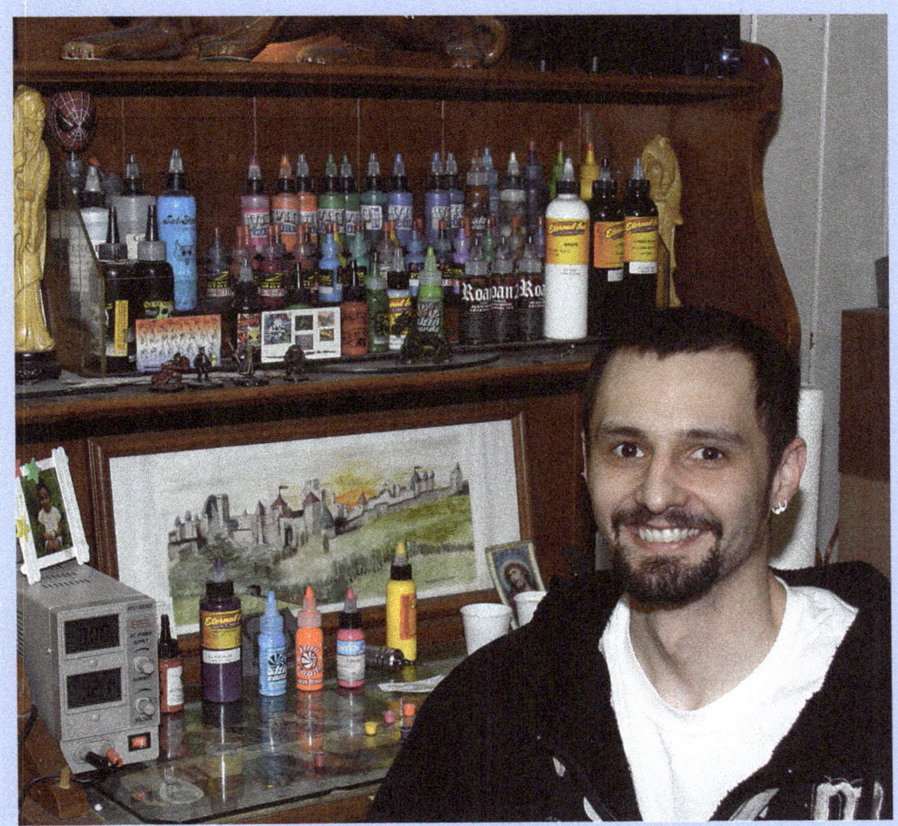

Tattoo Conventions

Ok, you've asked all the right questions, spoken with friends and decided the time has come to get yourself a tattoo. Assuming you already know the image, saying or illustration you want, the next question may be where to go to get it done? At this stage there are several avenues you can follow. Asking those who already have some ink might steer you in the right direction as long as the piece worn by your contact is similar to what you seek. Not every artist can create every style of tattoo so if your plan is fairly specific more research should be done.

Turning to the yellow pages, either online or in print will tell you where the local shops are located but probably won't shed much light on the styles offered at the shops listed. Of course you can always inquire at a local location about their styles, but getting through to them during a busy day of ink application often poses a problem. There is another way to sample the wares of many artists, face-to-face as long as your timing and geographical location lends itself to large gatherings.

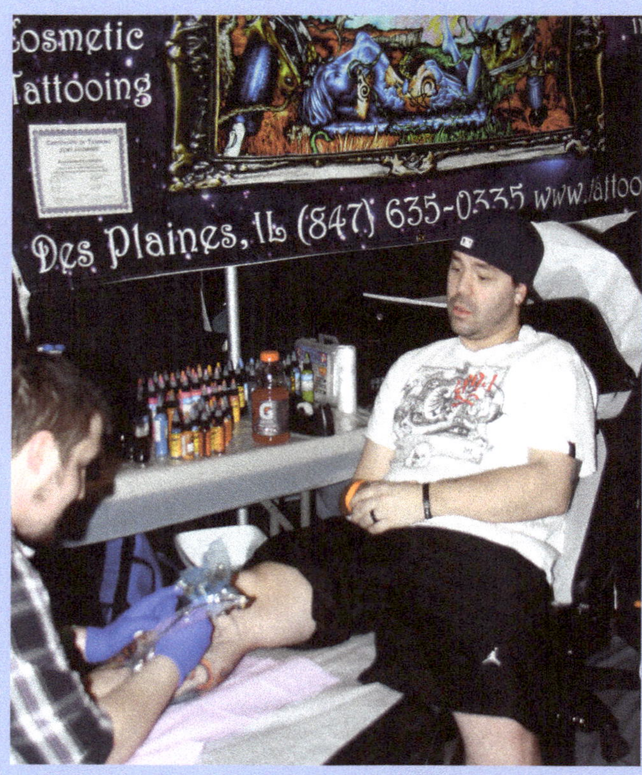

Perfection Dermagraphics created a tattoo for this book and the crew was on hand to provide clients with additional work at the event.

If you are lucky enough to have a tattoo convention traveling to a city near you, it will be the most efficient method of viewing different styles, designs and actual artists at work in a single location. As luck would have it, I was able to attend such an event that was hosted by Villain Arts of Philadelphia fame. They organize several of these events each year and use a number of cities to bring tattoo skills to the masses. The recent Chicago event was held at the Crowne Plaza Hotel in Rosemont, IL. It is close to the airport and the host hotel is a

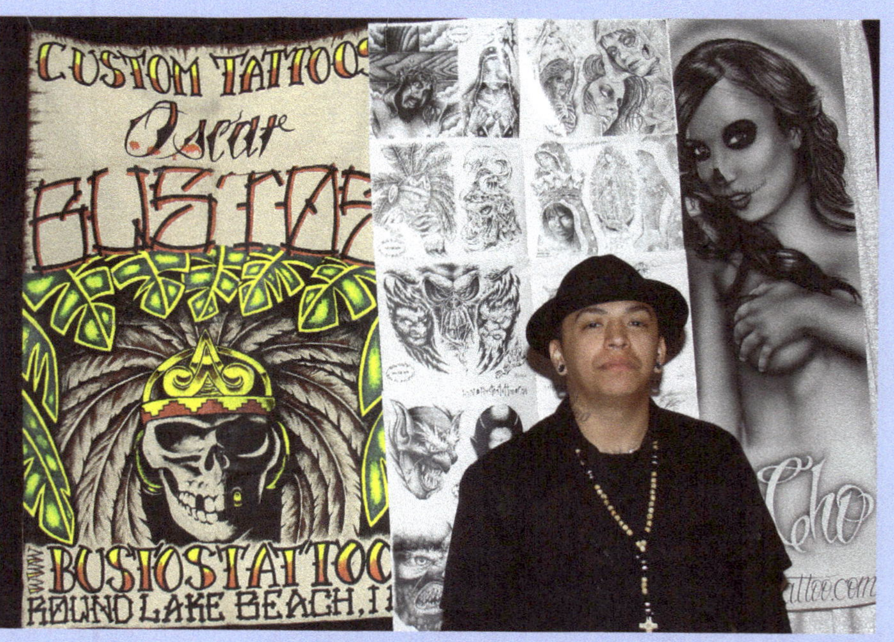

Oscar Bustos hails from a northern ILL location and was on hand among artists from many points on the globe.

high-quality venue for anyone attending an event or reserving a hotel room.

Listed in the convention booklet were almost 200 artists from around the globe. Walking the aisles of the ballroom it is truly amazing how many different styles of art can be placed onto the human skin. Every booth held a different artist or shop and offered up a colorful display of past efforts along with books of creations for your consideration. The artists are also on hand and happy to answer questions about your desired skin art. Many of those I stopped to talk with were available to do work on the spot, but at busier times during the event your options may not be as open.

It has been in my experience that even a glimpse of what you want can be expanded in detail and brought to life by a talented tattoo artist. A simple snake idea can be developed into a larger and more intricate design within moments of feeding the artist your input. Most of these artisans have unlimited skills when it comes time to create this form of art and are more than willing to assist your needs.

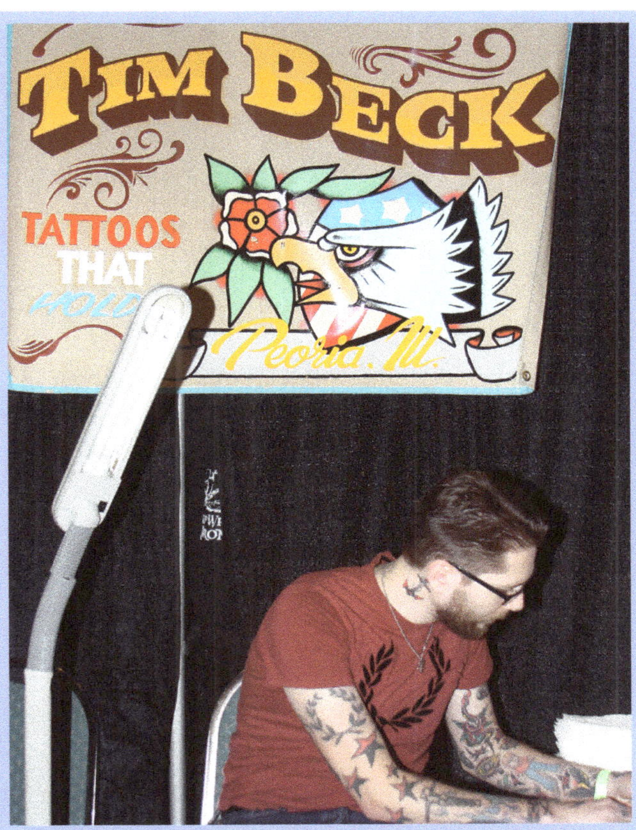

Tim Beck is another artist who created a tattoo for Wolfgang Publications and he was busy readying a new piece for a client arriving soon.

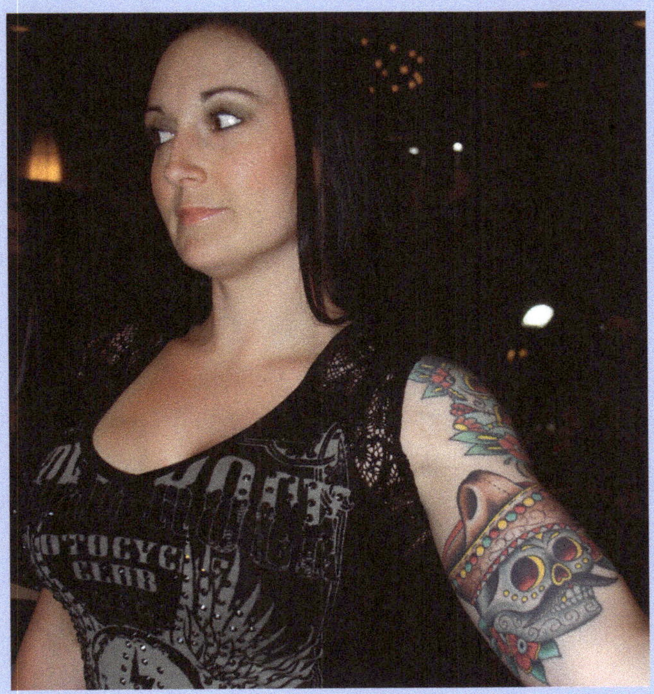

Jen Valentine was on hand to show Tim Beck how her last tattoo healed and to discuss the next segment of skin art on her wish list.

As with most forms of talent, rates of pay can vary from artist to artist and you need to get those numbers agreed to prior to setting needle to skin. Getting a tattoo that perfectly suits your desires may not be within your budget so a few moments should be spent to clarify this facet of the process.

All in all attending a large, well organized tattoo convention can provide the answers to all of your questions and even let you leave adorned with a piece of art that'll be yours forever.

You can search for this event as well as others online and Villain Arts can be contacted by e-mail, tattooedkingpin@yahoo.com or by phone 215-423-4780.

Others can be located with an online search but Villain Arts has been at the game for more than a decade, making them masters at the event organization game.

Chapter Seven

Joe Capobianco

Hope Gallery

When deciding to get a tattoo done, people can go about the process in one of several ways. If it's something "stock," they can walk into their local shop, pick a piece from the catalog and the work can begin. Since most people wish to create something original, the first step for them is to meet with their chosen ink person to discuss the art to be created. After a period of time, depend-

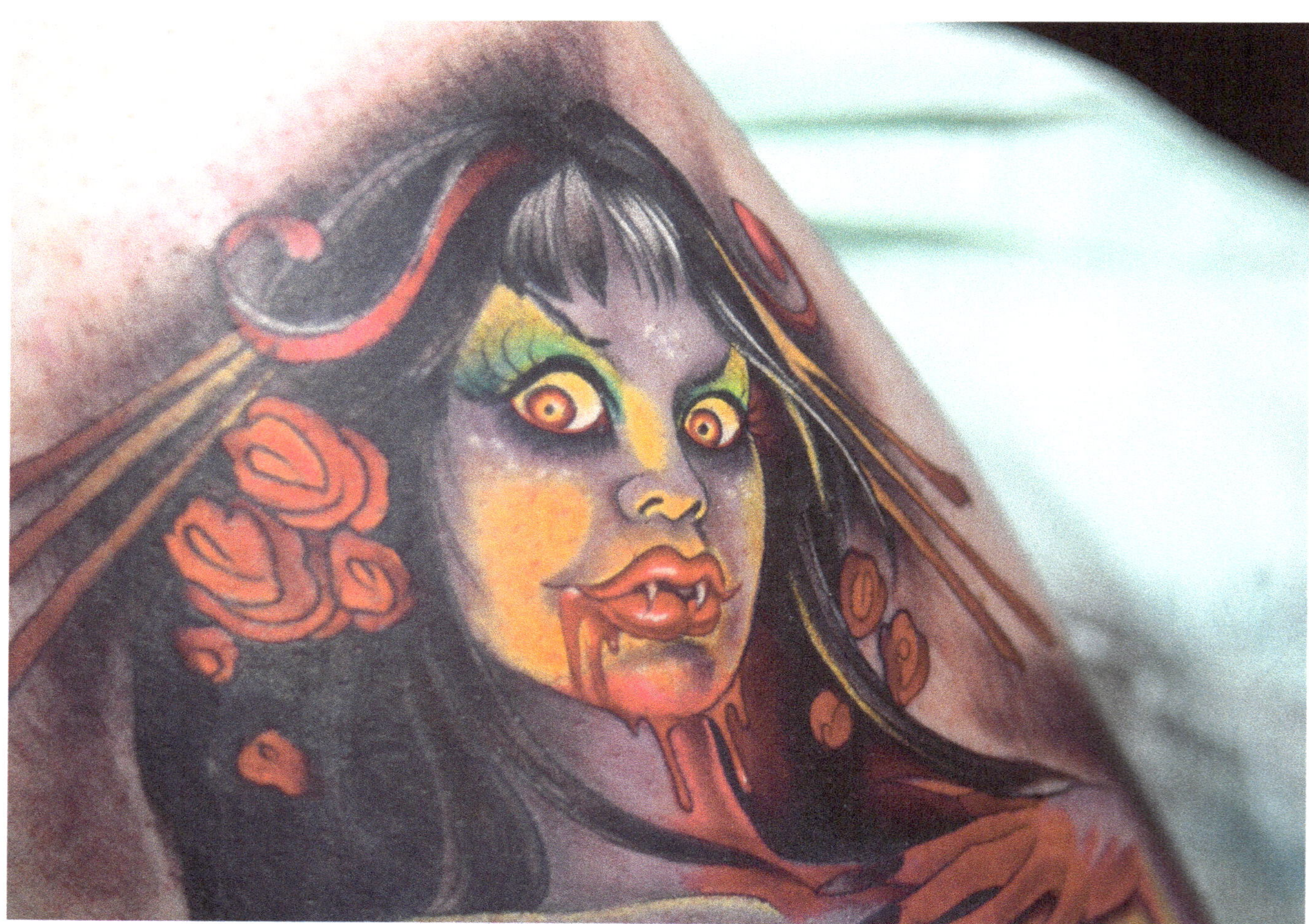

Erin had wanted a tattoo from Joe for nearly 3 years and booked her sitting 6 months in advance. Created during the festivities at the Hell City Festival, Erin was more than pleased with the results. Giving Joe nothing more than the theme, he drew up the art and turned it into a painting of the flesh.

ing on the request, the artist will contact the person saying the sketch has been completed for review. Once this process has been approved, the piece can be put onto the skin.

In the case of Erin's geisha-vampire piece, the path was a bit longer. Having seen Joe's work in numerous places, Erin knew she wanted Joe to do his magic. She has been getting tattoos for nearly a decade, but was willing to wait for the chance to work with Joe. Since she lives in Ohio, and Joe works out of his shop in Connecticut, they were hardly neighbors. After waiting three years for her opportunity, both Joe and Erin were scheduled to be at the Hell City tattoo convention in 2006. Seeing the chance to finally get some of Joe's art on her body, Erin made her appointment 6 months in advance. Joe typically doesn't book that early, but knew the Hell City event would be busy, and accepted the assignment.

Knowing Joe's abilities as an artist as well as a tattoo guy, Erin simply told him of her "vampire-geisha" idea and let his imagination and pencil run wild. Artists like Joe work best when not constrained by too much direction and prefer to fly by the seat of their pants. This is not to say that Erin would have accepted any old sketch for her calf, but had faith and confidence in Joe's work. When seeing the final drawing, she was immediately pleased and eager to get the ink started. Her initial desire was for the tattoo to represent Joe's talent, and to be recognized as one of his pieces. Many artists have a signature that runs through most of their custom work, and Joe is no different. His choices of colors as well as his use of shading and contours sets his work apart from the rest.

Besides Joe's vast exposure in the world of tattoos, much of his illustration and airbrush art has been published in several books. He was showing advance copies at the Hell City event, and would be debuting them on Saturday evening. While doing the tattoo we see here, Joe was deluged with questions about when and where people could buy their own copies of his latest books. The pages of his latest efforts were filled with col-

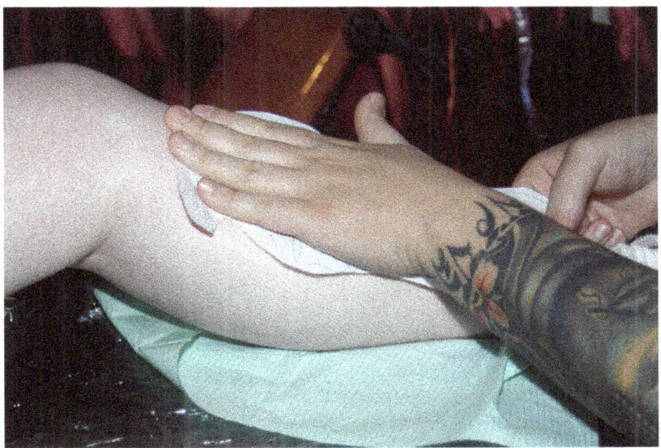

After moisturizing the skin, the heat transfer is put in place to check for size and position.

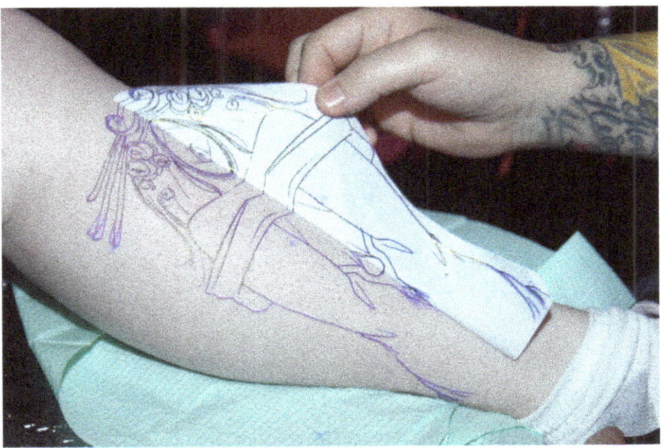

Satisfied with placement, the backing is removed to expose the guidelines beneath.

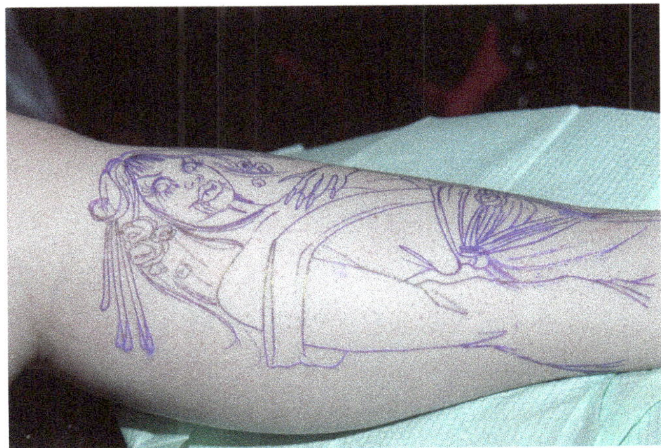

With the paper now peeled away we can see the beginning of the piece to be created.

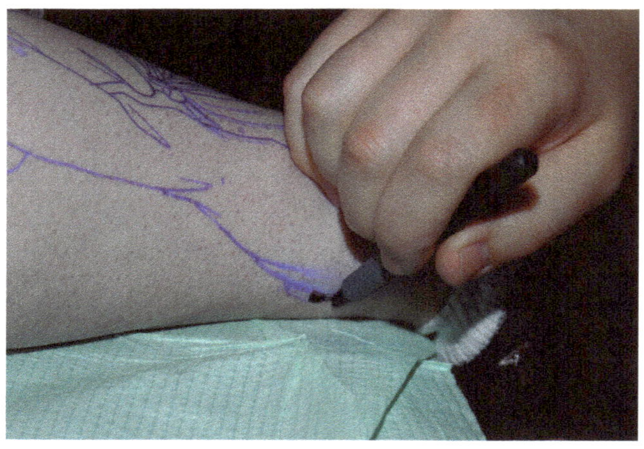

Joe uses an ink pen to define some of the more remote edges of the art before setting needle to skin.

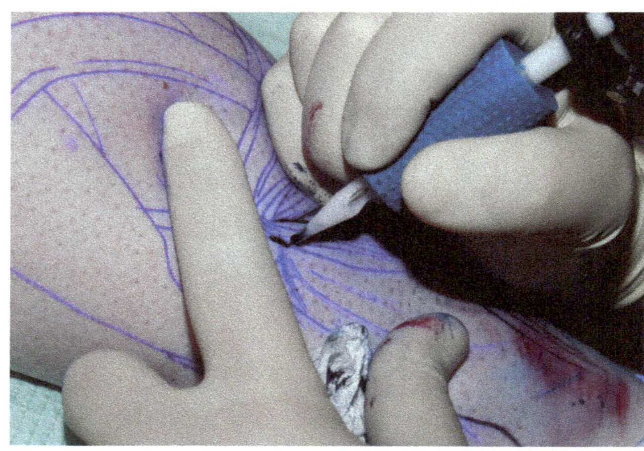

Seeing the finished piece long in advance allows Joe to create minute details that will enhance the finished piece.

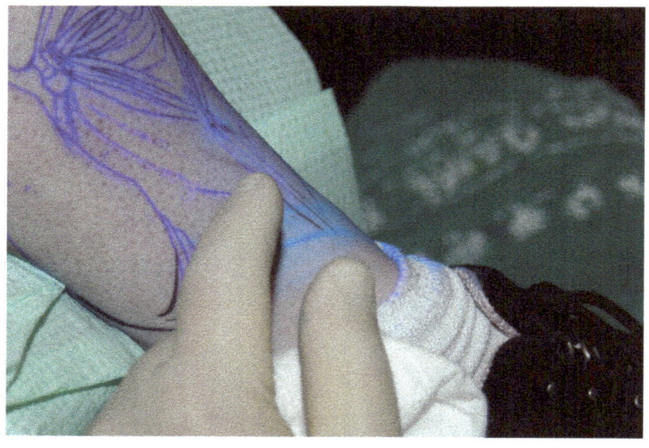

As is typically the case, the black outline comes first, but Joe needed to clear up a few imperfections before starting out.

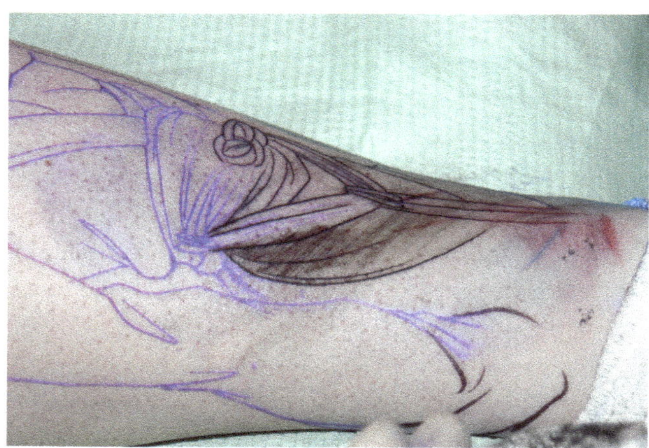

After a quick wipe of the excess ink we can see the outline work taking shape.

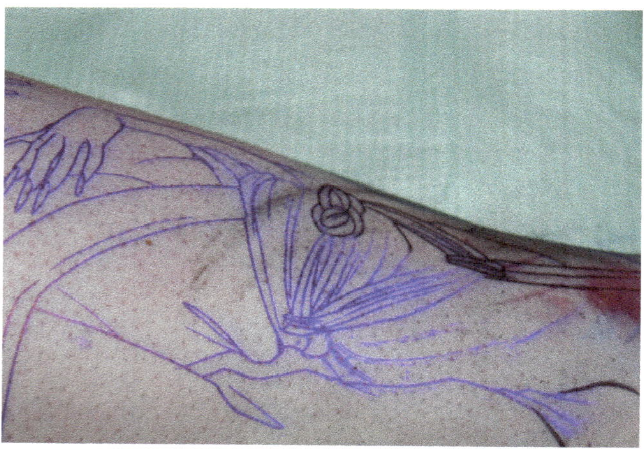

Using either a 3 or 5 liner needle, depending on the section chosen, the outline work begins.

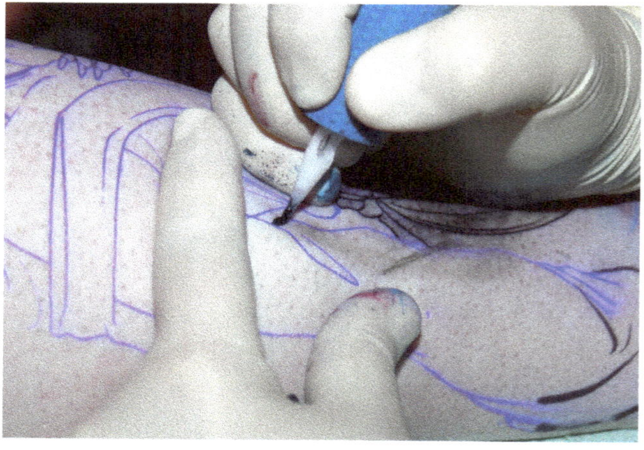

Details in the geisha's kimono will later become a major part of the art.

orful and fairly graphic illustrations of beautiful women, many of which wore smiles, and little else. You could see the pinup influence in his work, although it was not your typical approach to the art form.

When I asked Joe if airbrushing was similar to his tattoo art, he quickly explained that the two mediums were as different as night and day. The fact that he is so capable in both forms of art is evidence of his talents. Most people would be happy to possess the ability to do one or the other, let alone both.

Having no formal training besides high school art class, Joe's use of colors and textures in creating a tattoo or airbrush art are obviously innate. While certain aspects of any art form can be taught, a true artist seems to have been born with the ability to create the chosen illusions in the chosen medium. Despite his level of talent and exposure, Joe retains a level headed nature that makes him easy to deal with. This cannot be said of all parties who achieved any level of notoriety in their field.

During the creation of this book, I have learned that the tattoo machines are basically the same no matter where you go. Oh sure, there may be some models that are different in one way or another, but for the most part they are built using the same principles and design. This being said, it's amazing to see these same machines being used in such a variety of ways. Although each lays down ink using a needle or set of needles, it's the technique of the user that makes the magic happen. Much like a surgeon's tools, in the right hands, wrongs can be made right, but placed into my meat hooks, only bad things will follow. Since there are no rules or regulations as to who can own and operate a tattoo machine, one needs to do some research before having the needles taken to the skin. Opening a proper shop requires the usual litany of paperwork and approvals, but once purchased, a tattoo machine can be used in the convenience of your own living room. This is where the troubles can begin, although many talented tattoo artists did their

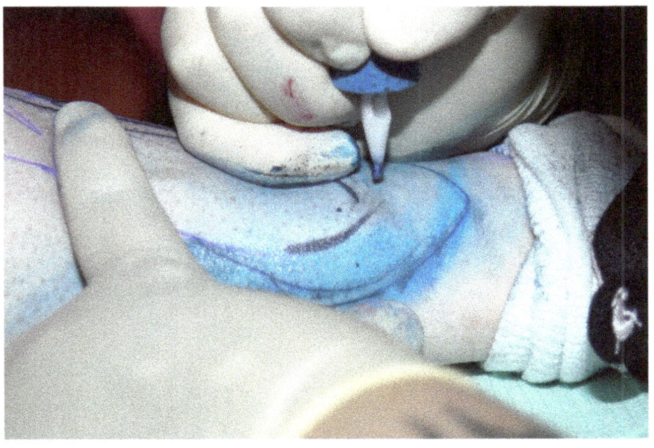

The early use of blue ink will assist Joe later as he returns to the location to complete the piece.

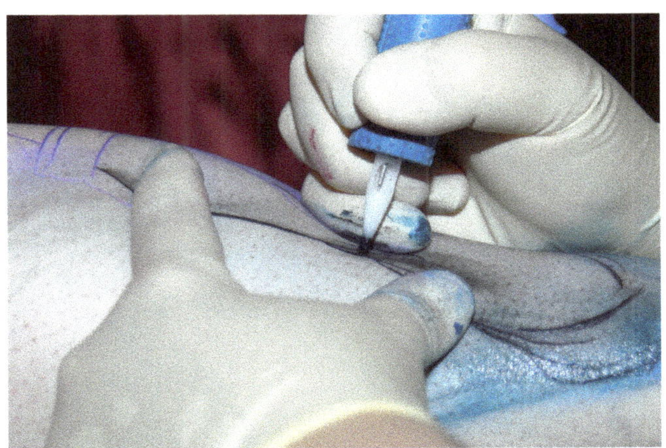

Picking up the black outline process again, Joe continues to define the shape of the kimono.

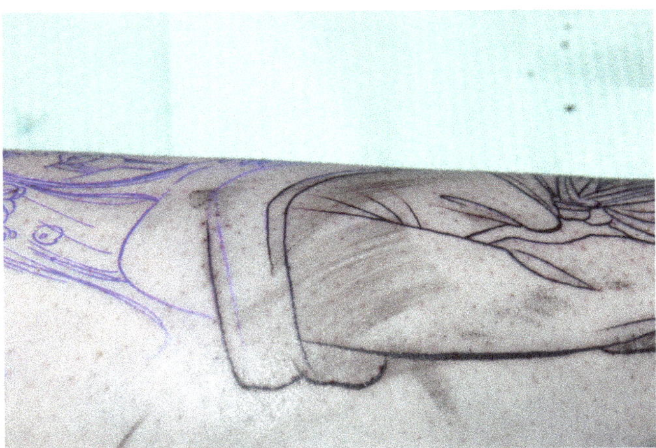

The fruits of his labor so far, we can see how much more work lies ahead.

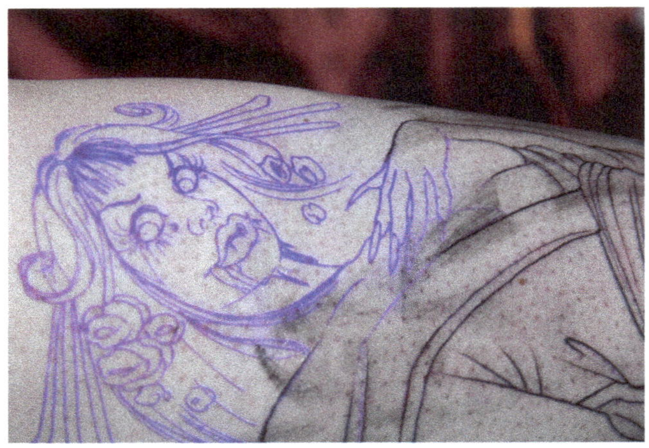

With the lower section of the art outlined, Joe will turn his attentions to the facial details next.

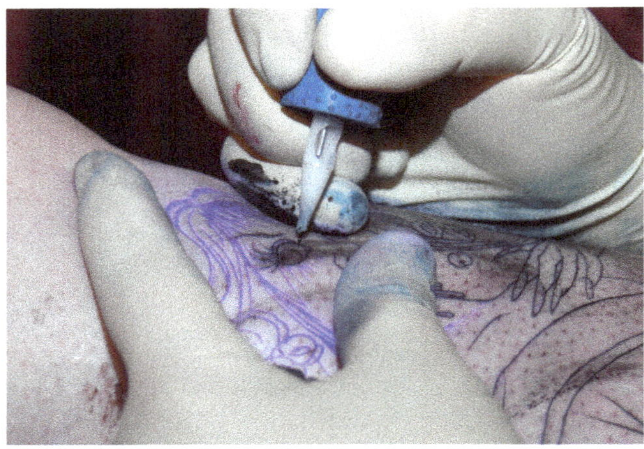

Lavish eyelashes will highlight the large eyes of the geisha.

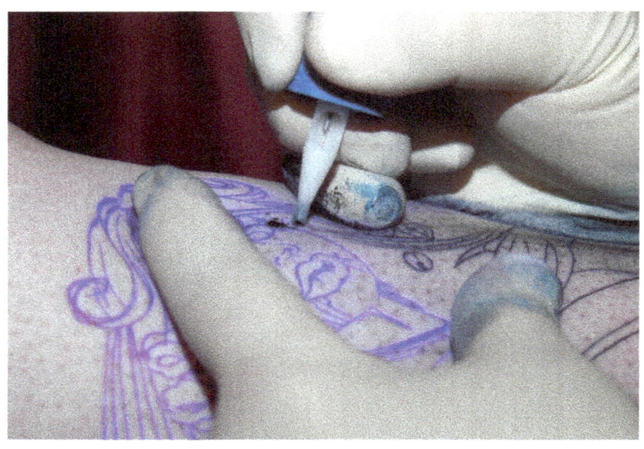

The tiniest of details are addressed first so as not to get lost in the flow of ink later.

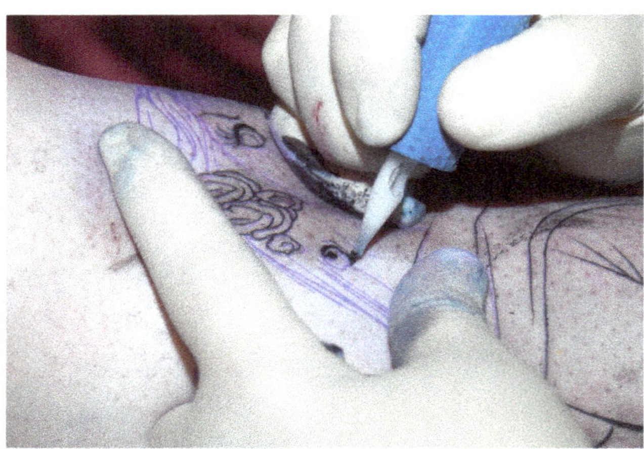

Moving away from the eyes for a moment, some additional details are added to the surrounding area.

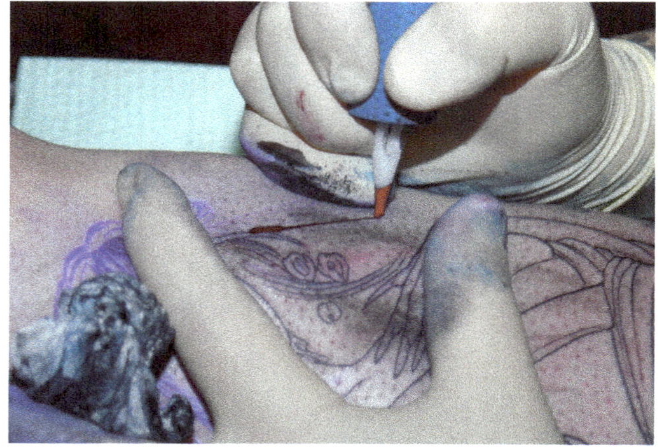

Joe again uses a hint of color before finishing up with the black work.

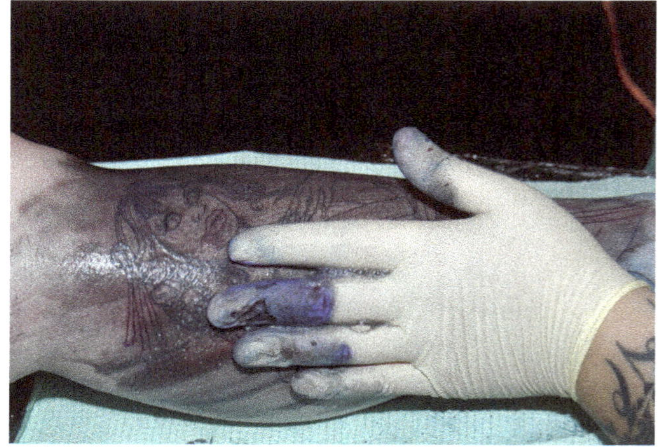

Wiping down the surface with moisturizer before wiping the tattoo clean for a quick review.

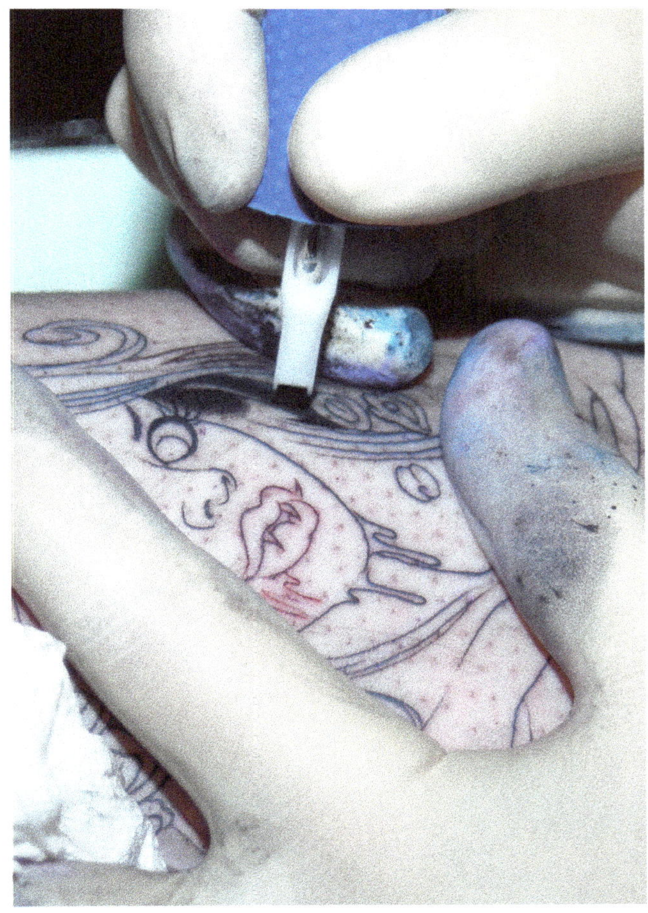

Using a larger 7 mag needle allows Joe to begin shading in the area around the face.

first work at home. It seems that "buyer beware" would apply when choosing the man behind the needles.

In the early stages of creating the sketch for a tattoo, Joe begins to see the colors that will be applied in the final piece. This level of vision is one of the traits that sets his work on the top shelf among purveyors of tattoo art. Small improvements are always added as a piece progresses, but his vision of the overall balance and hues that will be employed help make the actual process a thing of beauty. Being artistic by nature makes the application process seem easy to the untrained eye, but anyone who knows what goes into the creation of a tattoo will be stunned by Joe's efforts.

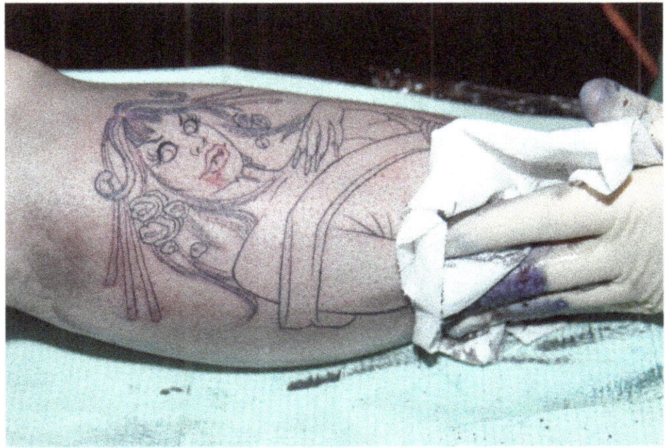

With the excess ink cleaned off, we can see the tattoo coming to life.

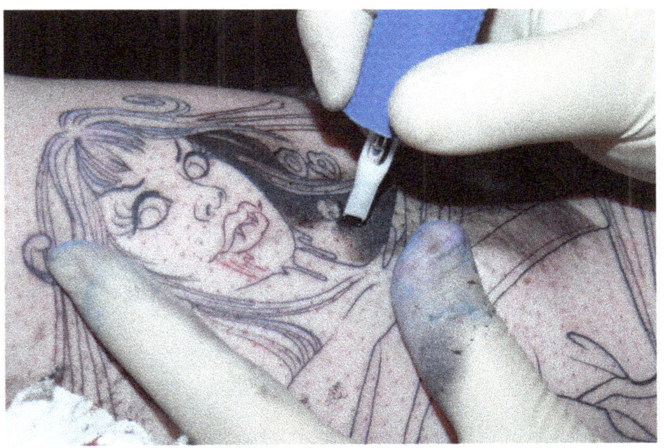

By adding the shaded areas to the piece, we can see the face become far more prominent.

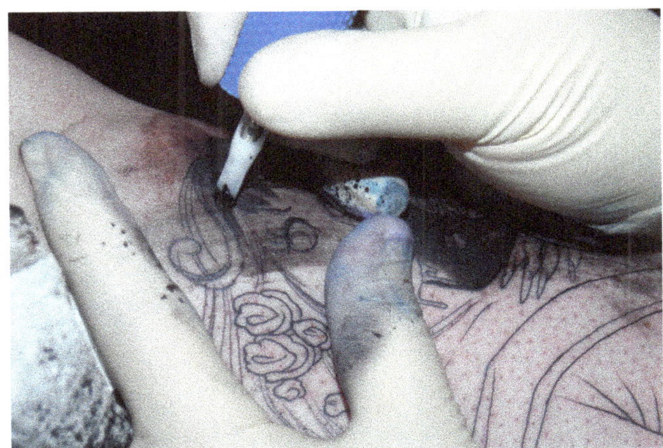

Moving to the hair, Joe begins to add large sections of ink to create shape and dimension.

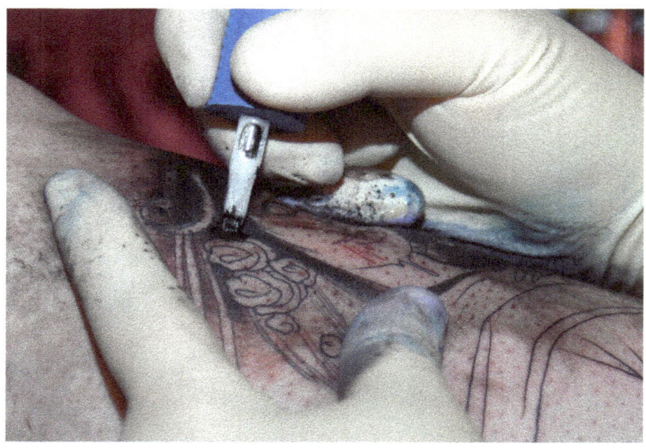

Using black around the roses in her hair will later allow the red petals to stand out.

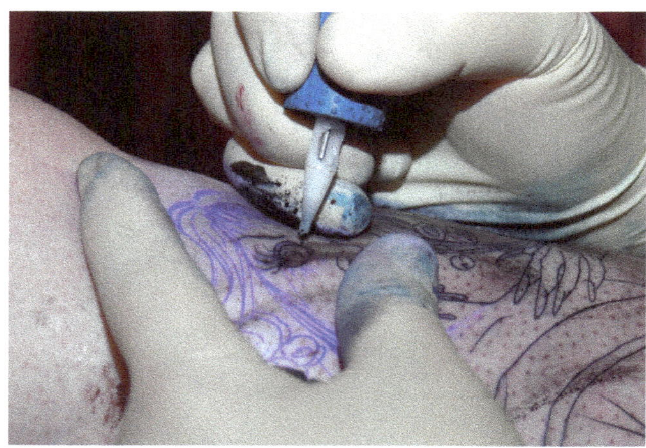

Larger areas of the flowing kimono are now shaded to add contours and shadow.

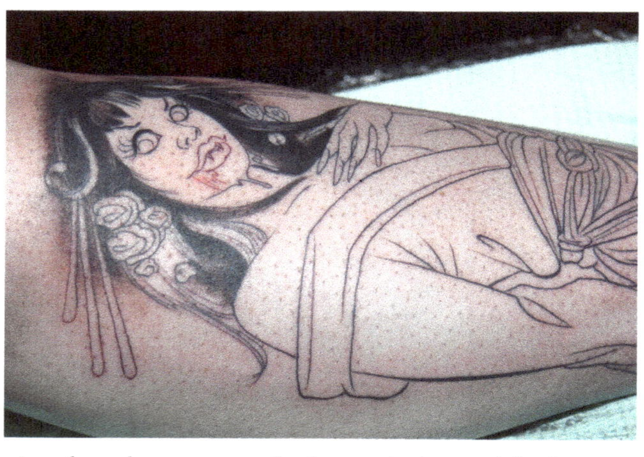

Another cleanup reveals the work done with the wider needle.

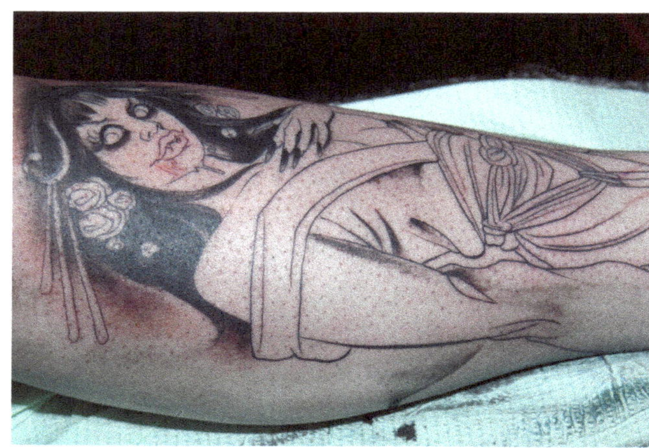

With the black work nearing completion, we can see the level of intensity that lies ahead.

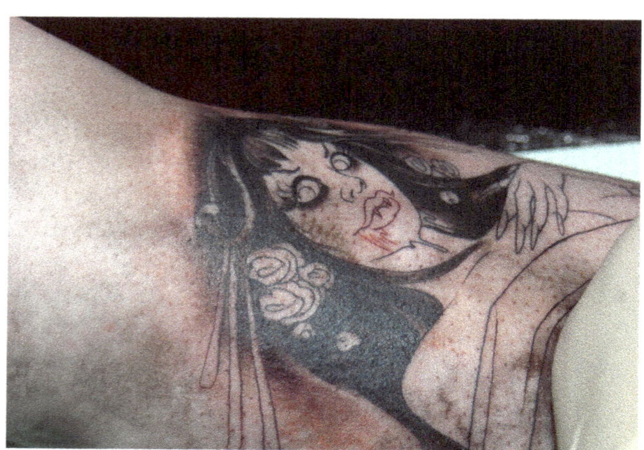

Every step taken shows us more detail and emotion as the face of the geisha-vampire receives attention.

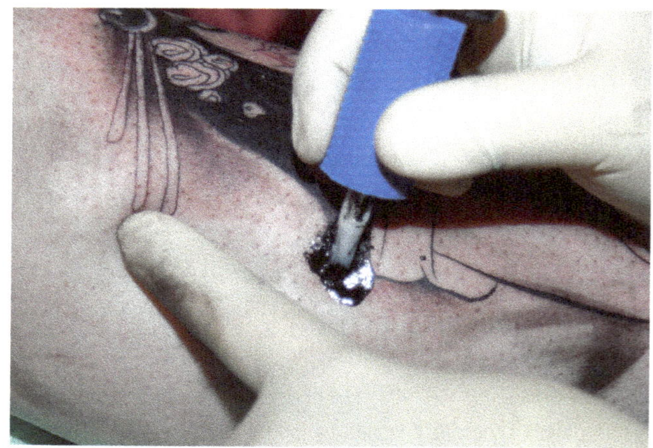

By placing areas of black outside the lines of the kimono, its shape and color will stand out with greater intensity.

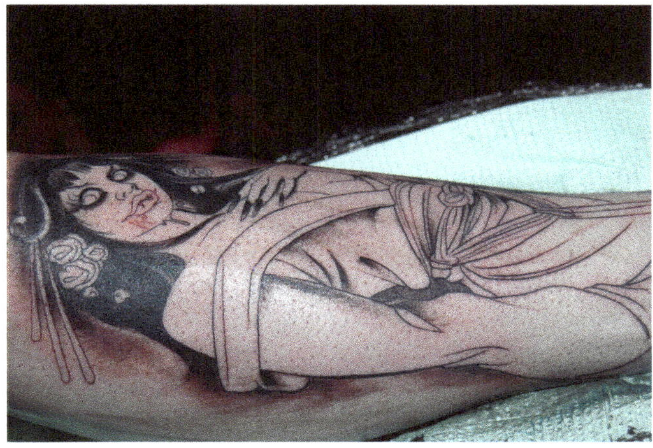

With the black work now completed, Joe can prepare to begin the application of colors.

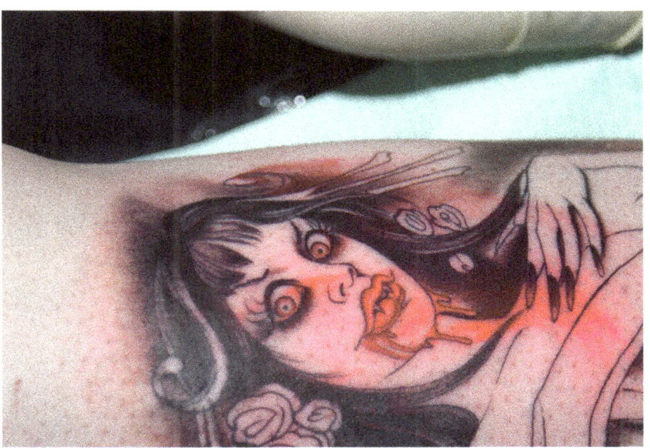

Now the red in the eyes and bloody overflow of the feast are added to the face.

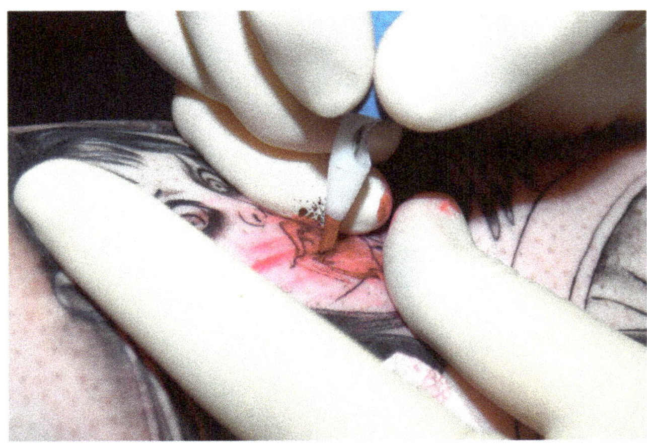

Illustrating a vampire right after a big meal, bright red ink is used to fill in the area around the mouth.

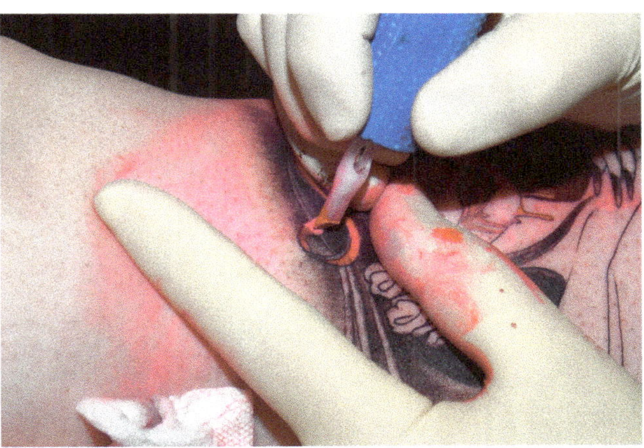

A few strands of red hair will help to bring life to the otherwise raven locks.

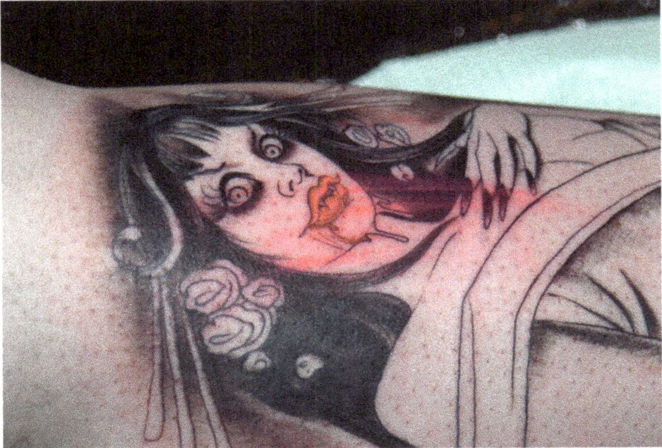

The red lips are only the first location for the "blood" of the tattoo.

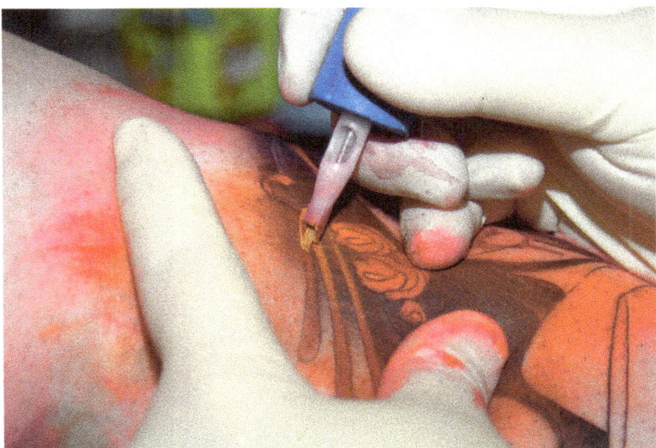

With the roses now filled in, Joe adds a bit of color to the decorations in the hair.

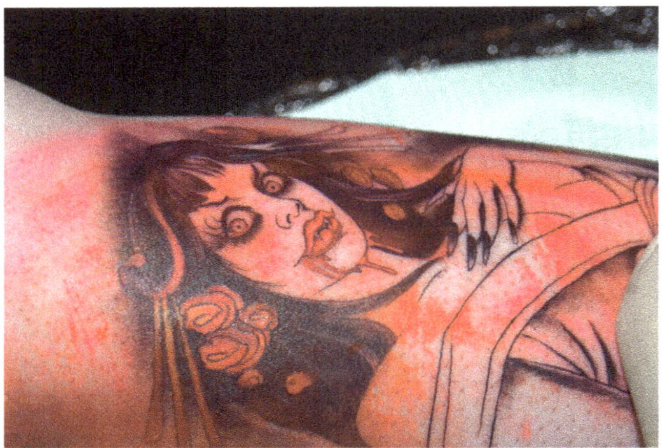

Being a vampire, we expected a high level of red to be used, and Joe hasn't disappointed us.

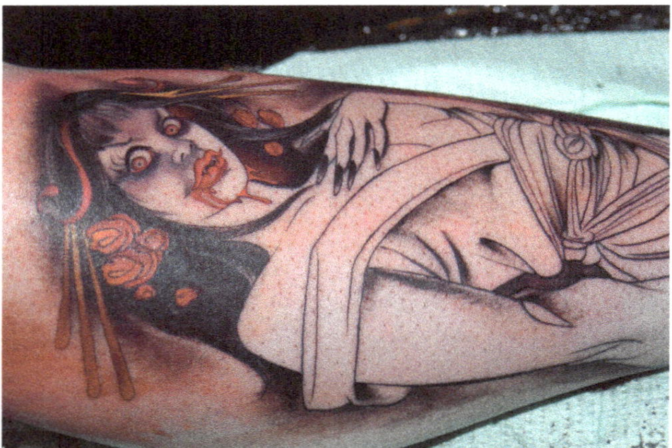

Wiped clean again, we can see the results of the first bloody steps in the piece.

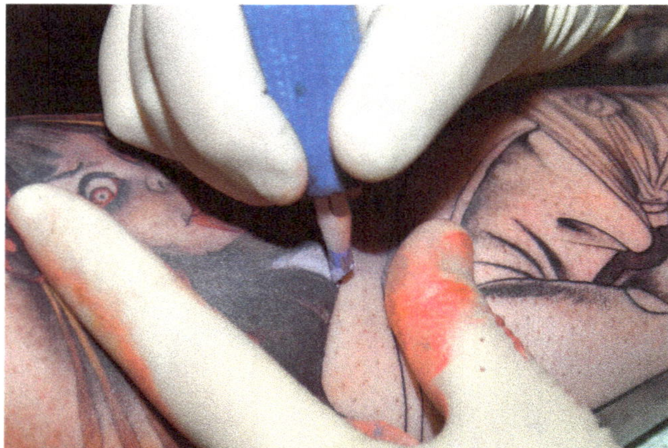

Using an ashen gray color will give the living-dead geisha just the right shade in her skin tones.

Q&A: Joe Capobianco

How long have you been doing tattoos?

It's been about 13 years since I got started doing work in this field.

What was your first tattoo?

My first piece as an apprentice was a tribal scorpion, and the first paid tattoo was a black and gray dragon's head on a guy's chest.

Any genre you are known for?

Although my work doesn't really have any specific niche, I do get a lot of requests for pinup work since my airbrush art is done in that style quite often.

Who or what inspired you to start doing ink?

I saw tattoos as a way to expand my art at first. Once I began doing it, I found that I enjoyed the process and fell in love with it.

What's your best known piece so far?

No one piece stands out, but my biggest was a full back project.

What's the story of the Hope Gallery?

I had worked with another group of tattoo artists in a shop, but the business went bad. Wanting to do things differently, I decided to open my own place and Hope Gallery was born.

What kind of art training do you have?

I took art class in high school, but no formal training beyond that. I began doing illustrations, and then switched to airbrushing before trying tattoos.

What changes do you see coming in the world of tattoos?

The actual hardware hasn't and probably won't change much, but more talented people are being seen, and each of them pushes the boundaries of the craft further than before.

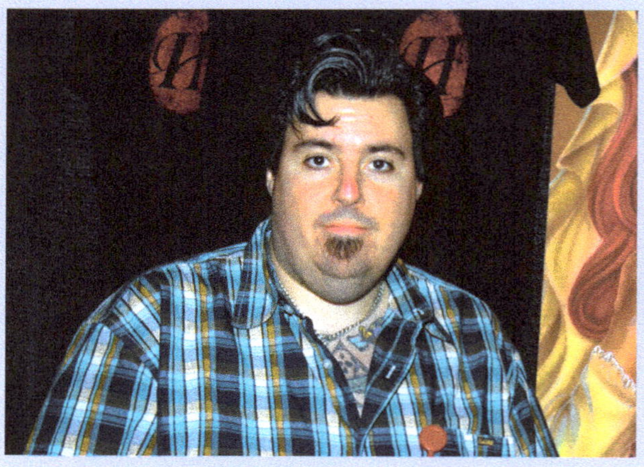

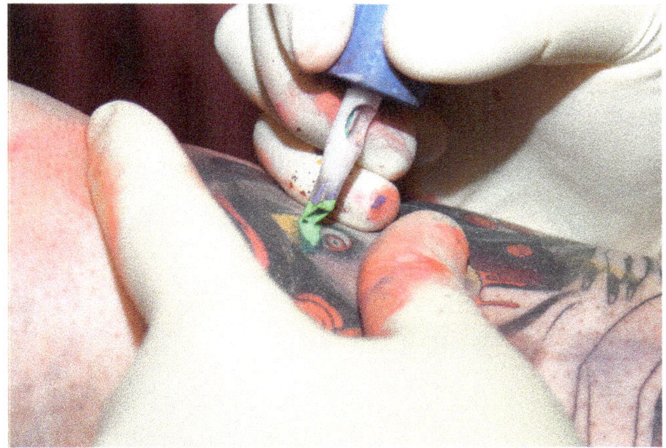

Small sections of yellow and green are now added to highlight the eyes.

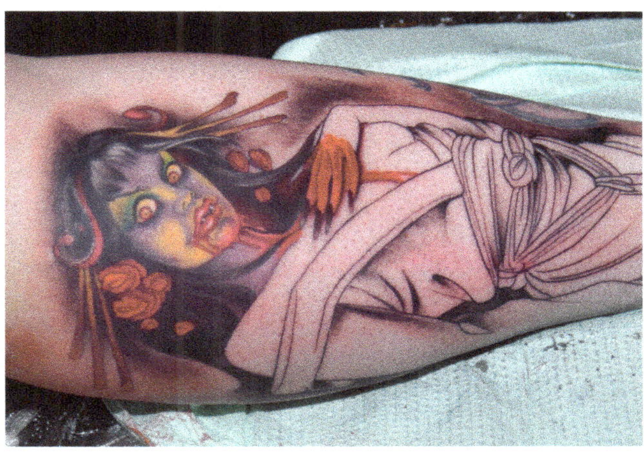

Cleansing the ink away, we now see the efforts taken on the facial region of the tattoo, but a few more finishing touches will be added later.

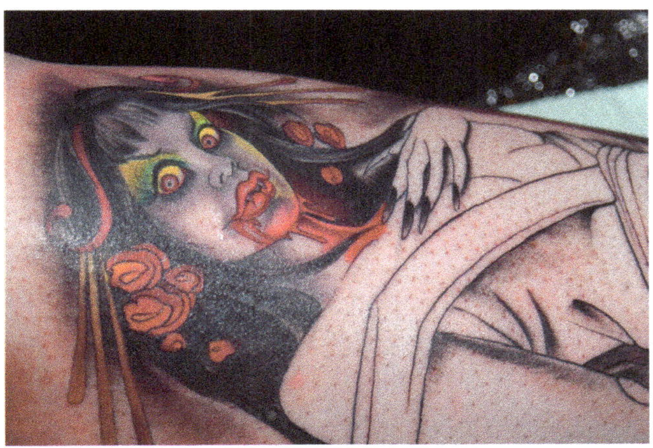

Joe's use of color and shading are bringing the dead to life.

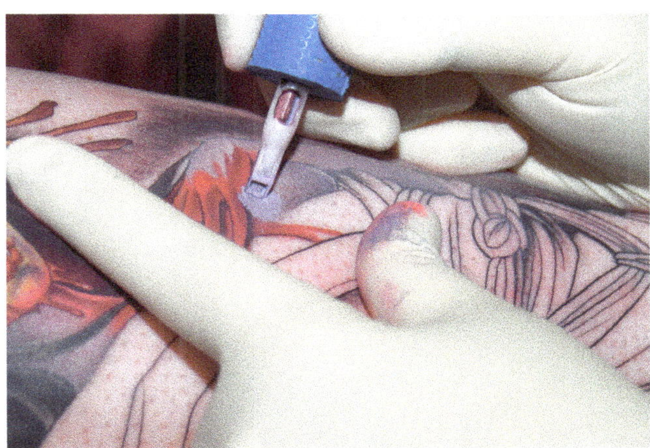

Even the flesh of her heaving breast will be done in the deathly gray color.

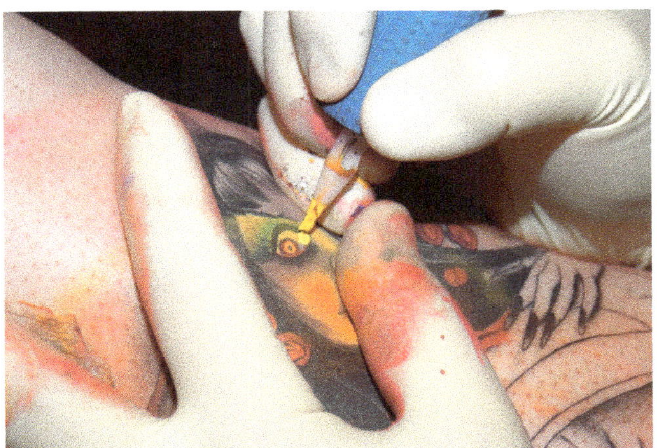

The yellow ink in the yes will bring a level of eerie beauty to the woman's face.

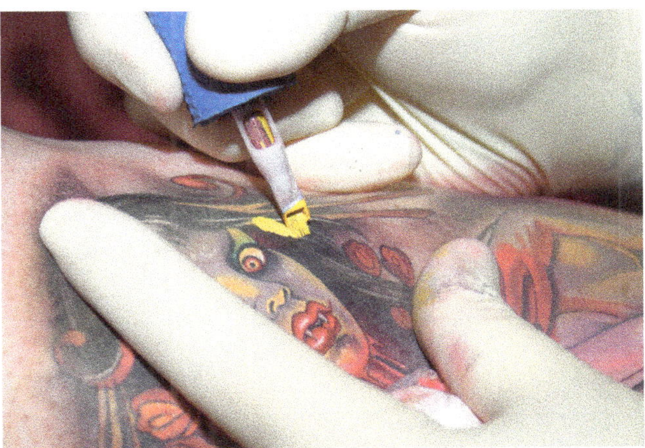

A few bright highlights are now added to the hair to create a sense of dimension.

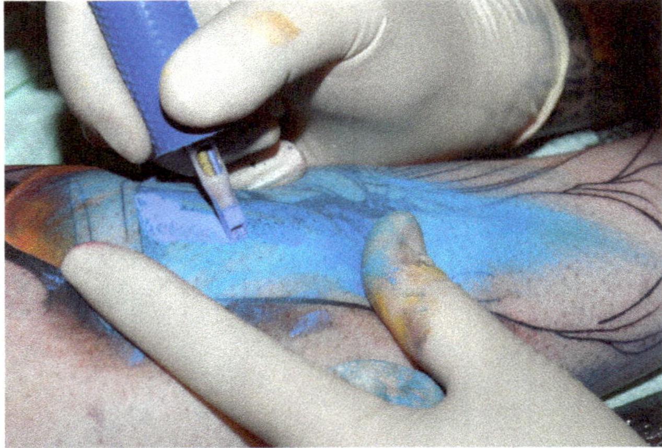

With blue as the primary color, large areas are covered in a short amount of time.

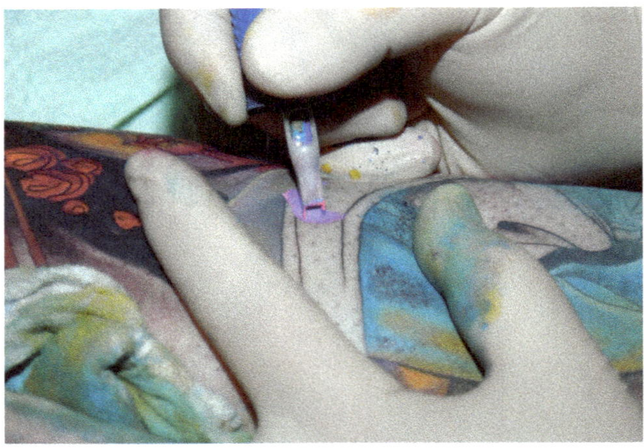

The sash of the kimono will be done in a dark lavender to offset the blue silk.

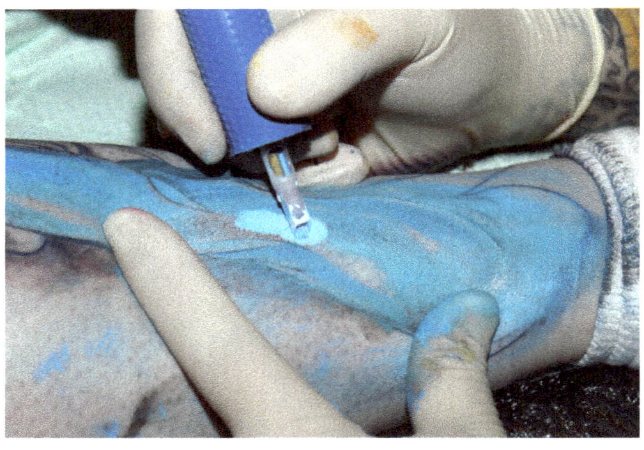

Working from dark to light, different shades of blue will be used as well as additional hues.

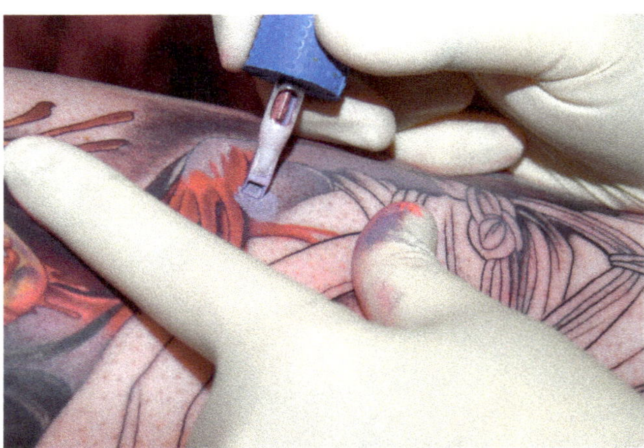

After a particularly heavy meal, the blood has flowed down onto the folds of her kimono.

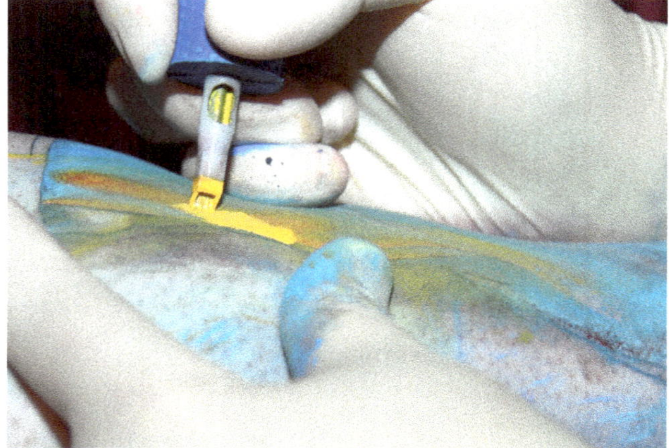

A bright yellow section will soon reveal contours not before seen in this piece.

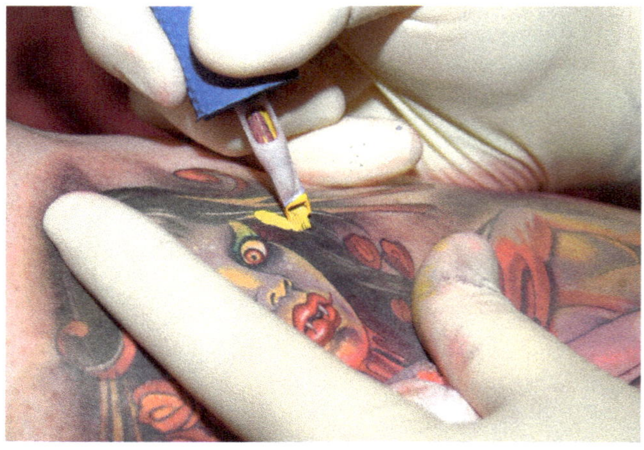

Additional shades of yellow will help to bring more shape to the flowing robe.

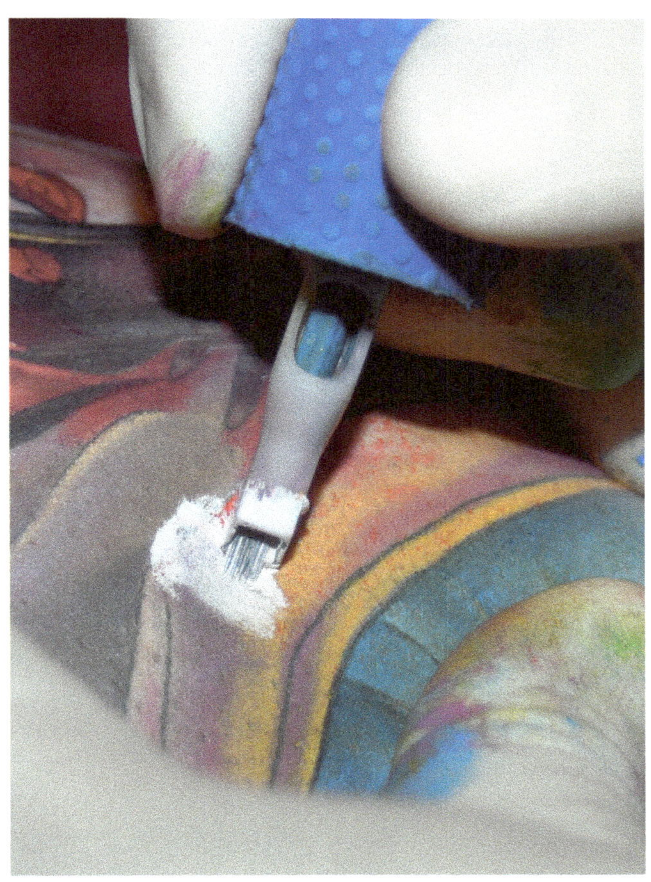

Final steps in any tattoo involve the use of white inks to add the last measure of contour to the previously applied inks.

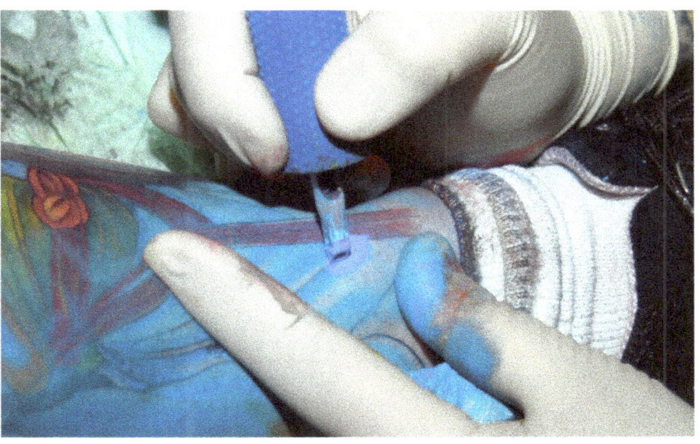

Even the simplest of shapes requires the use of a variety of shades to bring the needed detail to the finished tattoo.

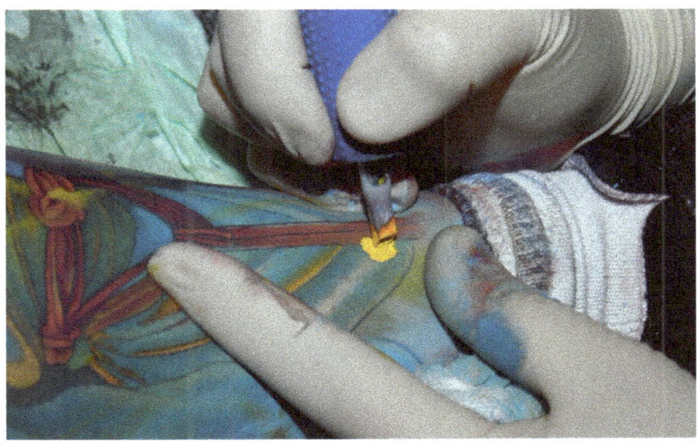

Final touches of yellow will complete the kimono and the entire piece of art.

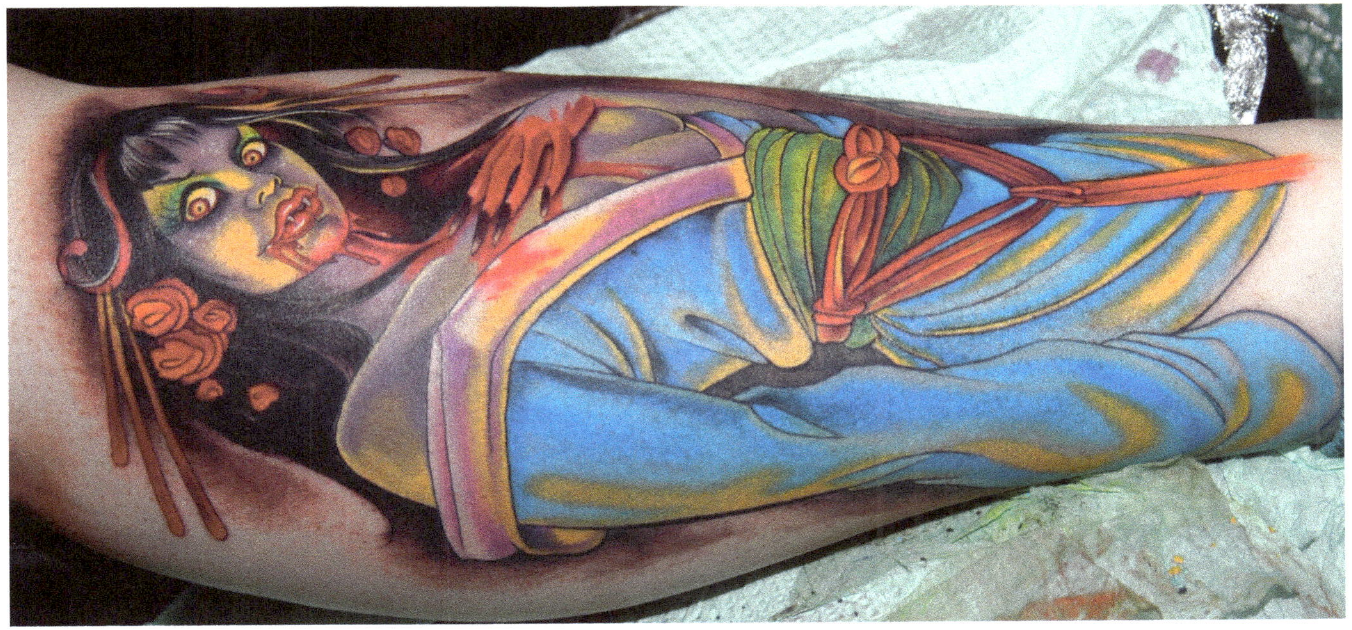

Overall, the tattoo screams of reality and makes a great showcase for Joe's abilities and talent.

Chapter Eight

Harley Freeland

Epic Image Tattoo Sequence

Although Harley's experience may be short in time it's obvious that his tattoo skills and talents are far beyond his years. With an early realization of his artistic ability in kindergarten his talent continues to develop and grow with every chance he gets to create an original piece of art.

Having begun doing tattoos only three years ago, Harley works hard to do the best art he can for as many customers as possible, and thereby expand his client base and exposure. Looking at

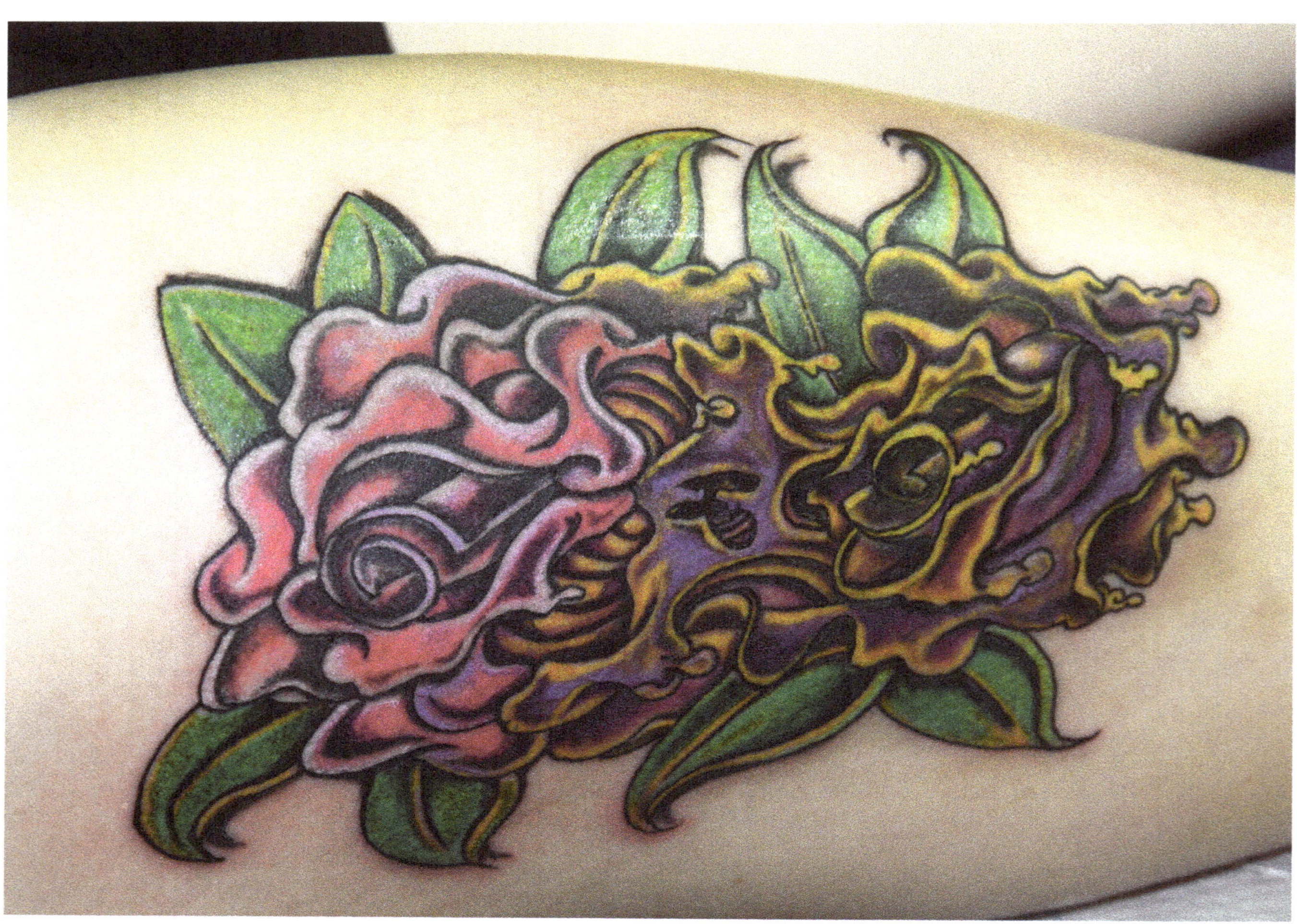

Nicole's thigh is now graced with the amazing design that was drawn and then tattooed onto her leg by Harley.

the array of art that decorates his shop it's obvious he lacks no talent in the creation of designs and examples of his ink is equally indicative of his skill level. If I were to guess at his experience level based on the art I'd have rated him at a decade or more of experience while the truth has it closer to only three years.

Epic Image is his first shop and has taken over the location of a previous tattoo parlor. He continues to improve the facility in appearance and convenience as he divides his time between two other jobs and his family. For me it's great to see a person of such a young age with a high level of skills and ambition - a willingness to work far too many hours each week.

He doesn't appear to use any radically different methods in creating his art but is careful to implement only the latest in gear and inks. When creating the piece illustrated here there was absolutely no blood drawn from Nicole's leg despite the size and complex nature of the art. A light touch is always welcome to those getting fresh ink especially the first-timers. He uses a variety of brand name equipment and supplies to achieve each piece and the expanding universe of tattoo supplies makes that an easy task. The line of Bloodline inks from Skin Candy and Kuro Sumi colors are some of his favorites with a diverse range of hues to pick from. Tatwax needles are his current preference and are often installed into machines from Superior, such as the Raven used in today's example.

With his budget still hampered by his newness to the craft he still creates his stencils by hand until he can add a heat transfer machine to his arsenal. The machines are a common sight at most ink shops but even at a few hundred dollars it remains elusive until additional income rolls in.

If the skills he exhibits are evident after only three years at his art form I can only imagine what he'll achieve after a decade or so has passed. Any competition at that point will face a daunting challenge to outdo Harley Freeland.

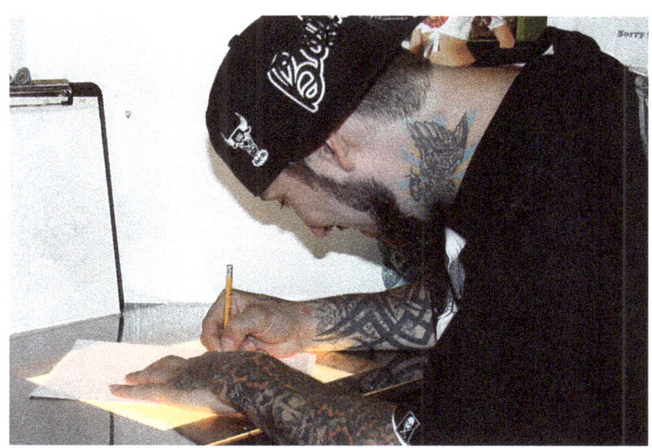

Harley puts some finishing touches on the design before manually creating the stencil.

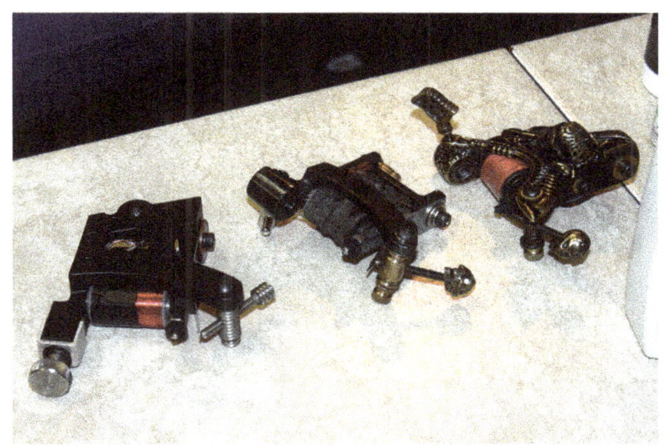

He preps a few machines prior to beginning, each with a different needle set for specific tasks.

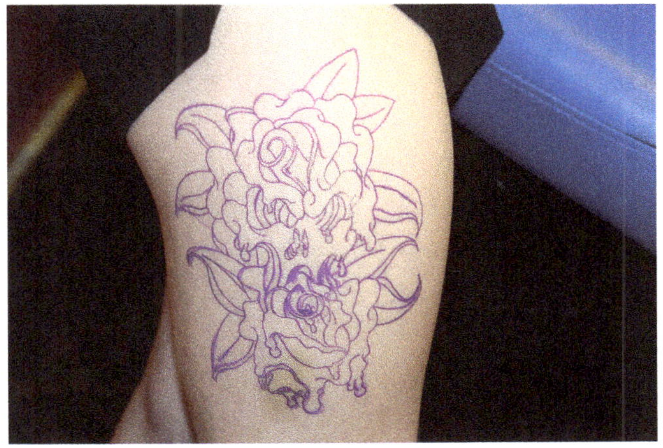

Nicole has had many pieces of tattoo art done before and all were created by Harley. The newest piece is being added to her thigh.

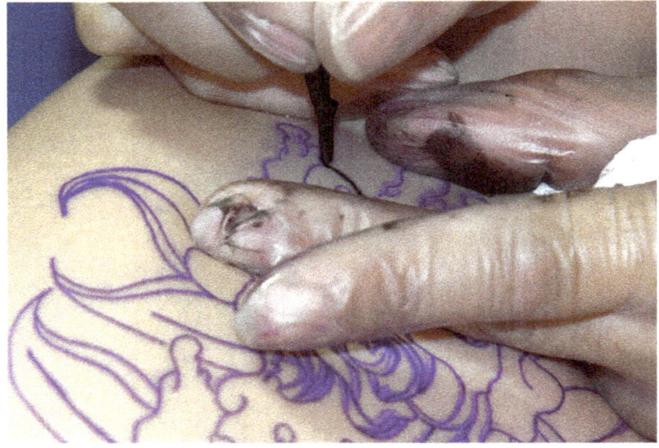

The black line work is created using a 7 round liner needle set and Kuro Sumi black ink.

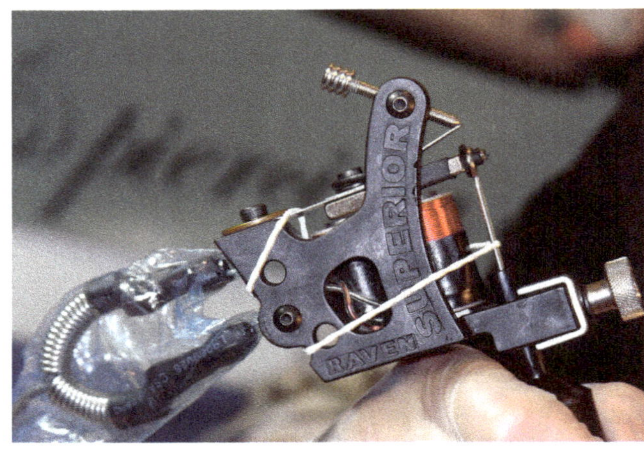

The next machine is equipped with a 7 Mag set of needles to create the wider shaded sections of the black base.

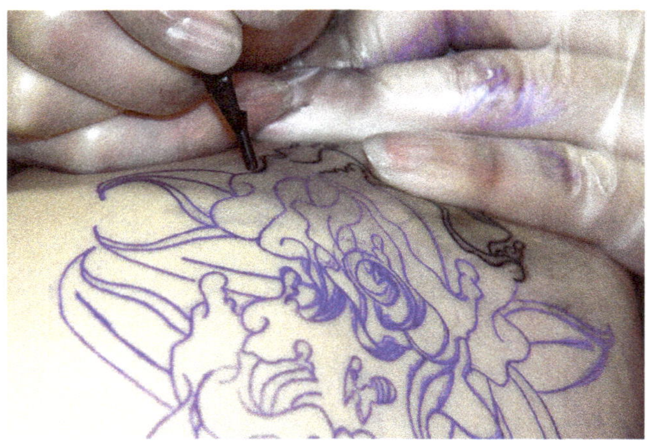

The outline process moves quickly while future steps require a bit more time.

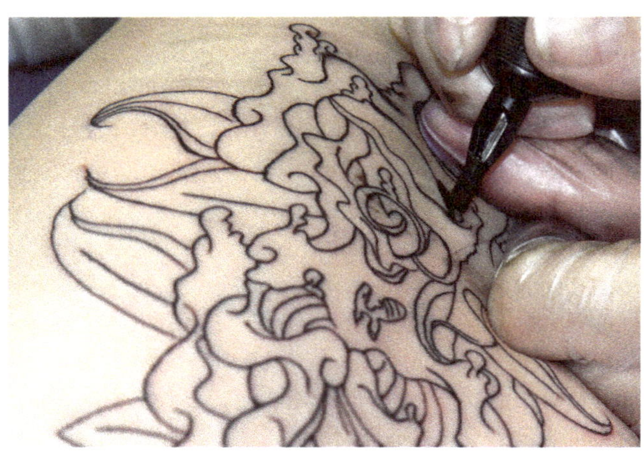

Shading is created using short, staccato motions, details are revealed quickly.

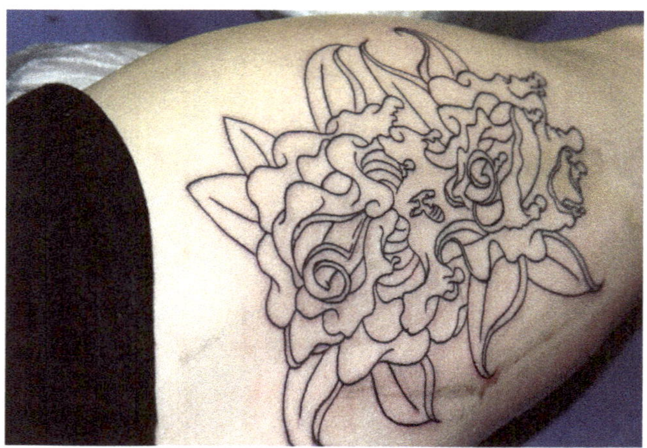

An early look at the ink with the outline complete, ready for shading to be added.

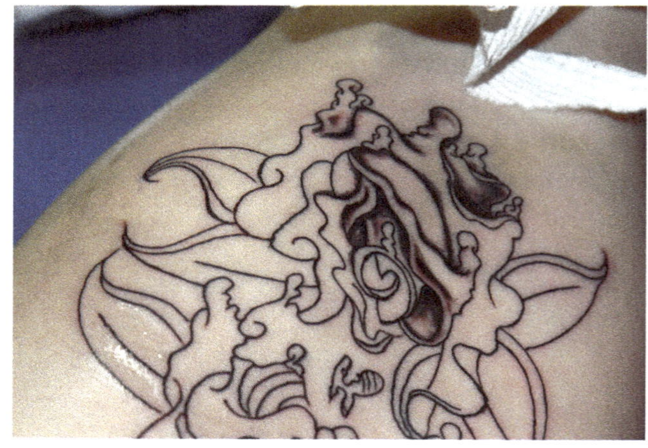

Cleaning the area of excess ink gives a much cleaner view and tells Harley what section gets attention next.

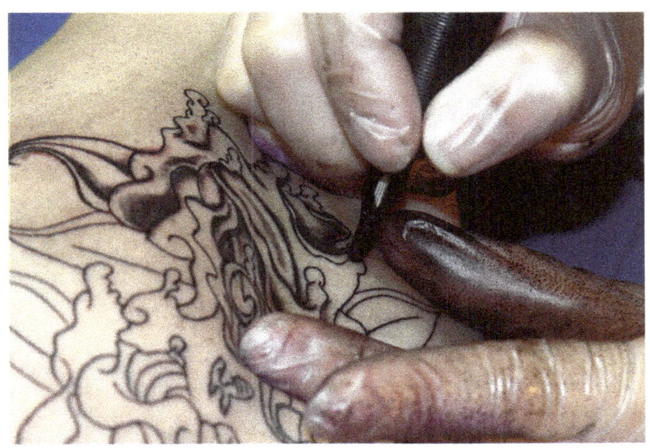

Using his fingers to hold the skin taught allows him to create a smoother surface, before applying ink.

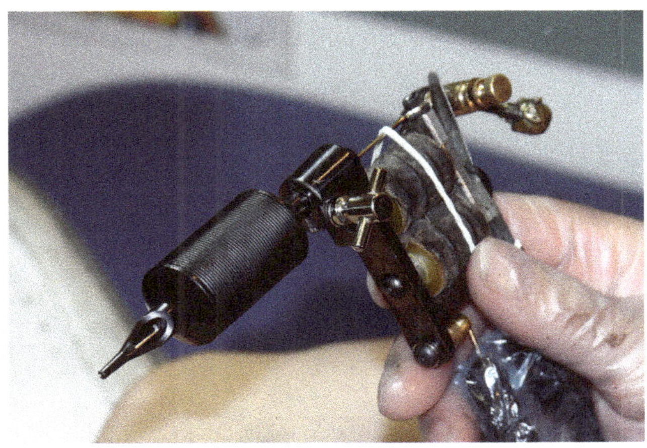

Fitted with an 8 round shader set of needles will allow Harley to add sharper bits of shading to the ink.

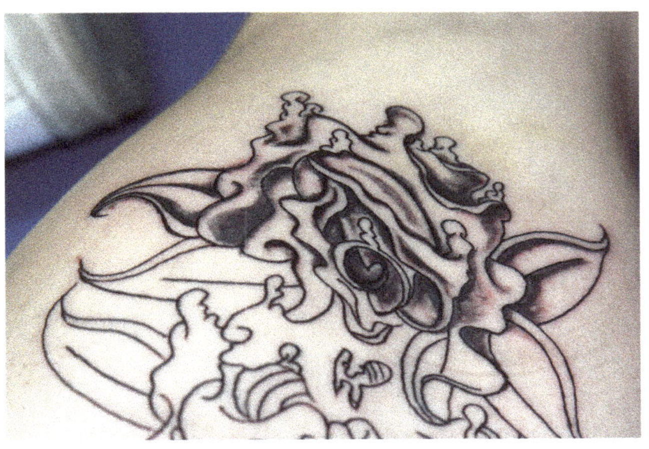

Another view when wiped clean shows how the shading adds so much depth to the art.

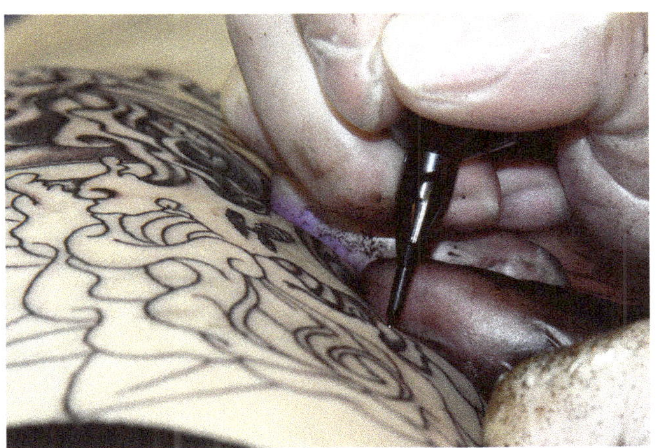

Using a much smaller set of needles will let Harley add finer focus to the shaded segments.

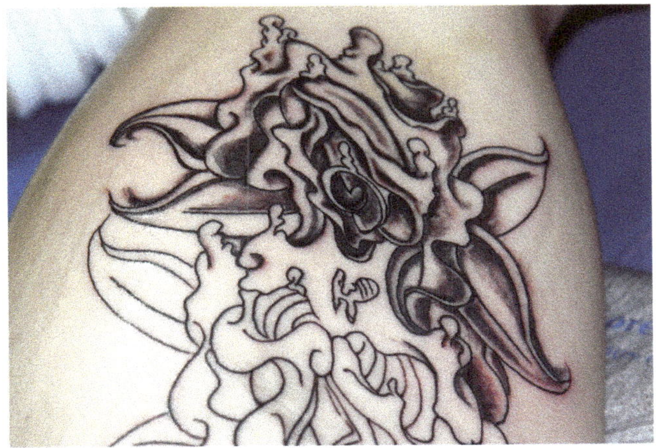

Having added the shaded section to the lower part of the tattoo means Harley will switch machines and begin adding some finer details to the skin.

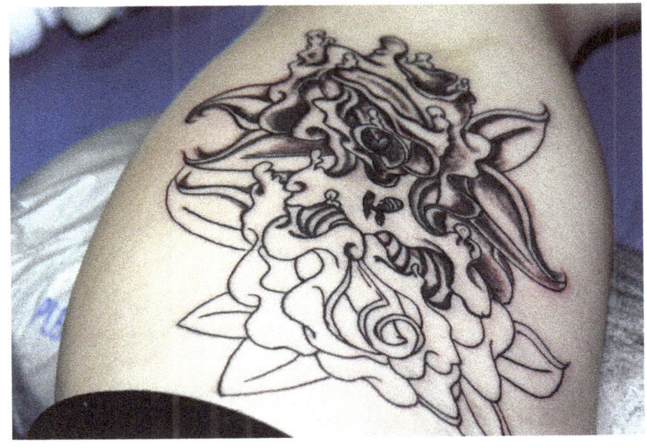

Periodically cleansing the area to check on progress we can now see how his efforts take shape, all with no trace of blood.

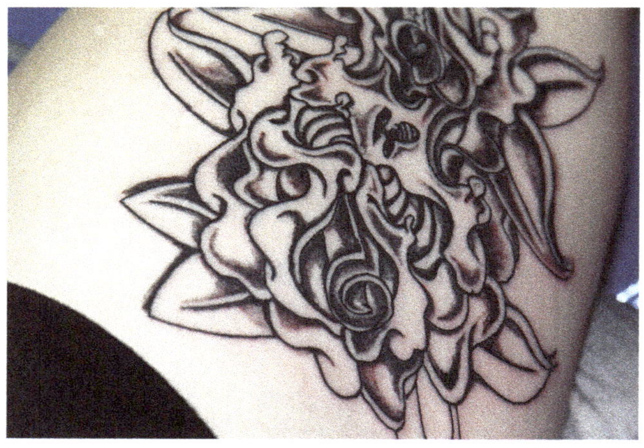

The added shading completed using the smaller needle set can now be seen as more depth is created with every step in the process.

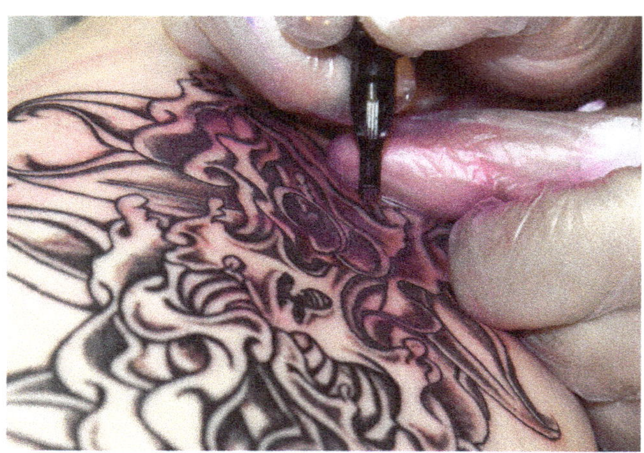

The first color adds some real intensity to the design and further use of colors will only enhance the theme.

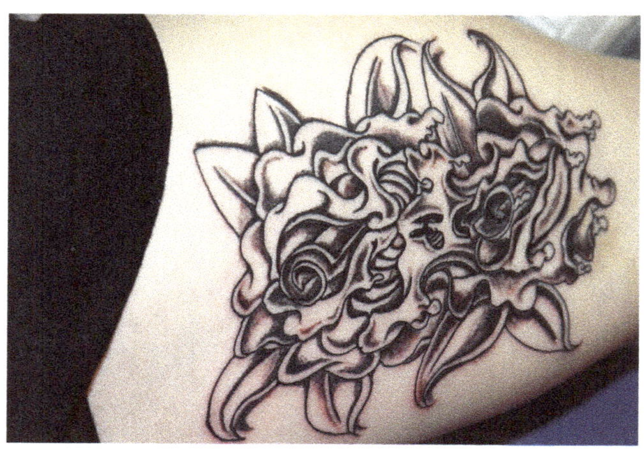

Returning to the larger 7 mag set of needles additional shading was added to the piece which measures about 6 in. x 9 in. overall.

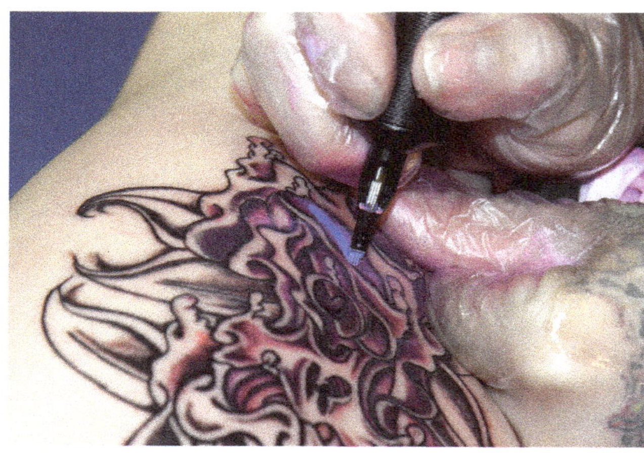

Staying with the 7 mag but switching to Bloodline Morning Glory ink will bring a more subtle change to the art.

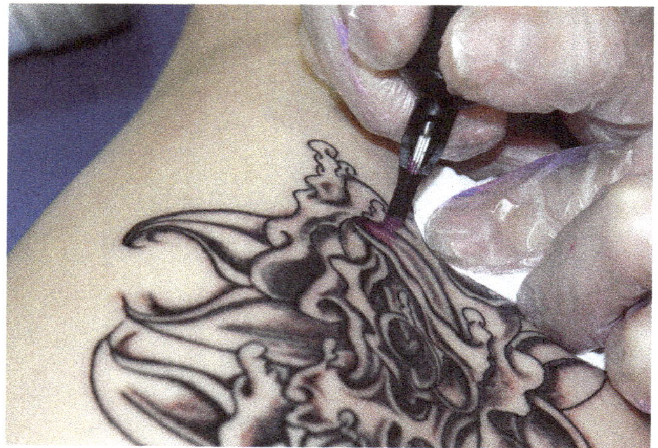

Loading the machine with Bloodline Violet ink and using the 7 mag set will give Harley a chance to fill in large areas of color.

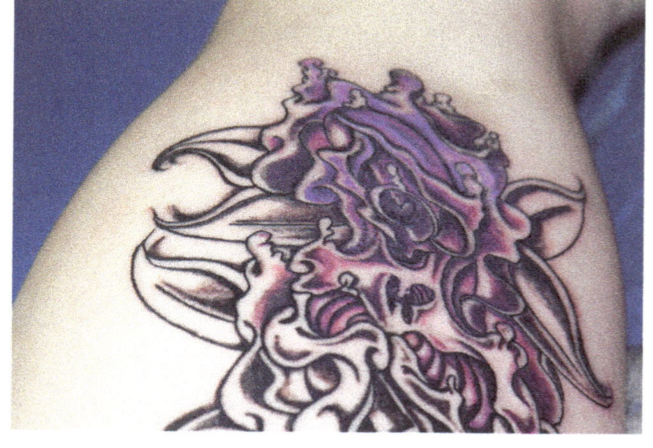

Before he changes to another color ink Harley previews his efforts so far and gets ready for the next stage.

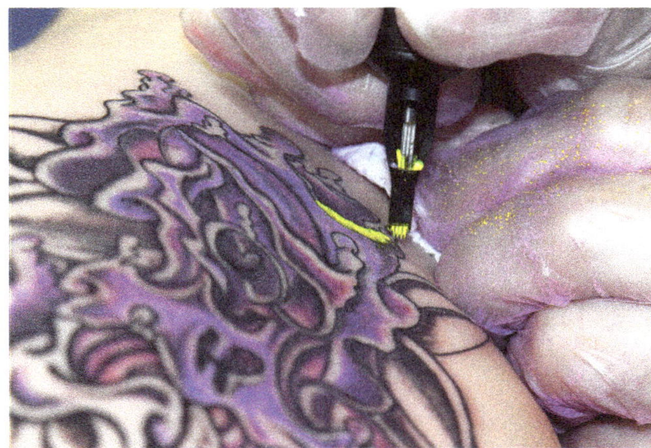

Choosing Bloodline Canary Yellow ink is a stark contrast to the dark ink already in place but adds more depth to the design.

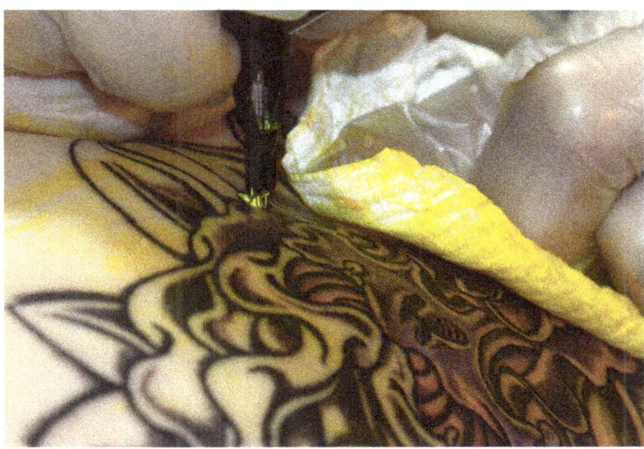

After reviewing the work he decides that additional Canary Yellow is needed and quickly adds fresh color.

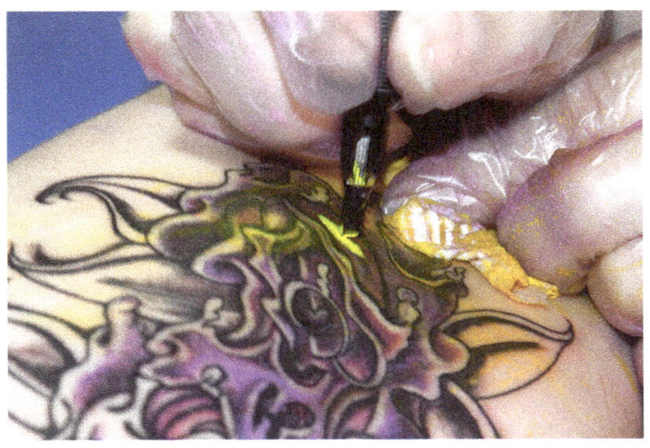

Prior to cleaning the area being dosed with Canary Yellow we can see the mess that's caused by adding each color.

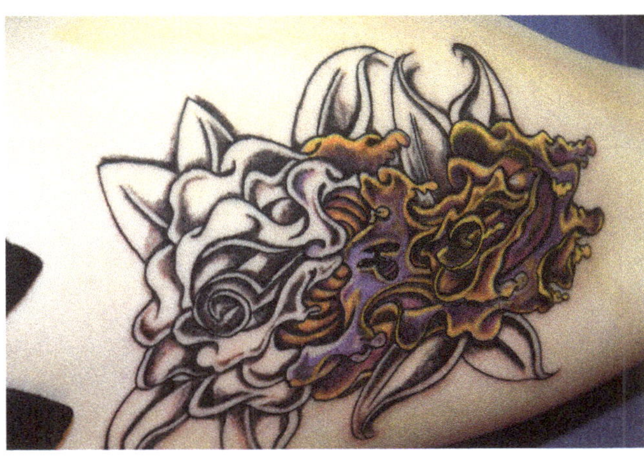

For now the first colors are done and he readies himself to bring another hue to the tattoo.

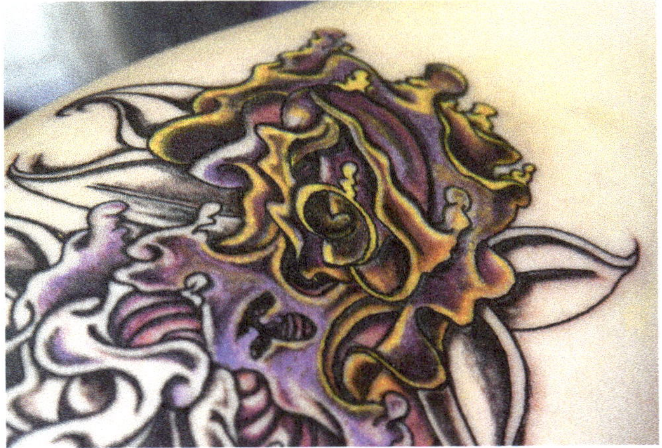

Once again cleaned of the excess ink we see how the bright yellow adds a new dimension to the art.

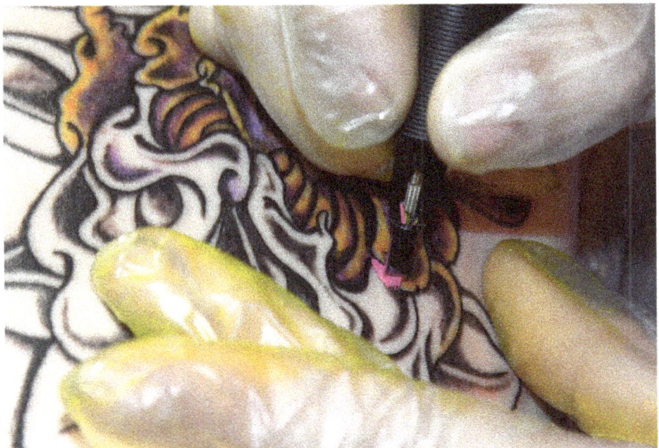

The same 7 mag needle set is loaded with Bloodline Magenta and Harley returns to the scene of the crime.

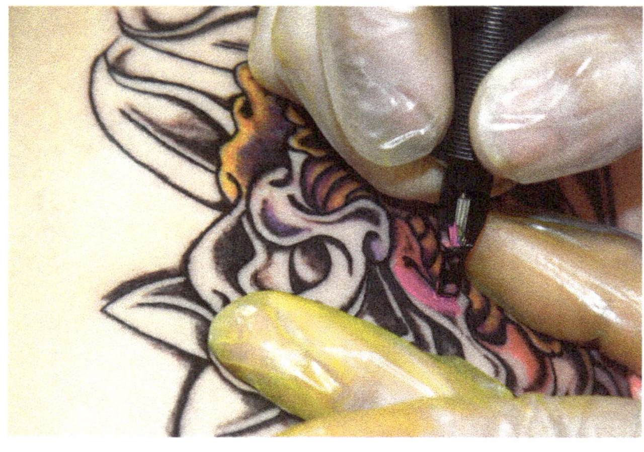

Some fairly large segments are filled with the colorful ink and will bring some vivid action to the finished piece.

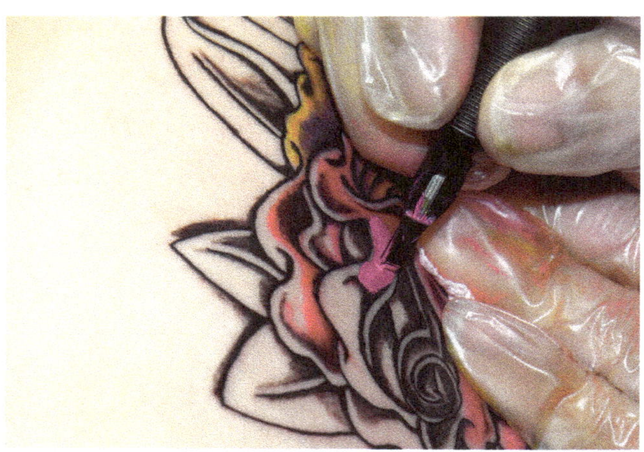

A few more dashes of magenta are laid down before he will once again wipe the art clean to review his efforts.

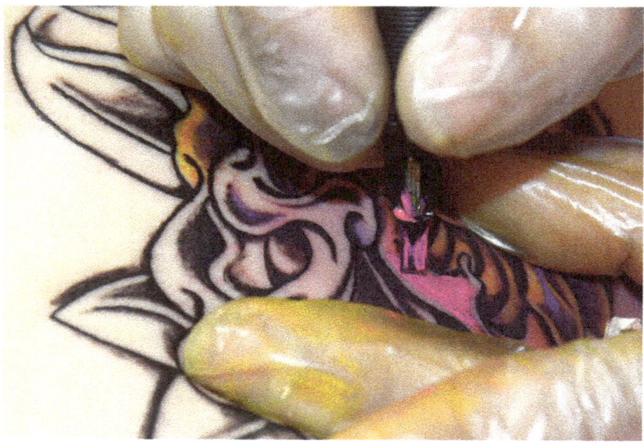

Having planned out the design in his head before even starting, Harley knows where he wants each color and what intensity to choose.

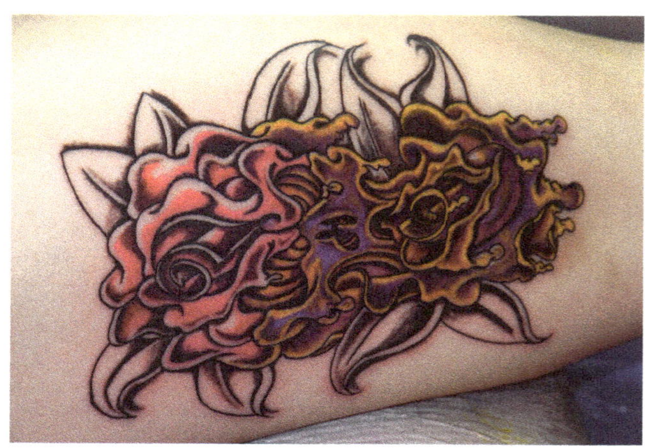

Standing back to view the design he can easily spot areas that require attention and which are OK as they are.

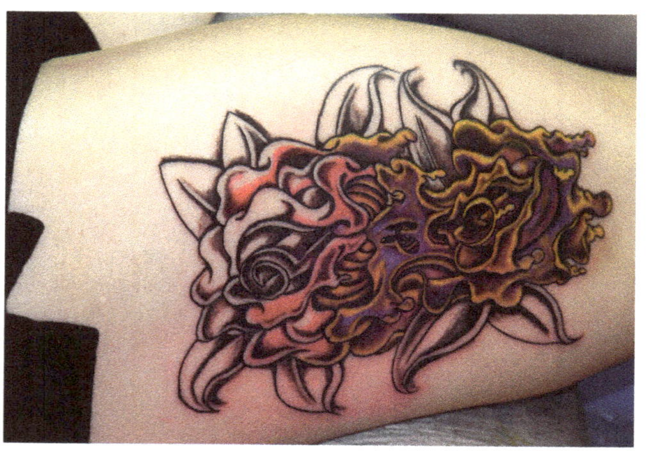

Taking another clean view tells Harley which direction to go next and when to select the next hue.

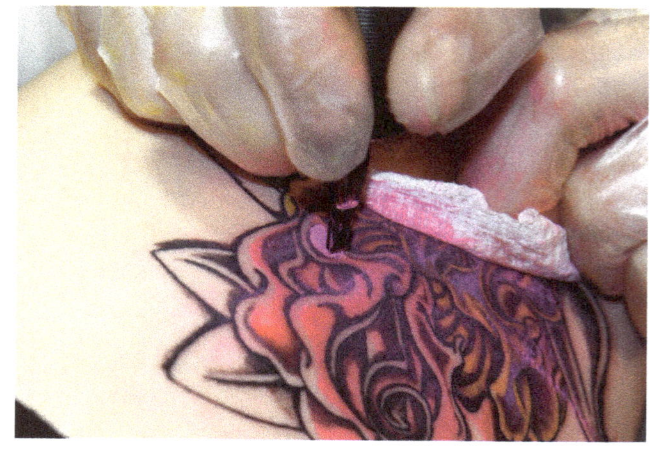

Sticking with the 7 mag needles he has now loaded Bloodline Rasberry into the machine to add an even brighter color to the layout.

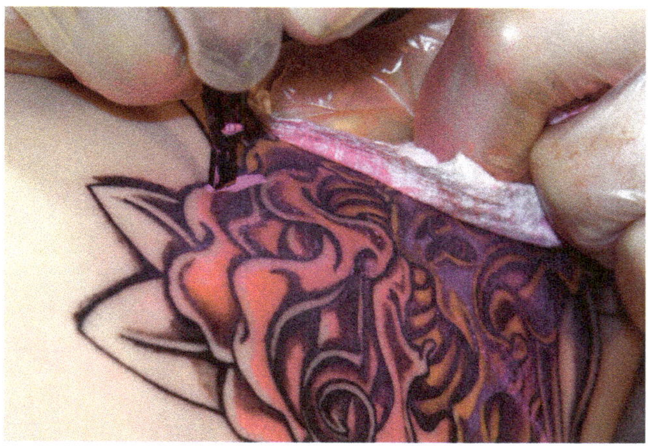

Moving swiftly but carefully Harley can easily monitor his own progress as each segment is moved further ahead.

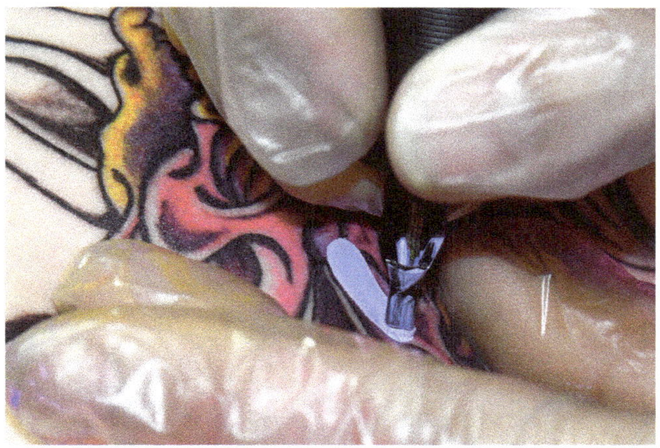

Tapping into the wide array of colors from Bloodline, Purple Rain is now selected for application.

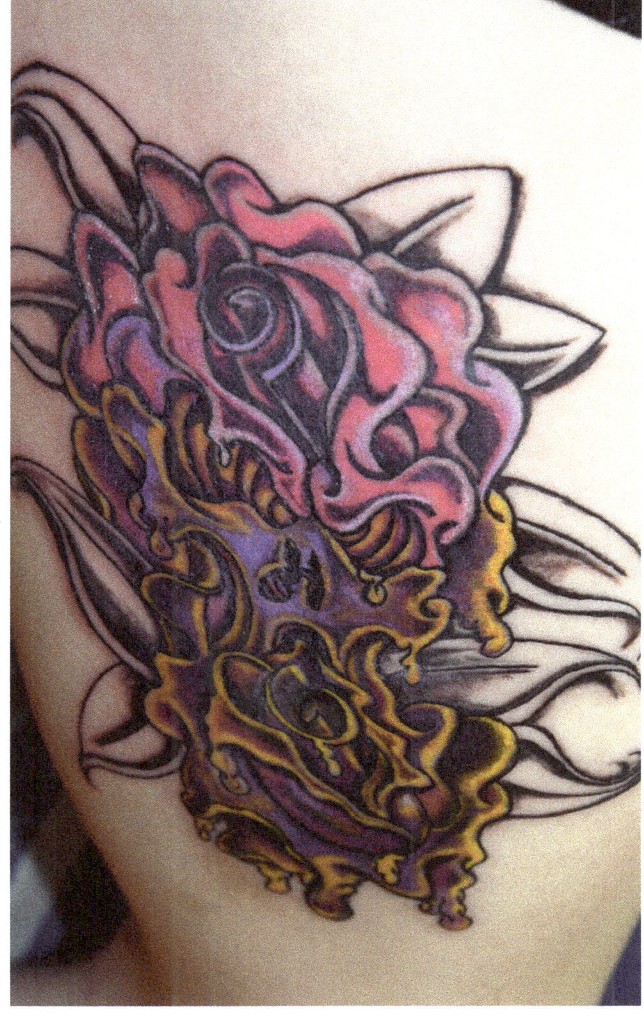

His use of a variety of purple, yellow and black can now be seen before the next batch of colors gets applied.

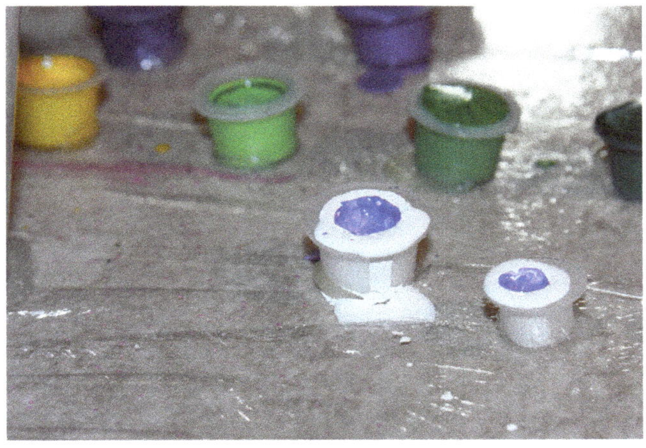

As Harley gets further along he turns to blending inks to achieve the perfect shade he needs for the tattoo being created.

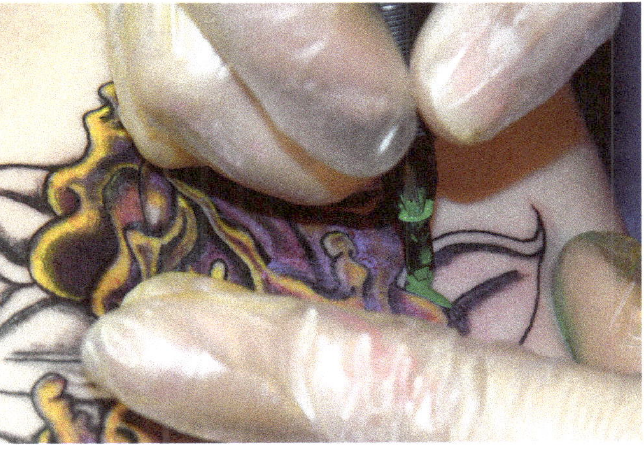

Turning his attentions to the leaves he chooses Bloodline Sassy Grass for the first shade of green.

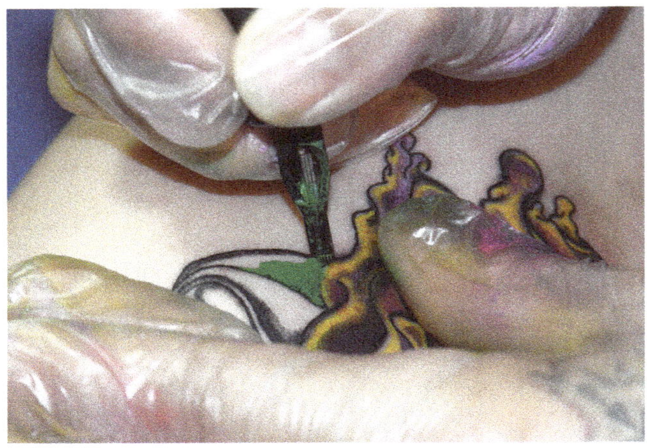

Still employing the 7 mag needle set he can fill in large spaces without a ton of effort.

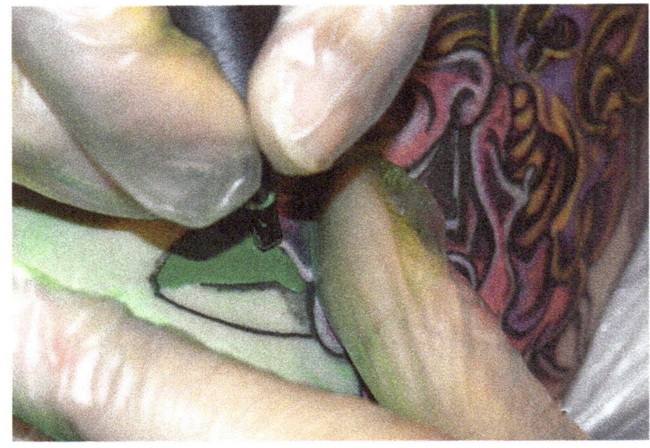

Despite the fact that the leaves are fairly similar in shape, Harley uses an altered motion for each to achieve a different texture from one to the next.

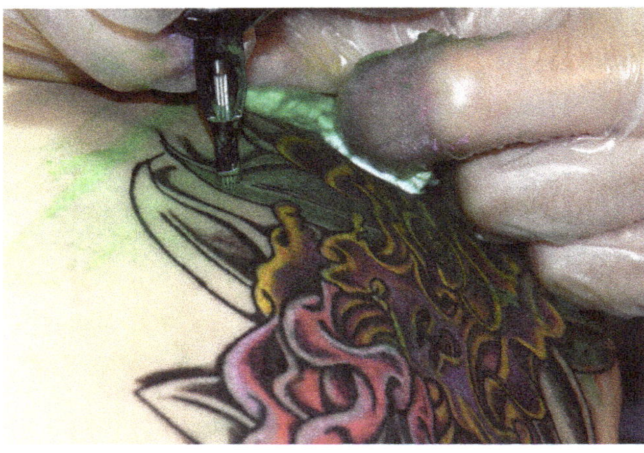

The grouping of needles found in a 7 mag setup are seen clearly here as a wide swatch of green is added to the leaf.

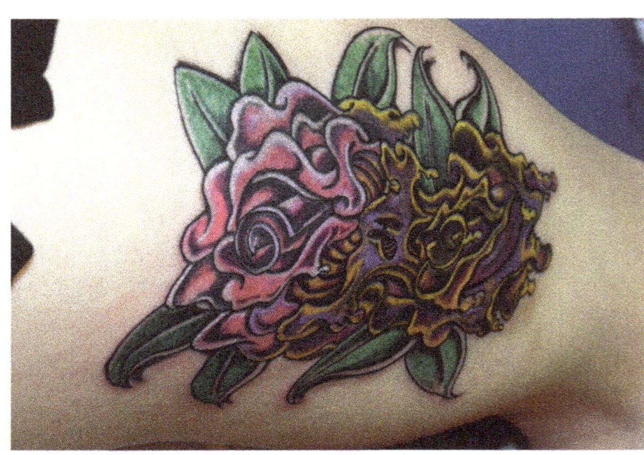

Slowly approaching the end of the process the palette of colors gets richer with every touch of the needle to the skin.

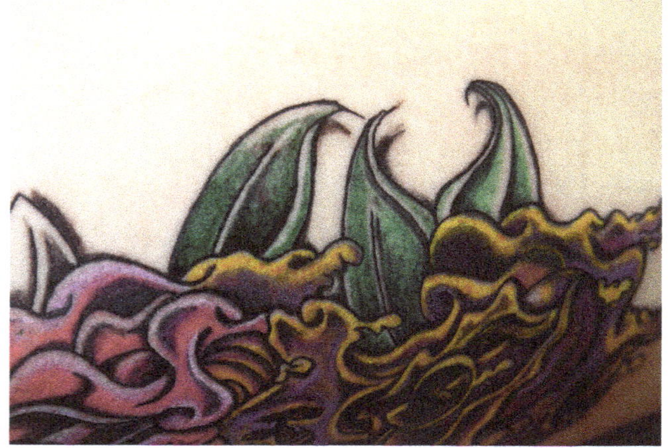

Another quick review of his efforts so far shows the first stages of filling in the leaves on the design.

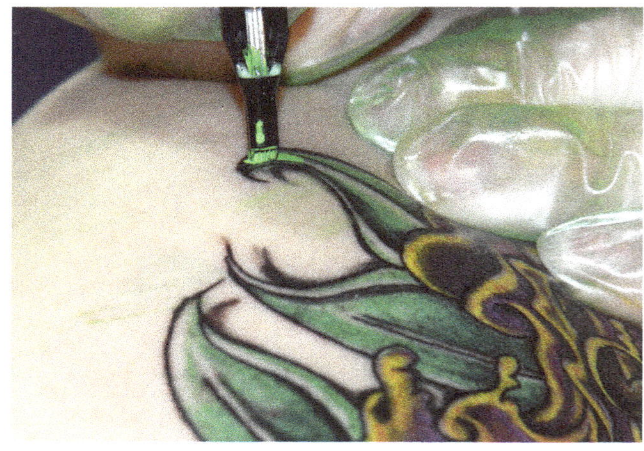

In an effort to add some subtle contours to the leaves, he now uses some Candy Lime ink to achieve the desired results.

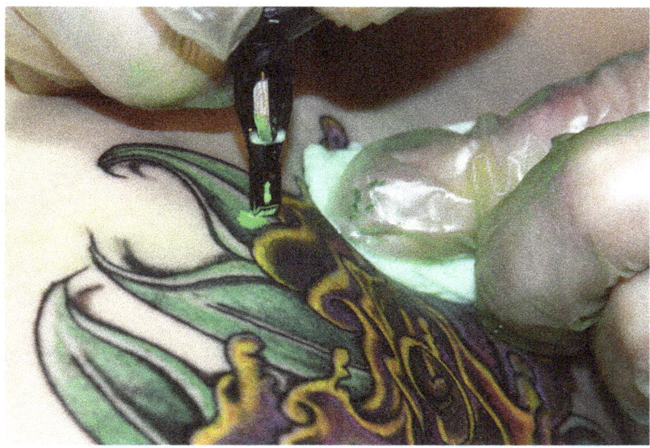

His hand motions are subtle yet bring more depth to the art with every movement as he builds up the colors on each portion of the art.

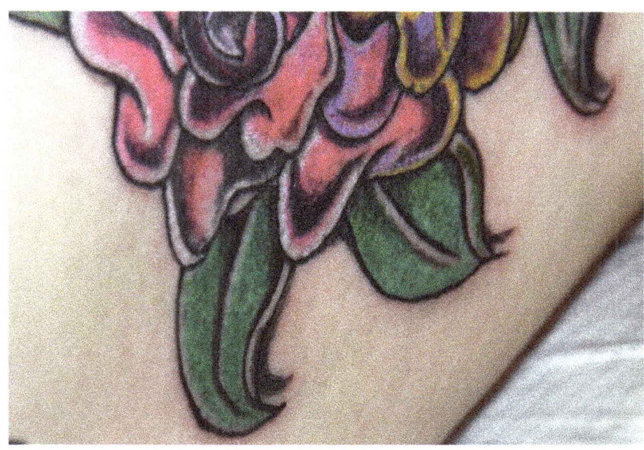

Completing the leaves is one of the last steps required as Harley nears the end of the tattoo process.

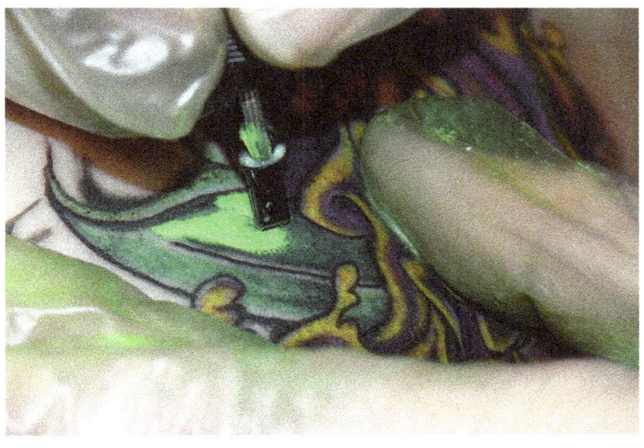

Adding a larger swatch of Candy Lime to the existing Sassy Grass creates a soft contour of colors that help to shape the leaf.

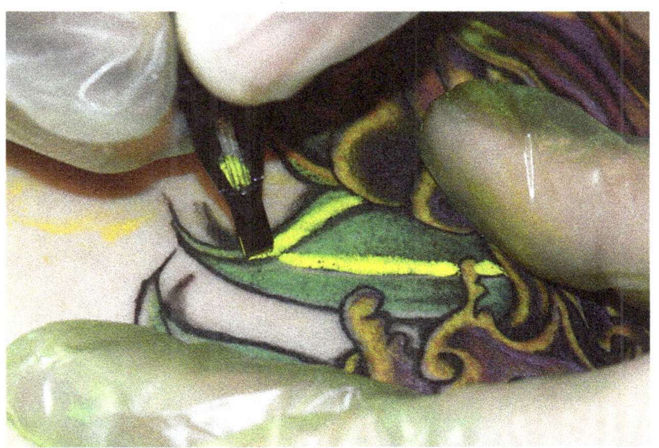

Returning to the Canary Yellow used previously...

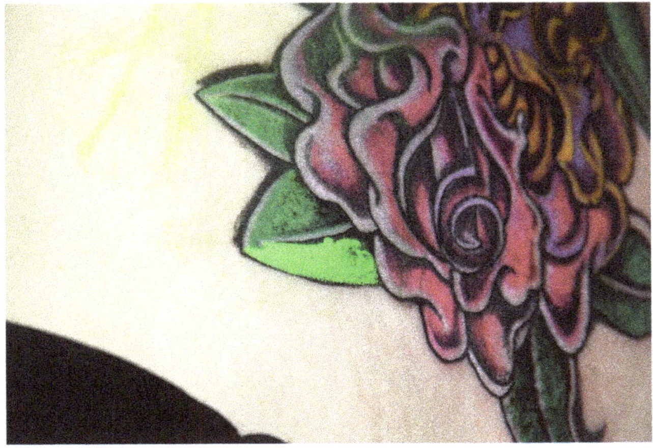

The results of his careful use of colors provide us with a life like sample of mother nature in the leaves.

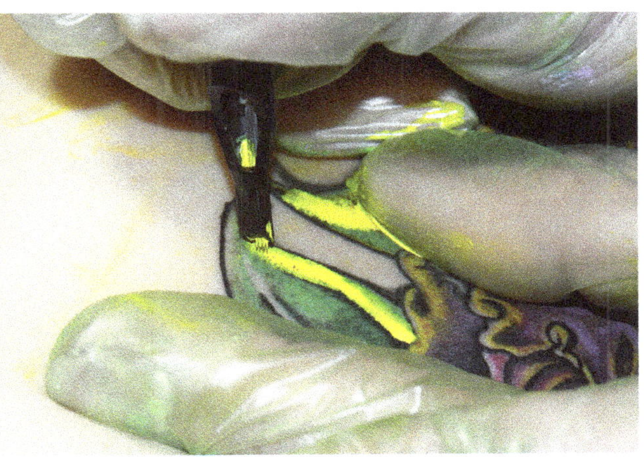

... Harley adds a few tiny details to the leaves for extra definition.

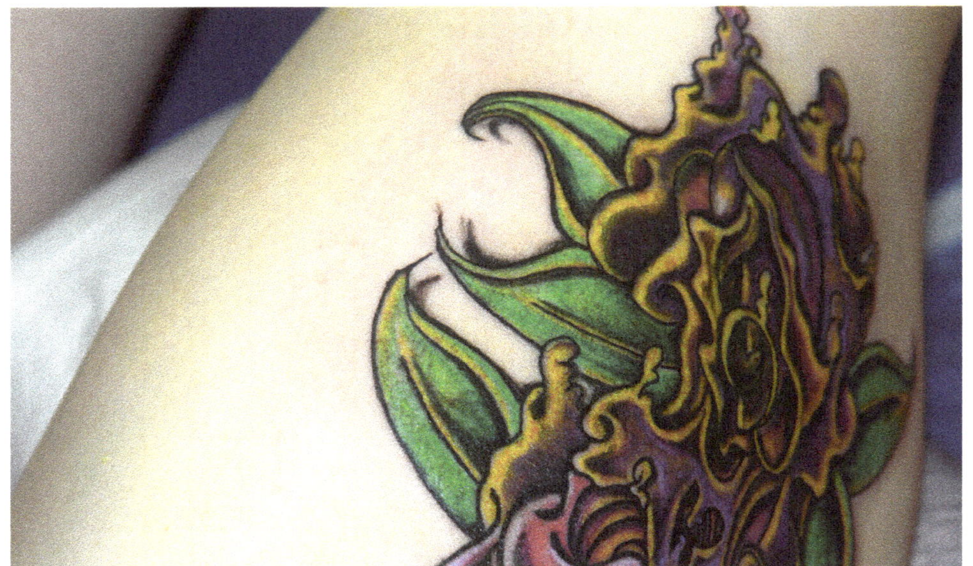

Nearly completed, Harley peruses his work and decides where to add a few hints of white.

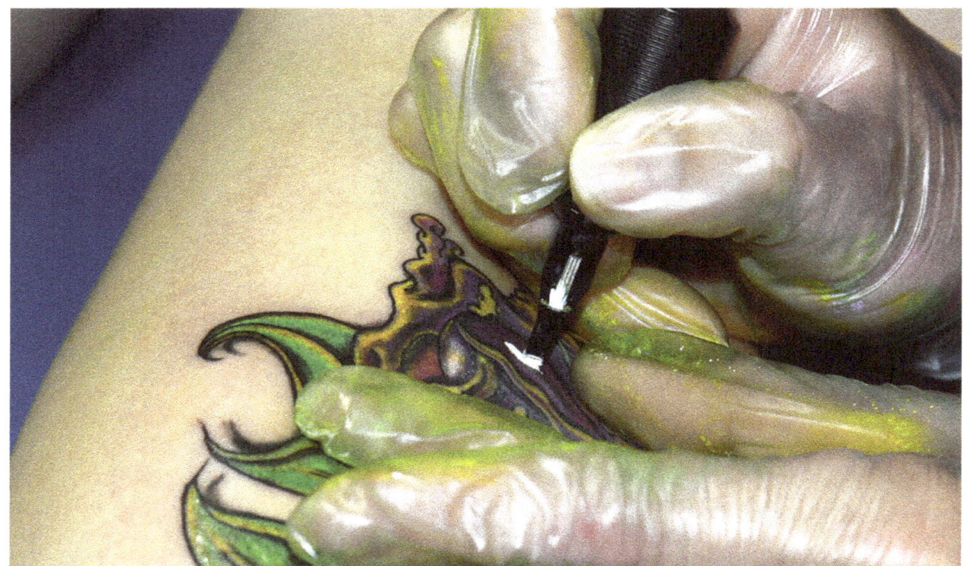

In most tattoos white is the final color used, applied sparingly only to accent the areas that require a hint of the bright hue.

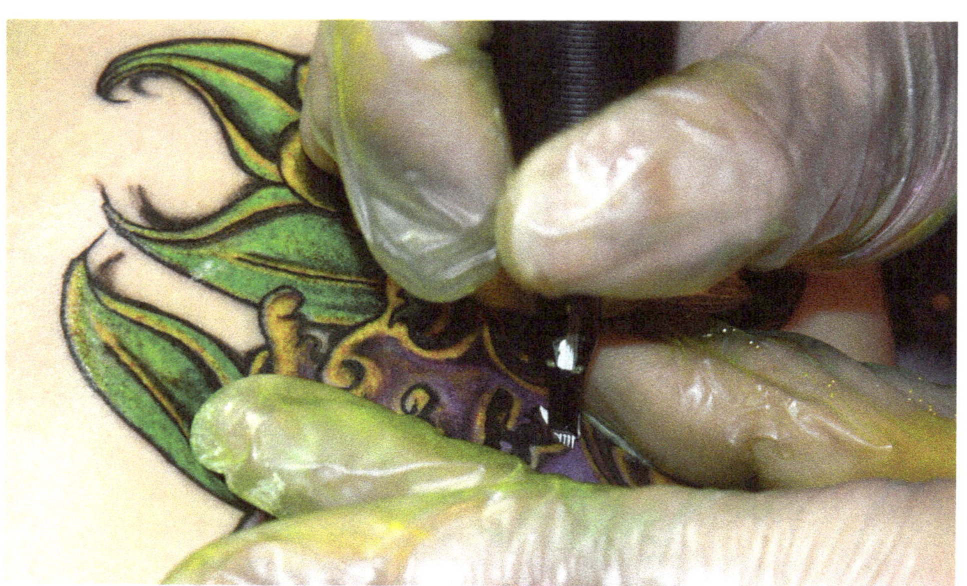

Compared to the time it took to create the rest of the design, adding a touch of white takes less than a few minutes and the piece is complete.

Q&A: Harley Freeland

When did people realize you had creative skills?

It was pretty early, I think in kindergarten teachers started to watch me as I doodled and drew things when I was supposed to be paying attention.

When did you get interested in tattoos?

I was really young and liked the colors and designs of those I saw. I also kind of liked the rebellious nature of the people who wore them although I wasn't sure what it meant then.

Who did you get your first guidance or instruction from?

Bruce Clevenger and Kip Edwards both showed me their own styles and from that I was able to begin my own process and designs.

Do you get inspiration from anyone in the industry?

I see new work all the time that inspires me, and Bob Terrel is one artist I continue to look to as an artist I admire.

When did you do your first tattoo and what was the subject?

It was in 2010 and it was a colorful piece of a biohazard logo with flames.

When was your first experience at a shop?

Once again it was 2010 at Legacy Tattoo here in Peoria.

Do you have a favorite style?

When I get the chance I like creating tats that fall into the "graffiti" style but at this stage anything that's a challenge is great.

What was your biggest piece so far?

I did a complete back at least once and they usually take several sessions to complete due to the complexity and discomfort experienced over such a long period.

What changes have you seen in the world of tattoos?

It seems as if people are leaning towards anime and cartoon designs more these days along with improved inks, colors and equipment upgrades.

How long have you been at this location?

It's only been about a year since we took the shop over and began making changes to the layout and décor to improve the appearance of the place.

Any plans for the future?

I hope to continue to improve this shop as well as attract more clients. Being kind of a newbie it will take some time to get fresh customers, but I think that over time it will become a full time thing for me.

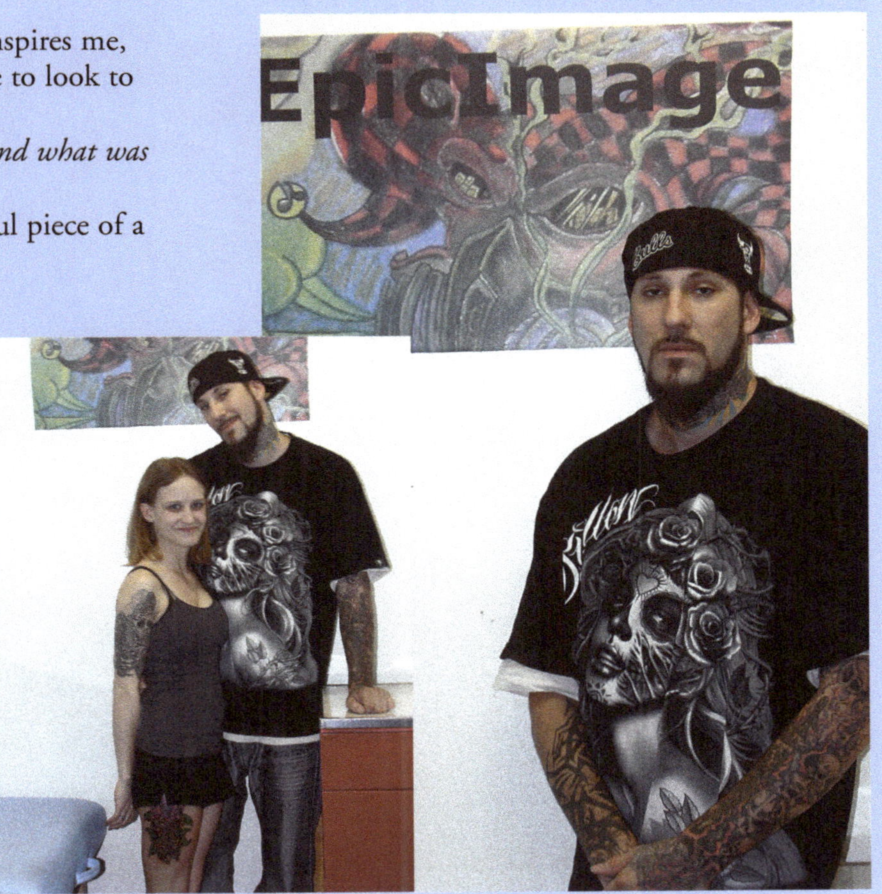

Harley and his significant other Nicole share the spotlight as she wears his latest design on her leg.

Chapter Nine

Chris Blinston

Big Brain 2 Tattoo & Piercing Studio

In some ways, Chris Blinston is like many of the other talented artists we have been introduced to in this book. He has no formal training in the world of art, but is still highly talented in creating the colorful tattoos we get to experience. Unlike many of the people we have seen, his work tends to lean towards the more realistic side of the scale. His chosen genre is in the "colorful realism" column by choice. He enjoys creating and applying tattoos that are nearly photographic in their detail, yet colorful enough to be real attention grabbers.

His first experience in the art world came while

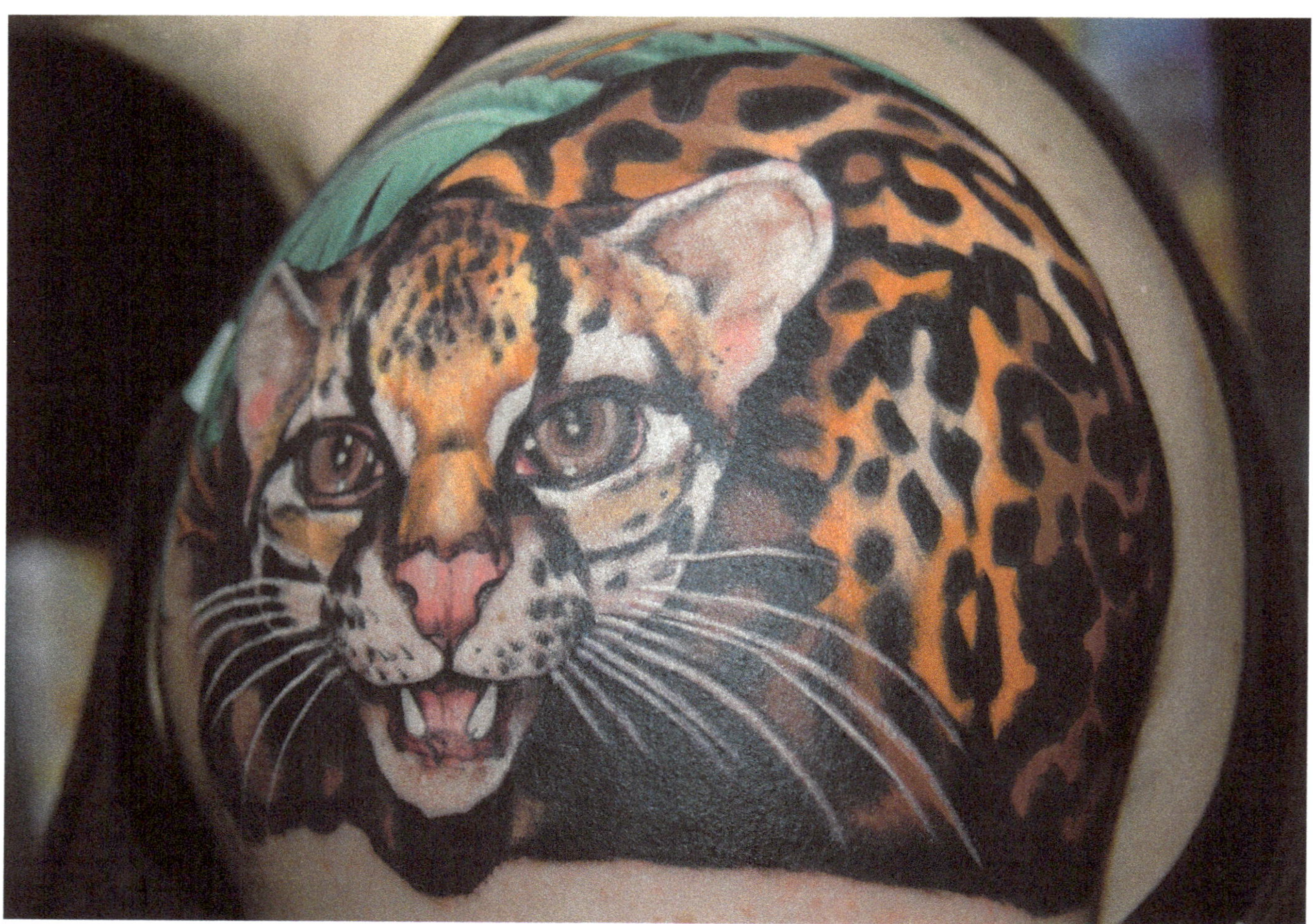

Another tattoo created at the Hell City show was this life-like margay image. Liam had also made plans to work with Chris again after having his first piece done while on his honeymoon in Florida. Chris creates a lot of his work in this realistic format, but can also produce tattoos in almost any genre requested.

he was still a youngster, but it was obvious that he was fairly gifted from the beginning. His early efforts at drawing and painting led him to his stint in the U.S. Marines, where fellow soldiers badgered him into turning his art into tattoos. He was not crazy about the idea at first, and didn't really enjoy the medium, but grew to see the challenges offered by the new form of art. As time went by his ability to translate illustrations into artwork on skin became apparent, leading to his opening of Big Brain 1 in Nebraska.

Once setting needle to skin, he begins his works with the standard black outline. Soon after this simple task has been accomplished he turns his efforts to making the piece a signature of his work. Bold use of outlining and shading are complimented by realistic use of colors and contours. Upon completion of this margay tattoo, we can almost feel the fur that covers the small cat's body. The eyes and mouth appear as menacing as they can from a cat that only measures about 40 inches in length. In life, the tail of the margay can take up nearly 16 inches of that number, leaving a medium sized cat to lead the way.

Another unusual trait of Chris' work is his use of a wide needle set to accomplish 98% of the piece. Many artists select and set up 2 to 6 different machines with their desired needle sizes loaded for ready use. Chris uses a smaller 7 round needle for the primary outline, then switches to a really wide 15 mag for the remaining work. By using the full width of the needles he can easily fill in large segments with a minimum of fuss. Turning the needles on their edge gives him a precise point to add small details to the piece. This method saves time and effort but does not compromise the quality of the work. In contrast to watching the other artists in this book use a range of needles, it was surprising to see the level of flexibility provided by the use of one large needle set.

Once Chris had applied the heat transfer art to the arm of the recipient, he turned to a set of felt tip markers to draw in some additional background for the piece. Since the person getting the ink had only supplied Chris with the image of the margay, it was up to him to create the balance of the required art. The addition of the foliage behind the cat delivered a more symmetrical balance and filled in the

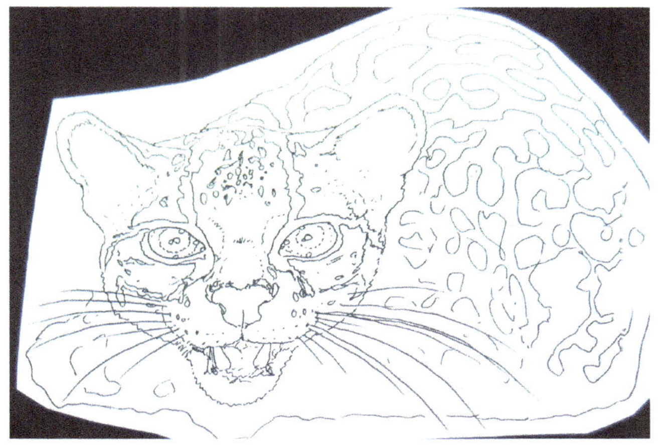

The sketch to become a tattoo has already been printed on heat transfer paper, and is ready for placement.

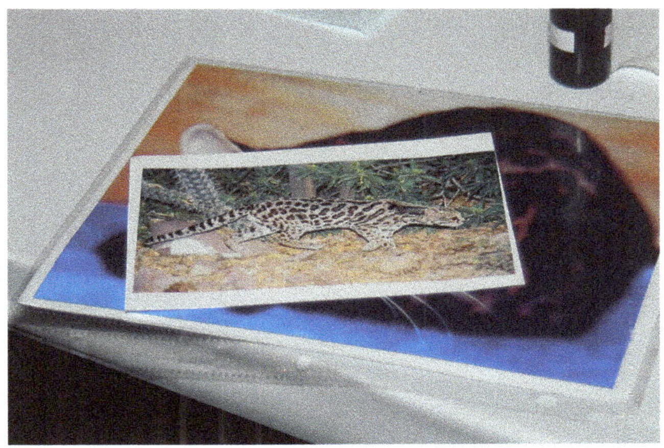

Providing additional detail information are these printed materials in photographic form.

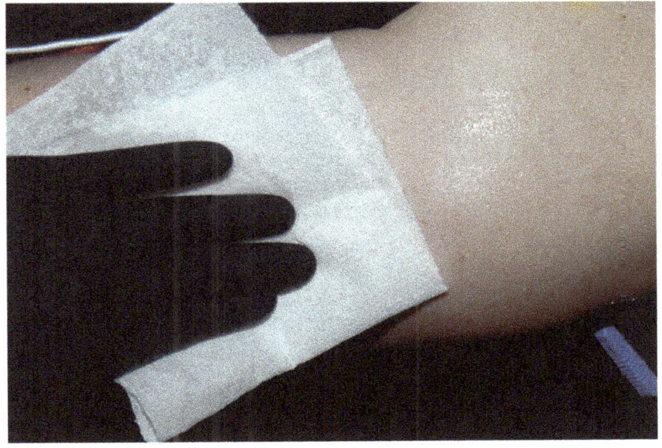

The target area is wiped down with a sanitizing solution.

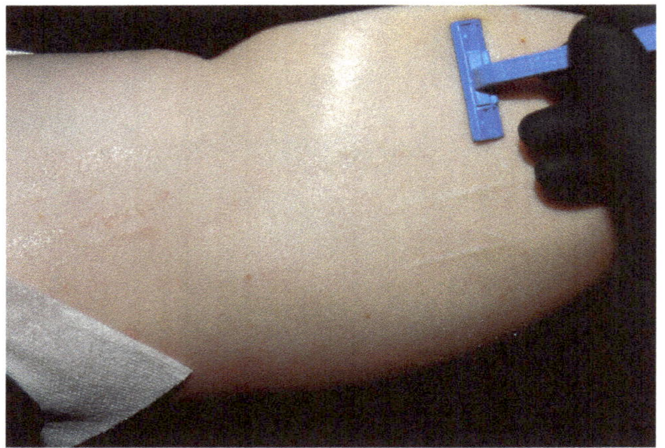

The affected area is then shaved for a clean work surface.

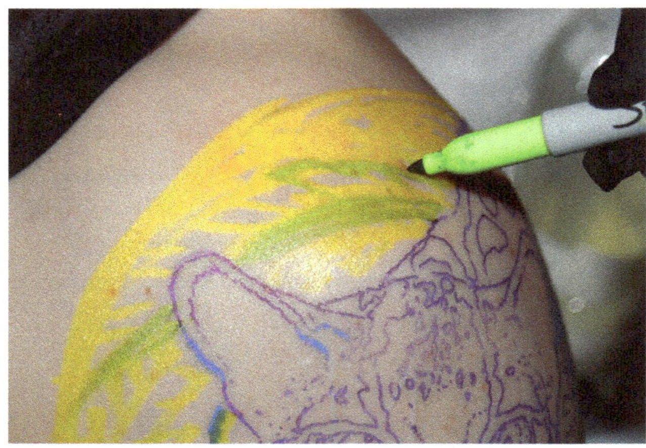

Chris wants to add some foliage to the image to insure a symmetrical tattoo upon completion.

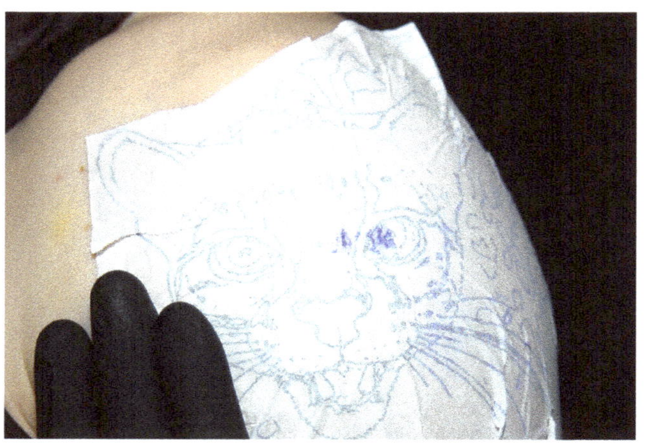

The heat transfer print is placed in position and rubbed by hand to make a clean print.

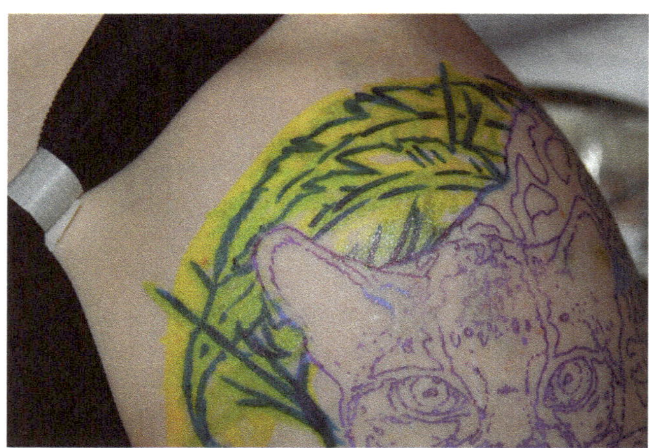

Using permanent markers, the additional details are drawn into place.

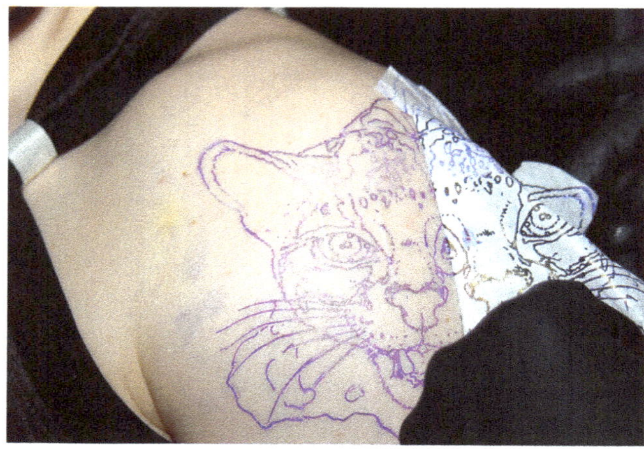

Peeling away the backing paper leaves the intended illustration.

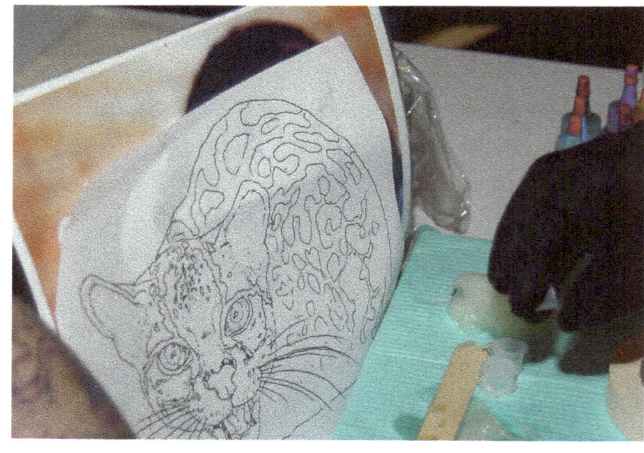

Set up for the tattoo begins with a copy of the original sketch on hand for review.

space nicely. Viewing how easily Chris added the broad leaves of the jungle greenery it was obvious that his talents went beyond the needle work he was known for.

The black and brown colors of the cat's fur were achieved by first laying down what seemed like acres of black ink. This process can seem quite confusing to an outsider like myself, even after witnessing several other tattoos being created. The mind of the tattoo artist is usually about 14 steps ahead of mine as they go about creating their art. Once the black ink has been completed, Chris begins adding the browns to bring life to the "fur." I still find it amazing that after what appears to be a random wash of ink, the resulting placement of the remaining color adds to the realism and drama with every sting of the needle.

Chris moves rapidly during the process, while carrying on a pleasant conversation. There are those of us who have trouble walking and chewing gum at the same time, but Chris is obviously not in that group. His concentration is unflinching as he plies his craft, and his speed belies the results of his efforts. This tattoo was completed at the Hell City tattoo convention in Columbus, Ohio, and he had hopes of finishing the piece in time to enter it into the contest being held. Prizes were being awarded for artwork done at the show, and another notch in their belts are always welcome, as tattoo artists do their best to stand out from the crowd. Sure, the level of their work is truly the yardstick they are measured by, but a store window full of gleaming trophies hurts no one.

With the larger areas of color being complete, Chris turned his attention to adding the lighter hues and numerous details that would bring the cat to life. Highlights in the mouth, eyes and ears really brought the level of detail to the forefront, exactly what Chris had planned. I am continually stunned by the results achieved by the single touch of the needle. While seeming complete to me, Chris, as well as the rest of the others in this book, know how to add the final 2% to the project, bringing the total to about 110% in my opinion. Their vision of the final piece and the ability to translate that into reality is what makes these artists truly remarkable.

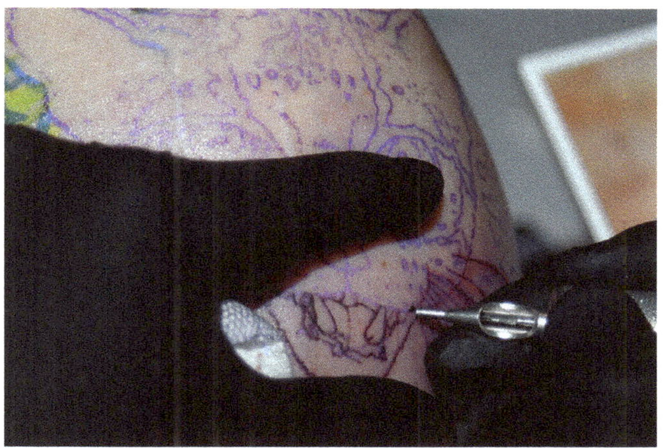

As usual, the black outline process is the first step in creating the art.

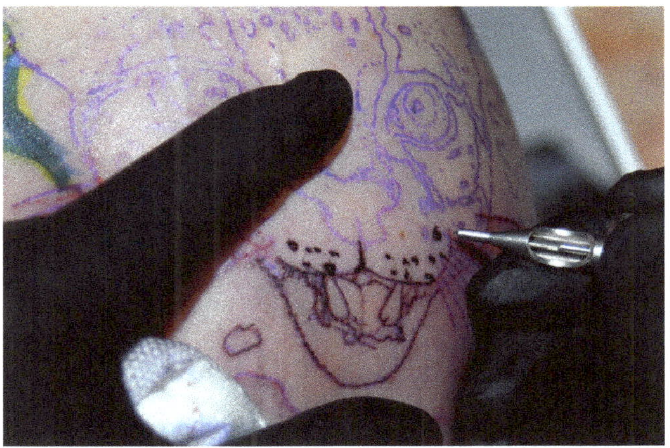

At this stage, a 7 round needle is used to do most of the basic outline on the piece.

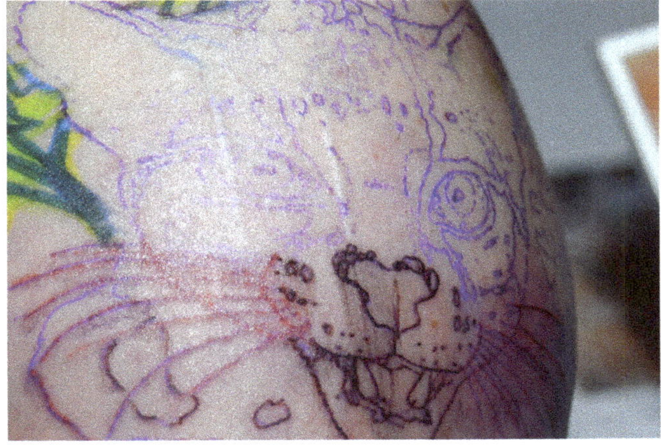

With a contest deadline looming, Chris works quickly to complete the basic outline.

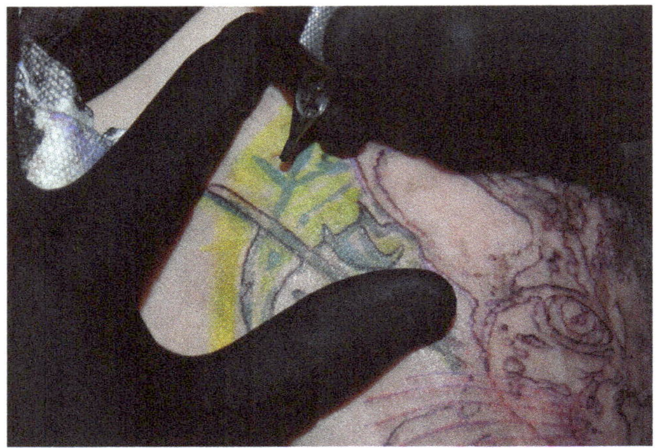

Moving to the marker area, Chris continues to add the required black outline.

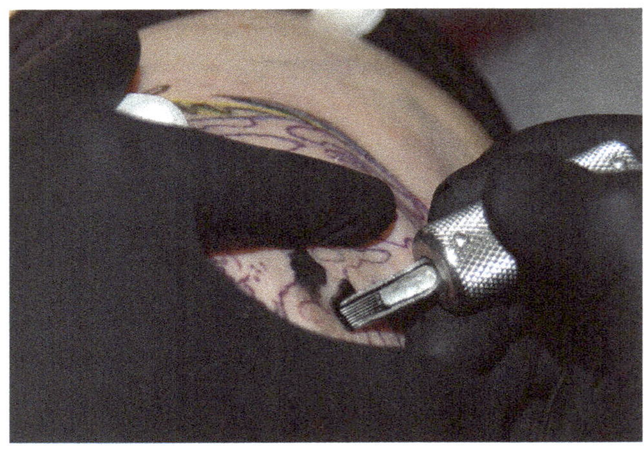

Chris switches to a 15 mag needle set for the balance of the tattoo, a style we haven't seen used in this book before.

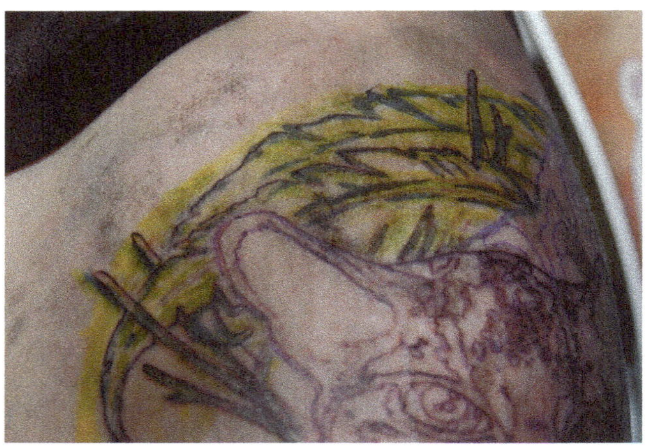

Within 15 minutes we can see the beginnings of the tattoo taking a more definite shape.

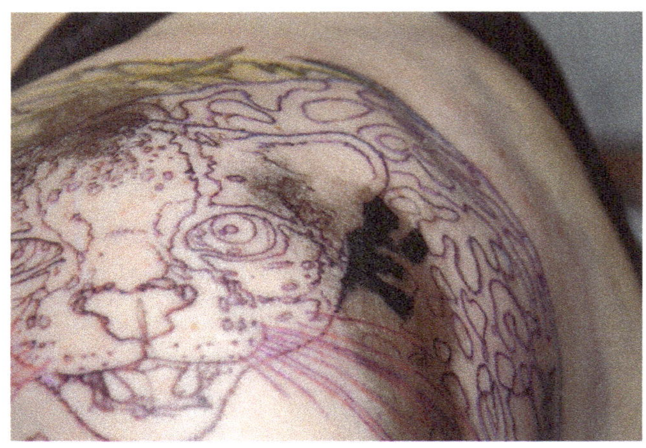

Large black areas get filled in quickly with the wide needles in action.

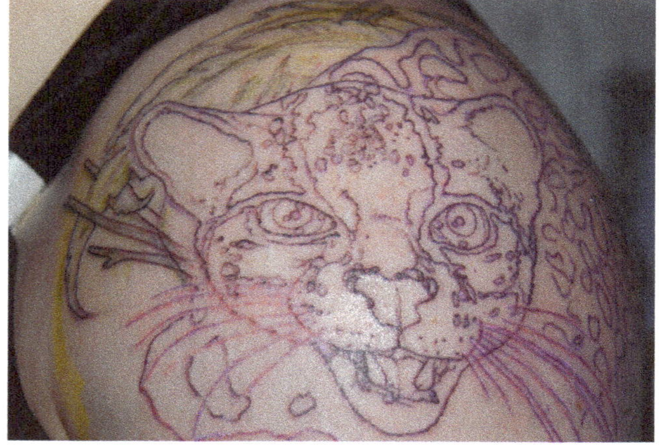

An initial cleaning reveals the outline work thus far.

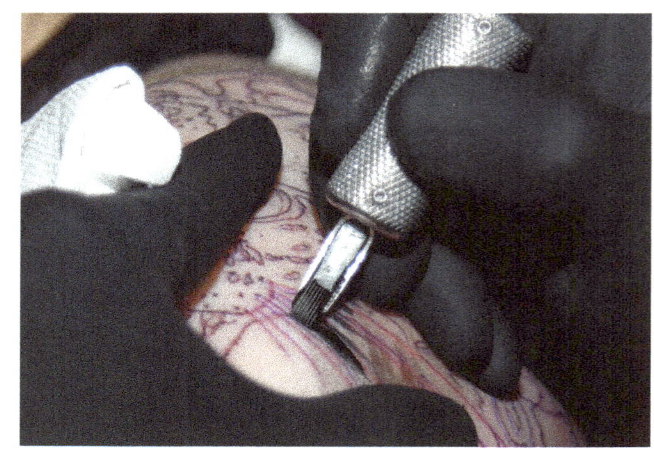

Chris works on the black areas between the brown first, covering a lot of ground in a hurry.

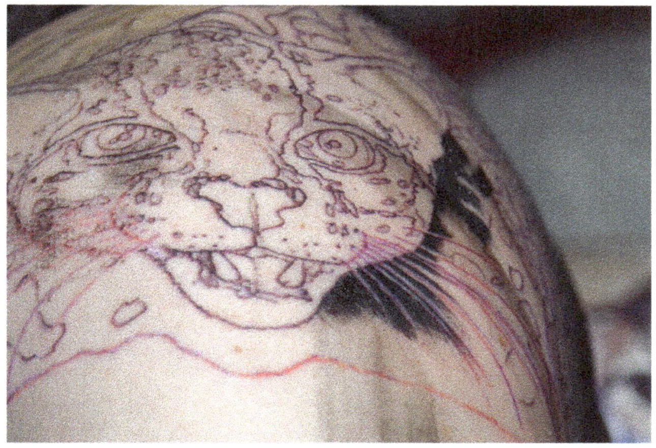

Applying ink around and between the whiskers of the margay will help to define them later on.

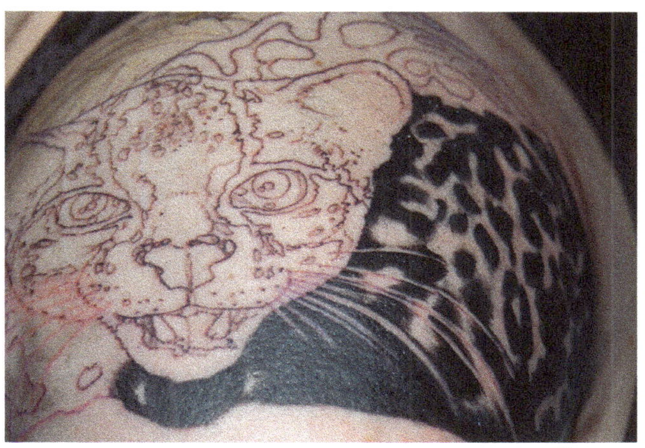

Only moments after beginning we can see the results of using the 15 mag needles.

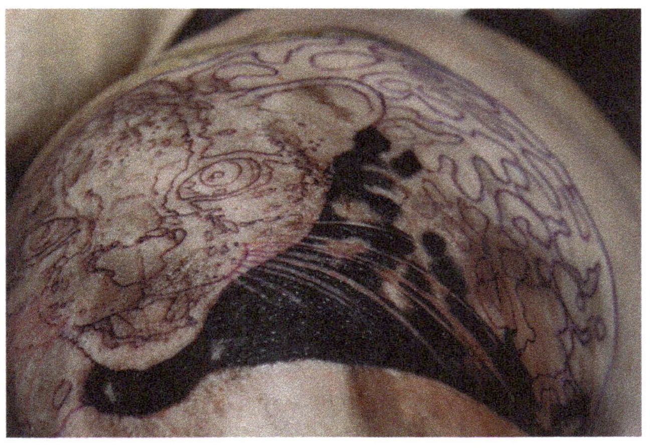

A large area has already been covered in black ink, setting the stage for the remaining efforts.

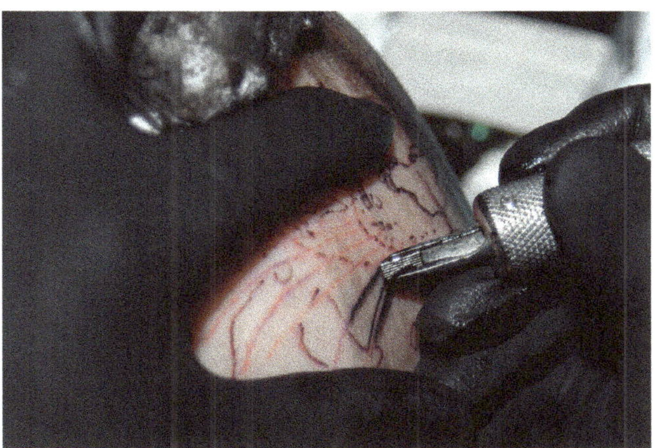

Moving to the opposite side of the face Chris begins to work around the second half of the whiskers.

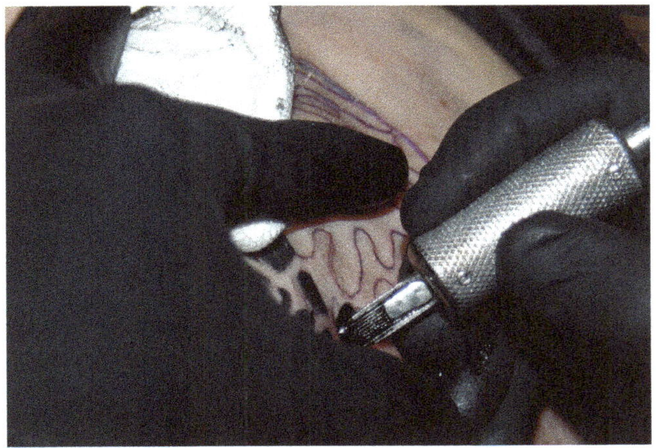

Similar to using a brush, the large set of needles lays down a swath of ink in a single touch.

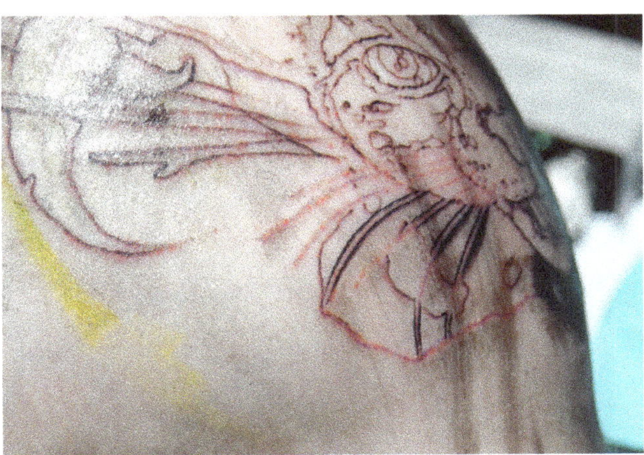

Even the smallest levels of ink can define the details that will soon become evident.

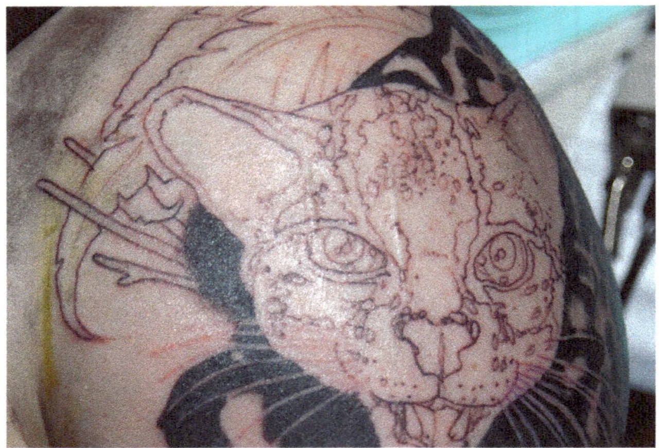

Now the entire underside of the cat's head has been defined with plenty more work to follow

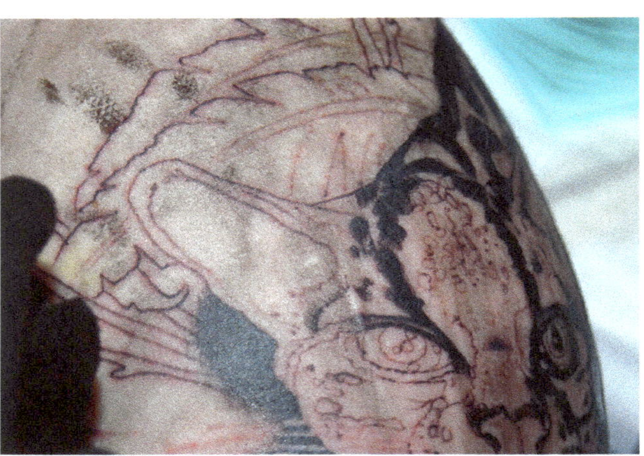

Additional facial definition is taking shape as the features are addressed.

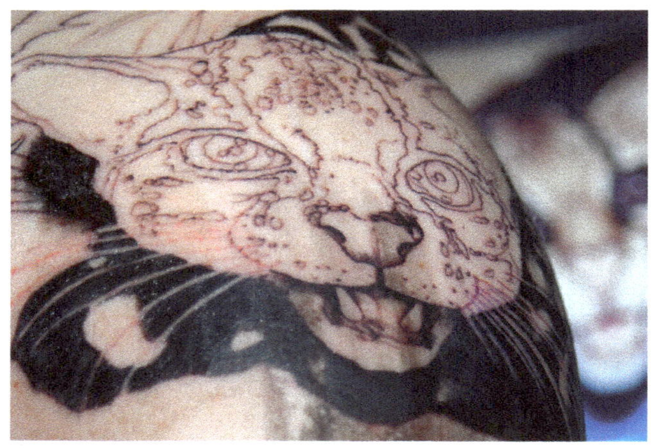

Moving into the facial area, Chris begins to outline the mouth and nose of the margay.

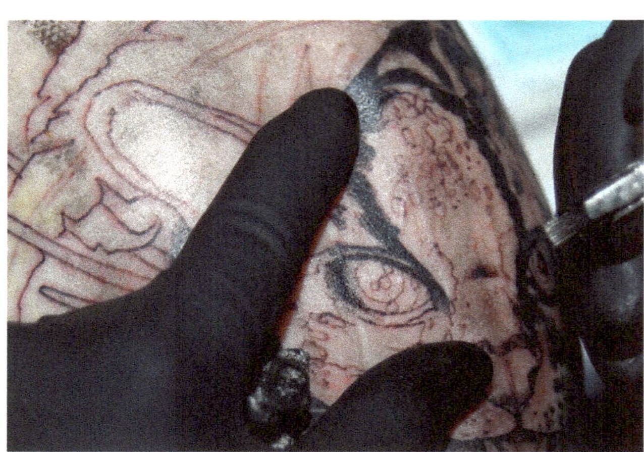

The dark region around the soon-to-be-lighter forehead of the cat can now be seen with clear definition.

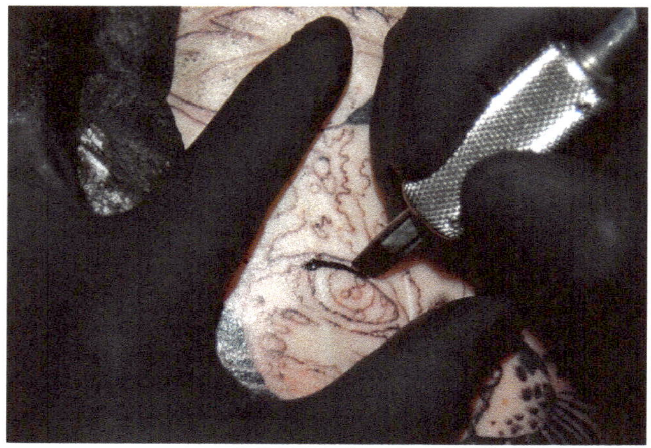

Turning the large needle set on its side allows Chris to do thin lines without swapping machines.

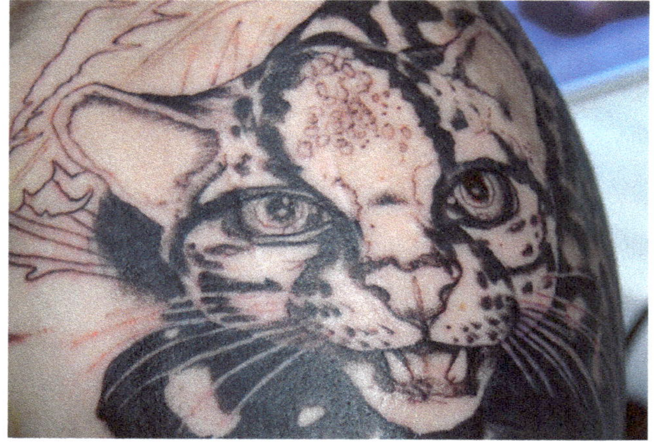

Both eyes, as well as the mouth, nose and whiskers have now been prepared for the next steps.

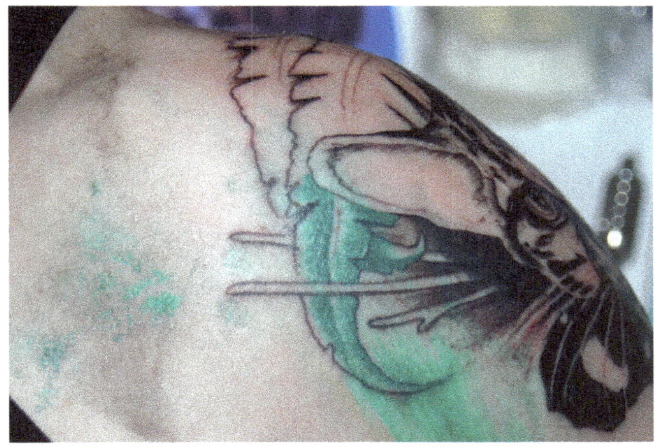

Work on the large, green leaves now begins and Chris continues to use the 15 mag needles.

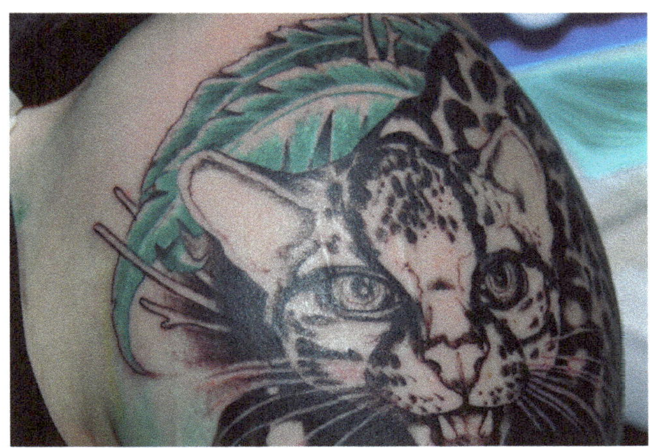

A clean swipe of the piece so far shows us the basic nature of the beast.

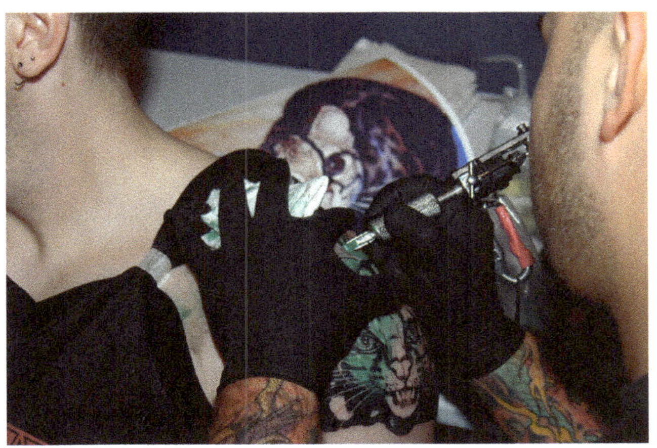

Chris moves to the top of the foliage to continue adding green ink to the mix.

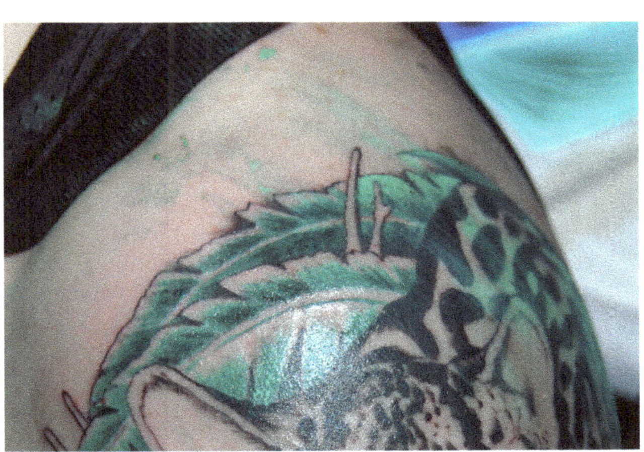

Additional details are added to the leafy background.

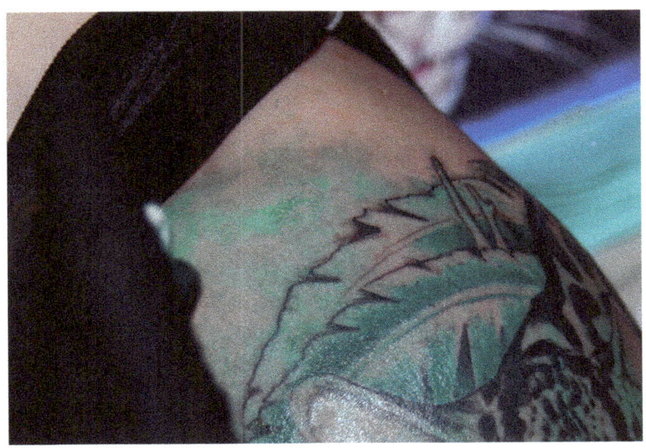

With the first shade of green now applied we can see the forest taking shape.

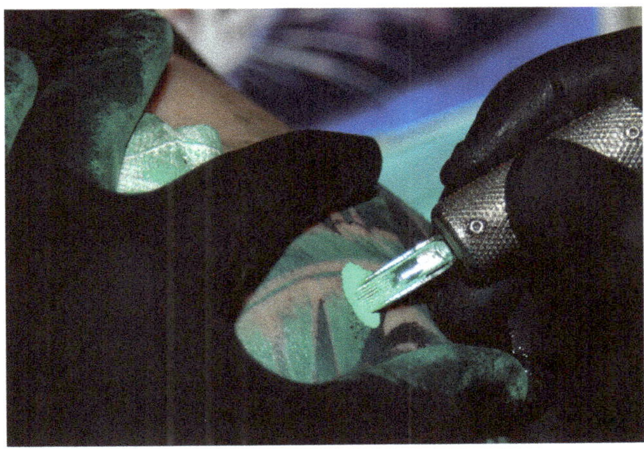

Shading the leaves will be done by using lighter shades of green on top of the dark base colors.

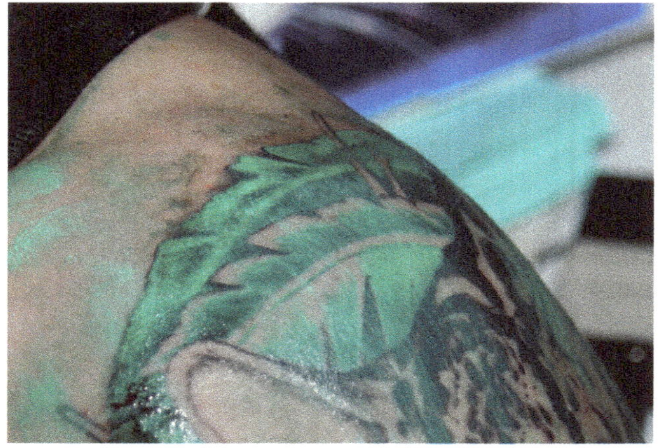

As the excess ink is wiped away we can begin to see the contours of each leaf snap into sharp detail.

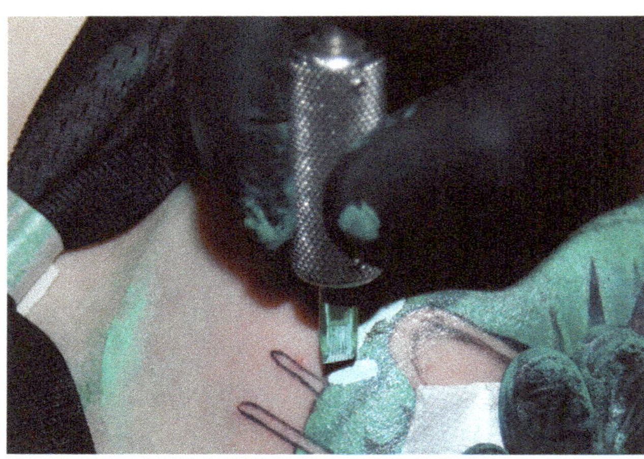

An even brighter shade of green is now applied on top of the darker hues to further add to the illusion of depth.

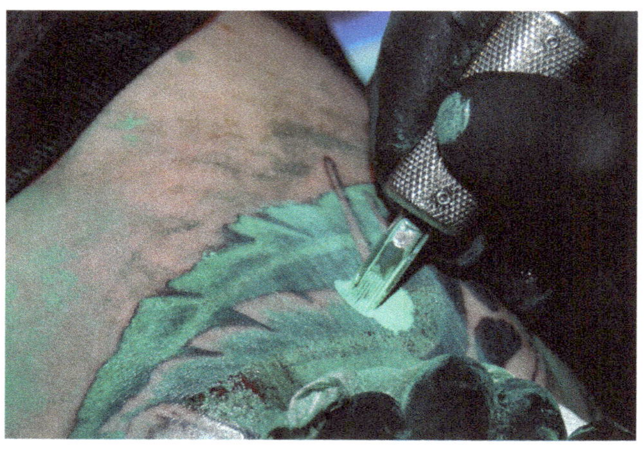

Large masses of color are laid down by the 15 mag needles as the background work gets close to completion.

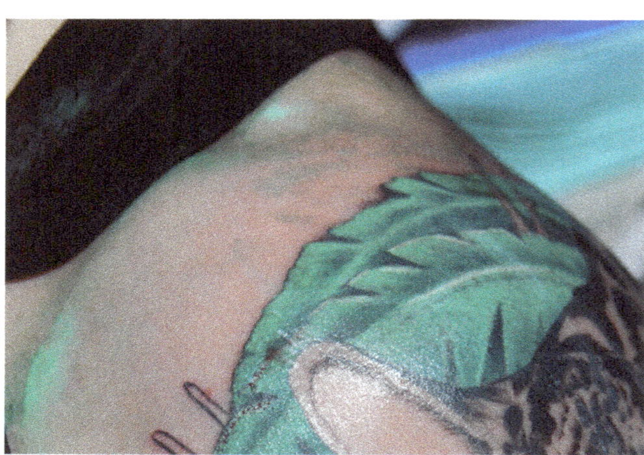

The results of the multiple steps can now be seen clearly as each leaf has become highly defined.

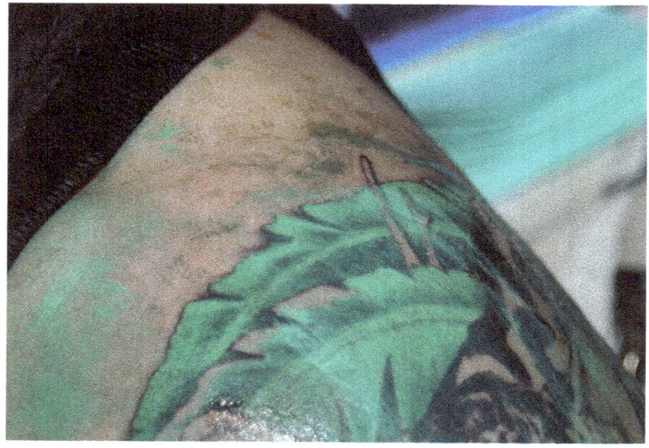

The forest behind the margay's head gets a little closer to looking real with ever passing step.

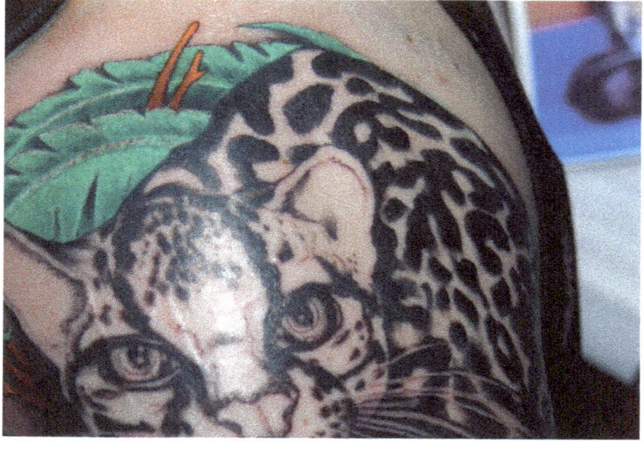

Two small red twigs now appear from the top of the foliage for a point of interest.

Q&A: Chris Blinston

How long have you been tattooing?

It's been a little over 9 years now.

What was the first piece you did?

A woman wanted a cherry on her breast. Being a beginner, I failed to compensate for the position of the piece in relation to the gravitational pull of the earth. She was happy with the cherry, but when she removed her bra later on, it stretched to look more like a chili pepper. Lucky for me, we both laugh about it now.

Do you have a favorite genre you work in?

I suppose "color realism" would be the best way to describe a lot of my work. I like using a bold outline and lots of colors to achieve a high level of realism.

Any particular inspirations or idols?

There are a handful of artists in the field that inspire me, as well as my Dad and my faith.

Do you have a piece that you are best known for?

A guy from New Orleans came in and wanted a crawfish piece. Using his entire ribcage I created a crawfish on a fork along with a lemon wedge. That piece has been seen in several tattoo publications.

See any changes in the field of tattoo art?

The entire business has accelerated as more and more talented people join the fun. I don't see much in the way of technology changes, but fresher talent raising the bar on the quality of the work.

Tell us about Big Brain 2.

As owner of Big Brain 1 with Smitty in Omaha Nebraska, I wanted a change of scenery and weather, so we opened Big Brain 2 here in Florida in 2005.

What kind of art background to do you have?

Although I got no formal art training or education, I was drawing and painting at an early age. While in the Marines in '96, some friends chided me into doing some ink for them. I really didn't like the medium at first, but I've grown to love what can be done using the human body as a canvas. I did a lot of sports logo art for Nebraska teams before getting into the tattoo world, but I like this much better.

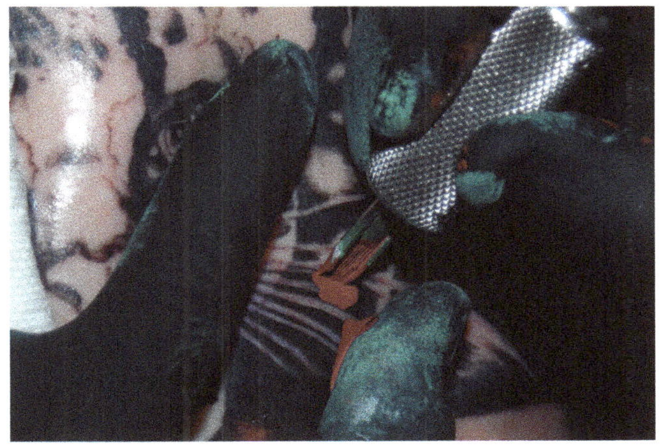

Brown ink is now applied to the fur of the animal to fill in between the black spots.

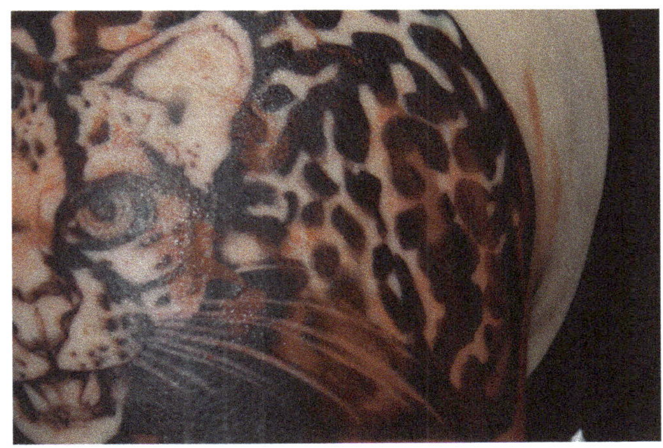

Early stages of the margay's "fur" can now be seen as Chris adds more color to the black areas.

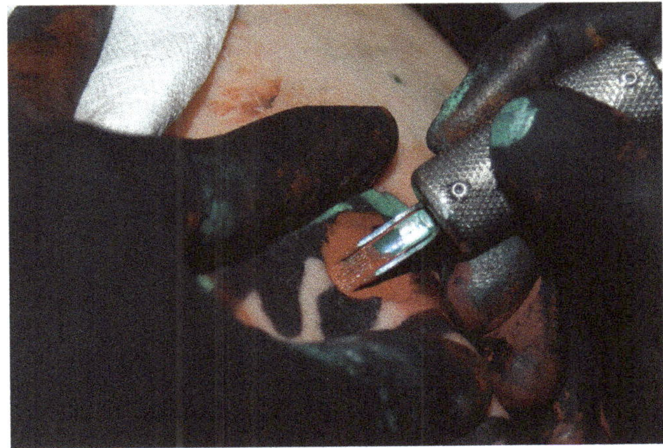

The wide 15 mag needle set makes filling in the large sections easier and a lot quicker.

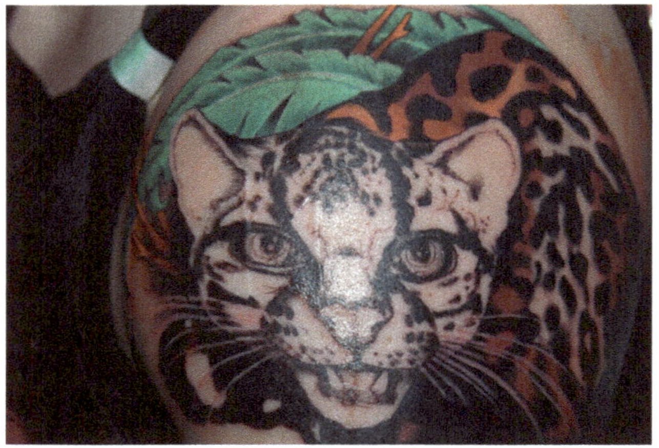

The addition of color can now be seen after the random ink has been wiped away.

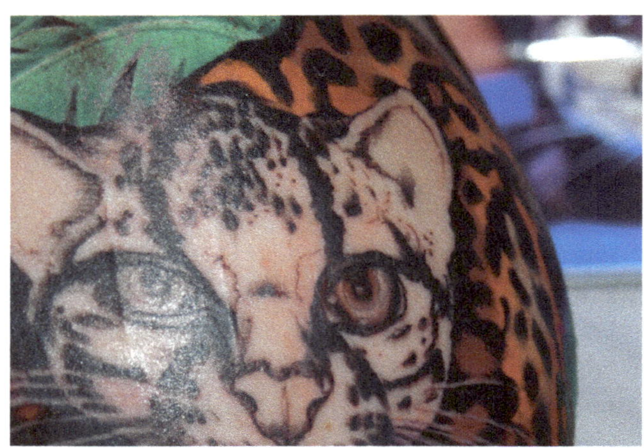

The subtlety of the eyes is now becoming more apparent as layers of ink are used.

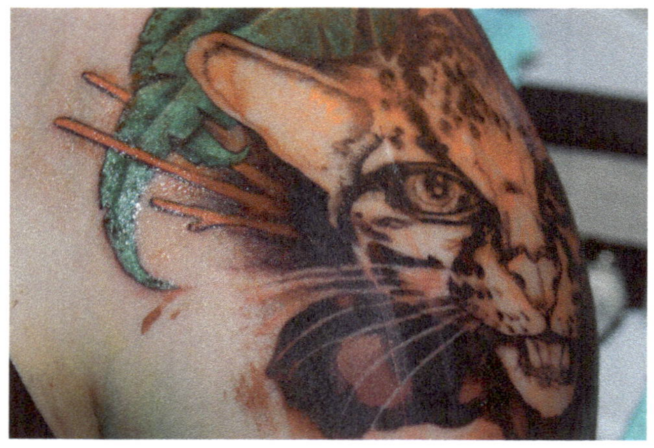

More shades of brown ink are applied to the left side of the cat's face as work continues.

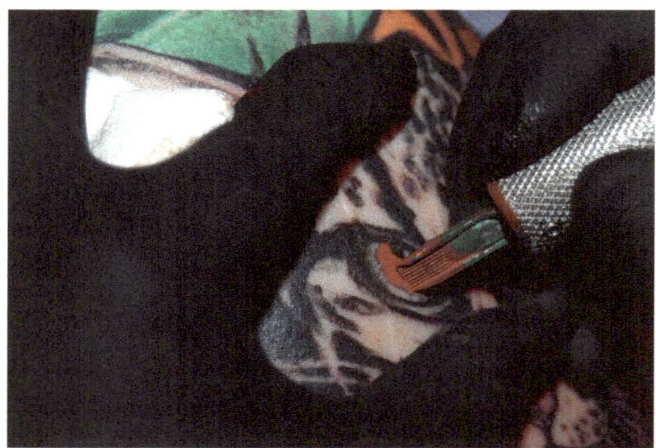

Turning his attentions to the left eye, the first slathering of brown is applied.

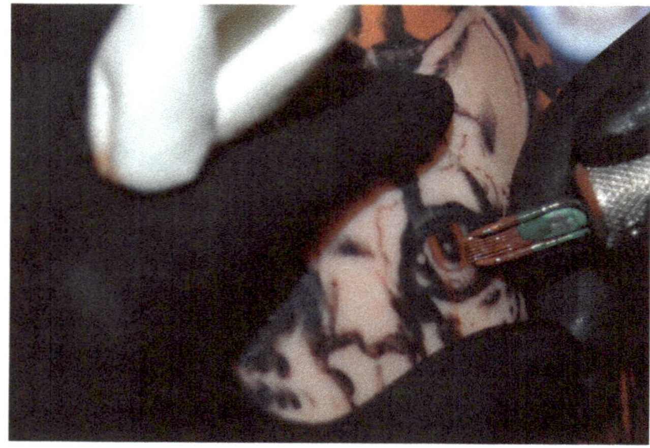

Chris' talents with the wide needles allow him to apply ink to much smaller areas without switching to a smaller set.

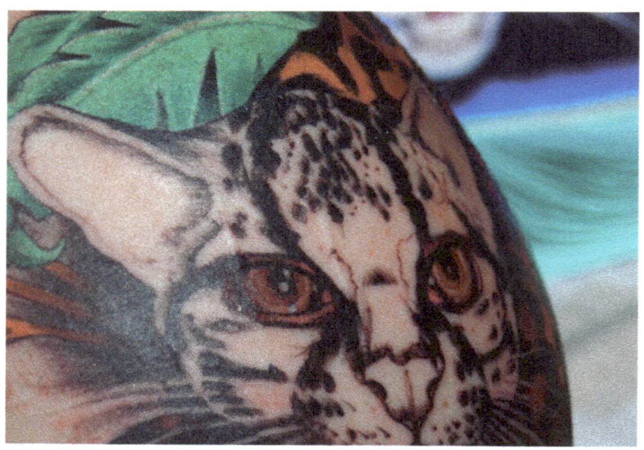

Both eyes are beginning to take shape, with additional steps still required to complete the illusion.

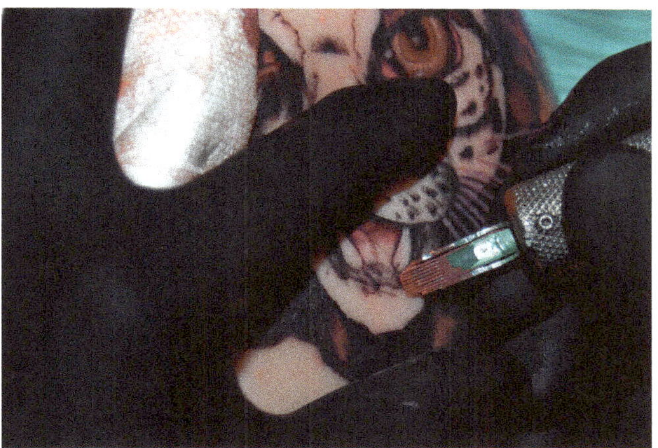

The fangs are to be held in place by the soon-to-be reddish gums of the snarling cat.

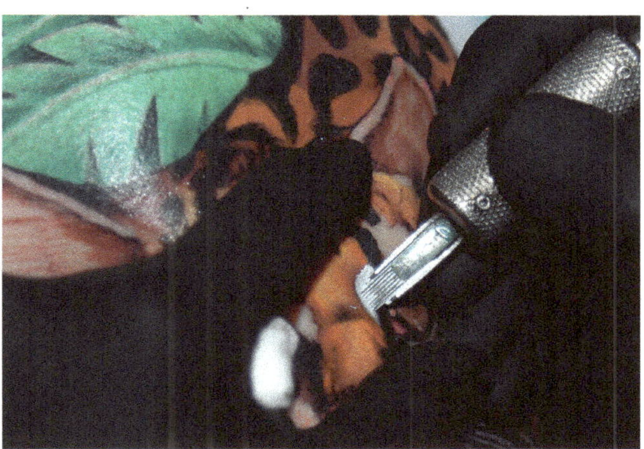

The right orb is now addressed as the bright white ink is layered over the darker base inks.

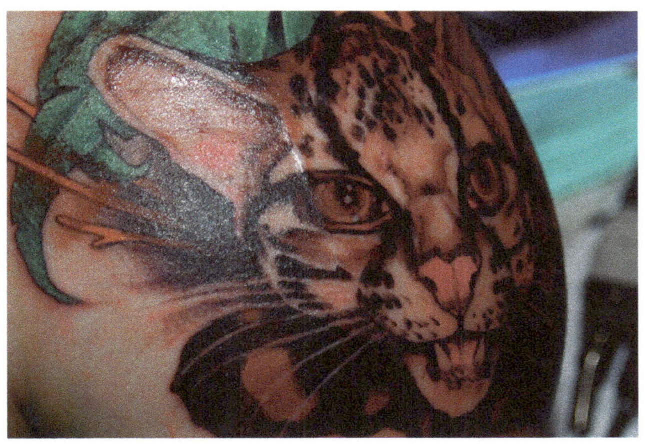

Mouth, tongue, eyes and nose are now nearing completion with only highlights of white to be added.

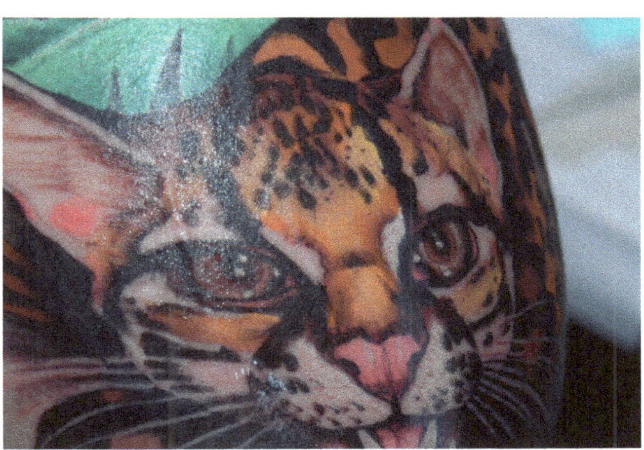

The eyes appear to be staring right at us after Chris' use of a multitude of colors and shading.

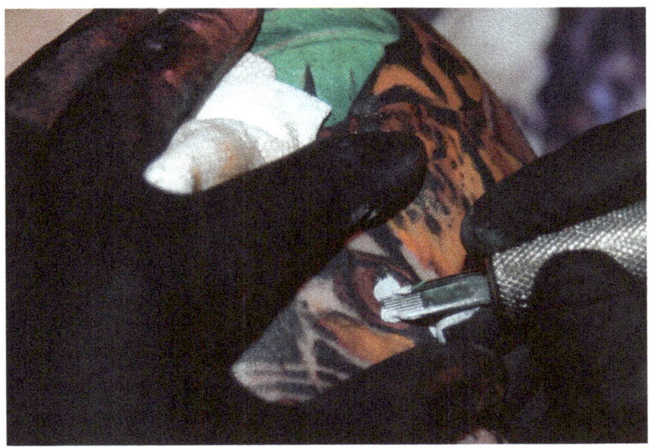

The whites of the eyes are now filled in for added intensity and realism.

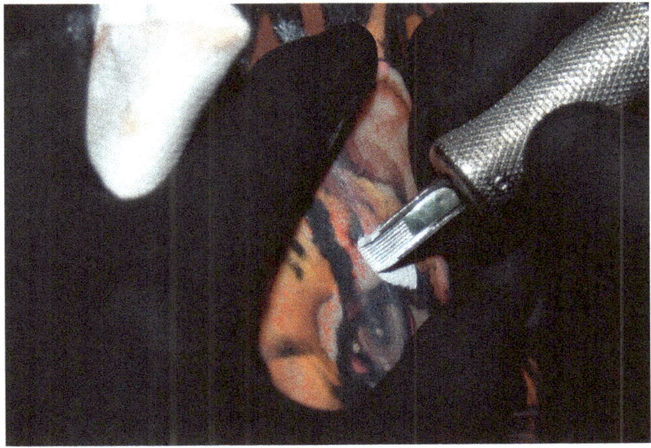

White ink is now added to the area above the eyes to bring more life to the margay's facial features.

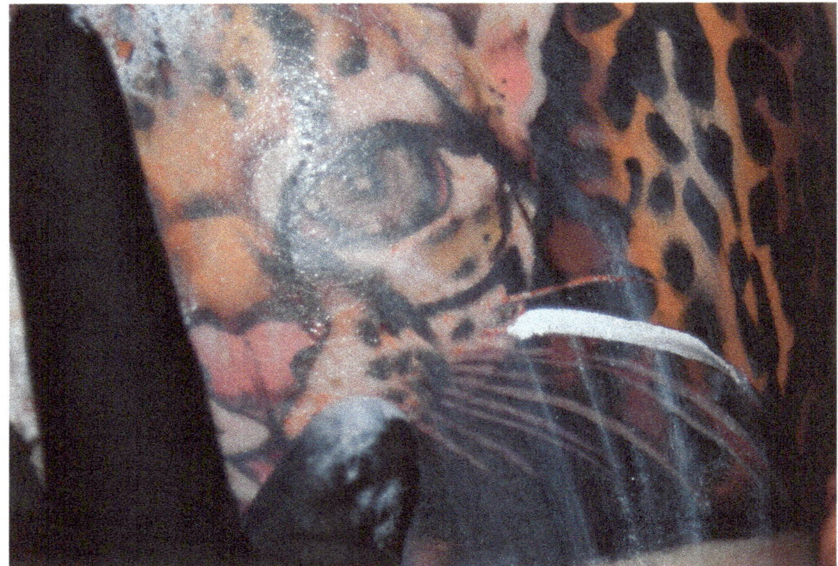

Each of the cat's whiskers will now be filled in with a wash of white before being wiped clean.

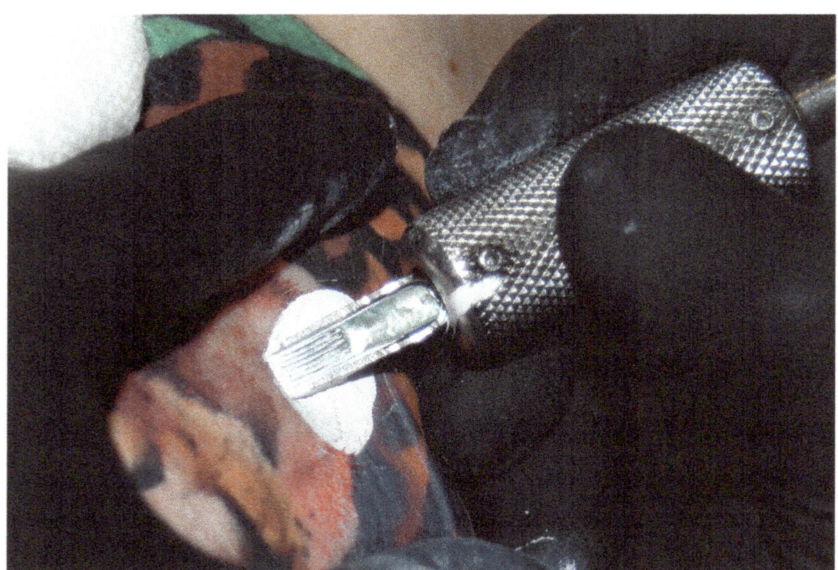

Never satisfied with the level of realism, Chris continues to brighten certain sections of the pelt with bright white ink for added depth and clarity.

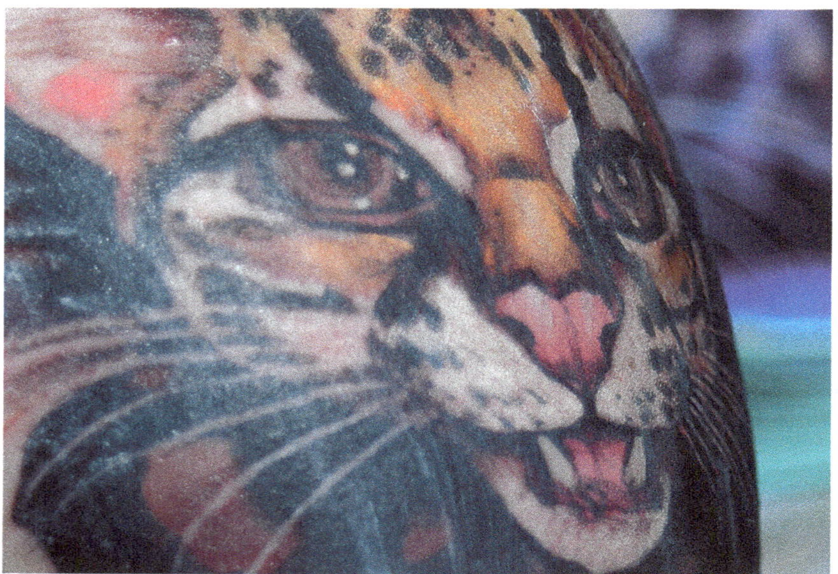

The results of his fastidious use of colors and details are quickly becoming obvious.

Bringing more depth to the insides of the margay's ears requires the use of lighter ink to contrast the darker hues already in place.

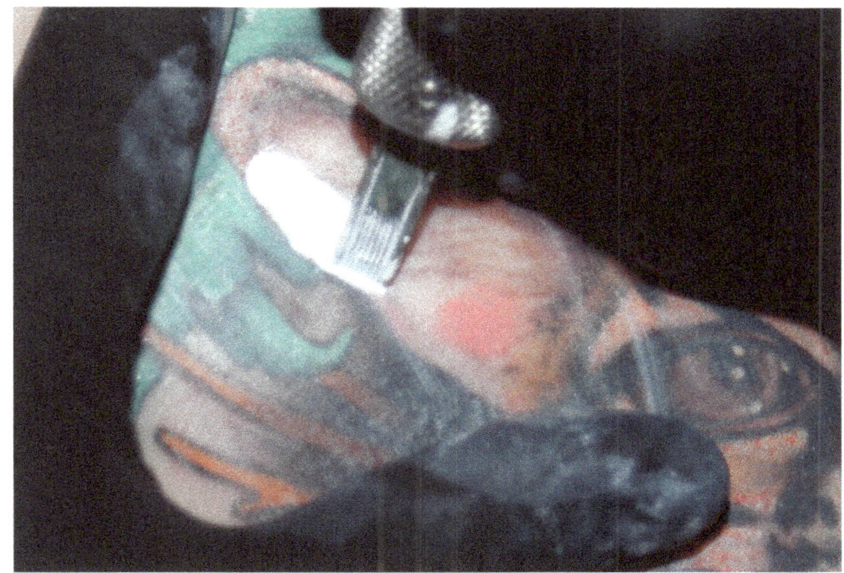

The left side whiskers have been highlighted with white to bring them into sharper focus.

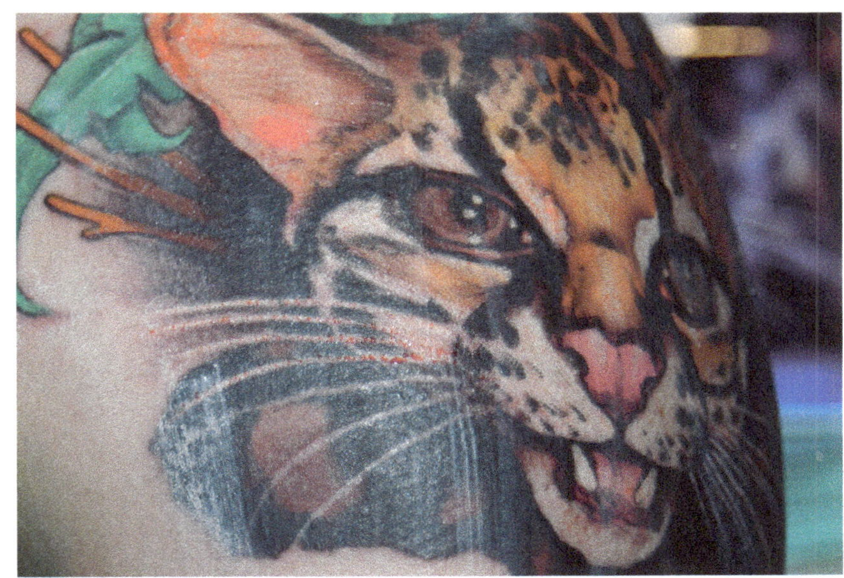

Having worked quickly to meet the contest deadline, Chris has produced this beautiful tattoo in less than 4 hours. No corners were cut, and Chris says that he usually works quickly once a piece is started.

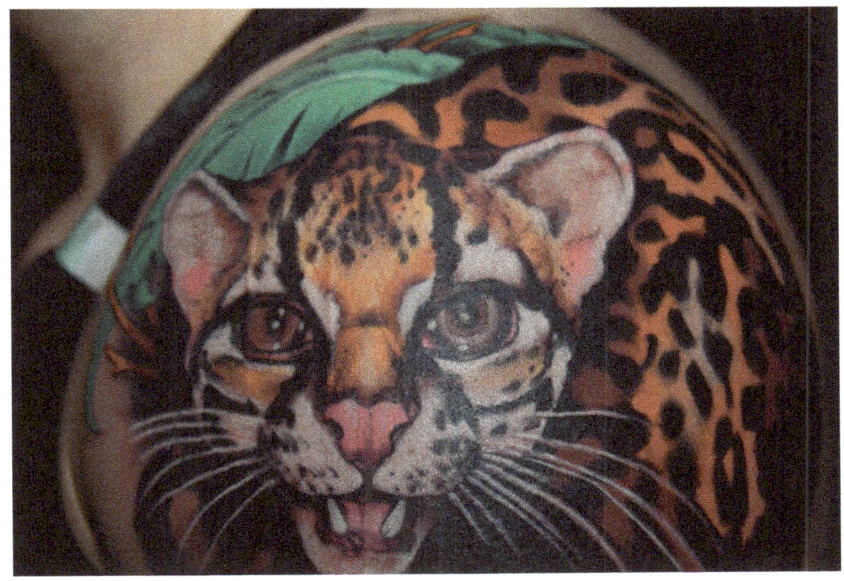

Chapter Ten

Scott Marshall

Vanity Tattoo

I discovered Scott Marshall after seeing some of his work on the forearm of a local hot rod builder. It was immediately apparent, even to a neophyte like me, that the tattoo was amazingly detailed, and produced by a skilled hand. After meeting Scott at the shop, I was able to view more of his efforts in several notebooks and on a video presentation he has rolling in the waiting room. Like most tattoo artists I have found, he is capable of creating nearly any type of tattoo a person could want, but still has his own favorite niche. Scott loves pinup art, and tries to incorporate it into his work whenever possi-

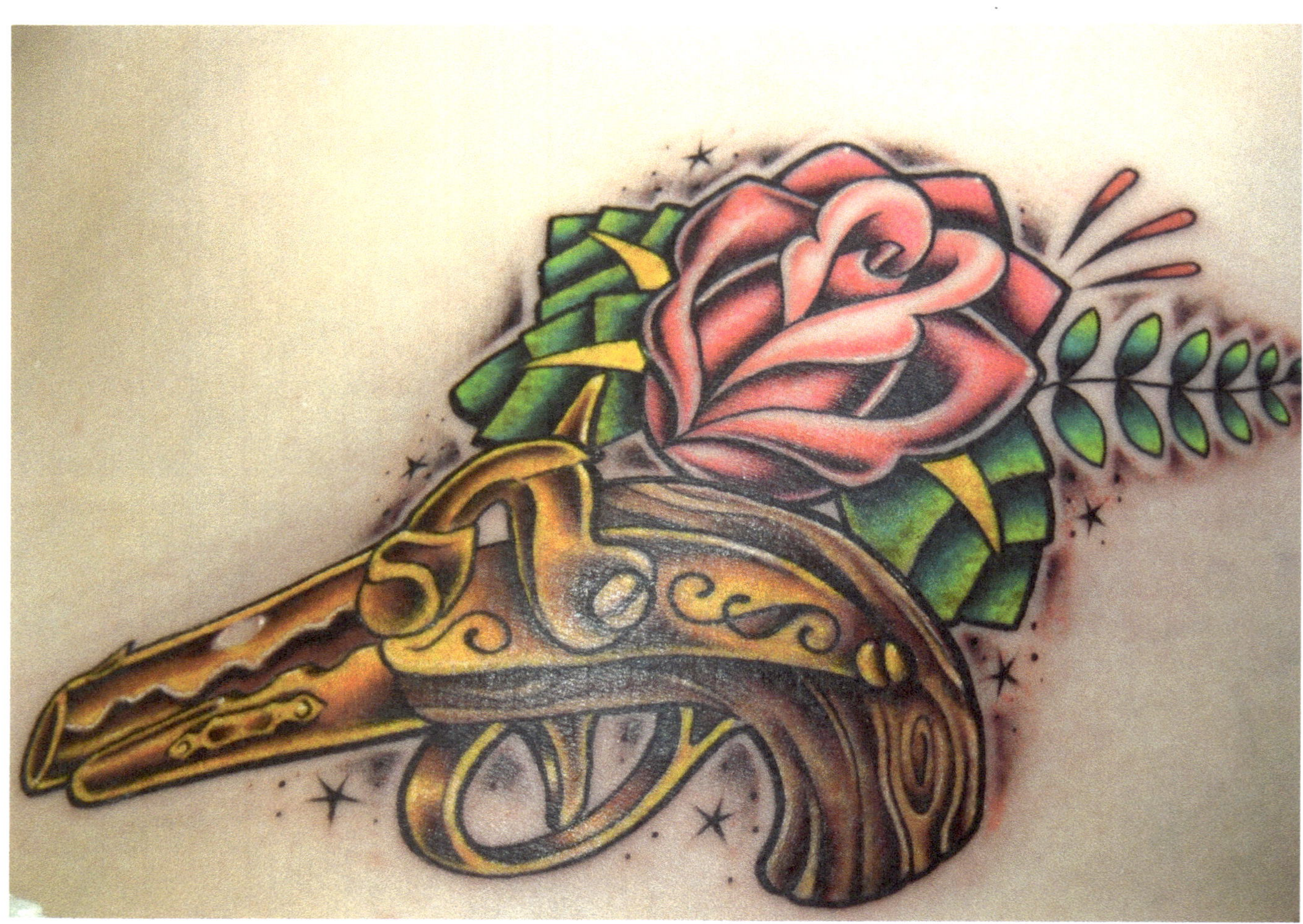

When Patricia agreed to have latest tattoo chronicled for this book, she gave Scott free reign in the design and location of the piece. She had no inkling of what he had in mind when arriving at Vanity Tattoo, but her past dealings with Scott put her at ease.

ble. His tattoo station is decorated with a wide variety of inspirational photos and related illustrations.

Unlike many tattoo mavens I have encountered, Scott began his career at the same shop he currently works out of. He has been at the same location for nearly a decade, while many other ink masters move around a lot, especially in their formative years in the business. Many will apprentice in one place, and then jump around from shop to shop until they land somewhere they like or open their own location. To find an artist of Scott's ability who has found a happy home so easily is rare indeed. I don't mean to stereotype here, but a typical trait for any artist is a restless desire to always move somewhere new to try fresh angles on his or her craft, no matter what the chosen medium. While this roaming around doesn't usually hurt anyone in the process, it does hamper the stability of ones work. With nearly a decade at one address under his belt, Scott has fallen into a rare category.

With a longstanding professional relationship between them, Patty gave Scott free reign when it came time for this tattoo. Knowing that Patty already had some ink on her right hip, Scott thought it would be cool to add a sister piece on the opposing hip. With no restrictions placed on him, Scott set his sights on doing something both different and traditional. By combining a vintage handgun and a red rose, the best of both worlds could be addressed. Using a historical reference guide, he selected a well known pistol for the art. Handguns of any sort are not too common in the tattoo arena, so Scott thought it would be an interesting addition to his collection.

With his art background, the creation of the rough and finished art took only about an hour. Once his blueline illustration was to his liking he created the crisp black drawing that would be his road map. Final placement and sizing were accomplished before transferring the art to Patty's hip. The location of the piece would give the illusion of Patty packing heat with the butt of the pistol just peeking over the top edge of her jeans. Scott used a few small dots of a felt tip pen to reference the location before applying the transfer to her skin. As in many things, measuring three times and placing once is a safe and sound method that avoids complications down the road.

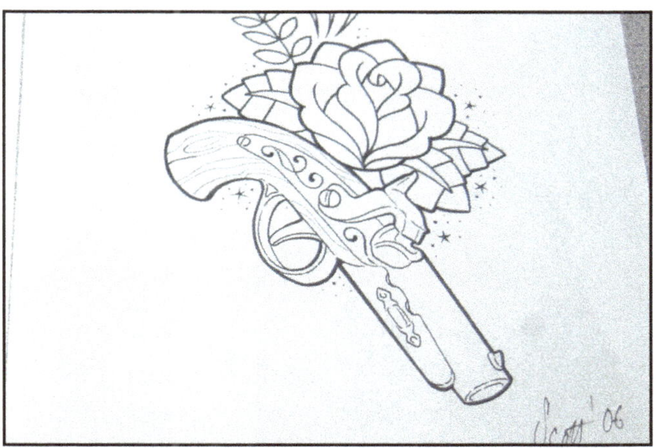

With no rules or suggestions from the recipient, Scott chose this pistol and rose motif for his newest piece.

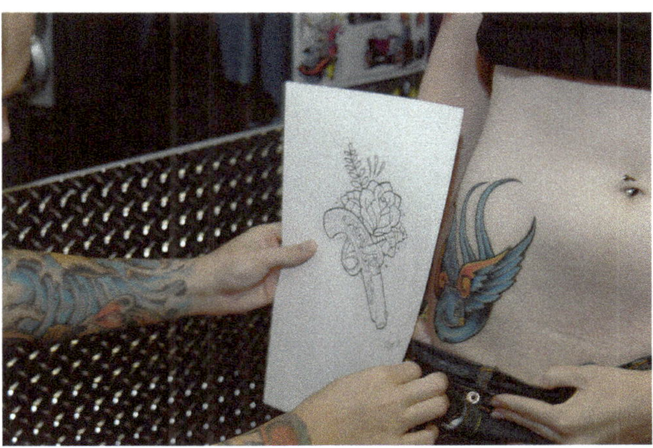

Comparing the new sketch to the tattoo found on the opposite hip, Scott makes sure that the 2 pieces will be similar in size.

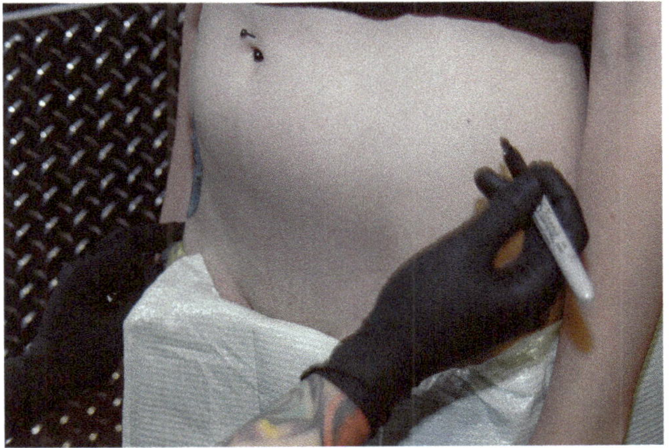

Using a felt tip marker he makes two reference dots that will allow him easier placement of the transfer.

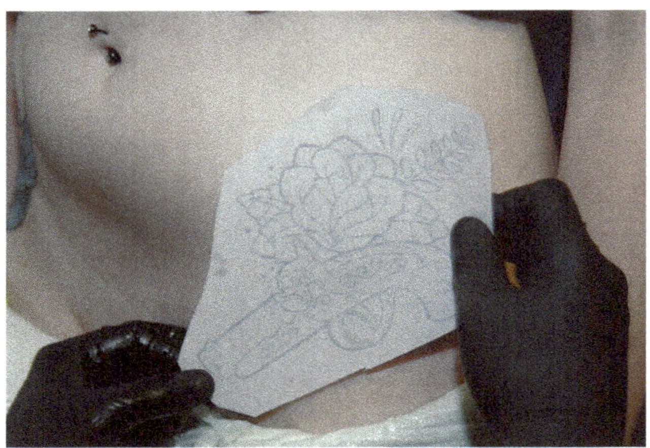

One final check of placement before he applies the art to the area to be inked.

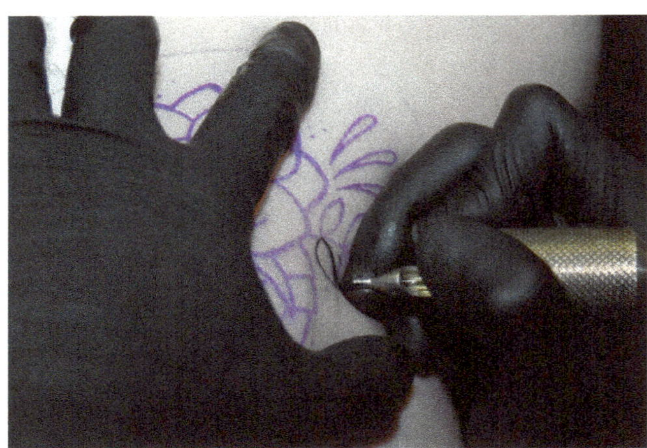

The small leaves of the decorative leaves will be the first black work to be addressed.

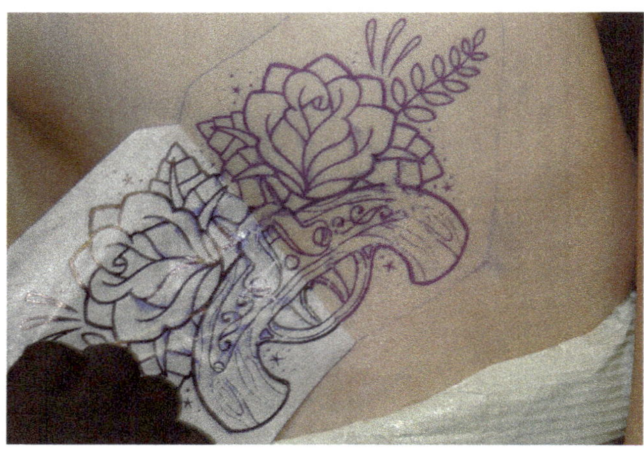

Peeling away the paper leaves the artwork on the skin, and will be his map for the finished piece.

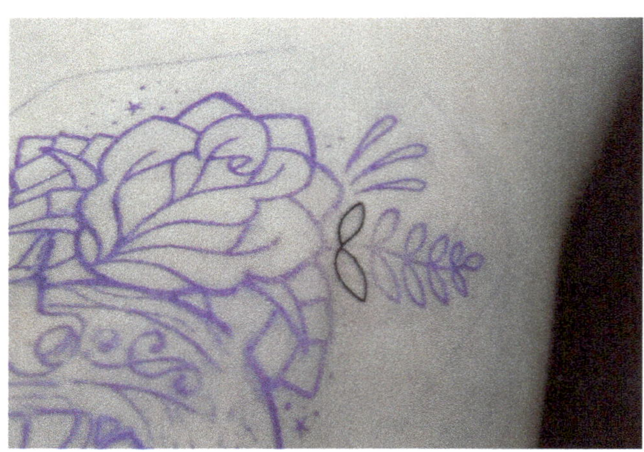

A 7 round needle is used for the basic outlines, seen here on the early stages of the art.

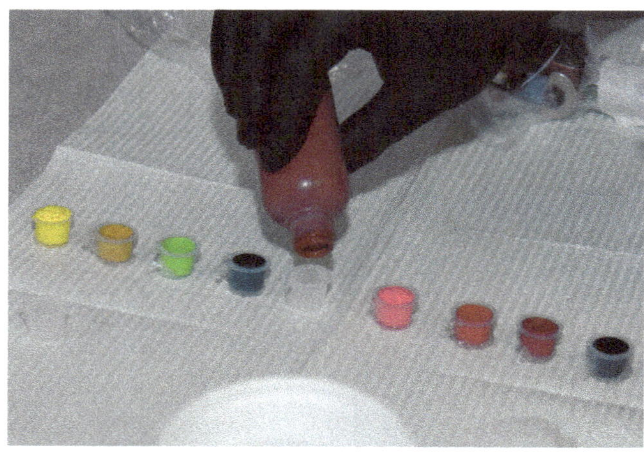

Scott now fills the cups with his preliminary inks, but others will be added later as he works on the tattoo.

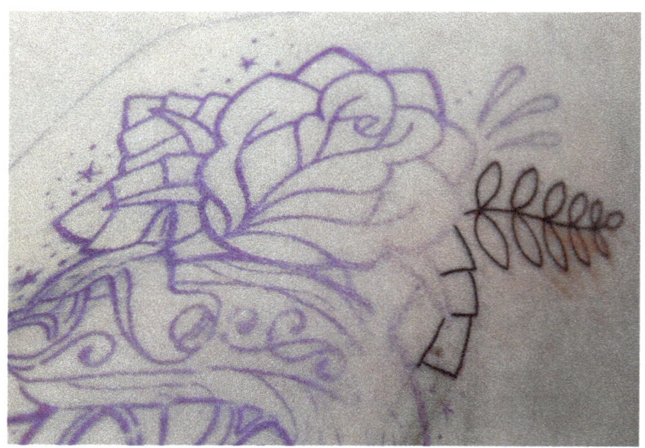

Scott moves from the completed leaves to those that will fall behind the rose as the outline efforts continue.

Once satisfied with the transfer and its location, a 7 round needle was chosen to begin the black outline. A clean line of equal width would first be applied to the entire piece before additional steps would be taken. In this segment of the process, Scott worked quickly and soon the completed outline was ready for review. After cleansing the area of stray ink, he checked to be sure that all portions of the illustration had been covered. Happy with the results, he went back to add bolder strokes to the more prominent aspects of the art. The use of the bolder lines help to accent certain aspects of the tattoo, as well as smoothing out any imperfections to the initial outline.

With the basic outline and bolder line work completed, Scott began the black shading of the tattoo. This step is crucial to the finished piece because the black shading will appear through the colors to be added later. Any shortcuts taken here would impact the detail and contours of the finished work. The petals of the rose, along with several sections of the pistol, were given a lot of attention in this step, and even in black we could see the shape of the subjects taking form.

Using a 7 mag needle for the shading, Scott again seems to work very quickly, but he could see the finished tattoo in his head long before it became obvious to the rest of us. A tattoo artist can adjust the "throw" of the needle to meet different needs. This refers to the amount of the needle that protrudes from the machine, and the potential depth the needles can go under the skin. A longer throw requires a higher level of finesse to avoid unnecessary pain for the recipient. The longer throw also allows a talented hand to create lines that are otherwise unattainable.

Although the classic rose tattoo has been seen perhaps a million times, Scott's application of shading, multiple hues and small highlights of bright blue set it apart from the rest. His addition of the small stars and pinpoints were another bit of subtle genius that keep his work ahead of the pack. I have learned to keep my mouth shut while certain bits are being applied until the needle stops its stinging. Often times, the artist can visualize the end result and can go about creating the desired effect without hesitation. What often seems like a random or care-

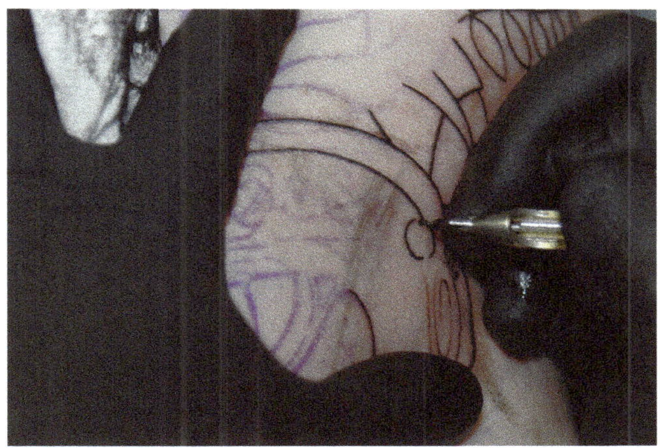

The first lines of the pistol are now added as work moves quickly over the blue lines of the transfer.

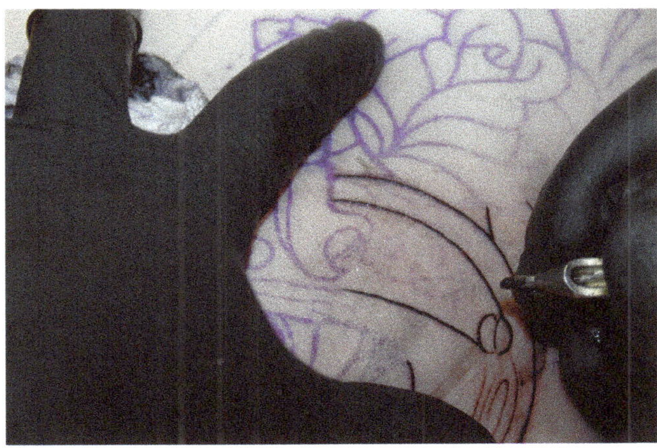

Additional details are added to the pistol grip which will make themselves more obvious later on.

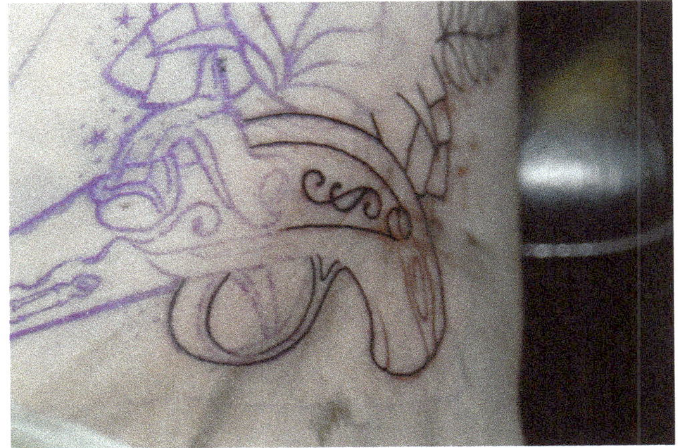

Outline work on the leaves and pistol scrolls can now be seen.

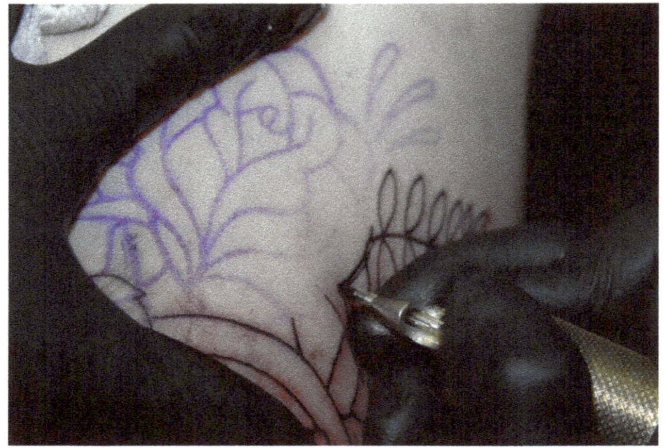

The rose petals are now given attention as Scott moves from place to place reducing discomfort for Patty.

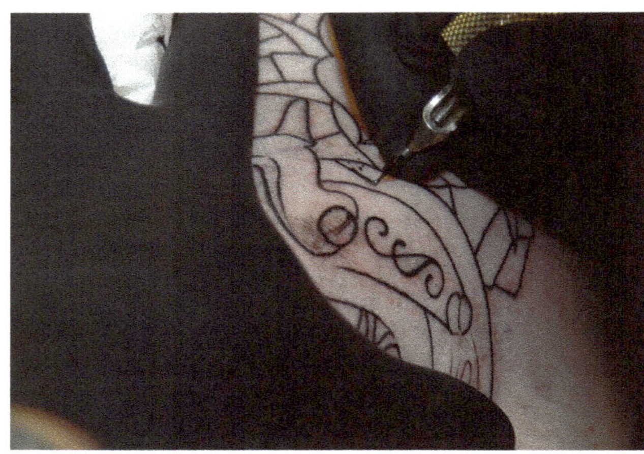

A small detail on the pistol's stock is now addressed.

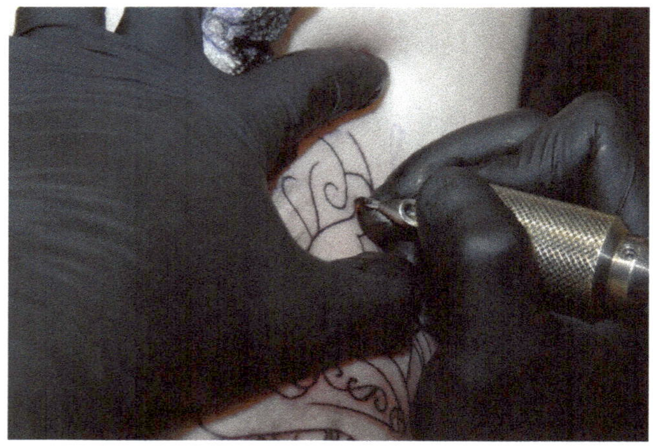

Interior lines of the flower's petals are now inked in with black as more of the blue line is replaced.

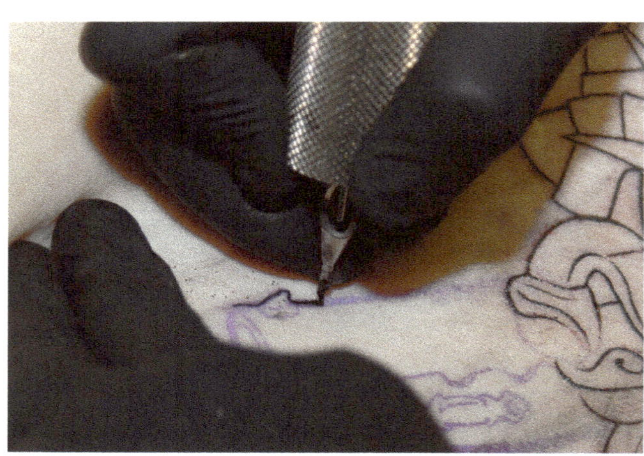

The gun's front sight gets a black outline for clarity.

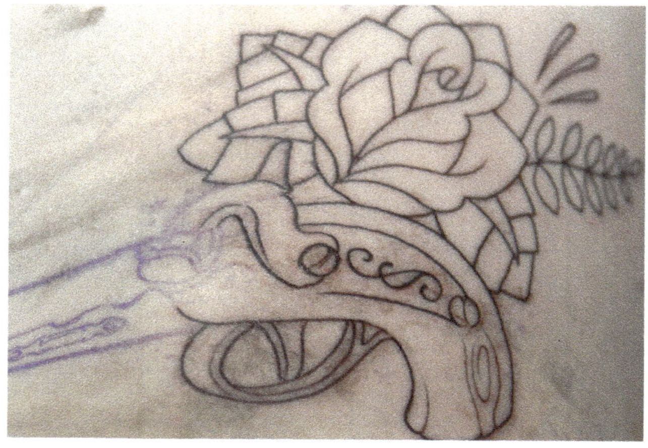

Outlines of the flower and most of the pistol are now complete.

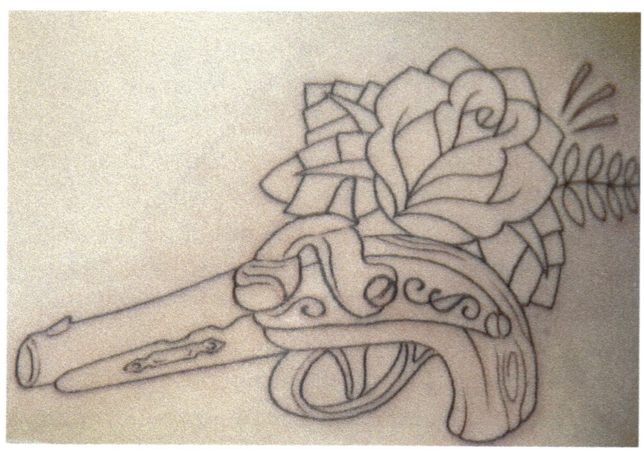

The primary outline is now finished and the application of color can begin.

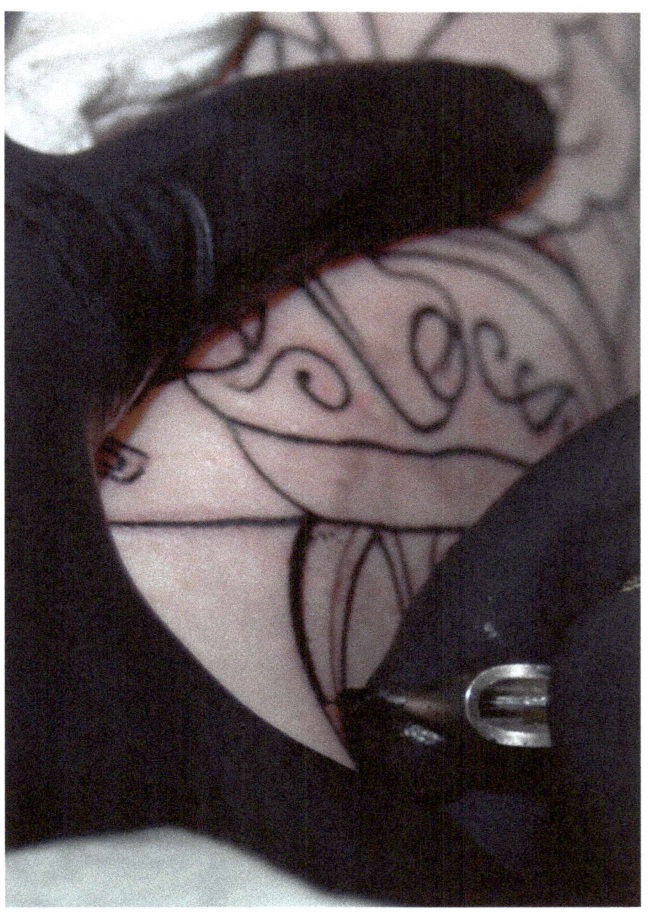

The trigger guard will be one of the first areas to get the bolder black outline for added definition.

less move plays out to the perfect touch of color or detail that I had no ability to envision. This is the reason we leave the work to the tattoo experts and avoid the "Do it yourself" kits we see advertised.

Nearing the end of this tattoo, Patty's discomfort level was growing, but that is typical as the skin has been rubbed raw by the repeated stinging of the needles. Being a veteran of the process she knew what to anticipate and the pain was well within her limits. She had some work done on her left foot two weeks previously, and she claimed that the pain of that region was far worse.

After Scott added a few more crucial details to the piece, he wiped the area clean and we waited a few moments for any last seepage before taking our final shots. As the healing process progresses, the colors will take on a new intensity and the true beauty of the tattoo will emerge.

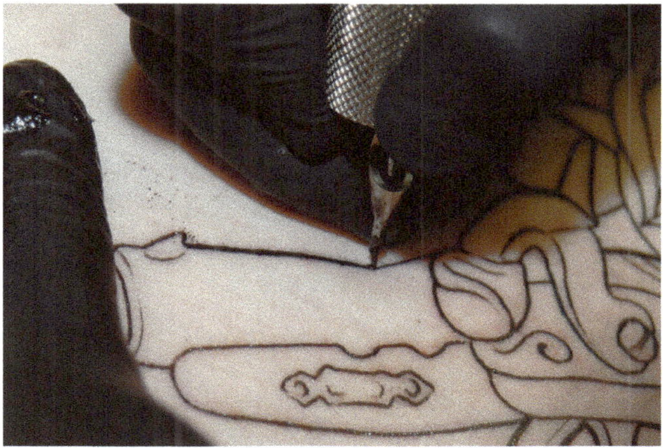

Only certain lines will be made bolder, such as the upper length of the pistol's barrel.

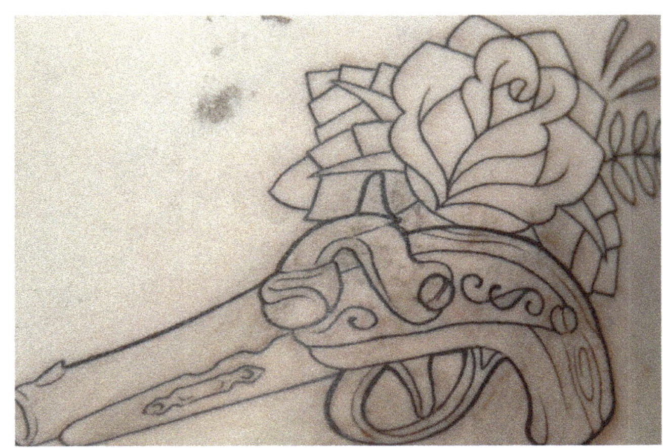

With the darker lines being added, we can now see the thought pattern that Scott has applied to the art.

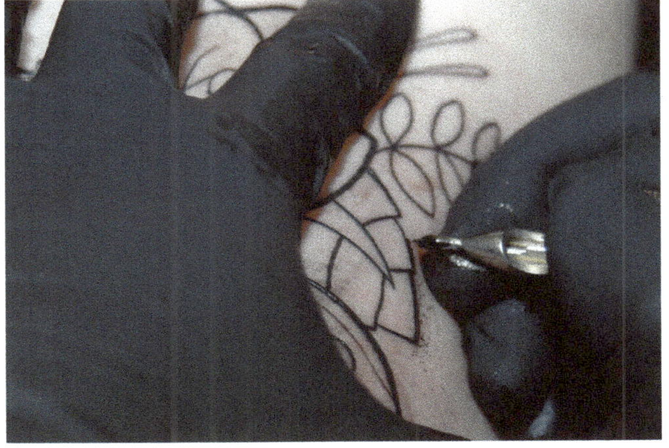

Each outline of the rose's leaves are now accented with the bold, black ink.

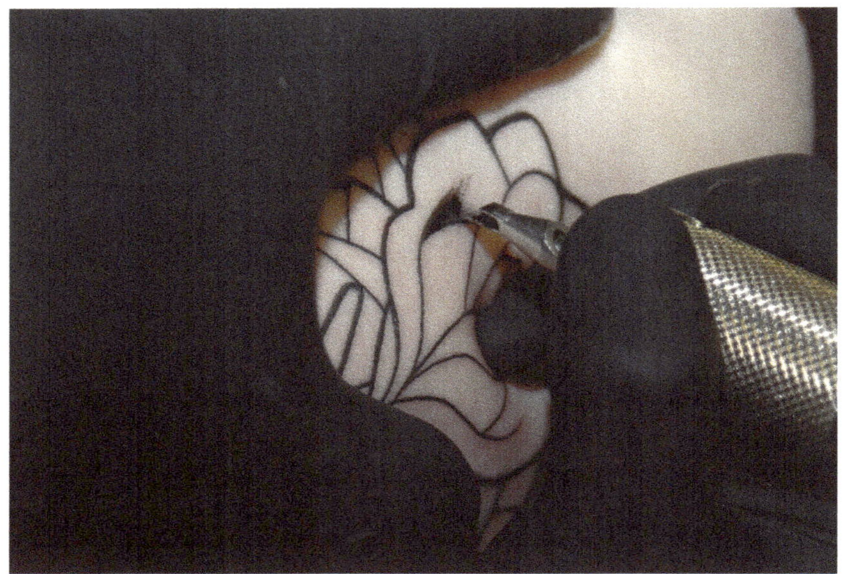

Black shading of the flower begins and is an important factor in the finished tattoo.

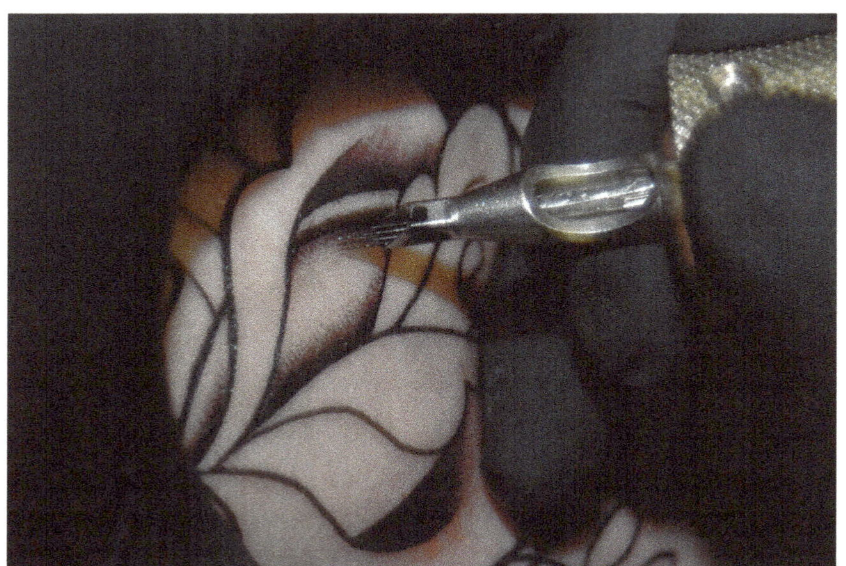

Careful application of the black ink provides the supple curves of the petals with the required details and contours.

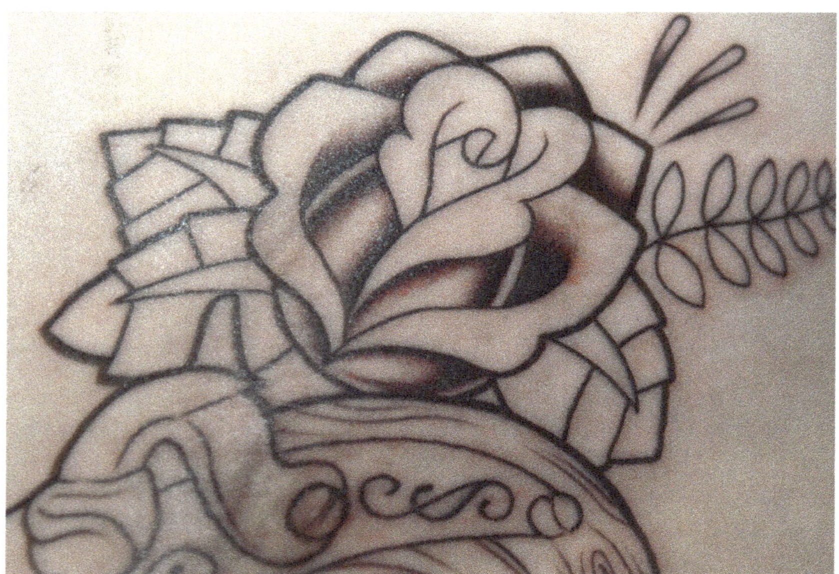

After cleaning the area we can now see the first efforts taken by Scott to create a 3-dimensional base for the soon to be added colors.

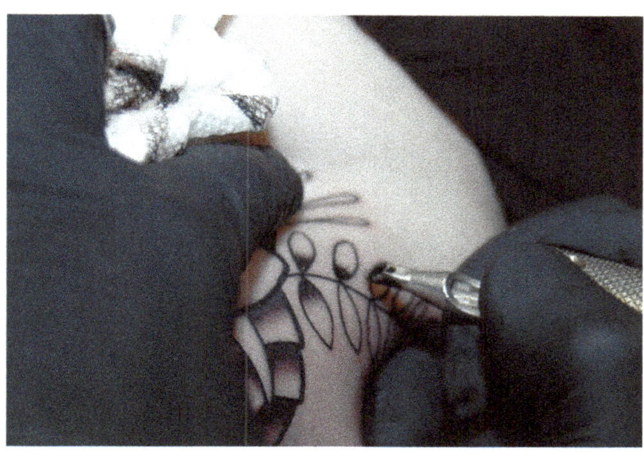

Shading is added to the smaller leaves to be sure that they are also a consistent part of the overall tattoo.

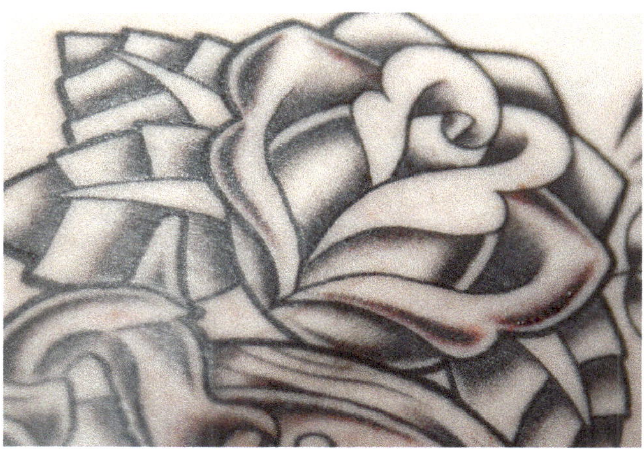

Additional shading has brought clarity to the petals of the rose.

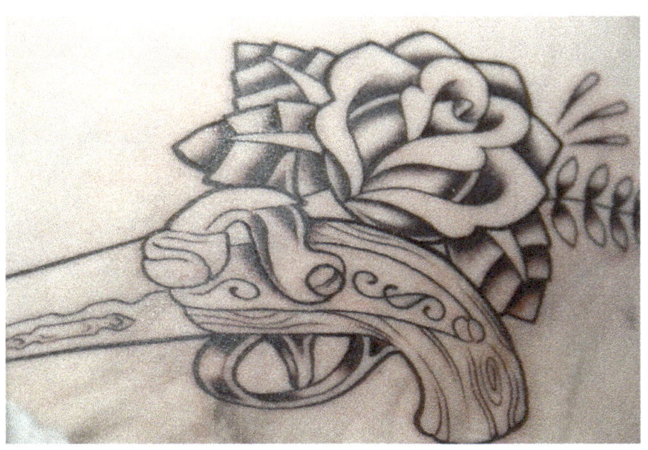

Basic black shading has now been added to the rose, leaves and pistol as the shapes of each item are better defined by Scott's hand.

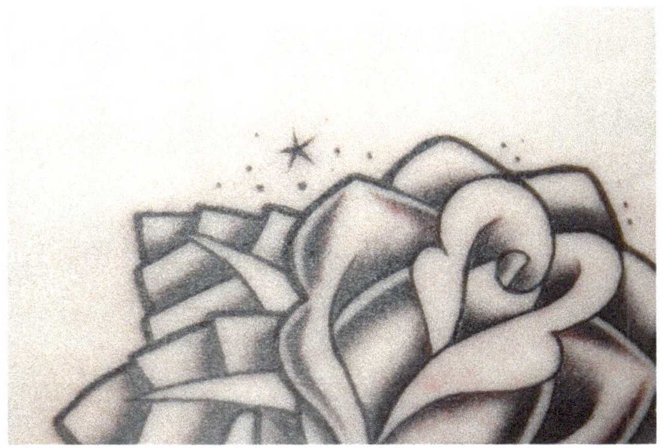

Small stars and hot spots are thrown into the mix to bring detail to the finished tattoo, and are often overlooked by other artists.

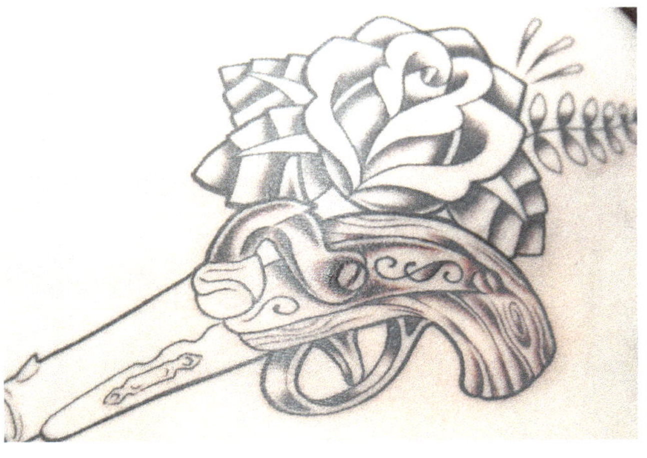

A clearer view of the progress so far can be seen after the unneeded ink has been cleaned away.

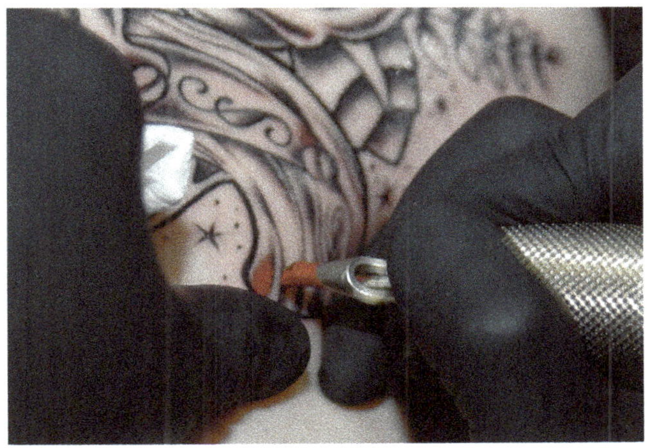

The first application of color ink begins with the brown used to fill in the grip of the pistol.

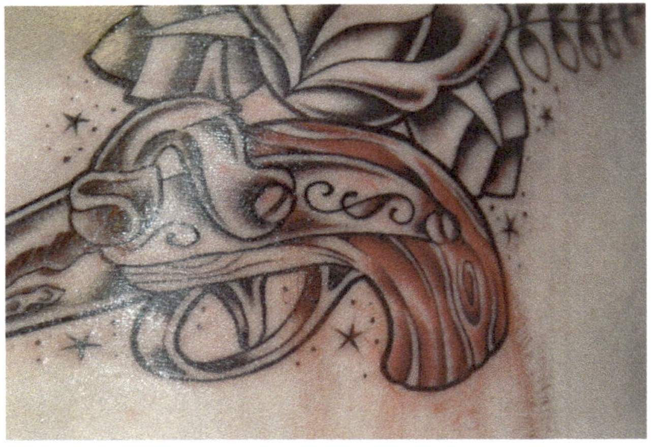

More of the pistol's wooden handle is filled in, and when combined with the previous black shading, Scott's genius begins to become more apparent.

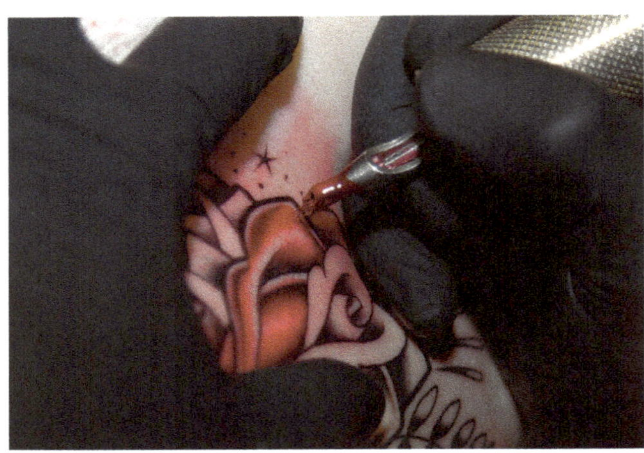

The browns of the pistol now complete, Scott turns his needle to the reds of the rose.

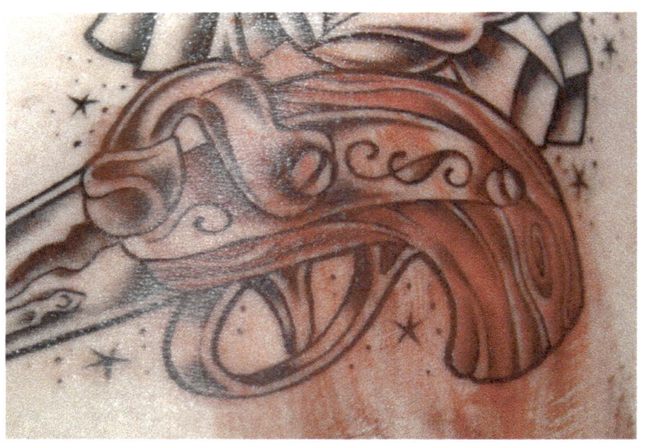

Before being cleaned, we can begin to see the contours of the rounded gun butt take shape.

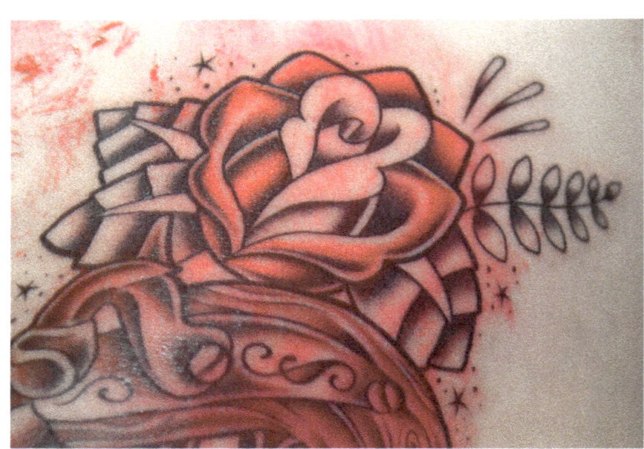

Red ink has been applied to the first petals of the flower with additional shades of the same hue soon to follow.

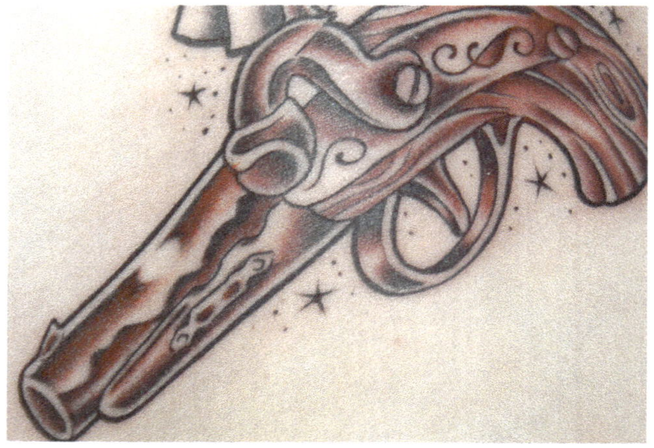

With the stray ink now cleared away, the remaining shape of the gun and its barrel are becoming more defined.

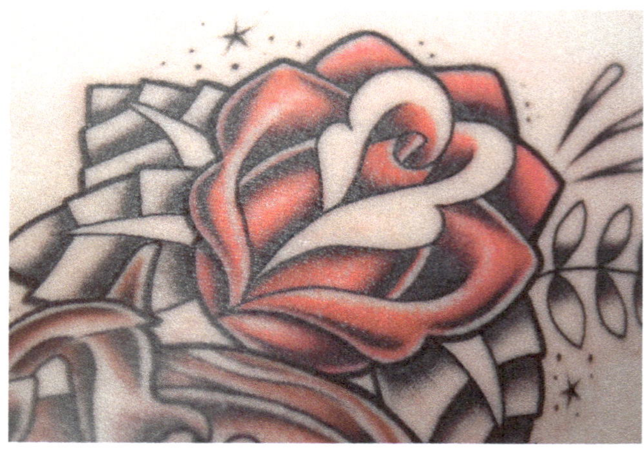

Wiped free of excess ink, the contours of the rose are now becoming more obvious.

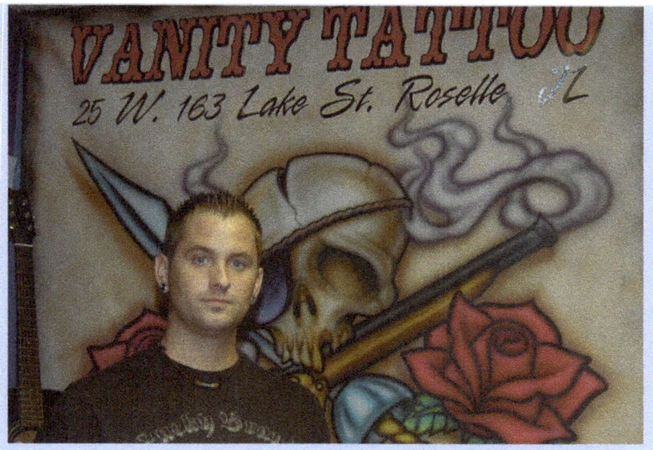

Q&A: Scott Marshall

How long have you been doing tattoos?

I apprenticed for two years at Vanity Tattoos, and began doing them in 2000, also at Vanity.

What was the first tattoo you did on another person?

The first tatt I did was a small moonshine bottle with a skull and cross bones on another tattoo artist.

Any special genre or style you prefer doing?

I have done a wide variety of pieces, but really like the pin-up art. Of course skulls, traditional and black and gray stuff, is great too.

Who or what inspires you today?

I guess the two people who inspire me the most would be Guy Atchison, who is huge in the tattoo world and Alex Gray, a really talented artist whose work I find amazing.

Do you have a best know tattoo?

I did an entire sleeve in black and gray in the H.R. Giger style that won an award in 2006, so I guess that is my biggest and best known tattoo.

Do you see any big changes in the tattoo world?

I'm not too excited about all the television exposure the art has been getting and I kind of like a more underground way of thinking.

Tell us more about Vanity Tattoos.

The shop has been here since 1996, and I began my apprenticeship with John, who has since become my best friend. I have been at this same shop from 1998 on as a tattoo artist.

What kind of background in art did you have?

I have always had an interest in art, ever since I was very young. I got my degree in illustration from the American Academy of Art in Chicago, and still do some airbrush and illustration work outside the tattoo field.

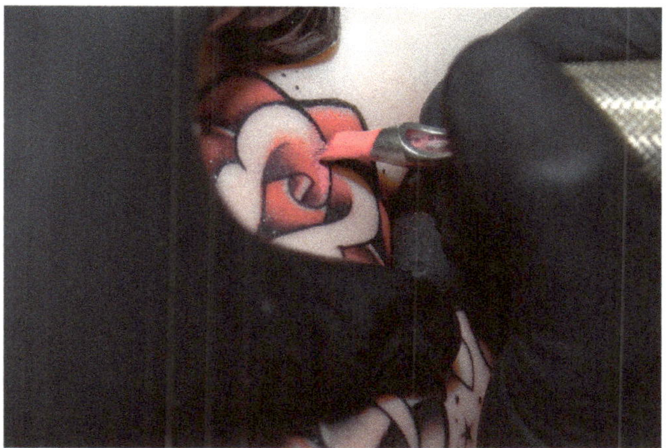

A brighter hue of red is now added to the blend bringing more depth and shape to the rose.

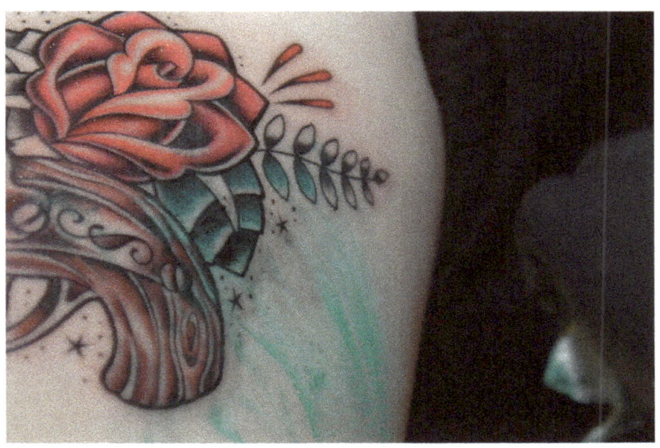

The leaves are tinted green and will greatly benefit the canvas of color when completed.

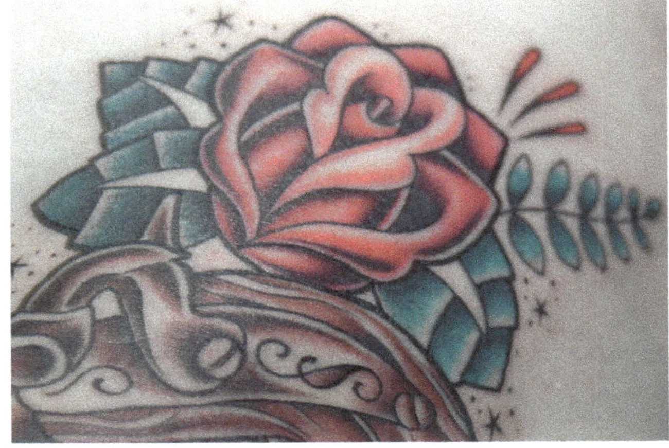

Scott's early mix of color and contour can now be seen as work continues.

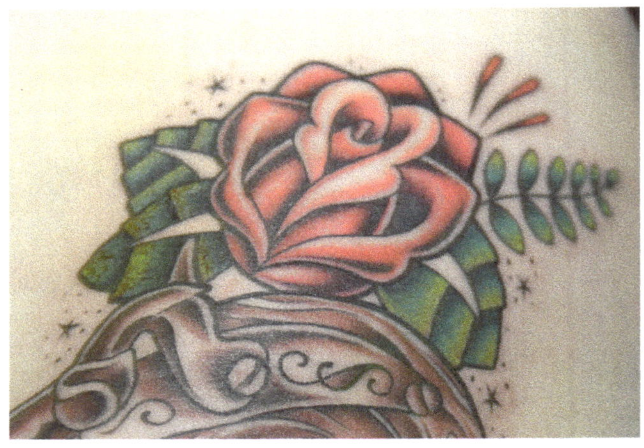

Use of a brighter green ink can also be seen now as the leaves receive more shape and color.

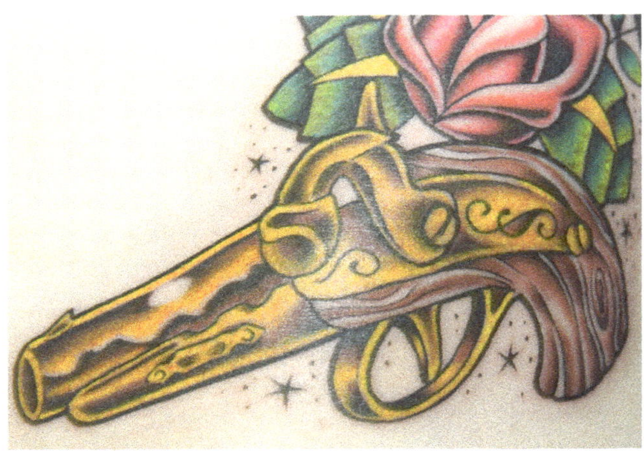

A preliminary wash of the art so far reveals the growing details and shapes of each bit of the tattoo.

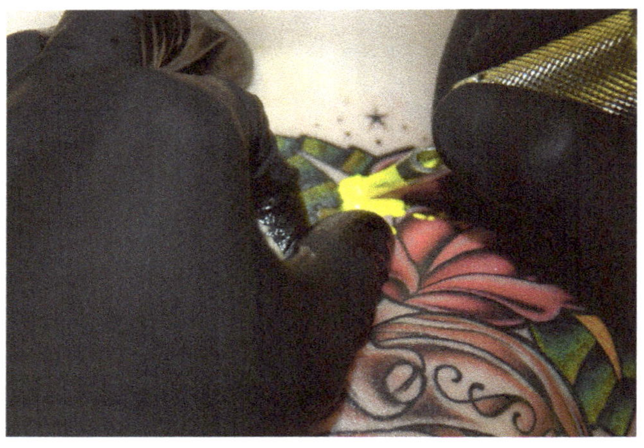

A wash of bright yellow ink is now applied to the leaves to bring more shape to the details.

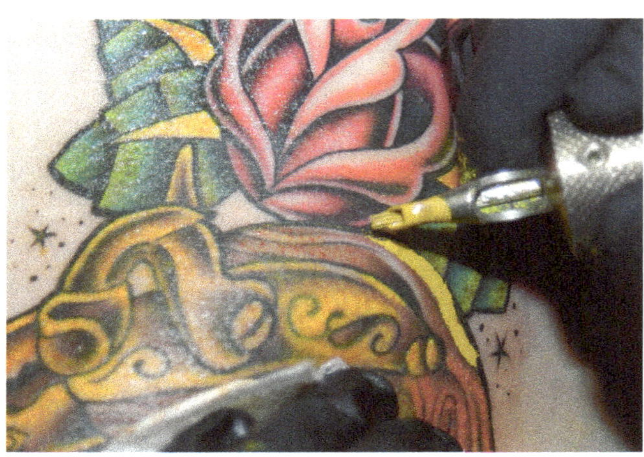

Mustard colored ink is now brought to the piece as a way of bringing more earth tones to the wooden grip of the gun.

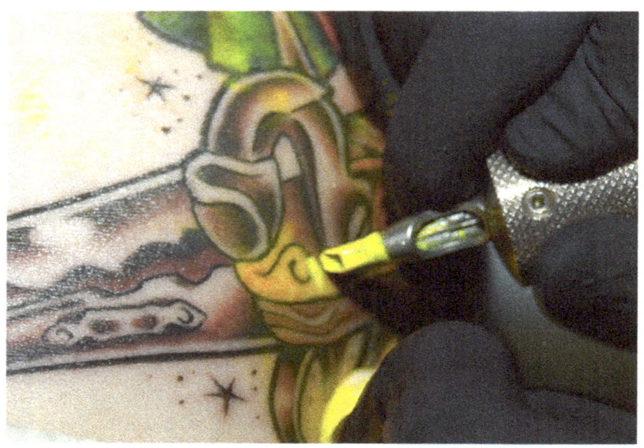

Components of the pistol are also given the yellow wash to add some golden highlights to the hardware.

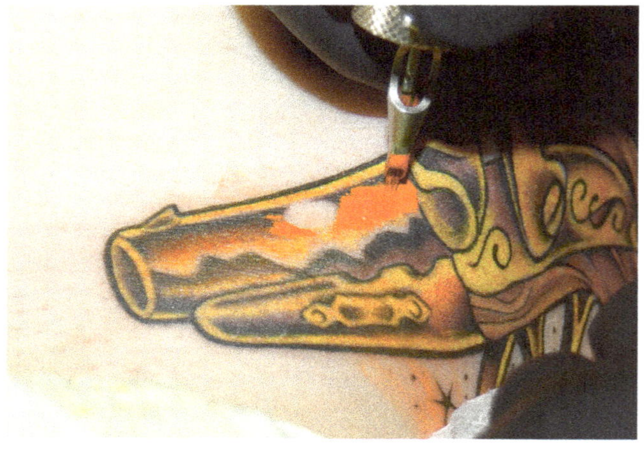

Bright orange ink is added to the fray as Scott brings more life to the barrel of the pistol.

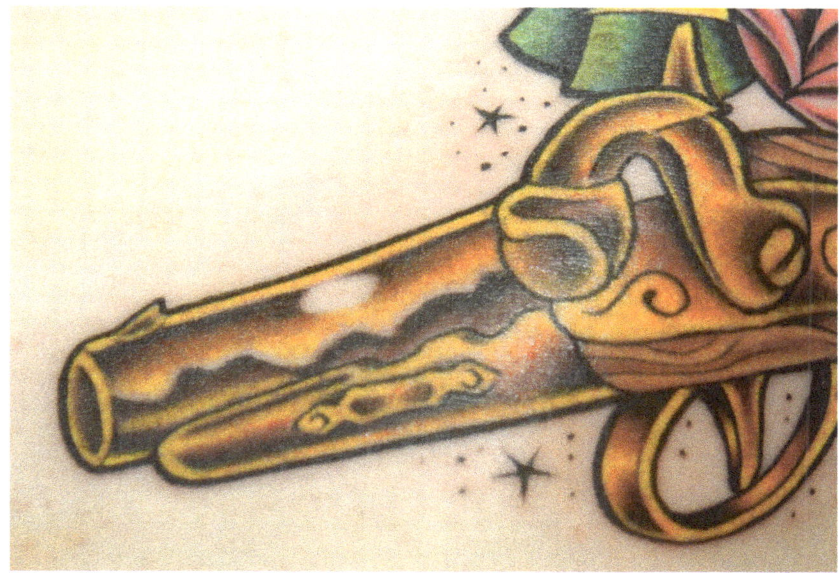

Appearing to reflect the warmth of the sun, the contours of the pistol's barrel grow in depth with every sting of the needle.

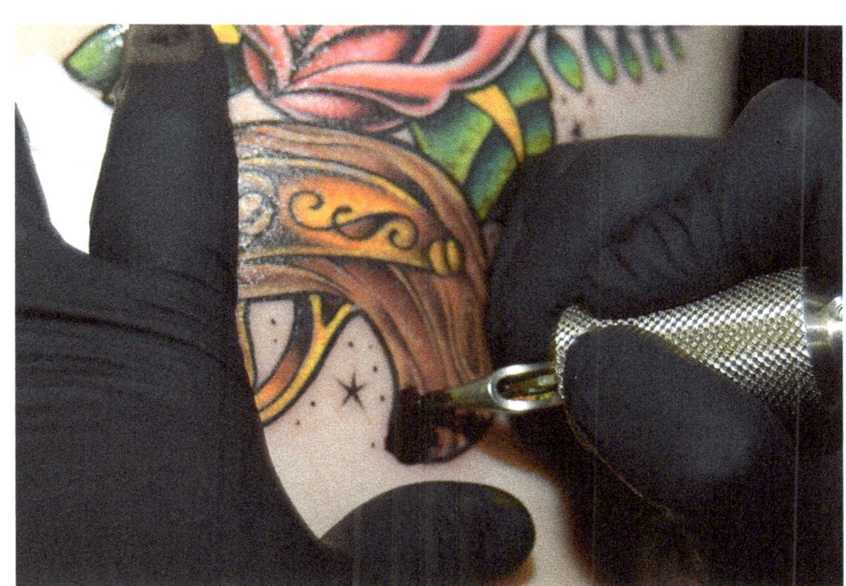

Dark brown ink is used to accent the wood grain of the pistol's handle.

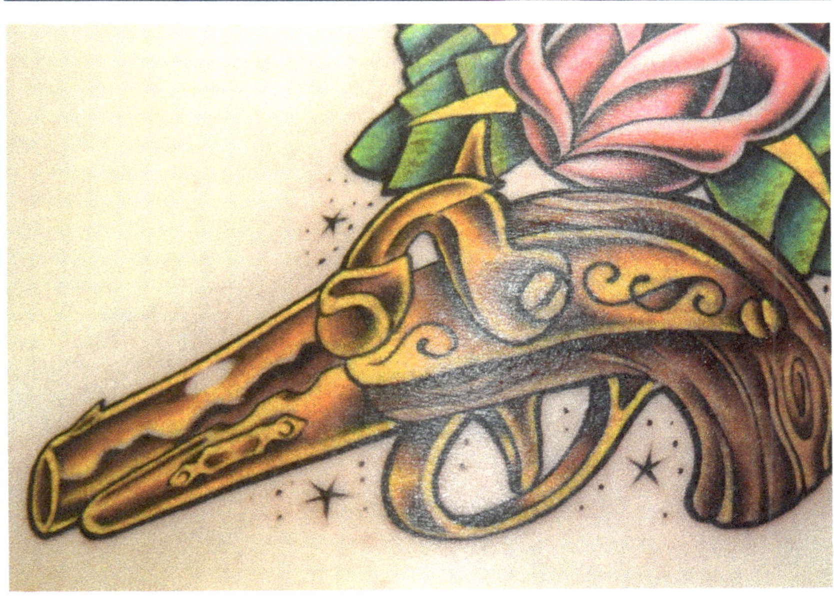

Again wiped free of the ink's mess, we find the piece developing rapidly and nearing completion.

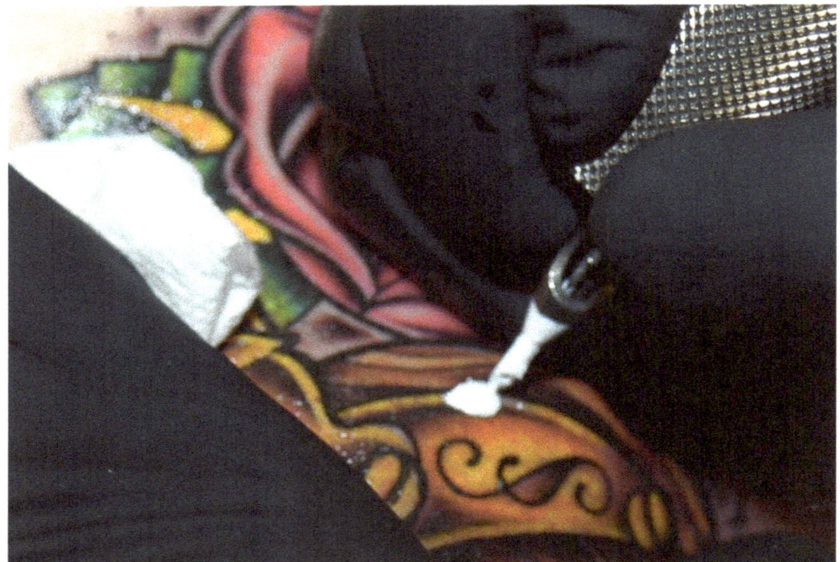

Highlights of white ink are added last to several places on the tattoo and will bring the final bits of life to the illustration.

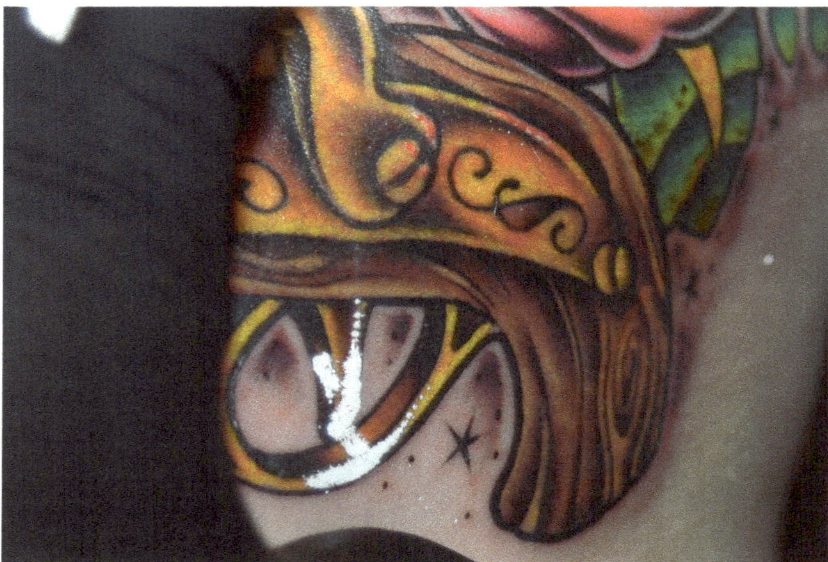

The trigger of the pistol receives a few of these white accents to add detail.

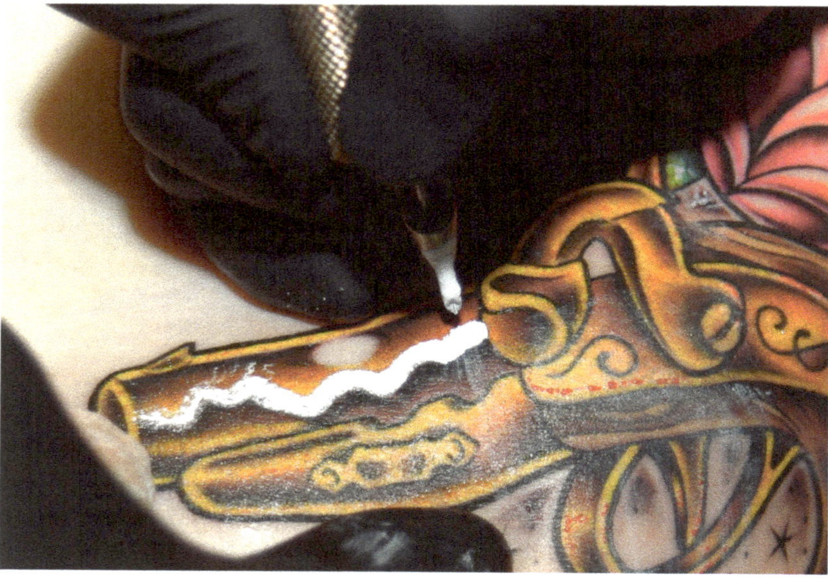

The reflective surface of the metal barrel receives some white ink to further enhance the contours.

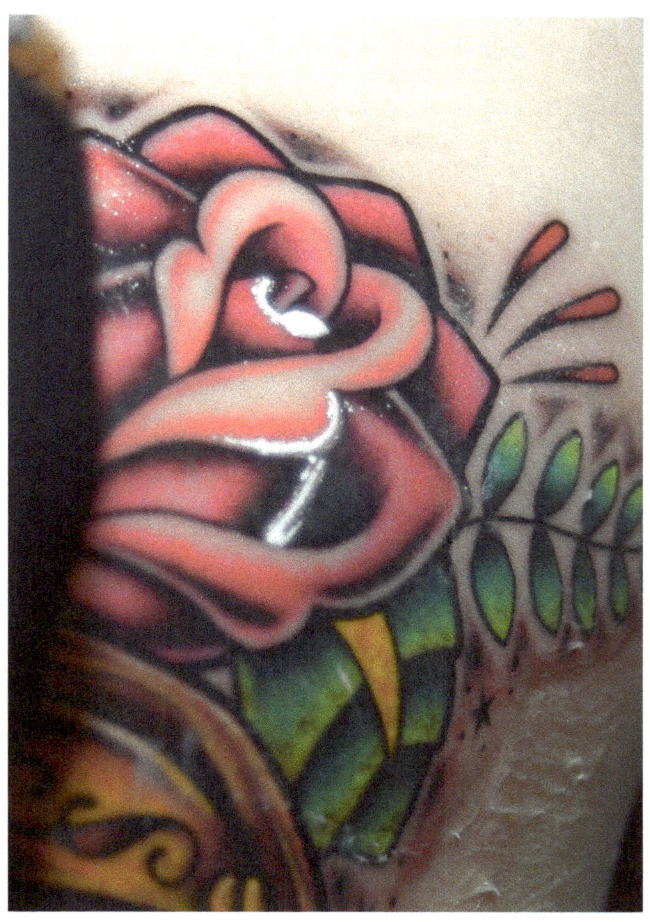

Scott now turns his attentions to the rose petals with touches of white to bring more depth to the gentle shapes of the flower.

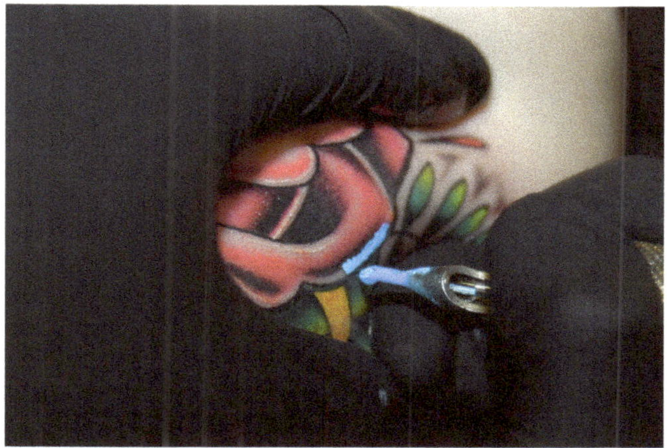

Bright blue ink is now brought to the project to add the final touches of color.

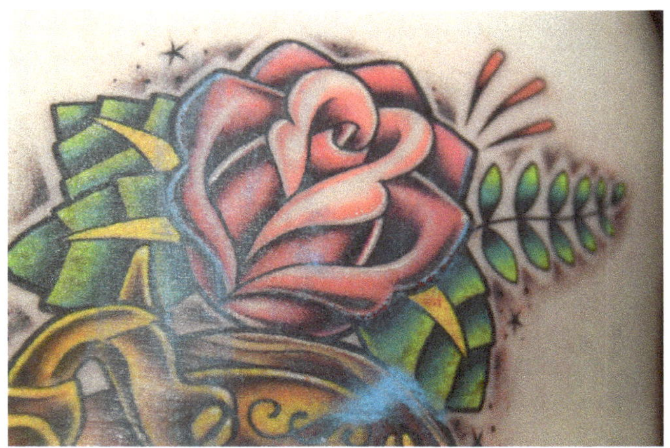

Although subtle, the blue ink has added another level of depth and detail to the piece.

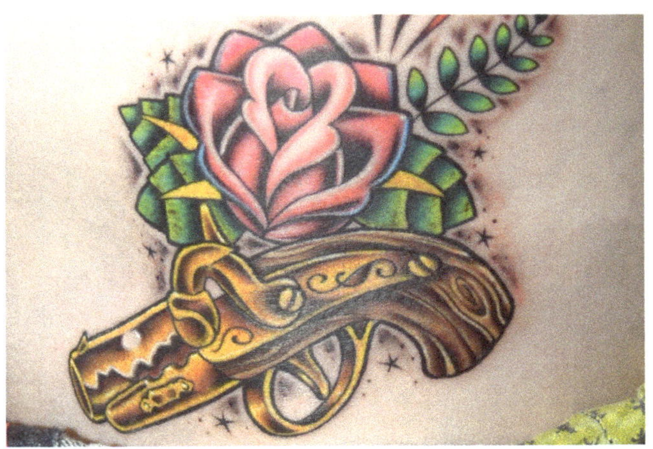

Scott has crated another piece of original art from scratch and has proven himself to be one of the best.

Wolfgang Books On The Web

http://www.wolfpub.com

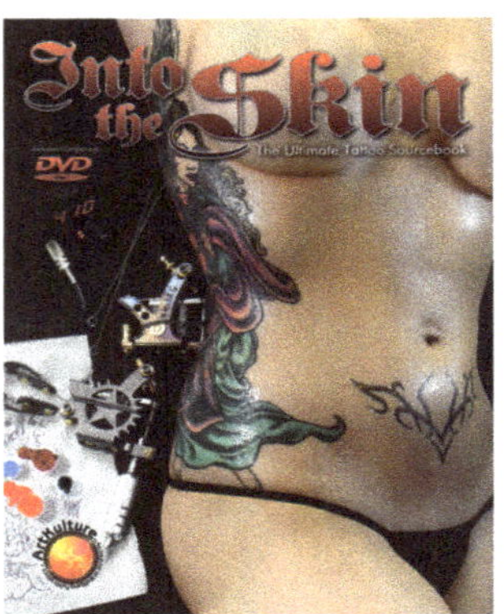

INTO THE SKIN WITH INCLUDED DVD

Into the Skin is a true Tattoo How-To book. From choosing the tattoo machine to picking the best needles for a particular situation, the information that tattoo artists need to create their day-to-day art is included here.

Ten tattoos are covered from start to finish, from sketch to competed art. Each step in the process is photographed and explained in detail. The companion DVD covers the tattooing process with a video camera. So whether you prefer to get you information from a book, or a DVD, the information you need is included in this new combination package from Wolfgang Publications and Superior Tattoo.

Whether you've been tattooing for five years, or five minutes, there is information here that will help with choosing and using your machine, picking needles, and applying color.

Eighteen Chapters 144 Pages $34.95 Over 200 photos, 100% color

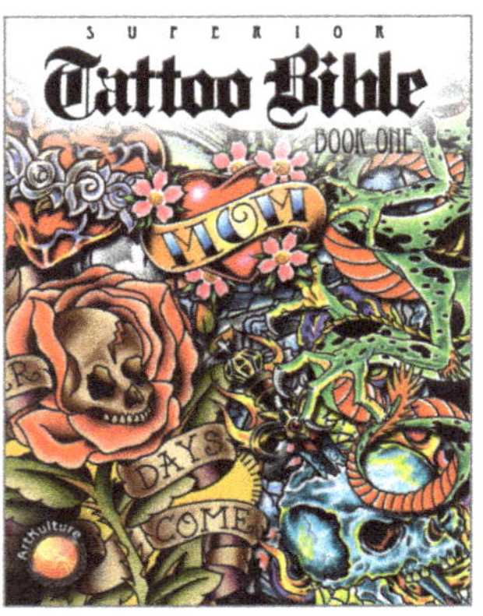

TATTOO BIBLE BOOK ONE

Whether you are preparing for your first tattoo or your twenty-seventh, you need artwork and designs that are just-right. Tattoo Bible, authored by Superior Tattoo, provides well over 500 pieces of unique flash art - flash never before compiled into one single book.

While most tattoo books available today concentrate on one specific genre, this Tattoo Bible covers many different genres and the ideas are endless. This is not just a book to add to your collection - this is your collection. You can combine different pieces of art from within the book, or just take them as is. This book is for you and your imagination to do with as you wish.

Published by ArtKulture, an imprint of Wolfgang Publications, with images that are both striking and very useful to both the tattoo shop, and the tattoo aficionado.

Ten Chapters 144 Pages $27.95 Over 400 photos, 100% color

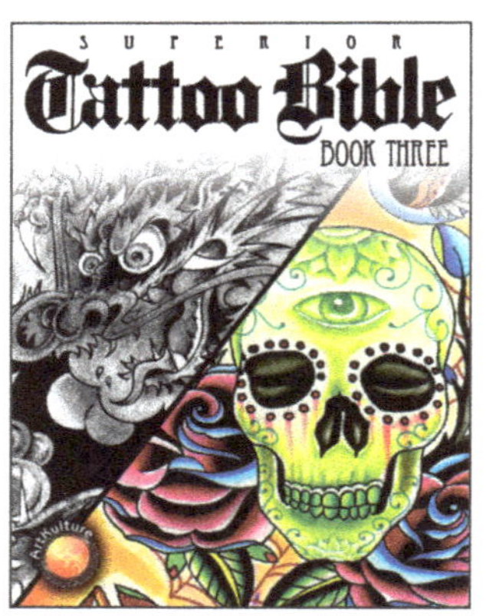

TATTOO BIBLE BOOK THREE

Book Three, the newest installment in the popular Superior Tattoo Bible series, continues the tradition of offering a vast collection of only the best tattoo artwork available.

Unlike the earlier Bibles, Book Three is a collection of designs from opposite ends of the spectrum. This book contains images from both the old school and the new.

With over 350 images, this new book is the perfect companion for any tattooist, from the aspiring novice to the seasoned vet; and a useful resource for tattoo aficionados looking for the art they need to create the ultimate tattoo design. Book Three showcases artwork from some of the most-recognizable names in the tattoo world, as well as the coolest, trendiest designs from some of the newest, up-and-coming talent in the industry!

Ten Chapters 144 Pages $27.95 Over 400 photos, 100% color

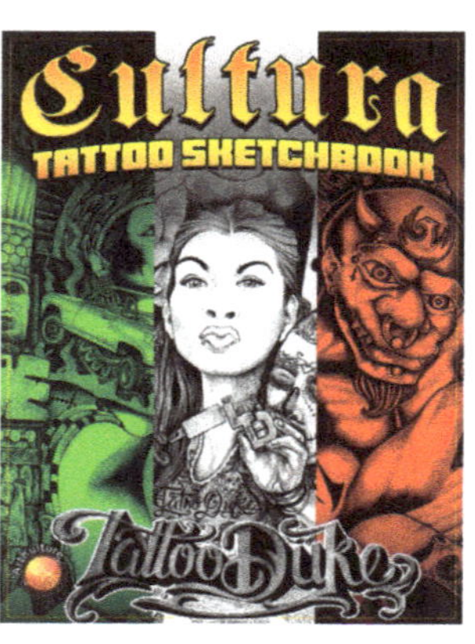

CULTURA TATTOO SKETCHBOOK

Here's a book that's inspired by the Mexican culture and history. Artist Tattoo Duke has gathered his collection of drawings, from fully rendered color images, to collages and unique hand sketches, and compiled them into this amazing reference source. Not only does this book feature artwork that could be described as "Gangsta" or "Street", but it also features Aztec warriors, Raza-style artwork, Graffiti Art, even American Indian themes. The key, as with all art, is the shading. When the shading is done correctly it changes the entire impact of the artwork, whether it's rendered in full color or simply sketched in black & grey.

This book features everything from beautifully, fully-shaded intricate collages, to simple sketches showing the design process. Tattoo Duke's artwork is a must for any artist/client that celebrates Mexican culture through tattoo designs.

Ten Chapters 144 Pages $32.95 Over 400 photos, 100% color

Wolfgang Publication Titles

For a current list visit our website at www.wolfpub.com

ILLUSTRATED HISTORY

Ultimate Triumph Collection	$49.95
American Police Motorcycles - Revised	$24.95

GUIDE BOOKS

Enthusiast Guide - Honda Motorcycles 1959-1985	$27.95

BIKER BASICS

Custom Bike Building Basics	$24.95
Sportster/Buell Engine Hop-Up Guide	$24.95
Sheet Metal Fabrication Basics	$24.95
How to Fix American T-Twin Motorcycles	$27.95

COMPOSITE GARAGE

Composite Materials Handbook #1	$27.95
Composite Materials Handbook #2	$27.95
Composite Materials Handbook #3	$27.95

HOT ROD BASICS

So-Cal Speed Shop's How to Build Hot Rod Chassis	24.95
Hot Rod Wiring	$27.95
How to Chop Tops	$24.95
How to Air Condition Your Hot Rod	$24.95

CUSTOM BUILDER SERIES

How to Build A Café Racer	$27.95
Advanced Custom Motorcycle Wiring - Revised	$27.95
How to Build an Old Skool Bobber Sec Ed	$27.95
How To Build The Ultimate V-Twin Motorcycle	$24.95
Advanced Custom Motorcycle Assembly & Fabrication	$27.95
How to Build a Cheap Chopper	$27.95

MOTORCYCLE RESTORATION SERIES

Triumph Restoration - Unit 650cc	$29.95
Triumph MC Restoration Pre-Unit	$29.95

SHEET METAL

Advanced Sheet Metal Fabrication	$27.95
Ultimate Sheet Metal Fabrication	$24.95
Sheet Metal Bible	$29.95

AIR SKOOL SKILLS

Airbrush Bible	$29.95
How Airbrushes Work	$24.95

PAINT EXPERT

How To Airbrush, Pinstripe & Goldleaf	$27.95
Kosmoski's New Kustom Painting Secrets	$27.95
Pro Pinstripe Techniques	$27.95
Advanced Pinstripe Art	$27.95

TATTOO U Series

Advanced Tattoo Art - Revised	$27.95
Cultura Tattoo Sketchbook	$32.95
Jim Watson's Tattoo Sketchbook	$32.95
Into The Skin The Ultimate Tattoo Sourcebook	$34.95
American Tattoos	$27.95
Tattoo Bible Book One	$27.95
Tattoo Bible Book Two	$27.95
Tattoo Bible Book Three	$27.95

LIFESTYLE

Bean're — Motorcycle Nomad	$18.95
George The Painter	$18.95
The Colorful World of Tattoo Models	$34.95

Sources

Adrenaline Tattoo
7513 International Drive
Orlando, FL 32819
407-345-8850

Art with Atattooed
269 Peterson Road
Libertyville, IL 60048
847-367-1966

Chris Blinston
Big Brain 2 Tattoo & Piercing Studio
3281 N. Federal Hwy.
Pompano, FL 33064
954-788-2334
www.chrisblinston.com

Larry Brogan's Tattoo City
14508 S. Archer Ave.
Lockport, IL 60441
815-836-8282

Joe Capobianco
Hope Studios
817 Chapel Street #2F
New Haven, CT 06510

Insight Studios
1026 N. Milwaukee Ave.
Chicago, IL 60622
773-342-4444
www.insightstudiosonline.com

It's Just a Little Prick
1051 W. Eldorado, Suite #1
Decatur, IL 62522
217-423-8282

Scott Marshall
Vanity Tattoos
25 W. 163 Lake Street
Roselle, IL 60172
630-529-3293

Ronin Tattoo and Body Piercing Studio
Kevin Harden
1161 B. Farnsworth Ave.
Aurora, IL 60504
630-585-7011

www.ingramcontent.com/pod-product-compliance
Lightning Source LLC
LaVergne TN
LVHW060616110826
845154LV00003B/96

* 9 7 8 1 9 4 1 0 6 4 3 8 2 *